WHAT ARE THEY TEACHING THE CHILDREN?

WHAT ARE THEY TEACHING THE CHILDREN?

Editor
Lynda Rose

Voice for Justice UK
Oxford

Wilberforce Publications
London

Published in Great Britain in 2016 by
Wilberforce Publications Limited
70 Wimpole Street, London W1G 8AX
Wilberforce Publications Limited is a wholly owned subsidiary of Christian Concern

and
Voice for Justice UK
PO Box 893 Oxford OX1 9PY

Wilberforce Publications ISBN 978-0-9575725-8-4

Voice for Justice UK ISBN 978-0-9929964-1-3

Printed in Great Britain by Imprint Digital, Exeter
and worldwide by CreateSpace

DEDICATION

For June Cash

The first thing that a totalitarian regime tries to do is to get at the children, to distance them from the subversive, varied influences of their families, and indoctrinate them in their rulers' view of the world.

Lord Hodge, in a judgment of the
United Kingdom Supreme Court, 2016

Contents

TRIBUTE TO JUNE CASH
FROM HER HUSBAND, TONY

My wonderful wife June was called home on 2nd May 2015. She had battled cancer for three years. However that never stopped her from fighting for the Kingdom of God in the UK. We both tried to do all we could to restrain, primarily through intercessionary prayer, our nation's rapid moral decline. We joined with other god-fearing people to form "Voice for Justice UK". VFJUK is a campaigning organisation that, amongst other things, seeks to inform and challenge people, especially our politicians and church leaders, about the decline in moral standards and 'British values'.

Since this term "British values" has become a buzz-word, June asked the question: *"Whose and what values are we referring to?"* She felt compelled, in response to this question, to make her own contribution to the national debate about British values, by writing a book which could be made available to the nation's opinion formers. June argued that a nation's values are defined by history and the struggles and sacrifices of our ancestors. She emphasised that these values are transmitted from one generation to another via the education of our children. In accordance with these insights, June started writing a history of education in Britain, documenting its Christian origins and the central role played by Christian churches, organisations and individuals in its subsequent spread and development. The following chapter, written by her, is the fruit of her research.

June was born in 1948. Following WW2 and five years of hardship and anxiety, Britain was saddled with enormous debt, and was still in a time of food rationing. However it was also a time of hope and development. Our nation still had an inheritance of Christian values, which were taught in our schools. June's primary education years were blessed by being in a traditional Church of England school with a much respected Head Master. Her secondary education was in a girls' grammar school, which also held strong Christian values and standards. The standards that June imbibed in those school years, 1950s and early 1960s, she endeavoured to pass on to our two daughters, who were in turn educated in the late 1980s and 1990s. Their state funded C of E primary school initially had a very strong personality as Head Mistress, who had run a well disciplined school since 1948. Very few children left her school who were illiterate or innumerate. Discipline was very good, but fair. Unfortunately, when she retired, she was succeeded by a Head Mistress who was a secular humanist.

One of the first things this new Head did was to dump a wonderful library filled with carefully graded books called "Wide Range Readers", which covered fiction with a moral theme, science, history, geography and many other topics. She then purchased books with content that June was appalled by, including: black magic, witchcraft, non-British legends and fairy tales, modern stories with non-Christian themes and rebellious children. Together we searched for the reason for this change. We discovered that in 1952 a meeting of British Humanists resolved to do everything they could to get their members into positions of authority within the state controlled teacher training colleges. By the late 1960s they had, to a great extent, succeeded in this aim. The graduates from the teacher training colleges became heads of department and heads of school by 1980. As a result, secular humanists obtained a stranglehold on British education. Our daughters went to school just as this new breed of teachers had established a new philosophy and set of values. We found that many of these values were in direct opposition to ours – for example, values relating to chastity, marriage, sexuality, abortion, respect and freedom of speech (for example to preach the Christian gospel, to criticise homosexuality, etc.).

You can see that June had been well prepared to write this book. As a youngster she had known what it was to grow up within a culture based on Christian values and standards. As an adult, she observed the erosion and rejection of those values. Sadly, June was unable to finish the book as the cancer stole her strength. She was so pleased, in her last few days, when VFJUK took on the vision to complete the book.

Tony Cash

INTRODUCTION
Lynda Rose

Revolution: *the forcible overthrow of a government or social order, in favour of a new system.*[1]

Colosssians 2:8: See to it that no-one takes you captive through hollow and deceptive philosophy, which depends on human tradition and the elemental forces of this world, rather than on Christ.

At first glance, one may wonder what these two apparently unrelated quotations have in common and – perhaps more important – how they are relevant to us today. But the answer is simple. We live in a time of unprecedented cultural, social, and political change. In fact, in the last fifty years the speed of transformation has been little short of phenomenal. However, what many do not realise is the extent to which this change has been orchestrated – a strategic shift so far-reaching and comprehensive that it is no exaggeration to say we are indeed experiencing a forcible overthrow of the traditional social order in favour of the imposition of a new value system. In short, we have undergone a revolution.

It has been a bloodless coup, it is true, starting without violence. But nonetheless, as demonstrated in the following essays, it was consciously planned and has been brought about by secular activists committed to the complete overthrow of the old Judaeo-Christian order, and transfer of power to a 'new' political elite.

But this brings us to our second quotation: on what is the nature of this 'change' based? Is it, as claimed by exponents, the natural and *neutral* cultural evolution of a society that has outgrown its myths and come of age? Or is it the imposition of a hollow and deceptive philosophy – of ideological totalitarianism – hell-bent on denying the Christian God, and bringing chaos in its wake?

We hear a lot today about 'British values'. Our former Prime Minister, David Cameron, labelled them, 'a belief in freedom, tolerance of others, accepting personal and social responsibility, respecting and upholding the rule of law'.[2] They are as British, he said, as the Union flag, as football, as fish and chips, and he is on record as saying that he wants them to be taught in every school.[3] Given the current challenges facing society, seen most clearly in the threat posed by Islamic extremism, you may wonder what is to argue. After all, in the interests of peaceful co-existence, who does not want everyone to share our views…?

Except… except that, despite what Mr Cameron said, British values are now very far from being what they were because, under pressure from LGBT activists, they have been redefined and rebranded – pulled into line by the Equality Act 2010, which has made some 'characteristics' far more equal than others, and imposes severe penalties on anyone who disagrees. It is these values that are being taught in schools, and they are being exploited not just to promote the new value system of the liberal secular agenda, but to silence and suppress all mention of religion, criminalising traditional Christian morality. Freedom of belief and speech, up to now the hallmark of our society, is increasingly tolerated only in so far as it supports the new value system, so that Christianity itself is now being 'rebranded'.

This book is dedicated to the memory of June Cash. Prior to her death in 2015, June was an enthusiastic member of Voice for Justice UK's core team, and our much-valued company secretary. She was a committed Christian, and cared passionately about children. And she was outraged by what she saw as their progressive indoctrination into sexual libertarianism, which she saw as causing great and obvious harm. With a view to exposing the damage caused by current education policies, and encouraged by myself, she began a report looking into the Christian origins of education in the UK. Sadly, she died almost before she had started, but in her final days in hospital she asked us to finish what she had begun, and we have continued with the support of her husband, Tony. To the last, June wanted to protect children, and she believed this could only be achieved by reaffirming Britain's Christian heritage, which, she said, was the only thing that would ensure genuine freedom of speech and belief.

INTRODUCTION

The overall contention of the book is that education today has become an ideological battleground. As well as analysing in detail the effects of certain policies relating to SRE (Sex and Relationships Education), and anti-bullying programmes that serve to normalise homosexuality, bisexuality and transgenderism, the collection of twelve essays making up the study examine the function and basis of education, its evolution, and its relationship to the broader topic of human rights.

Following June's introduction outlining the Christian roots to learning in the UK, the first part of the book (Chapters 2-4) explores the rationale for education – why and what we teach our children, how different societies have approached and interpreted the task, and the duty of parents to prepare and best equip their young to face the challenges of life. The first chapter, written by myself, unpacks the nature and function of education within society, with its central role in the historical transmission of identity and culture, arguing that from earliest times shared memories and the 'stories' people told didn't just equip the individual to meet the challenges of life, but actively helped form and strengthen 'community'. It was this same understanding that gave rise to the post-revolution Communist control of education in the Soviet Union, but in that case using it as an ideological weapon to destroy capitalism, in marked contrast to the Christian approach – committed to the exploration of truth, and inviting students to arrive at their own conclusions, even if unpalatable to the teacher!

Historian and film maker Philip Quenby follows this with a comparison of education in different cultures. Starting with Confucianism, he gives an overview of Zen Buddhism, Hinduism, Judaism and Islam, before moving on to Nazi Germany and Communist Russia. Edmund Adamus, Catholic commentator on Marriage and Family life, then explores the God-given duty and right of parents to train and equip their young – to pass on the faith – showing how this duty is being undermined by the imposition of secularist dogma.

The second part of the book (chapters 5-8) deals with current educational policies, analysing in detail specific programmes aimed at normalising such things as same-sex marriage and gender reorientation. Social analyst Anthony Busk examines the implementation and effect of SRE (Sex and Relationships Education) policy, explaining in detail how this impacts not just children, but also the rights of parents. As an example of a relevant teaching resource, Brian Hadley then examines CHIPS (Challenging Homophobia in Primary Schools), as promoted, with Government support, by activist charity Educate & Celebrate. Ostensibly aimed at tackling the problems of bullying among young children, their focus (as stated on Educate & Celebrate's website),[4] is on making schools 'LGBT+ friendly'. Having asked whether combating bullying is in practice a 'Trojan Horse' to promote an LGBT activist agenda, Brian questions whether the impact of this programme is intended to be not so much attitudinal change towards bullying, but rather the indoctrination of children into the unquestioning acceptance of a new ideology.

However, it is not only sexual rebranding that is the issue in education, because there appears also a systematic drive to undermine and suppress more general Christian input or influence. Whatever one's theological views, this is clearly evident in the prohibition against including 'creationism' in the scientific curriculum. Dr Alastair Noble, a noted scientist and educationalist, lays out the case for scientific examination of the notion of a 'Creator' or first cause, arguing that, whatever conclusions are reached, refusal to investigate is evidence of a closed mind and is itself unscientific. Current hostility to inquiry is, he argues, ideological, and based on no more than secularist opposition to religion.

Christian rights campaigner and activist Robert S. Harris follows this with a detailed examination of Christian assemblies, currently required by law but opposed by secularists and militant atheists, who argue that all forms of religion are indoctrination and have no place in public life. Arguing against this, Robert shows how Christian assemblies have been vital in building national identity, at the same time as giving lifelong benefits to children – not least familiarising them with the spiritual benefits and strengths of Christianity, testified to by many over the years as having proved invaluable in later life when faced with crisis. He maintains that, by contrast, the secularist drive to eliminate all trace of religion from schools offers no obvious 'benefit', flouts the law, and is a breach of democracy.

All of this has obvious implications for human rights, impacting both freedom of belief and freedom of speech, and the third section of the book (chapters 9-11) focuses on the attack on liberty. Setting out the Christian origins to the development of human rights law, educationalist Edmund Matyjaszek analyses the challenge to individual freedom posed by the Equality Act 2010, showing clearly the incongruities of legislation supposedly aimed at enforcing equality and tolerance, while making those who object subject to legal penalty. The position we are in today, he says, is that 'All men are equal', but certain 'protected characteristics' are more equal than others. Edmund's conclusion is that this is both a betrayal of British democracy and a challenge to the equality of all under God. In defending our right to proclaim the gospel of Christ, therefore, he concludes that we are fighting not just for ourselves but for the freedom of all.

Building on this, Dr Christopher Shell offers an in-depth analysis of the flaws and inconsistencies in what today we define as 'British values', many of which have led directly to the ills affecting modern society. Using carefully researched and comprehensive statistics, he shows the real impact of changed policies over the last fifty years, addressing a wide range of issues that encompass the sexual revolution, abortion rates, STDs, divorce, pornography, mental illness and much more. Having comprehensively shown and analysed the problems, in Chapter 11 he moves on to diagnosis and remedy, arguing that as top priority we need to jettison ideology in favour of plain, unvarnished truth.

Finally, drawing on her long experience fighting for human rights and helping those suffering abuse, Baroness Cox stresses the continuing and imperative need for Religious Education (RE) in all schools, including in particular knowledge of our Judaeo-Christian faith and heritage. A major influence in drawing up the provisions of the 1988 Education Reform Act, when she successfully campaigned for reinstatement of the requirement that RE teaching be mandatory, Baroness Cox emphasises the challenges being faced in society today. Citing as example the systemic abuse of women under sharia Law, she highlights the unique contribution to human rights of the Judaeo-Christian tradition, with its inherent respect for the individual as made in the image of God. Our fundamental freedoms, she says, are under threat. Therefore we must act now to defend them, and to promote and pass on our Christian heritage in and through education – before it is too late.

This book may prove uncomfortable reading for some but, if we are to have any hope of dealing with the many problems confronting society today, it is vital that we recognise and face up to the issues addressed. Not only is the wellbeing and future of our children at stake, but society itself is under threat. Education is a battleground precisely because the minds and hearts of the children hold the future. The ideological battle could not be more important. The values our young learn today, for better or for worse, are the values that will underpin our society in future generations.

I can do no better in ending this Introduction in repeating the final words of Baroness Cox:

> May we not leave our children to fight the battles we have not had the courage to fight, but may we strive to ensure that we pass on our spiritual, cultural and political heritage undiminished, that subsequent generations may flourish in peace and justice.

Notes
[1] The *Oxford English Dictionary*
[2] https://www.gov.uk/government/news/british-values-article-by-david-cameron
[3] http://www.dailymail.co.uk/debate/article-2658171/DAVID-CAMERON-British-values-arent-optional-theyre-vital-Thats-I-promote-EVERY-school-As-row-rages-Trojan-Horse-takeover-classrooms-Prime-Minister-delivers-uncompromising-pledge.html
[4] http://www.educateandcelebrate.org/

Chapter One

THE CHRISTIAN ORIGINS OF THE UK'S MODERN EDUCATIONAL SYSTEM
June Cash

King Alfred the Great – the English Solomon
Christianity was well established in the British Isles well before Alfred's reign. Referring to the period at least two hundred years prior to Alfred, Winston Churchill in his *History of the English Speaking Peoples* says, "There was no kingdom in the realm in which heathen religions and practices now prevailed. The whole Island was now Christian".[1] The Venerable Bede's description was of "A Christian England ... divided into seven kingdoms of varying strength, all professing the gospel of Christ".[2] As scholars studied the Scriptures, there was undoubtedly Christian education at that time – for example King's School in Canterbury, founded in 597 – but there was no widespread organised education for the poorer classes.

During his reign in the late 800s, King Alfred the Great recognised that Christian education was of supreme value to a nation, and therefore made it a foundational principle of his kingship. The inscription on his statue which stands in the market place of Wantage, the town where he was born, reads: "Alfred found learning dead and he restored it; education neglected, and he revived it; the laws powerless and he gave them force; the Church debased, and he raised it; the land ravaged by a fearful enemy, and he delivered it. Alfred's name will live as long as mankind shall respect the past".

Alfred's law revision recognised the Judeo-Christian principles already in place in the land. He wanted people to be able to read so that they could understand the laws, and thus obey them. So he "set to learning... all the free-born young men now in England who have the means to apply themselves to it".[3] Much was "based on the 10 commandments, given to Moses, fulfilled and interpreted by the love and compassion of Christ, continued by the teachings of the Apostles, and handed down through the ordinances of Church Councils down the ages."[4] Alfred said that there is only one way by which to build any kingdom, and that is on the sure and certain foundation of faith in Jesus Christ, and in Jesus Christ crucified, and it is on that foundation that I intend to build my kingdom".[5]

As an example to others, in later life he applied himself to learning Latin so that he could translate the writings of recognised sages for his subjects to understand and put into practice. He wrote in the Preface of his translation of Gregory the Great's *Pastoral Care*: "Without Christian wisdom there can be neither prosperity nor success in war".[6] In his translation of *The Consolation of Boethius* he wrote, "The pursuit of wisdom is the surest path to power. Study wisdom then, and when you have learned it, condemn it not, for I tell you that by its means you may without fail attain to power, yea even though not desiring it."[7] Working on this foundation for his rule, it is little wonder that he left to us a lasting legacy of his reign, the benefits of which are still with us today. It is not for nothing that the epithet "Great" was applied to him, our only monarch to have been so called.

Alfred "set the compass" for this nation's education. It is therefore no surprise that even 400 or so years later the colleges of Oxford, the oldest university in the land, were Christian – founded for the study of theology. Amongst the oldest colleges are University College, Balliol and Merton, the latter being established to support advanced theological study. Merton, opened in the 1280s, became the model for Peterhouse, the first college in Cambridge. On into the later Middle Ages, we see the establishment of yet more Christian-founded Oxford colleges: Exeter, Oriel, Queen's (1340s), New College (1379), Lincoln (1420s), All Souls, and Magdalen (1450s). The Arms of Oxford University depict an open Bible with words from Psalm 27, "Dominus illuminatio mea", translated "The Lord is my Light". Similarly, the names of many of the colleges of Cambridge University also reveal their Christian foundations:

Corpus Christi (founded 1352), Jesus (1496), St John's (1511), Trinity (1546) and Emmanuel (meaning "God with us"; 1546). For centuries the Universities of Oxford and Cambridge have produced a wealth of Christian leaders, theologians, scientists and numerous other academics. Their Christian influence on the nation and its history cannot be over-emphasised. That influence, however, did not stop at our own shores but reached throughout the English-speaking world.

It is undeniable that amongst the most influential of these Oxford-educated Christian men were the Wesley brothers, John and Charles, and George Whitefield. Their inspired teachings caused the nation's people to re-discover faith in Christ, and through this the nation was revived to its Christian foundations. The revival began in 1736 as the Holy Spirit anointed the preaching of George Whitefield. Prior to this he had felt "unable to even compose a sermon", and even on the day of his ordination in Gloucester Cathedral he found he was still not able to preach. But the very next morning, as he related, some words from the New Testament came with great power to his soul: "Speak out Paul!"[8] From that time onwards, great crowds gathered to hear him wherever he went. As people responded to his message on "The Necessity of the New Birth", their lives were gloriously transformed.

John Wesley's transforming "new birth" happened on 24 May 1738 as he sat in an Aldersgate meeting room listening to Luther's *Preface to the Epistle to the Romans*. He felt his heart was strangely warmed as Luther was describing the change which God works in the heart through faith in Christ.[9] It was not long before this inner fire spilled out in anointed preaching, just like George Whitefield, and by 1740 the Wesleys were also preaching to multitudes in the open air, with the resultant transformation of people's lives.

The outworking of all this was that Christians took seriously the Biblical injunction to look after the good of those around them. Christianity is not only a set of beliefs, but an inner dynamism which leads believers to work for the good of others and for the society in which they live. The life of the nation as a whole was therefore transformed as Christians worked to abolish slavery, set up homes for orphans, cared for the poor, established hospitals, educated the children of the working classes, etc., etc. And, indeed, so successful was the drive to promote child literacy that enthusiasm for learning to read spread also throughout the adult population – because people wanted to read the Bible.

The founding of today's education system

As early as 1751, a school was begun in St Mary's Church, Nottingham. Another early school was begun by a Nonconformist Christian, Hannah Ball, in 1769 in High Wycombe. However, these appear to have been one-off individual initiatives. The start of a deliberate movement to educate the children of the working classes came a little later with Robert Raikes and Thomas Stock, born in 1736 and 1750 respectively. Raikes was middle-class and owned a newspaper, *The Gloucester Journal,* inherited from his father in 1757. At that time, middle class children were either tutored at home or were sent to fee-paying local grammar schools or boarding schools. However, there was no widespread provision to educate the children of the poor and working class. Raikes was challenged when observing groups of ragged, uneducated, poor children roaming the streets and creating mischief. Among them were orphans and children whose parents were in prison. They were vulnerable to all sorts of exploitation, immorality and opportunities to participate in vice. Raikes recognised that vice would be better prevented than cured and that education would be the key. So concerned was he at the plight of these children that he consulted with his friend Thomas Stock, who was Curate of Ashbury in Berkshire. It was the era of the Industrial Revolution and such children worked long hours in factories and mills six days per week. Their only opportunity for schooling would therefore be on a Sunday.

In 1777, Thomas Stock gathered together the children of Ashbury in the parish church of St Mary's for day-long free education on Sundays. The mornings were devoted to instruction in reading, writing and arithmetic. Just as King Alfred, centuries earlier, had written that there would be no prosperity without Christian wisdom,[10] Raikes and Stock recognised that Biblical teaching would be imperative for the well-being of children's lives: "All our children will be taught of the Lord and great will be our children's peace thereby" (Isaiah 54:13). The Bible was therefore the focus of lessons in the afternoon. The numbers of children attending soon grew to such an extent that new premises were needed. Stock was therefore lent a cottage in the village by the Craven Estate. As commemoration, there is today a slate tablet in the chancel of St Mary's church Ashbury, which says;

> Be it remembered that in the chancel of this Church The Reverend Thomas Stock, Curate of this Parish, in the year 1777 opened a Sunday School. This later became the first of its kind in England to be housed outside the Church in a building of its own: still to be seen near the present school.

Since that time there have been two more school buildings, and the last erected still houses the Church school – but all four buildings stand in the village as a testament to the history of Christian teaching.

Thomas Stock moved to Gloucester in 1778, joining forces with Robert Raikes to open another school in 1780, run on the same lines as the pilot school in Ashbury. Within two years, several more schools opened in the Gloucester area. Once the success of these schools was established, Raikes published an article about them on 3 November 1783 in his newspaper, *The Gloucester Journal*. Several other publications reported on the work, with the result that soon around 4,000 schools had been set up in other English towns. Because Raikes owned a printing press, he was able to provide (at his own expense in the early years) reading and spelling books, as well as Bible study books and copies of the scriptures for the work of the schools. By 1785, 250,000 English children were attending such schools.[11] Raikes died in 1811. Such was the legacy of his success that, within twenty years of his death, the Sunday School movement in Great Britain was teaching 1,250,000 children every week, this number representing around 25% of the population. By 1851, 75% of working class children were receiving education through these schools. It is not surprising, therefore, that the Robert Raikes schools were seen as the forerunners of the English state system.[12]

This began formally in 1870, when the Government of the day passed an Education Act to provide for public elementary education in England and Wales. It stands as the very first piece of legislation to deal specifically with the provision of education in Britain. Most importantly, it demonstrated a commitment to provision on a national scale. Naturally there were many obstacles to be overcome, and at this point there was no move towards compulsory daily attendance at school, which would not have been feasible as some areas still did not have a school. An added problem, recognised by reformers, was that poor families depended on their children being employed for long hours daily in order to make ends meet, so that such a requirement would have been unreasonable.

In those areas where schools were present, "almost without exception they had been established by religious denominations". [13] It therefore followed that since some of these were the only school in their area, the Bill required that schools be open to all denominations, so that admission to all children in the district was guaranteed. Schools were not required to give up their connections with their founding denomination, so long as the religious teaching was non-denominational. Over and above that, the Government did not inquire into more than the secular education given in those schools: "Where the existing schools in any school district afford such an education as suffices for the requirements of the population – in the words of the Bill, where education is 'sufficient, efficient and suitable' – we propose to take no further steps".[14]

The Earl of Shaftesbury said that the majority of teachers were church attenders from all the Protestant denominations and that they kept clear of denominational distinctions, "but they all teach the great saving doctrines of Christianity". He went on to say,

> What has been the effect? I refer you to our colonies, to the numbers of those who have been sent out, and to those who are in the service of farmers and tradespeople, all of whom have been taken from ragged schools and drawn from the very depths of society, and of whom I can say that a large proportion keep up the character they acquired at school, and have never fallen into evil courses or disgraced the education they received at the hands of their excellent teachers. I can have no confidence in any system of education which is not based on the great doctrines of religion and which does not impart to the mind of a child a deep sense that it is an immortal and responsible being, that an invisible Eye sees into its inmost heart, and that there will come a day when it must tender an account not only of its actions but also of its thoughts.[15]

During the debate, Lord Howard of Glossop further added, "The feeling of this country ….is in favour of religious or denominational schools."[16]

In keeping with every other instance of training given – for example in the army, navy, the workhouse and gaols – religious instruction was an integral part of the school education system. Legislation to this effect has continued to the present day: seen, for example, in the 1996 Education Act, which makes it compulsory for an act of collective worship to be held in schools and that it is to be broadly Christian.

Is there any point?

In earlier times the greater mass of the population certainly thought so. For example, the benefit of Christian instruction was recorded in a report of 1840 on the state of education in Birmingham. It states that in 1838, the numbers of pupils enrolled on the registers of Sunday Schools was greater than that on day-school registers and that, "as a moral means the value of Sunday Schools cannot be too highly appreciated...they have the means of infusing the most powerful moral checks into the consciences of tens of thousands ... under existing circumstances, they stand foremost among the means of acting beneficially upon the dense masses of the population."[17] It is an observation that has been echoed by many since, as for example:

> Theodore Roosevelt, "A thorough knowledge of the Bible is worth more than a college education." And, "To educate a man in mind and not in morals is to educate a menace to society."[18]

> C.S. Lewis: "Education without values, as useful as it is, seems rather to make man a more clever devil."[19]

Education – the Ideological Battleground

For many centuries in this nation, instruction in reading, writing and arithmetic has always been accompanied by thorough Biblical instruction in the Christian faith, with its morals and values. From the outset it has always been overwhelmingly supported by public opinion. As recently as the 1950s the vast majority of children attended Sunday School and, as those who are old enough to remember will testify, there were as many children in school on a Sunday as on weekdays; those who didn't attend would have been seen as "unusual", though nothing would ever have been said. Yet during the 1960s there was a subtle change and an "unease" crept into the nation. The structured, safe society we had known began to be replaced by drug-taking, immorality, and rebellion against parents, seen in a general lowering of standards as the hippy movement got under way. At the same time there was a lowering of censorship across the media – well illustrated by what was hailed at the time the "ground-breaking" onstage nudity of the 1968 musical "Hair".[20] In this decade too, the Profumo affair – a major scandal for Westminster[21] – hit the headlines, and abortion was legalised,[22] while the idea of multiculturalism to accommodate the growing numbers of racially diverse immigrants began to take root and develop. New religions, ideas and philosophies – definitely not based on Christianity – were creeping in. This, paralleled by the growing determination of humanists to secularise society and remove Christianity from the public arena, saw the beginnings of an orchestrated conflict still being played out today. And one of the main battlegrounds was education.

Had we but known it, the social and cultural peace the nation had enjoyed for so long was being replaced by turmoil. Abraham Lincoln hit the nail on the head when he said, "The philosophy of the school room in one generation will be the philosophy of government in the next."[23]

Those challenging the established order knew exactly what they were doing, because theirs was a deliberate agenda to overthrow society as we knew it. At around the beginning of the last century, the view was put forward that in order to gain control of Europe and the West, Christianity would have to be expunged, thus causing society to collapse from within through immorality and loss of integrity, so making us weak and vulnerable.[24]

Ironically, Communist Russia, where the strategy was first developed, has itself already experienced this. Following the Bolshevik Revolution, sexual licence (including homosexuality) was legalised, resulting in such a meltdown of society that Stalin had rigorously to reinstate the old laws governing morality. Prior to that, the French Revolution had also taken the path of sexual licence in its attempt to overthrow the old social norms, which were viewed as oppression of the poor by the bourgeois class; once again, at the time, with disastrous effects.

In an age of bloody revolution based on man-made aspiration and philosophies, Britain could have faced similar upheaval, but mercifully this nation avoided tumult – due in the main to the Christian undergirding of our society brought about by the Wesleyan revival....

It is at this point that the manuscript stops. One can only speculate how June might have gone on to develop her ideas if illness had not intervened. As demonstrated by the above, she cared passionately about children and young people, seeing their education as a sacred trust. In tribute to her, therefore, Voice for Justice UK has edited and included her manuscript as the first contribution to this book. We hope the message will take root and bear fruit.

Notes

[1] Winston Churchill, *History of the English-speaking Peoples* (first published in four volumes by Cassell, 1956-1958; republished as one volume paperback by Skyhorse Publishing, 2011).

[2] The Venerable Bede, *The Ecclesiastical History of the English People* (Penguin Classics; Rev Ed edition, 26 June 1990).

[3] David Pratt, *The Political Thought of King Alfred the Great* (Cambridge University Press, 2007) p.120.

[4] See Nick Spencer, *The Bible and politics – Christian sources of British political thought,* http://www.jubilee-centre.org/the-bible-and-politics-by-nick-spencer/

[5] Alfred's Domboc, c.893 http://www.jubilee-centre.org/the-bible-and-politics-by-nick-spencer/

[6] Original text and translation at http://www.bible-researcher.com/alfred.html

[7] http://oll.libertyfund.org/pages/king-alfred-s-translation-of-boethius

[8] Robert Philip, *The life and times of the Reverend George Whitefield, M.A.* (Nabu Press, 2012) p.36.

[9] Dan Graves, 'John Wesley's heart strangely warmed', http://www.christianity.com/church/church-history/timeline/1701-1800/john-wesleys-heart-strangely-warmed-11630227.html

[10] Preface to Alfred's translation of Gregory the Great's *Pastoral Care* (Keynes & Lapidge, 1983) p. 126

[11] Elmer L. Towns, "History of Sunday School", Sunday School Encyclopedia, 1993

[12] Ibid.

[13] See http://hansard.millbanksystems.com/lords/1870/jul/25/elementary-education-bill

[14] Ibid.

[15] Ibid.

[16] Ibid.

[17] http://www.british-history.ac.uk/vch/warks/vol7/pp486-500

[18] See http://www.washingtontimes.com/news/2015/jul/28/w-scott-lamb-theodore-roosevelts-famous-quote-abou/

[19] Allegedly C.S.Lewis, *The Abolition of Man* (Harper One, 1944, copyright renewed 1974)

[20] Telling the story of a group of long-haired hippies living in New York, the show opened on Broadway, then was quickly followed by simultaneous performances across the US and Europe. The London production ran for 1997 performances.

[21] https://www.britannica.com/event/Profumo-affair

[22] http://www.legislation.gov.uk/ukpga/1967/87/introduction/enacted

[23] http://teach1776.ning.com/profiles/blogs/abraham-lincoln-philosophy-of

[24] See e.g http://www.academia.edu/3215366/_We_Are_Neither_Visionaries_Nor_Utopian_Dreamers_._Willi_Münzenberg_the_League_against_Imperialism_and_the_Comintern_1925-1933

Chapter Two

BATTLE FOR THE SOUL OF OUR NATION
Lynda Rose

What is 'education'?
We are unique on this planet in that we are the only species that seeks to educate our offspring beyond what is necessary for survival. A lioness will teach her young to hunt, a chimpanzee will pass on knowledge of how to crack a nut with a stone, or to fish for termites with a twig – and we too of course try to equip our young with the skills they will need to be safe and prosper in life. But for *homo sapiens* the communication of experience and knowledge goes far beyond food gathering and survival, because from earliest times (once language had developed) men and women gathered round the fire in groups to tell stories and sing songs – and when they found a cave, as often as not they graffitied the walls with beautiful images of animals and men out hunting, and delicate stencils of hands.

Why did we do this? Why do we still do it today?
Many complex theories have been put forward, especially in relation to cave art. But at least a part of the unconscious rationale must surely have been the forging of identity and communal worth, because it is through shared memories – and repetition of those memories – that the collective consciousness of 'the tribe' is first formed and then passed on. More than that, it is through the transmission of history, tradition and the perception of greater realities – of something beyond – that culture begins, and this is where common values are instilled, which allow individuals within the group to live together harmoniously and in peace.

At its most basic, this is education, and we know that from earliest times it has been important for the tribe or clan to remember and share its heritage in this way. Before writing developed, for example, we know that stories – whether of actual events or of myth – were carefully learnt and passed on orally from generation to generation by the wise man or priest. It was this transmission that told people who they were, bestowing identity and birthing the wider cultural and social organisation that defined the group as a whole. It taught individuals how to live.

We see illustration of this in the stories surrounding the Jewish exodus in the Bible. Over a forty year period in the desert, the rabble that came out of Egypt were forged into the Hebrew nation, with a common identity and shared belief in their God, Yahweh. And God knew exactly what He was doing when, having given the Israelites the Ten Commandments, He instructed them, 'These commandments that I give you today are to be upon your hearts. Impress them upon your children. Talk about them when you sit at home and when you walk along the road, when you lie down and when you get up....' [1]

It was an instruction to be given time and again, echoed in the many commands to 'remember' and 'not forget' the stories of deliverance, once the Israelites had entered the Promised Land. It was this repeated collective memory that allowed their survival as a nation through military defeat, exile, persecution and dispersion … right up to the present day.

Education, then, is not simply the neutral transmission of facts or knowledge. It forms character and ensures the survival of the group.

Christian approaches to education

Every society has sought at base to transmit its values, at the very least to encourage a work ethic that would benefit the whole. Historically, 'higher learning', which today we see as a fundamental human right,[2] was often reserved for the elite, a fact well illustrated in the educational history of Britain.

We know as fact that the Romans introduced schools to Britain, but when they left the schools did not survive, and were not reintroduced until the arrival of Augustine in 597AD. The saint's founding of churches is well known, but what is not perhaps so well known is that he also introduced two types of school: grammar schools, to teach Latin to would-be priests, and the 'song school', where sons of the nobility were trained to sing in cathedral choirs.[3]

The grammar schools, as suggested by the name, taught only Latin grammar and literature, because specifically they were training boys for entry into the Church's ministry. But the curriculum for the song schools was far broader, being based on the liberal arts and sciences of the Roman and Hellenistic schools and comprising grammar, rhetoric, logic, arithmetic, geometry, music and astronomy – all of which were seen as the basis for the later study of theology, law and medicine.[4] So, dating from this time, formal education in the British Isles was exclusively in the hands of the Church and was reserved first for the religious and second for the sons of the nobility – the future leaders.

For this reason, up until around the fifteenth century only about a third of the population could read or write, because for the common man it was seen as more important that they learn the skills needed for their work, and the values that would make them upstanding members of the community. Anything beyond that was regarded as not just unnecessary but even potentially dangerous, because of possible destabilisation of the class system – and unrest.

Nevertheless, over time and without any formal co-ordination, parish priests began to take on the task of educating children under their care, with the aim of equipping them for life. This was admittedly rather hit-and-miss at the beginning, with emphasis on practical skills and with no rules about attendance or age, but gradually children were 'taught their letters', and so began parish schools – the forerunners of our modern school system.

Though set within a framework of faith, however, it is important to note that the aim of parish schools was never *indoctrination*, but rather to help equip children with the skills they were going to need in later life. Thus, many boys were guided towards apprenticeships, while girls were taught cookery and how to sew. But the allegation that such an approach was fatally flawed because it was class based and failed to teach anything beyond the basic skills, is both misleading and unfounded.

As already noted, education of the lower classes originated in a desire to help them better their lot – to escape from poverty – and not from any desire to cement them as servitors into a capitalist system of exploitation (as alleged by the Marxists), from which they would never be able to break free. Contrary to what modern-day secularists would have us believe, Christian teaching did not deliberately exclude science, nor have certain areas of study ever been off-limits because of a perceived threat to faith. On the contrary, from earliest times Christian theologians – as seen, for example, in the writings of Augustine of Hippo and Aquinas – asserted that reason underpinned and was indispensable to faith, and a broad curriculum was always advocated so that believers could engage with non-believers from a position of strength. As clearly stated by Clement (who headed one of the earliest Christian schools in Alexandria at the beginning of the third century):

> Do not think that we say that these things are only to be received by faith, but also that they are to be asserted by reason. For indeed it is not safe to commit these things to bare faith without reason, since assuredly truth cannot be without reason.[5]

Similarly, Augustine wrote:

> Heaven forbid that we should believe in such a way as not to accept or seek reasons, since we could not even believe if we did not possess rational souls.[6]

Today secularists would have us believe that Christianity has censored and suppressed anything that might call into question the basics of the faith – that it has manipulated truth. But this assertion is itself perversion because, from its inception, Christianity has encouraged formal reasoning about God and His creation – so that we might more fully understand God's nature and intentions, and our relationship with Him. More than that, as pointed out by Rodney Stark,[7] science (defined as *explanations* of nature through systematic observation and research) was never the result of an eruption of secular thinking, but rather developed naturally from the view of medieval Christian scholars that all things were not just 'knowable', but that they *should* be known because of our God-given reason. To put it another way, they believed (1) that God is a relational being who reveals Himself progressively as our capacity to comprehend grows; (2) that God's creation of the universe out of nothing was in accordance with 'knowable' operating principles laid down by Himself; and (3) that the nature of reality – or revelation – only awaits increased human understanding. It is, therefore, God's will that we exercise His gift of reason, so that we might grow in knowledge. So Christianity has always encouraged enquiry and analysis. Indeed, as Stark asserts, science could never have existed without Christian theology, because historically it is the *only* religion worldwide that has encouraged such an approach.[8]

Other approaches to education

Compare this with the approach of other belief systems. Islam, for example, from its beginning condemned investigation into natural law as blasphemy, because of the logical constraint such findings would then impose upon Allah's freedom to act. To put it simply, rather than running on fundamental principles laid down at creation, the universe was regarded as sustained by Allah's will on a continuing basis, so that he retained *carte blanche* to do whatever he wanted. The Islamic system of study, therefore, was aimed at increasing *obedience* to Allah's precepts, as set down in the Koran via Mohammed (see further explanation below), but excluding any idea of gaining knowledge about Allah himself.

Or compare a Humanist approach, based on the idea that all things are ultimately 'knowable' through the application of reason. The theory is actually a variation of the Christian position, but denying a first cause or God. Logically, however, this is academically limiting, because if the researcher is unwilling even to contemplate the possibility of a Creator, it immediately means that certain lines of enquiry or investigation are off-limits. It imposes, in fact, methodological constraint, and may therefore lead to the suppression – whether conscious or not – of inconvenient data that throws doubt on the validity of certain assumptions.[9]

Communism and education

From Marx onwards, Communists regarded the education of the masses as vital to the success of the revolution. In their eyes the capitalist education system had been a tool for social engineering, aimed at empowering the ruling class (the bourgeoisie), while enslaving and exploiting those who lived by labour (the proletariat). In retrospect one can understand how this view took hold in Russia, because under the Tsar the peasants had received little or no education and 60% of the population had been illiterate (the condition of women was especially bad, with only 13% able to read and write). It is hardly surprising then that schools, the preserve of the wealthy, were seen as bourgeois institutions ideologically committed to servicing capitalism, while keeping the masses – on whose sweat depended continuance of the regime – firmly in their place.

With the revolution this clearly had to change. Under the new regime, the capitalist underpinnings of the old order had to be removed in their entirety – but at the same time it was recognised that knowledge was power, so top priority for the children of the revolution was education, and accordingly new schools and universities were set up, with education made free for all. In his book *The German Ideology*,[10] Marx clearly spelt out that ideas were not neutral, but rather ideological constructs[11] determined by the dominant social force or class, so from the start education was seen as a means of indoctrinating the proletariat into the socialist values of the collective. The People's Commissariat for Education, the authority established in the aftermath of the revolution, was ruthless in asserting control:

> In the matter of education, as in all other matters, the Communist Party is not merely faced by constructive tasks, for in the opening phases of its activity it is likewise faced *by destructive tasks* (italics added). In the educational system bequeathed to it by capitalist society, it must hasten to destroy everything which has made of the school an instrument of capitalist class rule.[12]

Revolutionary fervour did not stop, therefore, at mere reorganisation of the curriculum. Rather, for communists, the *entire system* that had made education a tool for class rule had to be dismantled and then reconfigured – and key to this was elimination of what was regarded as the pernicious influence of the church and family.

Marx had famously branded religion the opiate of the masses.[13] But for the new regime it was something infinitely more sinister than mere 'illusion', because the law of God was identified as one of the main tools of oppression, manipulated in the class war so as to maintain the status quo and produce 'blind slaves of capital'. To put it another way, religion was not just useless, it was opposed to everything to which the new order aspired – a counter ideology – and had therefore to be wiped out and destroyed. As stated by N.I. Bukharin and E. Preobrazhensky,

> The old school was intimately associated with religion – by compulsory religious teaching, compulsory attendance at prayers,

and compulsory church-going. The new school forcibly expels religion from within its walls, under whatever guise it seeks entry and in whatever diluted form reactionary groups of parents may desire to drag it back again.[14]

The same thought processes similarly branded the family an ideological construct of the bourgeoisie, aimed at perpetuating the values by which the ruling elite maintained their stranglehold on power. It too, therefore, became a target for destruction.

In bourgeois society, the child is regarded as the property of its parents – if not wholly, at least to a major degree. When parents say 'my daughter' or 'my son', the words do not simply imply the existence of a parental relationship, they also give expression to the parents' view that they have a right to educate their own children. From the socialist outlook, no such right exists. The individual human being does not belong to himself, but to society, to the human race. The individual can only live and thrive owing to the existence of society. The child, therefore, belongs to the society in which it lives....[15]

Education thus became a tool for re-education and indoctrination, ruthlessly replacing the old values with socialist dogma, aimed at emancipating the individual from perceived social pathologies and transferring allegiance to the State.

Unforeseen consequences
Some of the early social experiments were an obvious and dangerous failure. In 1917, for example, Lenin had decriminalised divorce, abortion and homosexuality – in one fell swoop abolishing what was seen as religious (and therefore capitalist) constraints on sexual behaviour. Speaking at a conference on Sexual Freedom in Berlin in 1923, the director of the Moscow Institute for Sexual Hygiene, Dr Grigory Batkis, stated:

Soviet legislation ... declares the absolute non-interference of the state and society into sexual matters, so long as no one's interests are encroached upon ... Concerning homosexuality, sodomy, and various other forms of sexual gratification, which are set down in

European legislation as offences against public morality, Soviet legislation treats these exactly the same as so-called 'natural' intercourse.[16]

The logic and motivation were wholly ideological, but sexual licence, with its inevitable deleterious effect on family life, began to undermine the stability of Soviet society. As a consequence, when Stalin came to power in the 1930s he memorably recriminalised homosexuality, labelling it a disease and making it punishable by up to eight years' hard labour.

Today, the social experiment trialed by the Bolsheviks in the wake of the revolution is largely over, seen internally not just as a failure, but as having dangerous consequences.[17] Perestroika has seen the rebirth of Russian enterprise and the emergence of a homegrown form of capitalism, but many of the old moral attitudes are similarly in the process of resurrection, and religion itself has been rehabilitated, with some 70% of Russians now self-identifying as Christian. Indeed, in a speech in 2014 condemning the godlessness of the West, President Vladimir Putin said,

Many Euro-Atlantic countries have moved away from their roots, including Christian values .... Policies are being pursued that place on the same level a multi-child family and a same-sex partnership, a faith in God and a belief in Satan. This is the path to degradation.[18]

It remains, however, important to understand the ideological frame that drove Communist change in the wake of the revolution, in order to comprehend what is going on in the West today – because we are inheritors of a deliberate programme of destabilisation, first articulated and implemented as policy in post-revolution Russia.

The Frankfurt School

When the Bolsheviks assumed control in Russia following the overthrow of the Czarist government, it was with the expectation that social revolution would catch fire and spread spontaneously across Europe and into America. This, however, did not happen – indeed, it showed signs of failing in Russia itself – and in 1922, on Lenin's initiative, a Communist think tank called the Institute for Social Research (the

I.S.R) and comprised of Marxist intellectuals, was set up to investigate the reasons for the failure.[19]

The group identified as the main problem the Judeo-Christian legacy, which they saw as underpinning Western/capitalist society. They argued that the religious teaching of transcendent purpose to life, and insistence on the importance of the individual as a moral being capable of decision and accountable to God, created a barrier to Communist insistence on a classless society that denied individual difference and the primacy of the State. Further, in their assessment, the hope and implicit trust generated by such belief militated against incitement to violent protest and revolution.

Based on this analysis, they then formulated a complex psychological strategy aimed at destroying all barriers impeding the spread of socialism – with the aim of bringing about the corruption, erosion and ultimate total disintegration of Western society. To this end they advocated such things as teaching sex and homosexuality to children, mass provision of contraception to school children, control and manipulation of the media, etc. Overall, there were three main objects: first, the demolition of the Family – which they correctly identified as one of the main building blocks of society; second, the destruction of religion – which, as well as providing a moral frame, they saw as giving hope; and, third, the promotion of sexual anarchy. As summed up by Willi Munzenburg, one of the plan's leading tacticians, 'We will make the West so corrupt that it stinks.' Because, 'Only then, after (we) have corrupted all its values and made life impossible, can we impose the dictatorship of the proletariat.' [20]

Even the Soviets saw these policies as too extreme, however, and in 1924 the group was expelled. Georg Lucaks, one of the main architects, ended up in Frankfurt, where he linked up with Felix Weil and went on to establish the infamous Frankfurt School, while Willi Munzenburg, who also returned to Germany and became instrumental in organising an extremely successful counter-propaganda campaign against both the Nazis and America, was subsequently hanged for his pains in the south of France (where he had fled in 1940) by a hit squad supposedly sent by Stalin.

STRATEGIC SPREAD

Education in the UK

In the UK, up until the nineteenth century, education was in the main the preserve of the Church, but the standard of provision was generally recognised as 'patchy', with one commentator even calling them 'pigsty schools',[21] and many children (as in pre-Communist Russia) received no schooling at all. A report of 1816, for example, found that of 12,000 parishes surveyed, 3,500 had no school, 3,000 had endowed schools of varying quality, and 5,500 had unendowed schools of questionable quality.[22]

Recognising the impact of the industrial revolution and exploitation of child labour, Peel's Factory Act of 1802 had tried to address the lack of provision by requiring employers to provide basic instruction in reading, writing and arithmetic. Overall, however, provision was plainly inadequate, and pressure began to mount for restrictions on child labour and for state-funded primary schools accessible to all, which would ensure basic standards. Thus began provision for state schooling, which, along with basic teaching in the three 'R's, aimed to teach Christian values and practical skills that would be of benefit to the child for life.

However, by the time of the Education Act of 1944, with its radical overhaul of educational provision, pressure was beginning to be exerted by a growing body of socialists, many of whom openly identified as Communist, who wanted to eliminate what they perceived as reinforcement of the class divide and objected to the use of state funds to teach religion.[23] We have already seen that a prime objective of the Frankfurt School was infiltration of Marxist ideologues into positions of influence, and here in the call of educators for removal of religion from education (including the daily act of worship laid down by the Act), we see the beginnings of the implementation of that strategy.

The subtle but insidious way such demands were introduced – most obviously in the name of *fairness* for the socially disadvantaged – should not blind us to the reality of an ideological assault committed to the destruction of Western culture. On any line of approach, it is hard to see how the banning of religion from all schools, including Church schools – in an avowedly Christian country – could do anything to help raise educational standards or ensure equality of opportunity. Rather, this should be seen for what it was – a beginning of the imposition of totalitarianism, intent on closing down debate.

As seen, this was a primary aim of the policy first set out by the political theorists of the Frankfurt School, and a part of their brilliance was undoubtedly the cynical ability to use and manipulate Western radicals, working to advance the cause of what they believed was socialist humanism. Munzenburg, perhaps the most expert propagandist the world has ever known, branded such individuals 'innocents', and joked that they had no idea they were working for Stalin.[24] The cult of political correctness that we see today is a direct consequence of the organised but covert manipulation devised in post-revolution Russia – and the goal is still the creation of chaos in order to allow the imposition of totalitarian control.

Make love, not war – the rise of flower power
The programme of Western destabilisation had always been envisaged as a 'long game', to be promoted by stealth so that the multiple targets would be unaware what was going on until too late. It was not until the 1960s, therefore, that the fruits began to be openly visible on any significant scale. A massive countercultural backlash – fuelled by a heady cocktail of post-war affluence, American anti-war feeling, sexual liberation, and 'mind-expanding' drugs – exploded onto Western culture with the force of a megaton bomb.

Led by the likes of Timothy Leary, William Burroughs and Allen Ginsberg; powered by the music of Dylan and the Beatles; symbolised by flower power and LSD ... it caught the imagination of the young who – already being taught to question Christian values in the school system – ostentatiously rejected what they termed the repressive authoritarianism of their parents and those in power.

Free thinkers in a brave new world?
Sadly, not. In reality, merely unconscious victims of covert Communist propaganda, hammered out in Moscow and Frankfurt, then channelled in the US through influential political theorists like Herbert Marcuse, darling of the New Left and open exponent of the Frankfurt School of

critical theory. Munzenberg's 'useful idiots' indeed.

Gay activism

With the ground for sexual anarchy well seeded and prepared, a couple of decades later the same strategies were then taken over and applied by the gay lobby in their struggle for 'equality'. In their highly influential book, *After the Ball: How America will Conquer its Hatred and Fear of Gays in the 90s*,[25] gay propagandists Marshall Kirk and Hunter Madsen set out their revolutionary plan for *rebranding* morality. Skilled marketing specialists (Kirk was a Harvard-educated neuropsychiatrist, and Madsen was an expert on public persuasion tactics and social marketing), the pair drew heavily on techniques reminiscent of the Frankfurt School. Their express object of course was not to bring about political revolution, but cultural transformation – yet, as we have seen, cultural alteration or rebranding is the bedrock of political change.

To achieve their ends, the pair aimed at recasting gays as victims – where necessary openly rewriting history. Their goal was not just acceptance, but the normalisation of homosexuality within society at large – laying the ground, in time, for the trumpet cry, 'Everyone is gay!' To achieve their ends Kirk and Madsen advocated, first, 'Desensitisation'; second, what they called 'Jamming'; and lastly, 'Conversion'.

They advised, for example:

> If gays present themselves – or allow themselves to be presented – as overwhelmingly different and threatening, they will put straights on a triple-red alert, driving them to overt acts of political oppression or physical violence. If, however, gays can live alongside straights, visibly but as inoffensively as possible, they will arouse a low-grade alert only, which, though annoying to straights, will eventually diminish for purely physiological reasons. Straights will be desensitized.[26]

Though again I am not suggesting that the pair were consciously employing strategies laid out by the Frankfurt School (although they might have been, because many of the techniques have undoubtedly been absorbed into mainstream marketing), the desired result was clearly the same – the overthrow of the existing value system in order to pave the way for 'revolution', defined this time as social and cultural conversion by way of orchestrated destabilisation.

It was exactly what the Frankfurt School had envisaged, and the obvious success of the campaign has in turn opened the way for further subversion – seen, for example, in the current campaign to normalise paedophilia, and once more using the same tactics.[27]

Again, as with Communist Russia, in the drive to bring about revolution we are seeing education being deliberately used to re-orient and change. For example, well known gay rights activist Peter Tatchell is now calling for mandatory LGBT inclusive sex education for children as young as five:

> ... equality and diversity education against all prejudice ... should be part of the core national curriculum and required teaching in every school. These dedicated lessons – by specialist trained teachers – should start from the first year of primary level through to the end of secondary education.[28]

It is a cry that is being increasingly taken up – not just by LGBT activists, but also by ordinary men and women who have bought into the lie that sexuality and gender are not biological, but rather the result of conditioning and choice. So not only are children now being officially taught that homosexual and heterosexual sex are exactly the same, but they are being actively encouraged by schools to *experiment* with both their sexuality and gender, before deciding what 'works best' for them.

No one of course should condemn another individual because of their sexual orientation – but many of the behaviours being taught in schools today are highly dangerous and, if followed, may well result in a shortened life span or a lifetime spent on medication.[29] More specifically, by encouraging generalised sexual experimentation, not only do we open children to the danger of STIs,[30] but also to diseases such as cancer[31] or hepatitis; to anal prolapse and tearing; or emotional and psychological damage.[32] The list goes on and on, and while advice on how to minimise risk and stay safe is given (usually with the rather simplistic 'use a condom'), the line taken totally ignores the fact that the risks would be non-existent if behaviours for which the body is not designed were avoided. Yet all biological, medical and scientific evidence suggesting a contrary view to the currently accepted liberal line is banned, and might even, if voiced, lead to criminal prosecution for breaching equality and diversity law.

These are the tactics of cultural Marxism – and they are dangerous. Freedom, enshrined in Christianity and one of the core values on which our nation is founded, has traditionally allowed open debate and criticism, and does not shy away from evidence-based truth. The suppression of truth in the name of equality is a denial of that freedom, and the imposition of totalitarianism.

Multiculturalism and Islam – why we should worry

For Muslims, knowledge is a sacred duty. But the knowledge they refer to is pre-determined and a form of *worship*, dedicated to acquiring greater understanding of the Koran. The website Islam Awareness defines it thus:

> The acquiring of knowledge is worship, reading the Quran and pondering upon it is worship, travelling to gain knowledge is worship. The practice of knowledge is connected with ethics and morality, with promoting virtue and combating vice, enjoining right and forbidding wrong....
>
> Not only should we seek knowledge, but when we learn it, it becomes obligatory on us to practise it...[33]

What is defined as 'secular' knowledge is also important. But, seen as the *second* branch of knowledge, it has to be integrated and set within the frame of religion, so that everything is taught in relation to the Koran.

As multiculturalism becomes a national mantra trumping all else, we see Islamic customs and teaching gaining ever-greater recognition in schools nationwide, with a corresponding decrease of emphasis on Christianity. This is true both in areas where there is a high Muslim population and areas where ethnic diversity remains relatively low. Thus, most schools today not only *celebrate* the Muslim festival of Eid, but increasingly the Christian character of Christmas (the main traditional Christian festival, along with Easter) is being either removed or minimised 'so as not to offend'. In fact, nationwide there seems to be a growing tendency to rebrand Christmas as nothing more than a generalised 'Consumer-fest'; and nativity plays, as reported in *The*

Independent on 14 December 2014, now regularly feature not just the baby Jesus, but spacemen, Elvis Presley, and any other loony addition that takes the fancy.[34]

The trend is especially odd, because we are told that Muslims don't mind our celebrations, because they too acknowledge Jesus as a prophet! While, however, at first glance this assertion appears welcome, we should beware, because such support serves only to downgrade Jesus, effectively making him subordinate to Mohammed, so that once again this functions as a covert attack – on both our society and 'established' faith.

The priorities of multiculturalism, which are inevitably leading to the marginalisation of Christianity in both our schools and culture could, as Islamic influence spreads, see in time a total prohibition on both the teaching and practice of Christianity. More than that, it is highly likely, on the evidence of countries where Islam holds sway, that we will in time see the active and violent suppression of Christians.

The irony of course is that secularists promote multiculturalism, and specifically Islam, as part of the drive to neutralise Christian influence, but they too will become targets for suppression if and when Islam gains ascendancy, because Islam is a species of theocratic totalitarianism that brooks no dissent, taking a hard line towards anyone not sharing their belief.[35]

It is fashionable these days to draw a distinction between moderate and radical Islam, and the former Prime Minister David Cameron, commenting on the Government's counter-extremism strategy in October 2015, expressly called for the Muslim 'silent majority' to make a stand and tackle what he branded 'extremism' within their own community.[36] Yet, while the majority of UK Muslims are no doubt peaceful, it is foolish to ignore the repeated commands of the Koran to kill unbelievers.[37] Islamic countries in general are strict in the enforcement of their faith, and persecution of Christians, even in apparently 'moderate' countries, is growing. We delude ourselves, therefore, if we imagine that devout Muslims in the UK don't wish to see this nation convert – they do, as evidenced by the creeping and seemingly inexorable spread of Sharia courts, the relentless pressure for provision of Halal foods, and the demand that our banking and finance systems be Sharia-compliant. So why should we believe that, as a group, Muslims will opt for secularist values and ignore the dictates of their faith if and when they gain greater power?

The myth of secular neutrality

The online Schools and Education page of the *British Humanist Association* proclaims: 'We aim for the UK to be a secular state with no privilege or discrimination on grounds of religion or belief.' [38] Similarly, the *National Secular Society* campaigns for the abolition of all faith schools, stating: 'A secular approach to education would see 'faith schools' phased out and ensure that publicly funded schools are equally welcoming to all children, regardless of their religious and philosophical backgrounds.' [39] The rationale is that such schools unfairly discriminate against the children of non-believers, in that they are selective and impose their views. Both groups also call for the disestablishment of the Church, and their stated aim is the removal of all religion from public life.

In other words, Christians are fine, so long as they keep their beliefs private and refrain from any public manifestation or comment. This is in fact already happening, and it means, in effect, that we are but a short step from the criminalisation of faith.

Secularists would have us believe that this is both just and reasonable, because they are neutral, and simply campaigning for a fairer and more equal society. But in reality what they are calling for is the right to substitute one ideology or religion for another, and their much-vaunted freedoms of belief and expression are mere cloaks to mask humanist indoctrination, with anything implying criticism rebranded as hate speech and bigotry.

It is clear that *secularism is an opposing belief system or religion*, and education is a primary source of conflict because of the power it has to shape young minds and ultimately transform the defining values of our culture. Secularism, just like Islam, will not allow peaceful co-existence with a rival, but seeks total subjugation. Whether knowingly or not, secularists are children of the Communist revolution, and their programme seeks to silence and shut down anything that calls into question and/or undermines the validity of their views.

Contrast this with the traditional Christian approach to education, which – though admittedly Christ-centred – encourages open and honest exploration and enquiry into everything, carefully weighing all evidence, in the belief that God has given us the gift of reason, which He wishes us to exercise.[40] This is not the case with Secularism, which, as we have seen, aims to *prohibit* any and all mention of God. In Humanist thought – whether dealing with creation, ethics, or religious instruction – anything that even hints at the divine would be strictly off-limits, because in the godless society in which they claim we live, man is supreme and responsible to no one other than himself. Man alone is the architect and creator of fate, so both religion and ethics are a social construct, and there can be no such thing as sin or moral constraint.

Battle lines
What we are seeing at the moment is a battle for survival, and Christians have been vulnerable because, by and large, we have bought into the lie that secularism is neutral, and that in these days of dwindling church attendance, non-believers have an absolute right to demand our beliefs do not impinge on others. In particular, we are told that we must be 'tolerant' of others, because it is the Christian thing to do – something non-Christians appear to imagine they are better able to interpret than believers themselves. The consequence is that we have been apologetic, entirely failing to appreciate that we are facing the insidious imposition of a different and hostile value system. But, as faith is held up to ridicule and – in face of our silence – Christians are increasingly blamed for every evil under the sun, so our society inexorably slides towards disintegration. The Marxist architects of destruction of the family would have been proud.

What can we do?
The only thing that has any chance of saving our society as we slide ever deeper into social collapse is a revival of the Christian faith, and of the core values on which this nation was founded: values of freedom, and of respect and care for all as made in the image of God. But first, as top priority, we have to recognise and acknowledge the nature of the attacks being launched against us, because only then will we have any chance of standing up to them. Only then will there be any possibility of success.

Second, we must be robust in challenging lies and distortion – whenever and wherever falsehood rears its head. Which means, as advocated by Clement and Augustine, that we must study to know the facts, so that, in love and speaking our truth quietly, *we can make a proper defence*. In short, we must educate ourselves! It matters not whether it is a question of history, biology, anthropology, social engineering, ethics ... or even of our much maligned faith – we must know the facts and take a stand. And we must act to defend our children, because they are the prize who will determine the future, and what they learn matters. Therefore, we must protect and safeguard what they are taught.

This is clearly rather daunting, especially for Christians taught to avoid confrontation and turn the other cheek, but all the evidence is actually on our side. Truth is on our side. The trouble is we have been cowed into apologetic agreement with those who claim neutrality and peddle anarchy – shot down by the weapons of supposed love and tolerance. However, it is neither hatred nor bigotry to insist on the truth, whether of science or faith, and we must stand on our right to speak and pass on our beliefs, turning the weapons of discrimination and intolerance back onto those who seek to silence and marginalise us.

The inescapable reality is that we are in an ideological war not of our choosing, which means, sadly, that there is no such thing as a safe middle ground where we can remain neutral. There is no such thing as a fence on which we can precariously sit. So now we must choose. We either defend our rights – our faith – or we give up altogether and submit to totalitarianism.

Specifics

In relation to education, this means that we must challenge the officially sanctioned programmes of study that are sexualising our children and robbing them of their childhood. We must call for a shift in emphasis in Sex and Relationship Education (SRE) – away from *sex* and onto *relationship* – calling for children to be taught first and foremost that they are special and of infinite value, and that the gift of love should not be trivialised by turning sex into a leisure-time activity, on a par with going for a pizza, or to the cinema with friends.

We need to denounce anti-bullying programmes and the like that are used as a cloak to indoctrinate and introduce children into harmful lifestyle choices, such as homosexuality or gender experimentation. Bullying is undeniably a major problem. A recent report by *Ditch the Label* found that 1.5 million young people (50%) had been bullied in the past year, and that 145,800 (19%) were bullied every day.[41] But, as the report went on to acknowledge, children are picked on for a variety of reasons, and the greatest identified cause is appearance related (52%), followed by a range including special educational needs, disability, low socio-economic status, ethnicity, etc. Conversely, only 7% of children surveyed reported being bullied as a result of attitudes towards their sexuality – yet many of the anti-bullying programmes being used in schools today concentrate on this aspect to the exclusion of all else.[42] So we need to call for a comprehensive approach that acknowledges this fact – demanding that such programmes look at the full picture, and not focus on one aspect to the exclusion of all else.

We need to insist too that our children are accurately taught biology and science, especially in relation to sexual health and wellbeing, so that they fully know the dangers attaching to sexual licence and immorality. This is not to import into teaching any 'judgement' on behaviours, but rather to ensure that children know the full facts, and that should they make a mistake (as children at some point inevitably do), we are there to help.

Above all, we must stand by the right of parents to decide what form and type of education we wish our children to undergo. Whatever the teaching of Marxist ideologues, children do not belong to the State. They 'belong' in fact to no one, but it is the duty of parents to ensure that they are best prepared and equipped to face the challenges that life will throw at them. The right of choice is the gift of God. The duty of educators is to help children to exercise that choice wisely.

Conclusion

As Christians we are called to love and respect all. But we are not called, in the name of tolerance, to accept that which causes harm. Our critics say we must not judge, and certainly they are right to the extent that ultimate judgment lies with God. But God has given us reason to discern between right and wrong, and He calls us to defend what is right and to oppose evil. Without doubt, education is one of the main areas of battle.

Our children cannot take up arms – they are there to receive and learn, not to lead the way – so it is up to us. If we are not to lose the values on which our society is founded, and all we hold dear, then we must make a stand – now, before it is too late.

Notes
[1] Deuteronomy 6:6-7
[2] 'Education is a fundamental human right and essential for the exercise of all other human rights. It promotes individual freedom and empowerment and yields important development benefits.' UNESCO http://www.unesco.org/new/en/education/themes/leading-the-international-agenda/right-to-education/
[3] *Education in England: a brief history*, Derek Gillard, 2011
See: http://www.educationengland.org.uk/history/chapter01.html
[4] ibid.
[5] *Recognitions of Clement*: book 2, ch. 69
[6] *City of God*. As quoted by R.W. Southern 1970a:49 *Medieval Humanism and Other Studies* (New York, Harper Torchbooks)
[7] Rodney Stark, *The Victory of Reason, How Christianity led to freedom, Capitalism and Western success* (Random House, 2005)
[8] Rodney Stark, *The Victory of Reason*, (Random House 2005, Chapter 1)
[9] Thus many scientists reject 'creationism' as being unscientific, arguing in favour of Darwinian evolution. But Darwin's theories of evolution are being increasingly called into question by geneticists and geologists, and the issue clearly needs further dedicated investigation. Nevertheless, as proudly trumpeted on the British Humanist Association website, the Government, under pressure, has banned wholesale all teaching of creationism in schools as pseudoscience. https://humanism.org.uk/2014/06/18/victory-government-bans-existing-future-academies-free-schools-teaching-creationism-science/
[10] Written 1845, published in 1932
[11] See Barry Burke (2000) 'Karl Marx and informal education', *The encyclopaedia of informal education*, www.infed.org/thinkers/et-marx.htm.
[12] N.I. Bukharin and E. Preobrazhensky: The ABC of Communism. S77 The Destructive tasks of communism https://www.marxists.org/archive/bukharin/works/1920/abc/10.htm
[13] Karl Marx, *A Contribution to the Critique of Hegel's Philosophy of Right*. (First published *Deutsch-Französische Jahrbücher*, 7 & 10 February 1844 in Paris).
[14] N.I. Bukharin and E. Preobrazhensky: The ABC of Communism. S77
[15] https://www.marxists.org/archive/bukharin/works/1920/abc/10.htm
[16] 'Russia's sexual revolution after 1917'. Colin Wilson *The Socialist Worker* https://socialistworker.co.uk/art/19929/Russia's+sexual+revolution+after+1917
[17] E.g. In light of its population crisis resulting from the high practice of abortion, in October 2011 the Russian Parliament put in place measures to discourage termination of pregnancy and strengthen families. See: http://www.nytimes.com/2011/10/22/world/europe/russia-abortion-restrictions-adopted.html?_r=0
[18] Reported in *The Washington Times*, 28 January 2014 http://www.washingtontimes.com/news/2014/jan/28/whos-godless-now-russia-says-its-us/?page=all
[19] Originally called the Marx-Engels Institute, under the directorship of D. Riazanov

[20] Willi Munzenberg, quoted by Ralph de Toledano, The Frankfurt School, manuscript 2000, p.5

[21] Giles 1946:35 quoted in Gillard D (2011) *Education in England: a brief history,* www.educationengland.org.uk/history

[22] Gillard D., ibid.

[23] See Brown, J.W.H. (n.d.) *The Education Bill,* (London: Watts & Co. for the Rationalist Press Association [forerunners of the Rationalist Association])

[24] 'The Innocents Club, The life and influence of Willi Munzenberg' Michael Newland http://www.heretical.com/miscella/munzen.html

[25] New York, Penguin, 1989

[26] ibid., pp. 147-157.

[27] See 'Paedophilia: bringing dark desires to light', Jon Henley, *The Guardian,* 3 January, 2013

[28] Peter Tatchell, *Make sex education compulsory and LGBT inclusive,* 5-02-15 http://www.petertatchellfoundation.org/sex-education/make-sex-education-compulsory-lgbt-inclusive c.f. David Cameron: teach children to treat gay people equally, *The Telegraph* 26 January 2010, http://www.telegraph.co.uk/news/politics/7079542/David-Cameron-teach-children-to-treat-gay-people-equally.html

[29] See e.g. http://factsaboutyouth.com/posts/health-risks-of-the-homosexual-lifestyle/

[30] In 2014, in England, there were approximately 440,000 new diagnoses of STIs, the highest number being to men who have sex with men, including a 46% increase in syphilis and a 32% increase in gonorrhoea. https://www.gov.uk/government/uploads/system/uploads/attachment_data/file/437433/hpr2215_STI_NCSP_v6.pdf

[31] It is reported that anal intercourse puts men at significant risk of anal cancer. See http://factsaboutyouth.com/posts/male-homosexual-behavior/

[32] Health care problems of lesbian, gay, bisexual, and transgender patients. http://www.ncbi.nlm.nih.gov/pmc/articles/PMC1070935/

[33] The importance of education in Islam http://www.islamawareness.net/Education/importance.html

[34] http://www.independent.co.uk/news/uk/home-news/rebranding-christmas-more-public-bodies-are-refusing-to-give-the-festival-its-name-for-fear-of-9923365.html

[35] E.g. 'I will cast terror into the hearts of those who disbelieve. Therefore strike off their heads and strike off every fingertip of them' Koran 8:12

[36] http://www.telegraph.co.uk/news/politics/david-cameron/11939380/David-Cameron-Extremists-and-hate-preachers-to-be-treated-like-paedophiles.html

[37] There are 109 texts in the Koran specifically calling Muslims to wage war on, and kill, unbelievers. E.g. Fight against them until idolatry is no more and Allah's religion reigns supreme. Sura 2:193; Unbelievers are enemies of Allah and they will roast in hell. Sura 41:14; Slay them wherever ye find them and drive them out of the places whence they drove you out, for persecution is worse than slaughter. Sura 2:191 etc.

[38] https://humanism.org.uk/campaigns/schools-and-education/

[39] http://www.secularism.org.uk/religion-in-schools.html

[40] This is not of course to imply that over the centuries Christianity has countenanced the co-equal acceptance of doctrines hostile to the faith. Examination and analysis of opposing or deviant belief is one thing, but acceptance of those doctrines as having equal or greater standing is quite another, and would be regarded as heresy.

[41] http://www.ditchthelabel.org/annual-bullying-survey-2016/

[42] E.g. Stonewall offers a range of resources specifically to designed 'to tackle homophobic, biphobic and transphobic bullying in education environments and help create more inclusive spaces.'
http://www.stonewall.org.uk/our-work/education-resources
These materials are now regularly being used in both state and church school education environments.

Chapter Three

EDUCATION: FUNCTION, IDEAS AND INFLUENCES
Philip Quenby

Education can be a slippery concept. Muriel Spark's 1961 novel *The Prime of Miss Jean Brodie*, set in a Scottish school against the backdrop of the Spanish Civil War, features a demagogic schoolteacher who lives through and manipulates her favoured pupils. At one point, Brodie is taken to task by the headmistress over what education means. She asserts that it is a leading out of what is within the child, deriving from the Latin *ex*, meaning out and *ducere*, meaning to lead. The headmistress prefers the Latin verb *educari*, meaning to feed, so that education is a feeding in. The exchange illustrates a fundamental dichotomy (amounting almost to schizophrenia) in how we approach education: is it *educere*, *educari*, or both? Linked to this is the question of whether we are in any meaningful sense able to educate ourselves. Again, literature points up how conflicted we are over this issue: Sartre's *Autodidact* (self-taught man) in *La Nausée* is an object of mingled pity, fun and bemusement, whilst Hardy's hero in *Jude the Obscure* wears his learning with a heavy sense of being looked down on merely for not having acquired it in the 'accepted' way.

What these examples illustrate is how thoroughly and deeply value judgements permeate any discussion on education. Once we move beyond the merely technical – how to feed and clothe ourselves, the mechanics of learning a foreign language or musical instrument, the programming of computers or use of tools – it becomes impossible to speak of what the function of education *is*. We can only articulate ideas of what we believe its function *ought* to be. Though some philosophers have valiantly tried to argue otherwise, moving from an 'is' proposition to an 'ought' proposition without making a value judgment along the way is something that so far has eluded our abilities. We are therefore stuck with it: the way we approach education and the kind of education we promote cannot help but reveal our deepest-held prejudices about the world – not just how we find it, but how we want it to be. It also shows what attitude we take towards those who are the objects or recipients of learning and how we seek to mould them into our desired image. Often we are not conscious of such things, but just because we are not deliberately trying to create a latter-day *Homo Sovieticus*[1] does not mean that we are inoculated against them.

One way to shine a light on the issue is to examine how education has been approached in other times and places. This chapter looks briefly at the examples of ancient Greece; Confucianism; Zen Buddhism; Hinduism; Judaism; Islam; Nazi Germany; and the Soviet Union. Attempts of this kind are of course fraught with difficulty: it is easy to object that they deal only in generalities; counter-examples and exceptions can almost always be found – even in the most homogenous and strictly controlled societies, dissenting voices are seldom far away. Yet that does not render such an exercise wholly valueless. Cultures based on these viewpoints have indisputably developed in quite distinct ways, to a degree that cannot be put down simply to differences in physical environment, external shocks or natural endowments of resources or manpower. Education and attitudes towards it have clearly had an impact, albeit that these influences have combined with other factors in ways that we might now find difficult to disentangle. Investigating the past therefore gives us a tool with which to assess what we believe to be good and bad about the approaches that others have adopted, and a means by which we might measure the likely results of our own educational experiments.

Ancient Greece
In education as in so much else, Athens and Sparta represent opposite ends of the spectrum. All ancient Greek city states agreed on the health and military benefits of physical fitness and trained boys accordingly, but Sparta took this approach furthest. Females as well as males were schooled in ways defined and controlled by the *polis*:[2] the former to

become the wives and mothers of soldiers and the latter to be the rank and file of Sparta's armies. In a highly militarised society, service of the state was deemed the highest good and this service was to be rendered primarily through war or preparation for it. The logical consequences were: complete subordination of the individual to the state; elevation of the state to a role in the upbringing of children which elsewhere was left with parents; concentration on what was directly relevant to things military and disregard of what was thought extraneous or effete; ethics built on concepts of duty, honour, service, loyalty and physical bravery; disregard for life, expressed in the killing of infants deemed unfit for service of the state or likely to be a burden to it, and the ruthless exploitation of a class of slaves (*helots*) whose labour left citizens free to devote themselves to war.

Since that is an outlook so far removed from our own, it is worth reflecting on how this kind of education worked in practice. Boys[3] were removed from their families at the age of seven to live in barracks, where they remained until being allowed to marry at the age of thirty. Harsh discipline, designed to accustom youngsters to physical discomfort and pain, was rigorously enforced. Boys were deliberately underfed and under-clothed so as to encourage them to forage, steal and endure deprivation; academic learning was kept to a minimum; fighting between students encouraged; weapons-handling, drill and tactical exercises constantly practised; courage praised and cowardice penalised; music and dancing taught not for their own sake but to enhance movement in combat. Towards the end of their teenage years, youths were expected to hunt down and kill a *helot*,[4] failure in this task being punished. To us, this looks like morality turned on its head: the deliberate infliction of pain; inducements to theft; conniving in murder; promoting survival of the fittest; treating the weak as embarrassments at best and disposable commodities at worst; sublimating all personality into the commonality of nationhood and national survival.

Athens was considerably less militaristic than Sparta, its *polis* less prescriptive and intrusive, its ideas about learning less rooted in what was thought to be needed for the survival of the state in war. Athenians viewed education as a key aspect of individual identity and reputation, rather than as an essentially corporate exercise or group endeavour.

Consequently, their approach to it was not solely or primarily utilitarian, allowing for the pursuit of intellectual growth as well as physical prowess and valuing the search for knowledge regardless of how immediate its practical applications might be. The (relatively few) who could afford it would therefore study mathematics, natural sciences (what we would now call biology and chemistry), rhetoric, geometry, astronomy and meteorology. Music and dance were considered worthwhile in their own right instead of merely as means of achieving greater battlefield manoeuvrability. Philosophy[5] was highly esteemed. The resulting intellectual achievements had a huge impact on other cultures in the classical and mediaeval world and continue to resonate today. It is, however, worth remembering that Athenian culture differed fundamentally from our own: for all that there might be democracy for the few, there was no thought that slavery might be morally repugnant; women remained very much second-class citizens; the only restraints on the exploitation of empire were practical, not ethical.

Confucianism

The parameters of Confucian education were set both by Confucius[6] himself and his later interpreter Mencius. Confucius considered that the goal of knowledge 'is to know man' and that we must look within to find truth, since 'Tao cannot be separated from us for a moment.'[7] Thus knowledge in the truest sense equates to self-knowledge, technical accomplishments being of correspondingly lesser importance. Truth exists not in books but in man himself, and to know man is to find truth. Since human nature is thought to be essentially good, learning is a means to recapture the original virtue that has been obscured or perverted by circumstances. It follows that education is not about imparting facts so much as receiving guidance that will allow an opening of the mind: 'The way of great learning consists in illuminating innate virtues.' Consequently, teaching focussed less on conceptual analysis of structured arguments than on personal encounter between teacher and student, reflected in Confucius's preference for aphorisms rather than systematic reasoning. The aim of these was not to convince at an intellectual level but to cause disciples to ponder and digest the true meaning and implication of what was said.[8]

Confucianism valued thinking (*ssu*), though it used the term in a different sense from that implied by the Western tradition that derives in large measure from ancient Athens. In speaking about thought, Confucius meant not simply abstract speculation but something that belonged to the heart as well as to the brain – the pictograms for *ssu* comprising *t'ien* (meaning, field) and *hsin* (meaning, heart or mind). Hence thinking did not merely involve rationalisation or computation, but encompassed what we would term the psychological dimension, involved considerations of ethics and values, and necessitated reflection on the origin of knowledge and the means by which anything can be known. In the *Analects*, Confucius opined, 'He who learns but does not think is lost.' Mencius concurred, stating of the search for Tao that, 'If one thinks, he will get it. If one does not think, he will not get it.' Mencius believed the human mind esteems *li* (reason) and *i* (righteousness) so that to think is to do so reasonably and morally, and thought that anyone who studied without using the mind would be wasting their time. In this tradition, the ultimate objective of thinking is to know oneself, gain self-illumination and understand human nature, not so as to acquire a particular skill or profession, but in order to become fully human, a 'superior man'.

Teachers were expected to configure teaching to the qualities of individual students, guiding them to develop their inner natures, moving at a pace suitable to them and teaching by example as much as by formal instruction. Confucius thought that, 'if a ruler sets himself right, he will be followed' and by analogy that good education would be like 'the north polar star, which remains in its place while all the other stars revolve round it'. Whilst those who did not want to learn could not be taught, teachers could help students overcome obstacles, though they could not give them good nature or force them to learn. In fact, formal schooling was in many ways viewed as the least important part of the educational process, which encompassed the entirety of life and in which the home played the primary role. It was the job of parents to nurture the innate abilities and talents of their offspring; they bore the main responsibility for inculcating *jen* (humanity), *li* (propriety) and *i* (righteousness); it was they who should encourage youngsters to live as a 'superior man' in whatever their station in life might be. A child's good nature and moral worth was reflected in relationships with parents and grandparents, which in turn reflected relationships within society, so socialising a child was of prime importance.

As the litany of Chinese achievements in many fields of endeavour makes clear, Confucian concepts of education were no absolute bar to technological progress: gunpowder and printing, for example, were developed in China long before they became known in Europe. Nor did Confucian emphasis on loyalty, filial piety and social harmony necessarily condemn Chinese society to become fossilised: the meritocracy inherent in Confucius's belief that anyone could live as a 'superior man' helped give rise to the imperial examination system which survived into the early years of the twentieth century, and this provided a means of advancement regardless of wealth or social background.[9] Nevertheless, as the full extent to which China had fallen behind the West became apparent from the middle 1800s onwards, a number of Chinese intellectuals began to criticise their Confucian inheritance, attributing to it the nation's relative technological and social backwardness. The New Culture Movement which arose in the early decades of the twentieth century, for example, advocated replacing Confucian cultural norms with ones based on Western standards embracing democracy and science. Criticism of Confucianism was taken up by the Communist Party (reaching hysterical proportions during the Cultural Revolution under Mao Zedong) and its educational legacy remains the subject of debate in China even today.

Zen Buddhism
Unsurprisingly given the interplay between Buddhism and Confucianism, Zen shares many Confucian ideas on learning.[10] It holds that education is an opening of the mind; that the role of teaching is not simply to impart information but to help students gain access to original abilities or qualities which have been obscured or lost; that students cannot be forced to receive instruction; that daily life and physical labour is as much a part of education as academic study; that logical argument is of limited usefulness; that truth requires practical application if it is to be fully apprehended; that a teacher should be alert to the opening of a student's mind and should foster this through his own personal experience, facilitating fresh viewpoints on the part of the student through

which a new person will emerge. As eighth century Zen master Ch'ing-yuan put it: 'Before I had studied Zen for thirty years, I saw mountains as mountains and waters as waters. When I arrived at a more intimate knowledge, I came to the point where I saw that mountains are not mountains and waters are not waters. But now that I have got its very substance I am at rest. For it is just that I see mountains once again as mountains and waters once again as waters.'[11]

Hinduism

Sharing with Buddhism the conviction that the world of the senses and all connected with or derived from it is illusion, Hinduism has traditionally considered theoretical knowledge inferior or unworthy. Yet at the same time it believed that mankind has an obligation to explore truth, seeing personal experience as a vital and necessary step towards the ultimate goal of attaining freedom from a cycle of birth, death and rebirth. Consequently it did not discourage scientific enquiry as long as this was undertaken in conformity with Hindu teaching. An uneducated man was thought on a par with the animals, since he lacked what would enable him to transcend his physical self, whereas someone who became educated thereby received a second, spiritual birth. Education (*vidya*) was valued as a means of realising the four aims of life: *dharma* (virtue), *artha* (wealth), *kama* (pleasure) and *moksha* (liberation) – a mechanism for achieving spiritual insight through which desires would be controlled; religious duties properly performed; impurities of egotism, attachment and delusion mastered or overcome; liberation achieved.

Knowledge was classified according to that which was lower (being acquired through the senses and pertaining to the material aspects of human existence) and that which was higher. The former was the realm of rites and rituals, scholarly study of the Hindu scriptures and what touched on everyday living; the latter was knowledge of Atman and Brahman,[12] gained through personal experience and its attendant self-realisation. Though higher knowledge was to be preferred, it was admitted that this alone is insufficient, for lower knowledge is needed to navigate the world of illusion – which all must do in order to progress towards recognition of the value of higher knowledge and to acquire a state of mind receptive to this enhanced level of understanding. Experience and the performance of religious duties were thus part and parcel of spiritual progress, salvation not being gained by fleeing the vicissitudes of life but by inner transformation brought about by confronting and overcoming the challenges that come our way. Lower knowledge could be gained through teaching within the family, apprenticeship in a trade and so forth, but higher knowledge required the pupil to seek out a guru (teacher).

Gurus were revered as removers of darkness, a god in human form, Brahman himself. They came in various guises, from relatively lowly *upadhyayas* to revered *acharyas* and even wandering *charakas*. *Acharyas*, blessed with knowledge both theoretical and practical, taught for free in *Gurukulas*, where students would live as part of the master's household. The relationship was a fatherly one, for though parents were responsible for the physical welfare of their offspring, the guru was responsible for their spiritual welfare, discipline and eventual growth into responsible adults. He was to show the way by example and through spiritual knowledge gained through his own experience, *sadhana* (practice) and insight. (Like Confucianism, Hinduism elevated knowledge which derived from direct experience, this being thought more spiritually valuable than reading of books, contemplation of profound questions or living as a hermit.) Instruction was oral and students were required to learn verses of the Hindu scriptures by heart. Having mastered all subjects to the guru's satisfaction (a process that could take years) they were then free to leave.

Gurukulas were usually located away from population centres (often in forests). Life for students was hard: they would need to serve their guru for years before being trusted enough to receive advanced instruction and had to beg for food, as gurus had no obligation to feed them. There were more substantive problems, too: the *Gurukula* tradition militated against inter-disciplinary cross-fertilisation by propagating a fragmented educational model; unconditional submission to the guru was required; once a student had enrolled, there was little parental say or control thereafter over what was taught, or how; the austerity demanded of students was often excessive; instruction was frequently hidebound and resistant to innovation, adhering rigidly to Hindu scriptures and traditions; there was no independent oversight, so that the quality of teaching was hugely variable; reliance on oral teaching and students learning everything by heart meant the educational process took much longer than it might otherwise have done; teaching was highly centralised, as the guru had the final say over everything; no females were admitted; and access to *Gurukulas* depended on caste, the lower orders being entirely excluded.

The caste system was a pernicious influence throughout Indian society, segmenting it into groups which were determined purely by accident of birth and militating against widespread education by ability. At its most restrictive, the caste hierarchy trapped many in lowly positions by circumscribing movement and contact between the castes, closing occupations to people other than members of approved castes and requiring different social groups to live apart from each other. The degree to which development of the caste system can justly be attributed to Hindu teaching is a matter of debate and it is fair to say that elements within Hinduism (as within other religions such as Jainism, Sikhism and Buddhism) have roundly rejected it.[13] Be that as it may, Brahmins (the priestly caste) were certainly jealous of their learning and clung to oral teaching as a way of ensuring that it was not disseminated to those at the bottom of the social scale. Lower castes were forbidden to study the Vedas (Hindu scriptures) or any subject outside their occupation, strict penalties being imposed on teachers and pupils who disobeyed.[14]

There was indeed a more general reticence about who should receive learning for, in the hands of someone evil or immoral, knowledge was thought to be a destructive force. It brought power which could be misused and hence should be taught only to those who were mentally disposed towards it; qualified to receive it by virtue of their current knowledge and degree of discipline; and fitted to use it properly through having cultivated the necessary virtue. Though this attitude was understandably most prevalent with regard to higher knowledge, it seems to have rubbed off in other areas, too. Even at the vocational level, there was a tendency for certain instruction to be imparted secretively under oath and only to qualified students. Though some of the craft guilds of western Europe might have had similar rules at various points, in India restrictive practices of this kind were buttressed by the caste system. Overall, the climate for learning tended to steer those of higher caste towards the metaphysical whilst substantially excluding those of lower caste from learning what fell outside their permitted caste functions.

Judaism

The *Torah*[15] commanded Jews to 'teach [God's decrees and laws] diligently unto thy children' (Deuteronomy 6:7, KJV). Later interpretations translated this into a duty to read the *Shema* (the central statement of Jewish monotheism found in Deuteronomy 6:4–5) twice a day and to learn the Torah so as to be able to teach it themselves. In addition, some took the instruction to 'write ye this song for you' (Deuteronomy 31:19) as a requirement for all adult males to inscribe their own Torah scroll. Consequently, the ability to read and write was highly prized. Initially the duty to instruct children lay upon the father as head of the household, but in 75 BC the influential Pharisee Simeon ben Shetah argued for mandatory schooling at public expense, and high priest Joshua ben Gamla followed this up in 64 BC with a statement that children should start instruction at the ages of six or seven. The result was that literacy levels in Jewish communities tended to be relatively high, causing Jews in medieval and early modern Europe to be valued for this skill even though simultaneously discriminated against and often persecuted.

The standard educational text was the *Mishnah*,[16] with instruction according to its six categories: *zeraim* (meaning 'seeds', dealing with agriculture); *moed* (meaning 'festivals', dealing with the sabbath and related regulations); *nashim* (meaning 'women', dealing with marriage and divorce); *nezikin* (meaning 'damages', dealing with civil and criminal law); *kodashim* (meaning 'holy things', dealing with dietary laws, sacrifices, temple observance and the like); and *tohorot* (meaning 'purities', dealing with laws regulating purity and impurity). In practice the curriculum was much broader than this might suggest, since proper understanding of these matters was thought to require instruction in such things as basic mathematics and accountancy, chemistry, physics and animal biology, geography; history, pharmacology and more. Judaism did not teach a distinction between mind and matter of the kind espoused by elements of ancient Greek philosophy.[17] Instead, it embraced the unity of Creation and advised seeking wholeness in body, mind and spirit – a set of beliefs which tended to translate into a holistic view of education.

The impact of Jews on almost every field of educational endeavour is extraordinary: people of full or part Jewish ancestry account for 22% of all individual Nobel Prize recipients between 1901 and 2015.

Islam

Muslim theories of education lean heavily on the work of Al-Ghazali (1058–1111),[18] for whom education involved not just intellectual but also religious, moral and physical training. Ingesting information was only part of this process, since learning had to be put into practice: true learning would affect behaviour and true knowledge could only be gained after becoming thoroughly versed in the Koran. Such knowledge would draw the soul closer to God and thereby increase its happiness. Consequently, the aim of education was to cause people to follow the teachings of Islam so that they would achieve salvation and hence eternal life. Worldly goals were of correspondingly lesser worth: "O Disciple! How many sleepless nights have you passed reading science and poring over books — but I do not know its purpose. If it was for worldly ends, to gain its baubles, win its honours and to boast over contemporaries and equals, woe to you, and again woe! Yet if your purpose was to breathe life into the Sacred Law of the Prophet, to develop your character and break 'the soul commanding evil', then blessing on you and again blessings."

Since the avowed purpose of knowledge is to help man attain true happiness and this comes from drawing close to God, it followed that the religious sciences were superior to (and contained greater truth than) secular sciences. So whilst the latter might be useful, they took second place to the former. Al-Ghazali classed revealed science (knowledge of God, his books, his prophets, the kingdoms of earth and heaven, *shari'a* law) as true knowledge, and worldly learning (metaphysics, mathematics, logic, non-revealed sciences, politics and ethics) as mere techniques.[19] Each branch of knowledge was then divided into elementary, intermediate and advanced levels and a list of books given to aid study at each level. Investigation of the revealed sciences[20] and their ancillary disciplines such as linguistics and literature was obligatory, other subjects optional. Further subdivision produced categories of subjects that were permitted, alongside those that were reprehensible and forbidden, and though there was seen to be no contradiction between mathematics, logic, politics and ethics on the one hand and religion on the other, nevertheless there was a suspicion that these (like music, dance and art) might prove gateways to subjects that were off limits, so they were looked at askance. Overall, the effect was to restrict the acceptable parameters of learning.[21]

Al-Ghazali thought the main responsibility for education lay with the family. Believing children to be a blank slate at birth, he emphasised the importance of environment and the early years in forming character. He considered women intellectually inferior to men and thought their instruction should be confined to the basics of Islam. Seeing the relationship between teacher and pupil as like that of father and son, from which each could benefit and to which each should contribute, Al-Ghazali (who worked as a teacher himself) emphasised the part that teachers play as examples to students, their role not being limited to teaching particular subjects but instead encompassing every aspect of the pupil's life and personality. Early introduction to the fundamentals of Islam was recommended, to be achieved through inculcation, memorising and repetition: at this initial stage, Al-Ghazali saw no need for understanding of what was taught, since that would come with later exposition and practice.[22] Though recognising that a scholar should seek after truth, Al-Gazali nevertheless acknowledged that there might be limits on teaching truths which could prove harmful or cause people to doubt Islam or their own reason.[23]

These ideas helped ensure that science in the Muslim world was increasingly subordinate to religion; effectively undermined any attempt to develop scientific method by their rejection of causality;[24] entrenched views of the inferiority of women; tended to downgrade learning that was not religious; categorised various subjects as unworthy of study and others as forbidden; weakened independent enquiry in all disciplines, creating reliance on existing authority rather than encouraging innovation, creativity and discovery; and elevated the derivative and imitative, validating rote learning as the prime method of early instruction. As a result, by the seventeenth century Western Europe had already opened up a significant scientific lead over Islamic nations – a gap which widened over succeeding centuries as scientific method propelled further advances. Partly in reaction to the shortcomings of the existing educational arrangements and the increasingly obvious gulf with the West, nineteenth and early twentieth century Muslim leaders often sought to put in place education on more Western lines. This attempt was at best a partial success and in large measure the dispute between *Falasifa* (philosophers) and *Fuqaha'* (the religiously minded) continues.

Nazi Germany

Immediately on coming to power, the Nazi regime set about politicisation of the entire educational system through controlling appointments of teaching staff and by manipulating the curriculum. The avowed aim was to fulfil Hitler's wish that 'a young German must be as swift as a greyhound, as tough as leather, as hard as Krupp steel', the ultimate objective a population equipped to carry out the project of conquest and racial purification set out in *Mein Kampf*. New textbooks were issued, Jewish teachers sacked and the Aryan staff who remained subjected to indoctrination; propaganda given prominence on notice-boards and in classrooms; schools explicitly required to educate their pupils 'in the spirit of National Socialism'; Nazi racial theories taught, and all other subjects used to inculcate National Socialist ideals. Adherence to this programme was enforced through a National Curriculum which emphasised physical training[25] and progressively downgraded the academic learning available to women, whose access to higher education was increasingly curtailed. Nazi ideals of womanhood centred on the three Ks – *Kinder* (children), *Küche* (kitchen), *Kirche* (Church) – and the instruction available rapidly came to reflect this.[26] Meanwhile, elite schools to train future leaders (*Nationalpolitische Erziehungsanstalten*) were set up and run by the SS, featuring even greater emphasis on physical pursuits which would be of use in war.

History and biology bore the brunt of Nazi tampering in education, but no aspect of learning was immune. Interior Minister Wilhelm Frick asserted that the purpose of history was to teach 'that life was always dominated by struggle; that race and blood were central to everything that happened in past, present and future; and that leadership determined the fate of peoples'. The Armistice that ended the First World War was portrayed as a stab in the back by internal enemies; the Versailles Treaty as an unparalleled betrayal on the part of its German signatories; and this and the economic problems of the immediate post-war period as the work of Jews and Marxists whose constant aim was to keep Germany down. Biology was hijacked by concepts of racial superiority, blood purity and eugenics; geography employed to emphasise the territories that had been stripped from Germany by the victorious Allied powers, and her consequent need for *Lebensraum* (living space); and science was used to teach ballistics, military aviation, bridge building and the impact of poisonous gas. Even mathematics was given a special twist as pupils were asked to calculate artillery trajectories, fighter-to-bomber ratios, the cost of looking after the mentally ill or socially undesirable, and the like.[27]

Teachers were kept in line by a vetting system run by local Party officials, backed up by the threat of being informed on by their pupils, who would be reminded of this duty to the *Führer* as part of their *Hitlerjugend* (Hitler Youth) training. Any teacher considered disloyal was sacked and promotion was dependent on political soundness as much as talent. Within a relatively short time the authorities had weeded out Jews, political undesirables and those with an independent streak, so that by 1936 something over 32% of teachers are reckoned to have been members of the Nazi Party and fully 97% joined the Nazi Teachers' Association – much higher percentages than for the equivalents in other professions and a measure of the importance of education to the entire Nazi project. Such rapid Nazification of the teaching profession was all the more striking because in the years before Hitler came to power many teachers had been members of the (soft Left and avowedly democratic) Social Democratic Party. Not only that, but the shortcomings of the new system swiftly became apparent: as early as January 1937 one army officer was complaining, 'Our youth starts off with perfectly correct principles in the physical sphere of education, but frequently refuses to extend this to the mental sphere ... Many candidates applying for commissions display a simply inconceivable lack of basic knowledge.'[28]

Soviet Russia

Education was seen to be an instrument of securing and advancing the Bolshevik revolution just as it was a means of spreading Nazi ideology. Inheriting a national literacy rate of barely 25% (a legacy of war as much as of Tsarist inefficiency or inertia), the Soviet regime moved quickly to set up universal schooling.[29] Adult literacy classes were run through night schools and, for the first time in Russia, education for children was made compulsory so that almost full literacy was achieved by the 1970s. Progressive ideas were adopted: the sexes were treated equally (in theory at least), a programme of sex education was instituted, excessive corporal punishment frowned on, scope given to minority languages and cultures in place of the forced Russification of former years. Schools were controlled by the state and heavily subsidised, families co-opted through parents' committees, collective farms and social groups enlisted, youth organisations like the All Union-Leninist Young Communist League (*Komsomol*) and Young Pioneers used – all to help instil Marxist-Leninist values as well as to teach purely academic subjects. In accordance with the ruling philosophy's emphasis on corporate (class) identity, collective responsibility was emphasised: parents could rely on co-workers or neighbours to help care for their children if they were taken ill, for example, but could equally expect to be taken to task by the authorities if it was thought that their parenting skills were not up to scratch.

Responding to the ambitious development targets set by a series of Five Year Plans, Soviet education placed heavy emphasis on mathematics, science and engineering – subjects which fitted well with the self-proclaimed rationalism and supposedly fact-based foundations of the dialectical materialism propounded by Marx. These skills were harnessed for prestige projects at home (characterised by building massive dams, irrigating vast areas for cotton production, reversing the flow of rivers and the veneration of heavy industry) and also to show the superiority of the socialist system on the world stage. The Soviet space programme was a dazzling accomplishment for a nation which only forty years earlier was regarded as one of the most backward European nations, whilst its nuclear arsenal was an uncomfortable reminder of the mailed fist within the velvet glove of revolutionary communism.[30] Biological determinism was used to buttress Marxist views on the nature of man and society; history and literature sanitised to meet the needs of the state; and inconvenient facts were massaged or omitted entirely – everything bent towards proving the truth of the promised dictatorship of the proletariat and inevitability of the coming state of abundance.

For schools were not only places to acquire technical skills and neither were they simply factories to churn out future workers and citizens in the mould of the New Soviet Man; they were also visible symbols of a socialist moral order based on secular conscience and complete equality. Ethics derived from a mixture of duty to the state and conventional morality, the teaching of religion having been banned by the avowedly atheistic regime. Instruction in a collective lifestyle and socialist values was expected over the course of a few generations to lead to the eradication of all social problems, since this was the logical outcome if human nature could indeed be perfected just by providing the right environment, as Marxists believed. Consequently, children were intensively schooled so as to mould them into the most competent citizens they could be. Yet despite sometimes impressive results, the system had a number of serious flaws: a monolithic, hierarchical and bureaucratic structure; rigidity of administration and ideology; the invariable habit of making students repeat a grade, regardless of circumstances, if they failed to meet accepted standards; unwillingness to acknowledge disabilities or differences in individual aptitude. Calls for reform went largely unheeded, criticism (as in politics, where self-censorship and group-think prevailed) being suppressed.

Conclusion

The snapshot of examples contained in this chapter illustrates some of the questions which differing approaches to education have raised: Is it desirable primarily for its benefit to individuals or because of its repercussions for society? Should it be strictly utilitarian or are there some things which have educational value regardless of practical usefulness? Ought it to extend to body, mind and soul or only to some of these? Must a rounded curriculum comprise music, sport, art and literature or can one or more of these be dispensed with? Is there any subject which is indispensable? Are there some fields of study which should be discouraged or even banned? Does education comprise a search within or ingestion from outside? Is it the servant of objective truth and morality or the process by which the state moulds and imposes its own ideas of these things? Can there be any meaningful education at all if truth and beauty are absent? Is it possible to make worthwhile assessments about whether one kind of education is preferable to another? The answers which have been given on these issues are as varied as humanity itself, being both a reflection of the societies which spawned them and an influence on their developmental trajectory. Whatever view we take, education clearly matters: it is a prime determinant of values as well as of technical competency and hence a key to our future as well as a means of understanding the past and making sense of the present.

How does all this relate to modern Britain? Whether intentionally or not, and whether actively or by default, we have begun to give answers to many of the central questions about education that are fundamentally different from those that would have been given a generation ago. We may think this is all well and good (and whether we do or not, we have to recognise that democracy necessarily requires acquiescing in policies that have been approved at the ballot box, even if we do not agree with them), but we might also suspect that much of it has been imposed without consultation. How do sell-offs of school playing fields fit with a quest for *mens sana in corpore sano*? [31] To what degree can present-day schooling be said to cater for the soul as well as for mind and body when the legal requirement for a daily assembly that is 'primarily Christian in character' is honoured more in the breach than the observance? Does the imperative of economic efficiency too often take priority over the pursuit of beauty and of learning for its own sake? Does state propaganda intrude in ways and in areas that are unwarranted? Has the role of parents been progressively undermined and sidelined in ways that are damaging or unhelpful? Are the mantras of equality ultimately inimical to education in the best traditions of Western thought?

These are some of the issues touched on in this book. They deserve to be confronted head-on so that we can make informed decisions about them as a nation – for we get the education no less than the government we deserve.

Notes

[1] Latin for 'Soviet Man': since Marxists believed mankind was formed by environment, it followed that people could be improved by altering their circumstances and the Soviet system would cause a better kind of human to emerge – the New Soviet Man. The term *Homo Sovieticus* was an ironic play on this idea, signifying someone indifferent to the results of their work, lacking initiative, keen to avoid responsibility, passively accepting of authority, incapable of critical thought.

[2] Primarily the city-state, but also capable of referring to citizens or citizenship – from which we derive the words 'polity' and 'politics'.

[3] Girls likewise received state schooling until the age of eighteen or thereabouts, being taught to run and wrestle, to throw discus and javelin, to sing, dance and play musical instruments. These accomplishments were regularly put to the test in competitions such as the annual footrace at the Heraean Games.

[4] Each Autumn the state would formally declare war on the *helots*, whose killing was not considered murder. The *Crypteia* was a group of citizens used to spy on and control the *helots*.

[5] Literally: the love of wisdom – the study of ideas about knowledge, truth, the nature and meaning of life; the rational investigation of questions about existence and ethics.

[6] Confucius lived from 551-479 BC. In China he is sometimes known as *Wan-shih Shih-piao* (the teacher of all ages).

[7] Tao, the primordial essence or fundamental nature of the universe, also encompasses an intuitive knowing which cannot be grasped fully as a concept but only through being lived out.

[8] Hence the *Analects* (a collection of Confucius' sayings) consist of short dialogues between the master and his disciples. These are not designed to explain truths completely, but to provide an aid by which students might open their own minds.

[9] A turning point seems instead to have come with China's decision to close itself to the outside world. From 1410-20 the Ming dynasty's fleets sailed far and wide, with Admiral Zheng He leading an expedition to East Africa which reportedly comprised 62 junks (amongst them, the largest vessels ever built up to that time), 225 support vessels and 28,000 men. Yet these expeditions were subsequently curtailed and there were various (intermittent) attempts to ban seaborne or coastal trade. In 1792 the Emperor Qianlong told George III's trade mission that 'Strange and ingenious objects do not interest us. We have no use for your country's manufactures.'

[10] Becoming a Buddha involves fully apprehending one's own nature: 'Enlightenment is your own nature. Originally it was entirely pure. Only avail yourselves of this mind and you will immediately become a Buddha.'

[11] The *kung-an* (a collection of dialogues between Zen masters and their disciples) adopts Confucius' approach of brief aphorisms rather than lengthy logical exposition, being intended (like the *Analects*) as pointers to aid students on their personal journey of discovery.

[12] Atman is a Sanskrit word meaning the soul or inner self; Brahman is eternal truth, the universal principle or ultimate reality behind the universe.

[13] Four *varnas* (meaning, colours) or idealised human callings are referred to in ancient Vedic texts: Brahmins (priests), Kshatriyas or Rajanyas (rulers, administrators

and warriors), Vaishyas (artisans, merchants, tradesmen and farmers) and Shudras (labourers). By implication there is a fifth element outside the *varna* system, comprising tribal peoples and Untouchables (Dalits). It is uncertain precisely how and when an overarching caste system emerged and precisely how inflexible this was at various points. The word caste is thought to derive from the Portuguese casta, meaning race, lineage or breed. Shaivism (one of the four main sects of Hinduism, which reveres the god Shiva as Supreme Being) rejected caste rules.

[14] It is arguable that other aspects of Hindu teaching were detrimental to national development. The idea that crossing the sea would result in losing *varna* (caste) status was a hindrance to trade and exploration, with their attendant benefits for wealth creation and access to foreign learning.

[15] Meaning 'teaching, instruction, scribe or law', Torah is generally used to describe the Law on which Judaism is founded, contained in the first five books of the Bible (the Pentateuch, otherwise known as the Books of Moses). Sometimes this is extended to include the entire body of Jewish law and wisdom.

[16] The *Mishnah* (meaning, 'study by repetition') contains a series of expositions on the Torah. It was later supplemented by the *Gemara* (meaning, 'study'), a series of rabbinical commentaries on the *Mishnah*. The *Talmud* (meaning, 'instruction or learning') is the body of Jewish civil and ceremonial law contained in the *Mishnah* and *Gemara*.

[17] Such dualism has at various times influenced Christian thinking. It is still to be found in the Olympic ideal (the cult of the body) and the ascetic principle (which regards all matter as tainted).

[18] Jurist, theologian, logician and philosopher, he bears the title *Hujjatul-Islam* (the Proof of Islam).

[19] A similar rationale allows Nigerian Islamist group Boko Haram to feel no compunction about using Western technologies whilst simultaneously proclaiming that Western education is forbidden.

[20] In Al-Ghazali's classification there are four revealed (or Arab) sciences: (1) the Fundamentals (the Koran, the teachings and practice of Mohammed, the consensus amongst other respected authorities and the teachings of the companions of the Prophet); (2) the Branches (Islamic jurisprudence and ethics); (3) the Means (linguistics and grammar); and (4) the Accessories (reading, Koranic exegesis, the sources of Islamic jurisprudence, annals and genealogy). Non-Arab sciences included medicine, astronomy, chemistry, mathematics, philosophy, logic, poetry and history.

[21] Al-Ghazali lived at a time of conflict between the revealed (Arab) sciences (*fuqaha'*) and the non-Arab sciences (the philosophers, or *falasifa*). His treatise *Tahafut al-Falasifa* came down in favour of the former, who eventually prevailed.

[22] Islamic education for adults was initially carried out at mosques by *fuqaha'* (experts in Islamic jurisprudence) whilst children were taught reading and writing at associated schools by *mu'allimin*. Later the *kuttab* gave elementary instruction to the masses, with *mu'addibin* (educators, tutors) providing home schooling for the children of the élite. In due course higher educational institutions emerged, including *madrassas*, 'houses of science and wisdom', Sufi hermitages, brotherhoods and hospices (though mosques continued to be used, too). The elementary curriculum mainly comprised learning the Koran and the basics of Islam, together with reading and writing, and perhaps some arithmetic, poetry and grammar. Likewise the higher curriculum at first focussed exclusively on religious instruction and associated disciplines. This changed during a

period of openness to Greek, Persian and Indian learning which helped drive the Islamic Golden Age of the eighth to the thirteenth centuries before subjects such as mathematics, medicine, astronomy, natural sciences and logic once again began to disappear from the curriculum from the eleventh century.

[23] This position seems to have been influenced at least partly by the assassination of a number of prominent thinkers and the burning of their books.

[24] Al-Ghazali denied that the world is governed by scientific laws, asserting instead that it is maintained, governed and driven by the direct and continual intervention of God.

[25] Boxing was made compulsory in upper schools and PT became an examination subject both for grammar school entry and for the school-leaving certificate. A pupil who did not meet the required standards in PT could be expelled and even prevented from continuing their education. The mania for physical fitness extended to teachers, too, those under fifty being obliged to take part in PT courses.

[26] Kirche (Church) being either the Roman Catholic Church (Hitler having concluded the 1933 *Reichskonkordat* with Pope Pius XII and thereby effectively negated challenge to his regime from that quarter) or the state-sponsored *Deutsche Evangelische Kirche*, which peddled a bastardised form of Protestantism acceptable to the regime. In fact, Nazi ideology was self-consciously pagan and thoroughly opposed to Christianity, which from a Nazi point of view had the twin defects of being weak at best and pacifist at worst; and of being Jewish in origin. The failure of the Church establishment to stand up to Hitler led Karl Barth, Dietrich Bonhöffer and others to set up the breakaway *Bekennende Kirche* (Confessing Church) so as to provide a clear Christian witness in the face of Nazism.

[27] A typical mathematics text featured the following question: 'An aeroplane flies at the rate of 240 kmph to a place 210 km away in order to drop bombs. When may it be expected to return if the dropping of bombs takes 7.5 minutes?'

[28] Letter from Colonel Hilpert to the *Frankfurter Zeitung* dated 16.1.37.

[29] The First World War and the Russian civil war that followed almost immediately afterwards had a catastrophic effect on education. Literacy had increased from 24.8% in 1897 to 56% by 1916, but was back down to 25% by 1920.

[30] The militaristic side of the Soviet system made itself felt in the discipline and parades foisted on students, as well as in the terminology used to describe them – words like 'unit commander' and 'guard.'

[31] Meaning 'a healthy mind in a healthy body', a phrase originally used by the Roman poet Juvenal in his *Satires* but later taken up by educational theorists as diverse as the Englishman John Locke (1632–1704) and the Prussian Heinrich von Treitschke (1834–96).

Chapter Four

NATURAL LAW: THE PATRIMONY OF PARENTS
Parents for Eternal Life
Edmund P. Adamus

The purpose of this chapter is very simple: to restate what to some is obvious but which to many is perhaps unknown and, at best, an unrecognised or under-valued natural instinct arising from the bond between parent and child – that is to say, the instinct to protect and help flourish. This value or universally acknowledged natural and moral principle is also held dear by many across the world and in history as a *spiritual* principle (one intrinsic to one's faith) and, as such, one that is mandated directly to parents by God. To that end, I shall outline the principle of the parent as the primary educator and protector of the child, reflecting on how it is respected or ought to be respected. I shall list some of the major threats to this natural value. I shall then cite some of the legal framework in the UK, within which parents might begin to reclaim something of their inalienable rights, and conclude with an exhortation to a unified Christian response to the most critical issues of our era.

According to the weekly columnist 'Pastor Iuventus' who writes in the London Catholic Herald magazine, the journalist and papal biographer George Weigel says the following about culture:

> Culture is what men and women honour, cherish and worship; what societies deem to be true and good and noble; the expression they give to those convictions in language, literature and the arts; what individuals are willing to stake their lives on.[1]

In other words, if culture is defined by something for which you would be prepared to lay down your life, then for who else would parents be willing to sacrifice even their lives, if it were necessary, but their own offspring? The family homestead therefore lies at the heart of what we mean by culture, because it is defined by that for which we would sacrifice our lives – i.e. children. This dynamic, which generates life and love in a home, makes parents not just the procreators of their children, but in fact the transmitters of life and love for the whole of the life of the child, not just in infancy and childhood but right through to adolescence and young adulthood.

The family is the natural primary and fundamental unit group of society and, as a moral institution possessing inalienable and imprescriptible rights, antecedent and superior to all positive law. In the prevailing climate of liberalism and accelerating secularism, there is an unrelenting attack on family, and especially the rights of parents as primary educators and protectors of their children.

Yet history and human experience teach us that within the family parents address vital issues – such as life, faith, morality, Christian values and virtues, social and political principles. In most cases they also provide a clear understanding of the unique status of marriage between a man and woman and the desire for parenthood.

In a speech in 2006, Pope Benedict XVI reasserted these truths and indeed went further by acclaiming them as three non-negotiable principles, including the absolute rights of parents:

As far as the Catholic Church is concerned, the principal focus of her interventions in the public arena is the protection and promotion of the dignity of the person, and she is thereby consciously drawing particular attention to principles which are not negotiable. Among these the following emerge clearly today:

– protection of life in all its stages, from the first moment of conception until natural death;

– recognition and promotion of the natural structure of the family – as a union between a man and a woman based on marriage – and its defense from attempts to make it juridically equivalent to radically different forms of union which in reality harm it and contribute to its destabilisation, obscuring its particular character and its irreplaceable social role;

– the protection of the right of parents to educate their children.

These principles are not truths of faith, even though they receive further light and confirmation from faith; they are inscribed in human nature itself and therefore they are common to all humanity. The Church's action in promoting them is therefore not confessional in character, but is addressed to all people, prescinding from any religious affiliation they may have. On the contrary, such action is all the more necessary the more these principles are denied or misunderstood, because this constitutes an offence against the truth of the human person, a grave wound inflicted onto justice itself.[2]

Given the historical background and context, it seems beyond comprehension that as recently as 2006 such a statement needed to be made, and still needs to be echoed and repeated over and over. In 1949, when the *Universal Declaration of Human Rights* (UNDHR) was drafted and agreed, as memories were still raw and fresh from the worldwide atrocities against human dignity, the language could not have been more stark in Article 16 (3):

> Whereas disregard and contempt for human rights have resulted in barbarous acts which have outraged the conscience of mankind …
> The family is the natural and fundamental group unit of society and is entitled to protection by society and the State.

In her book on this topic, the former US Ambassador to the Holy See and legal expert, Professor Mary Ann Glendon states that the drafting committee of the UNDHR was so appalled at the Nazi regime's utilisation of the educational system to indoctrinate children it added the following line to Article 16, clause 13: '*Parents have **a prior right to choose the kind of education** that shall be given to their children*'[3] (emphasis added).

The right is 'prior' because it is rooted in nature and instinct that parents (in the vast majority of cases) know always and everywhere what is best for their children. We cannot over estimate just how important this truth is, yet it seems almost impossible nowadays to even dare to proclaim against the backdrop of almost 100 years of compulsory education in the UK. Of course, no one denies the evident benefits of good education, and the social/cultural value of a good school community, which can add enormously to a child's personal development. But it also doesn't do us any harm to stop and remind ourselves that such a universal approbation for education from an early age did not always exist, as for example evidenced in a letter to the *Catholic Herald* newspaper in November 2007.[4]

> I came across a scrap of newspaper among the belongings of a dead relative. The scrap was undated and gave no indication of the name of the newspaper from which it came but on one side it had an advertisement for Manchester Civic Week — October 2nd to 9th 1926 — and on the other it bore the following report: 'The present organisation of elementary education in this country is depriving the men and women to a very large extent of their rights as parents,' declared Cardinal Bourne at a crowded meeting of Catholic women in the Free Trade Hall, Manchester, yesterday.

This growing climate of anti-parent sentiment began to gather momentum behind the academic phenomenon known as 'the Frankfurt School'. In 1922, Lenin organised a meeting to consider why the Bolshevik Revolution had not swept into Europe and America. At this meeting, Willi Munzenberg recommended 'that intellectuals be organised and used to make 'Western civilisation stink' because only then could the dictatorship of the proletariat be imposed. Georg Lukacs, who was also present, developed the idea of *'Revolution and Eros'* — sexual instinct used as an instrument of destruction. In 1924, Lukacs moved to Frankfurt University in Germany, where he chaired the first meeting of a group of Communist-oriented sociologists, a gathering that was to lead to the foundation of the Frankfurt School.

In essence, the Frankfurt School believed that as long as people in Western Europe and America had hope based upon the belief in God, society would never reach the state of hopelessness and alienation which it (they) considered necessary to provoke a socialist revolution. According to one of its leading thinkers, Jurgen Habermas, the Judaeo-Christian legacy in Europe and America had to be destroyed. Amongst the long term methods they recommended:

> The most negative destructive criticism possible of every sphere of life for the breakdown of culture lay in the breakdown of the family:

- teaching of sex and homosexuality to children
- removing parents' rights as primary educators of their children
- destroying traditional relationships between men and women
- denying the specific roles of father and mother
- the destruction of the authority of the father
- the emptying of churches. [5]

With the arrival of Hitler, the Frankfurt School relocated to the USA from where, with the vast commercial, academic and media resources available, it was enabled globally to export its toxic agenda. As long ago as 1946, Dr Brock Chisholm, a Canadian liberal who later became the first Director of the World Health Organisation, said: 'The concept of right and wrong is a barrier to developing a civilised way of life. This concept of right and wrong should be eradicated. Children have to be freed from … prejudices forced upon them by religious authorities … parents are dictators and suppressors of the child's best nature. Sex education should be introduced … eliminating the ways of the elders, by force if necessary.' [6] That kind of language ought to have prevented him even getting the job, instead his philosophy most likely enabled him to acquire the role, given the all-pervading influence of the Frankfurt School.

We see continued 'fruits' of this anti-parent thinking in modern academe even now. Professor Jeffrey Shulman of Georgetown University Law Centre wrote, in 2004, *The Constitutional Parent: Rights, Responsibilities, and the Enfranchisement of the Child.*[7] This book aims at ending the 'erroneous' legal belief that parents have a right to control the education of their children. No, says Shulman, they only have a duty to educate them, and if they fail to educate them as the state sees fit then the state can take control. His reading of parent/child law reveals only 'the notion that the state entrusts the parents with educational custody of the child, and does so only as long as the parent does his or her duty to serve the best interests of the child.'[8] Note: God no longer entrusts the rearing and education of the child to His co-operators in creation, since they as co-creators have engaged in acts suitable for procreation, but rather it is the State who giveth and the State who taketh away – when it deems the parents' plan for education is not 'in the best interests of the child.'

What are these best interests? According to Shulman, it is not the acquisition of truth but 'intellectual incitement' that will prepare the child to make 'free and independent choices'. The parents fail if they restrict the spectrum of available knowledge and thereby fail to 'prepare the child for obligations beyond those of familial obedience'. Freedom of choice is the ultimate good; indeed it has rapidly become the ultimate god. Education, according to Shulman, enables 'children to leave their homes and leave behind the ways of their parents or at least it means giving children the choice to do so'. Well, that would depend on the ways and values of the parents to be left behind. Undoubtedly, some might well come in for some legitimate criticism.

However, this view of education is really about 'liberating' children from traditional values of Christianity, handed down from generation to generation through the guidance of the family. But, according to Shulman [and many who think like him], the law of parent-child relationships must 'protect' children from this sort of 'protection'; ensuring that children receive a public education that can provide the children with a much needed respite 'from the ideological solipsism of the enclosed family.' Public education, according to Shulman, 'disrupts the intramural transmission of values from parent to child. It threatens to dismantle a familiar world by introducing the child to multiple sources of authority – and to the possibility that a choice must be made among them. Indeed the open world of the public school should challenge the transmission of any set of closed values.'[9]

Catholicism denounced this as far back as 1929 with the encyclical from Pope Pius XI *Divini Illius Magistri n32-3*:

> The family therefore holds directly from the Creator the mission and hence the right to educate the offspring, a right inalienable because it is inseparably joined to the strict obligation, a right anterior to any right whatever of civil society and of the State, and therefore inviolable on the part of any power on earth. That this right is inviolable St. Thomas proves as follows: The child is naturally something of the father ... so by natural right the child, before reaching the use of reason, is under the father's care. Hence it would be contrary to natural justice if the child, before the use of reason, were removed from the care of its parents, or if any disposition

were made concerning him against the will of the parents. And as this duty on the part of the parents continues up to the time when the child is in a position to provide for itself, this same inviolable parental right of education also endures.

Pius continues in the same vein but with even more forthright language about the role of the state in paras 34-35:

The wisdom of the Church in this matter is expressed with precision and clearness in the Codex of Canon Law, can. 1113: Parents are under a grave obligation to see to the religious and moral education of their children, as well as to their physical and civic training, as far as they can, and moreover to provide for their temporal well-being.

On this point the common sense of mankind is in such complete accord, that they would be in open contradiction with it who dared maintain that the children belong to the State before they belong to the family, and that the State has an absolute right over their education. Untenable is the reason they adduce, namely that man is born a citizen and hence belongs primarily to the State, not bearing in mind that before being a citizen man must exist; and existence does not come from the State, but from the parents.[10]

The Common Law Duty of Care

Teachers have a duty of care to pupils, which derives from the 'common law'. The 'common law' is law developed through decisions of the Court, as opposed to law which has been determined by Parliament and set down in statute. Traditionally, the term 'in loco parentis' was used to describe the duty of care that a teacher has towards a pupil, to the effect that a teacher has a duty to take the same reasonable care of the pupil that a parent would take in those circumstances. 'In loco parentis' was originally embodied in the nineteenth century common law principle that *a teacher's authority was delegated by a parent,* so far as it was necessary for the welfare of the child.

The issue of what are parental rights in education, in particular to choose the education parents wish their child to receive, is well enshrined in English Law, where the phrase 'in loco parentis' sums up pithily the relation between parent and school and, by proxy, any organisations such as state or church providing schooling: the latter is only 'in place of the parent'.

Like so much that relates to education, this stems from the view of education embedded in the canon law of the Christian Church (Catholic in England to 1534, and thereafter Anglican, with a broadening from the mid nineteenth century onwards to include other Christian denominations; subsequently extended to other religions, but with the same concept intact).

The origin of this is of course is the Fourth Commandment: 'Honour your father and your mother, so that you may live long in the land the LORD your God is giving you' *Exodus 20:12 (NIV)*.

The 1992 Catechism of the Catholic Church spells out the terms of this education very clearly:

Para 2221: The role of parents in education is of such importance that it is almost impossible to provide an adequate substitute. The rights and the duty of parents to educate their children are primordial and inalienable.

Para 2223: Parents have the first responsibility for the education of their children ... The parent(s) delegate their duty to educate to other bodies but they never abrogate it. This role of parents as what is often now called the 'Primary Educator' is based on divine law from a Christian point of view, and this view has long been incorporated in the law of the land. This is then delegated to, in education, teachers, and this is noted in the law also....

It is now mainly governed not just by Education legislation, but also, fittingly, by Human Rights Law. However, the overarching Equality Act of 2010 has introduced elements that have confused the issue as far as parental rights are concerned, a confusion exacerbated by varying policy diktats from the Department of Education. But it is important to state that the rights under English law still follow this ancient principle of parental responsibility. Where it is overridden by overly zealous teaching personnel, governing bodies, and Ofsted inspectors misapplying the law, the actual rights of parents need defending and amplifying all the more. After all, manifestation of religious belief and conscience is supposed to be among the nine legally protected characteristics under the 2010 Equality Act.

The primary law is contained in the following Article of the European Convention on Human Rights of 1950 (following the Universal Declaration of Human Rights proclaimed by the General Assembly of the United Nations on 10 December 1948) and incorporated into English Law by the Human Rights Act 1998.

Protocol 1 Article 2

No person shall be denied the right to education. ***In the exercise of any functions which it assumes in relation to education and to teaching, the State shall respect the right of parents to ensure such education and teaching in conformity with their own religious and philosophical convictions.***

And, as already stated, the Equality Act 2010 lists certain 'protected characteristics', which includes Religion or Belief, defined in the following way:

(1) *Religion* means any religion and a reference to religion includes a reference to a lack of religion.

(2) *Belief* means any religious or philosophical belief and a reference to belief includes a reference to a lack of belief.[11]

Therefore the Christian faiths and their acknowledged scriptures and teachings are supposed to be legally 'protected' under the Act in exactly the same way as is, for example, sexual orientation. This is of enormous importance for parents, especially in relation to sex education, or what is now referred to as RSE (Relationships and Sex Education).

Section 405 of the Education Act 1996 provides the right of parental withdrawal from all or part of SRE (Sex and Relationship Education) provided at school, except for those parts included in the National Curriculum (this is the Science part of the National Curriculum which only specifies matters relating to reproduction in humans at KS3 onwards, i.e. 11 years and older). This enshrines in law the principle behind Article 2 above, the right of parents to ensure *teaching in conformity with their own religious convictions*. So, in theory at least, this encompasses any teaching on 'diversity' which would directly offend Christians who hold the scriptural or catechetical views on sexuality, gender and marriage; meaning that a conscientious Christian parent, or any parent, would have the right to withdraw their child from such lessons if they so wish.

There is also the argument that the very existence of SRE/RSE as a 'subject' imports a value of seeing sexual relations as a matter of 'study' or as 'technical', i.e. value-free. But this actually embodies a value of detaching it from the whole person and the values or beliefs of that pupil or their family; and itself encourages or incorporates a value in the idea of being 'value-free'. This can lead a child to see sexuality as a technical or non-personal issue, which in effect is just another form of teaching as to the role of sexuality in human life. Unless the state is to lay down a law about how sexual relations are to be viewed – a prerogative of such political systems as Apartheid, Nazism or Communism, which seek to control the whole person and subjugate him or her to the state or the party – there will be a real diversity in opinion as Christians, and many Jews, Muslims and others, are never going to conform to modern ideas of sexuality and gender. It may be wise for the state to recognise this reality and not adopt the approach of these failed ideologies of repression and control.

Parents are still able to insist on education in conformity with their religious convictions, and withdraw their children from RS, RE or SRE/RSE. Should that change, it would present an irreconcilable conflict with Article 2 of the Human Rights Act.

In summary
1. Parents have the right to ensure education is in 'conformity with their own religious ... convictions'.
2. Religion is a protected characteristic of the law and therefore its adherence and proclamation in the entirety of its teachings is protected.
3. It is therefore a denial of the human rights of parents if their children are taught contrary to the religion of the parents (to be ascertained as in 2 above).
4. Parents have a legal right to withdraw their children from RS, RE or SRE, excepting where such teaching is a part of, and included in, the Science Curriculum.

It is also to be noted that at present SRE/RSE is NOT obligatory at all for Primary School children, and only for Secondary School children in the maintained or state sector. Yet despite this, seemingly as result of pressure from both external and internal sources, more and more primary schools, even Catholic ones, are adopting sex education policies and materials.

All schools of a religious nature have the right to frame SRE in accordance with their religious ethos. It remains to be seen if there is a 'conflict of laws' inherent in the 'protected characteristics' of the Equality Act, but Christians have no reason to hesitate in adhering to and proclaiming – in both public and private – their full beliefs, and insisting their children are educated accordingly.

Some of the consequences of 'moral neutrality'
Even a cursory glance at some UK statistics shows the appalling consequences when the religious and moral formation of the young does not proceed from the family home where, ideally, children are cared for by conscientious parents.

According to a report by the BBC on a WHO survey into under age sex conducted by Edinburgh University in 2004, 40% of girls aged 15 or under admitted having sexual intercourse – the highest of any of the 24 European countries. The figure for boys was the second highest in the survey.[12]

UK teenage pregnancy and abortion rates are the highest in Europe.[13]

45% of British children are born outside marriage (and the figure increases year on year).[14]

Birth control 'experts' are responding to this with demands for compulsory sex 'education' from five years of age upwards (though this has so far been prevented from making it to the statute book).

In 2002, the Journal of Health Economics published the results of a 14-year study conducted in 16 areas around Britain.[15] Dr David Paton of Nottingham University Business School, who led the study, claimed the findings cast serious doubt on the policy of improving family planning services for teenagers.

Although family planning may make sexually active teenagers less likely to get pregnant, it seems that it also encourages others to start having sex. Some of these will get pregnant through contraceptive failure and, if anything, the overall effect of expanding family planning services for under-16s has been to increase pregnancies and abortions.[16]

Even the organisations which take part in birth control and sex education programmes concede that they have failed. By 1986 the Alan Guttmacher Institute, a research arm of the International Planned Parenthood Federation, which openly supports liberal abortion laws and widespread access to contraceptives, had concluded:

... neither pregnancy education nor contraceptive education exert[s] any significant effect on the risk of premarital pregnancy among sexually active teenagers. [This is] a finding that calls into question the argument that formal sex education is an effective tool for reducing adolescent pregnancy.[17]

Dr Judy Bury, former director of the Edinburgh Brook Advisory Centre, admitted:

There is overwhelming evidence that, contrary to what you might expect, the provision of contraception leads to an increase in the abortion rate.[18]

Jean Malcolm, another Brook Advisory Centre director, also conceded:

It's partly because of greater availability of contraception that there are more pregnancies. I suppose it's almost inevitable.[19]

Yet virtually all secondary schools, including many Christian schools, welcome into their premises certain government funded agencies. These agencies are committed to giving schoolchildren, under the age of 16, access to abortion, abortifacients and other contraceptives *without parental knowledge or permission*. Parents resist pointing out that, morality apart, this policy flies in the face of the best scientific evidence, in which *all* high quality studies show that *parental notification* in the case of abortion requests reduces underage abortion by 10–20%, and that under age births rates are either reduced by a few percent or remain unchanged.

Compare this with the famous Gillick Case of 1984. A courageous Catholic mother of ten children, Mrs Victoria Gillick, took the Department of Health to court to prevent the prescription of contraceptives to under age children without parental permission. The Court of Appeal agreed with her. For the next ten months doctors were forbidden to give contraceptives to under-age girls without parental permission. In this period the contraceptive uptake fell. The abortion and teenage birth statistics did not rise. They fell. Why? Because for a brief period the state actually strengthened and legally supported the inalienable rights of parents.[20]

Parents are the primary educators

What do we mean when we say that parents are the primary educators of their children? We mean everything!

- We mean that parents begin to teach their children from the moment their children are conceived and born.
- We mean that parents teach their children during the children's infancy and childhood.
- We mean that parents are the first, and most important and indispensable, teachers of their children.
- We mean that unless the children are taught and primarily formed by the parents, the children will be getting only a substitute education.

We mean all of this when we say that parents are the primary educators. But we mean much more. After all, there is a primacy in what the children are taught. They can be taught how to walk and to talk. They can be taught how to read and write. They can be taught how to eat and drink and take care of their things. They can be taught arithmetic and spelling, and history and geography. All of those things they can be taught and *should* be taught. But what they mainly need is to know why God made them; why they are on earth at all; why they are in this world; and that they are here in this life in order to prepare and train themselves for the world to come.

In a word, children are to be taught that their short stay here in time is preparation for the world that will never end. They are to be trained for heaven. That is why the subtitle of this chapter is: 'Parents for Eternal Life'.

Having said this, we are now in a position to get to the principal message. It can be explained in a single all important statement: 'Under

God, parents are the first in time, first in authority, first in responsibility, first in ability, and first in dignity to educate their children for eternal life.'

How are parents to become primary educators?
Needless to say, the vision we are describing can remain just that, a vision. It can be an ideal or even only a dream. But God intends it to be a *reality*. This, I am convinced, is the providential reason that God has allowed so many forces of error and evil to plague the modern world – and with emphasis in our own Western society.

'Where sin abounds,' St. Paul tells us, 'there grace even more abounds.'[21] In His providence, God wants to wake parents up from their lethargy. He wants them to open their eyes to failures and see what is going on. He wants them to come out of the dream that so many parents are still sleeping in — and arouse them to the gravest, and I mean *gravest* duty they have before God. What is this? *To pay whatever price they have to, in order to educate their children for eternal life.*

Of course, this will not be easy. Of course, parents with this faith-vision will be criticised, even ostracised. Of course, parents will have to give up many things that the modern world has provided in such profusion, for their own and their families' enjoyment here on earth. But the price is worth it. When Christ told us: 'Take up your cross daily and follow me,' this has a specific poignancy for those to whom God has granted parenthood.

To be the primary educators of their children for eternal life is not easy for parents. It never has been since the dawn of Christianity. But in today's world, intoxicated with its own pride, addicted to its own pleasures, indoctrinated in its own propaganda that only temporal life exists and eternal life is a mirage — to become parents of eternal life demands *heroism*.

Parents for eternal life
So the litany of secularism goes on. Its principal target is our children. This then brings us face to face with the *gravest* duty of believing Christian parents. They must be convinced that their primary responsibility as parents is to steer their children toward the life of heaven. Yes, parents are the primary teachers of their children in all that pertains to the children's

lives here on earth. But that is not all. The parent's most fundamental duty is to prepare their children for eternity. Parents *must* teach their children from birth the following:

- God created us to know, love and serve Him in this life, in order that our souls may reach heaven.
- Parents must teach their children that *everything* in this life is to be a means of leading us to our heavenly destiny.
- Parents must teach their children that, while everything in this life is intended by God to lead us to heaven, not everything is to be used in the same way.
- Some of the persons, places, and things in our life are to be enjoyed.
- Other persons, places and things are to be endured.
- Other persons, places, and things are to be avoided. Why? Because they can easily lead us to sin.
- And finally, there are persons, places and things that God asks us to surrender. It is an invitation from God to sacrifice what we like in order to express our greater love of God.
- Parents must teach their children that they have a fallen – I stress the term *fallen* – human nature. We are not *naturally* prone to do what God wants, but what we want.
- Parents must teach their children that if they are going to cope with their natural tendencies to pride, lust, anger, envy, greed, avarice, and gluttony, they need the constant help of God's grace.
- Parents must teach their children that to obtain the necessary light to know God's will and the necessary strength to do it, they need to pray, be fed by Sacred Scripture and take an active part in the worshipping community.

All of this is locked up in the simple statement: *Parents are parents for eternal life*. God gives them children *in* this world, but not *for* this world.

Parents, in God's plan, are to conceive and give birth to, and nurture and educate their children for life after bodily death. After all, the only purpose that God has in having them become parents here on earth, is that they might raise families for everlasting life in heaven. Parents must always keep this vision clearly in their minds. '*We are fathers and mothers of children for heaven.*' Our one hope is to be at rest in heaven with our families, our children and grandchildren and great, great grandchildren, in the everlasting City of Jerusalem which is our heavenly home.

Christians of the East and West, breathing with both lungs of the Mystical Body of Christ, must unite in order to protect our families and our faith. We must replace what Bishop Egan of Portsmouth called 'the strangling counter-culture of death.'[22] There is no alternative. This obligation is God-given in the Commandments. *'Honour your father and your mother...'* It is affirmed by Jesus Christ in His teaching. It is affirmed in His life. *'But He went down with them to Nazareth, and lived there in subjection to them ... And so Jesus advanced in wisdom with the years.'*[23]

This right is fundamental. It is founded upon parental transmission of life to, and love for, their child. The Social Doctrine of the Russian Orthodox Church teaches –

> Children become fruits of their love and communion, and their birth and upbringing belong, according to the Orthodox teaching, to one of the most important goals of marriage.

This right is **inalienable** and **irreplaceable.** Again the Social Teachings of the Russian Orthodox Church teaches:

> The role of family in the formation of the personality is exceptional; no other social institution can replace it. The erosion of family relations inevitably entails the deformation of the normal development of children ... it is so dangerous to distort the traditional parents-child relationship, which, unfortunately, has been in many ways endangered by the contemporary way of life.[24]

And more recently, in the post-synodal apostolic exhortation Amoris Laetitia, Pope Francis declares in article 84: "It is important to reiterate that the overall education of children is a 'most serious duty' and at the same time a 'primary right' of parents. This is not just a task or a burden, but an essential and inalienable right that parents are called to defend and of which no one may claim to deprive them. The State offers educational programmes in a subsidiary way, supporting the parents in their indeclinable role; parents themselves enjoy the right to choose freely the kind of education – accessible and of good quality – which they wish to give their children in accordance with their convictions. Schools do not replace parents, but complement them. This is a basic principle: 'all other participants in the process of education are only able to carry out their responsibilities in the name of the parents, with their consent and, to a certain degree, with their authorization.' Still, 'a rift has opened up between the family and society, between family and the school; the educational pact today has been broken and thus the educational alliance between society and the family is in crisis.'"

The schools of the *Civilisation of Love* are our homes, where our children learn to love by knowing that we love them. A mother who values her maternal vocation and her importance in the home nurtures the femininity and future motherhood of her daughters. She sets a clear, strong and attractive example of womanhood for her sons. The dignified and masculine behaviour of fathers is a model for their sons. It inspires respect, admiration and security in their daughters. The greatest lifelong gift loving parents can give their children is a brother or sister. Children naturally absorb sound attitudes on love, marriage and the *true* meaning of human sexuality from their parents.

Each child has his or her own rate of maturation and children should be individually taught the truth and beauty of chastity, modesty and sexuality by their parents, who alone are in the position to know *what, when and how*. Forbid, and where possible resist, any instruction on sexuality which may damage your child's innocence. Families must pray and worship together. Firm but gentle and consistent encouragement must be given to our children to intensify their Christian identity, so that they might live godly lives.

Only then will they will have the necessary courage to give witness to their faith and morals. Families do not survive alone, so form associations of families. Encourage clergy to see the vital and interdependent relationship between the family and the Church. In conclusion: There is *no* alternative to the *Civilisation of Life*. It *is* possible to build this civilisation. The *Civilisation of Love* is *God's civilisation*. It is *our* civilisation and the birthright of our children and grandchildren.

My sincere thanks for their invaluable help, advice and encouragement in writing this paper to: Dr Thomas Ward, Founder and President of the National Association of Catholic Families and Corresponding Member to the Pontifical Academy for Life; and to Edmund Matyjaszek, Principal of The Priory School, Isle of Wight.

Notes

[1] *Catholic Herald*, 23 April 2015.
http://www.catholicherald.co.uk/magazine-2/spirituallife-magazine-2/2015/04/23/why-polands-culture-is-healthier-than-britains/
[2] Address to EU Parliamentarians, 30 March 2006.
https://w2.vatican.va/content/benedict-xvi/en/speeches/2006/march/documents/hf_ben-xvi_spe_20060330_eu-parliamentarians.html
[3] M. A. Glendon. *A World Made New: Eleanor Roosevelt and the Universal Declaration of Human Rights.=*, Random House NY (2001).
[4] https://reader.exacteditions.com/issues/3169/page/1
[5] T. Matthews, editor of CF News, *The Frankfurt School. The Quiet Revolution rolls forward*. http://www.cfnews.org.uk/PEP.htm#1
[6] B. Chisholm, Speech given at the Conference on Education, Asilomar, California, 11 September 1954.
[7] Yale University Press (2004).
[8] Ibid., Chapter 1, Sacred Rights or Sacred Trust?
[9] Ibid.
[10] http://w2.vatican.va/content/pius-xi/en/encyclicals/documents/hf_p-xi_enc_31121929_divini-illius-magistri.html
[11] http://www.legislation.gov.uk/ukpga/2010/15/section/10
[12] See BBC news online 3 June 2004, http://news.bbc.co.uk/1/hi/health/3773659.stm
[13] http://www.fpa.org.uk/news/uk-has-highest-teenage-birth-rates-western-europe
[14] http://www.ons.gov.uk/peoplepopulationandcommunity/birthsdeathsandmarriages/livebirths/bulletins/parentscountryofbirthenglandandwales/2015-08-27#births-within-marriagecivil-partnership
[15] David Paton, 'The Economics of Abortion, Family Planning and Underage Conceptions', *Journal of Health Economics, 21* (2 March, 2002).
[16] Breakdown Britain [2007] *Social Justice Policy Group,* Chairman: Rt. Hon. Iain Duncan Smith.
[17] 'The effects of sex education on Adolescent Behaviour', *Family Planning Perspectives* 7-8/86 pp 162-169, Alan Guttmacher Institute.
[18] *The Scotsman*, 29 June 1981.
[19] *Edinburgh and Lothian Post*, 11 January 1992.
[20] *Gillick v West Norfolk & Wisbech Area Health Authority* [1985] UKHL 7. The decision was subsequently reversed on appeal to the House of Lords.
[21] Romans 5:20.
[22] *Catholic Herald,* 26 September 2012.
http://www.catholicherald.co.uk/news/2012/09/26/new-bishop-asks-the-faithful-to-fight-strangling-counter-culture-of-death/
[23] Luke 2:51
[24] Dr T. Ward. Speech to Rhodes Forum Dialogue of Civilisations, '*Towards a new Civilisation of Life: Parents the Primary Educators and Protectors of their children*', October 2011.

Chapter Five

THE SECULARIST SIEGE
– WITHIN AND OUT OF SCHOOL
Anthony Busk

'For modern society, a colossus with feet of clay, we shall create an unprecedented centralisation, which will unite all powers in the hands of the Government. We shall create hierarchical constitution, which will mechanically govern all movements of individuals.'
Adolf Hitler (circa 1920)

A new socialism?

The programme of Hitler's National Socialist Movement was born in 1920, and affirmed that the party would uphold a positive Christianity! However, this meant a non-biblical, non-ecclesiastical Christianity, which would bow to the movement's ethical principle of '*the common good before the individual good'*.[1] The programme closed with the assertion: '*In order that all this may be carried out, we demand the creation of a strong central power in the Reich, unconditional authority of the political central parliament over the whole Reich and its general organisation....'*[2]

Today, Secularism is the panacea vigorously promoted by some politicians and activist movements, manifested fundamentally in the curbing of Christian influence across society and government. It is more than the aspiration to legally separate church and state – although that is an objective – rather, it is the removal of principles of law that are upheld in the Bible as good for the individual and society. Goodness is redefined as the outcome emerging from a fluidity of opinions, where there is no reference to biblical teaching, other than by mere accident. The National Socialist Movement from the beginning freed itself from conventional ethical standards, which opened the way for any kind of behaviour or law to be justified, placing what was termed 'the common good' before the individual good.

Both in communist and socialist movements, there are underlying aims, or ideologies, which to their adherents represent the 'common good'. Because there is no respect for biblical teaching determining right from wrong, activist movements do not hesitate to employ strategies that trample on the very democracy allowing their existence. Using a veneer of legality, but with an increasing arrogance and contempt for the law, militant activist groups are today systematically imposing their regime of despotic 'values', and at the same time taking legal steps to prevent opposition.

The principal tool used by secularist movements is the equality argument – a fundamental tenet of communism: that every person should be as equal as possible, and any attempt to thwart equality must be condemned by the law and society. The judiciary, acting as an arm of the government, must punish any individual or organisation which refuses to be 'politically correct', particularly using precedent within equality legislation as the touchstone. In order to enforce its values there is no place for dissent, and freedom of speech is only acceptable within boundaries dictated by government, through the law.

Interpreting National Socialism's aims, to obtain equality in accordance with 'British Values', requires '*a strong central power in the UK, unconditional authority of the political central parliament over the whole of the UK and its general organisation....*' Marxist teaching follows a similar pathway where, to achieve supreme equality, a country's leadership must exert '*absolute control over the common citizen's personal choices – including his or her education, religion, employment and even marriage*'.[3]

British history is peppered with power struggles, often a tension between the application of biblical doctrine to society by an independent Parliament, and the absolute rule of monarchs, claiming the 'right of kings'.

Magna Carta personified the immense struggle to robustly establish a rule of law undergirded by Judaeo-Christian teaching, which has proven to be good for the nation and many other countries throughout the world.

As one traces recent history in relation to one important facet – traditional marriage and the family and education – one has to ask whether recent trends and government pronouncements are a political strategy whose roots are found within National Socialism and communism.

The Equality Act

The controversy over the abandonment of ethical values within the sphere of sexuality can be traced to legislation culminating in the Equality Act, which came into force on 10 September 2010. An understanding of the Act's requirements is necessary to appreciate what is happening within our educational system, and the subsequent influence of activist movements. Central to the Act is a public sector equality duty for nine protected characteristics which include, amongst others, gender reassignment, sex and sexual orientation, marriage and civil partnership, disability and race. Sexual orientation includes orientation towards persons of the same sex, persons of the opposite sex, or persons of either sex.[4] Direct discrimination occurs:

> When one person discriminates against another because of a protected characteristic, where the other person is treated less favourably than how others would be treated.

Indirect discrimination occurs *when a person is disadvantaged compared with others who do not share a similar characteristic.*[5]

A condition of Indirect Discrimination is that the person alleged to be discriminating *cannot show [the behaviour] to be a proportionate means of achieving a legitimate aim* (Section 19(2)(d)). The Government's website[6] specifically includes harassment and victimisation as discrimination.

These are important definitions, because they make it clear that the objective is to overcome the negative social and cultural effects of an individual's beliefs or behaviour. Discrimination against groups of people can be socially divisive. However, the support given to a person with 'protected characteristics' must not elevate a person in such a manner that others are relatively demeaned or disadvantaged. Its purpose should be to bring equality and not dominance or favouritism. This is very important.

The Equality and Human Rights Commission (EHRC) provides Technical Guidance applicable to groups with protected characteristics (which includes sexual orientation), including one such guidance applicable to schools. However, before examining that application, it is worthwhile having a closer look at the Equality Act itself in the area of *Public Sector Equality Duty* (S.149) (PSED) introduced in April 2011, initially referred to in *Part A* of that report.

This approach is helpful because of the campaign that Stonewall and others are pursuing, which gives the impression to schools and local authorities that PSED is all about halting 'homophobic bullying'[7] and their belief that those affected should have a pedestal position compared to all other groups – with or without protected characteristics.[8] It is necessary to have objective standards with which to judge the validity of the policies of Stonewall or any other organisation seeking to provide professional guidance to schools. Approaches to gender reassignment, sex, and sexual orientation will therefore be discussed in this context.

Gender Reassignment

A person has the protected characteristic of gender reassignment if the person is proposing to undergo, is undergoing or has undergone a process (or part of a process) for the purpose of reassigning the person's sex by changing physiological or other attributes of sex.

(Equality Act, Section 7(1))

This definition describes someone who has made a decision to change their gender, which may be evidenced by physiological changes or 'other attributes', such as clothing. It excludes a girl who perhaps exhibits 'tomboy' characteristics but who does not seriously intend to become a boy. There should be a clear decision made by that person to change their gender. This raises the question of whether, on age grounds alone, a comment or desire by a child to change her gender should be taken seriously. To create an environment in a class where children are told they may be born with the wrong body can be coercive and manipulative. A boy from a dysfunctional home where sisters are better treated may temporarily feel it would be better to be a girl, and try to emulate that gender and consequently be led to believe that he is gay.

The Act does not require that a pupil should be locked into a gender reassignment programme by the school where there is transient behaviour. This could be interpreted by both children and staff as unreasonable and could be discriminatory against other groups. Sections 7 (2) and (3)[9] simply reinforce the definition of a transsexual person. When a pupil has been categorised, this label is assigned, and from the school staff's point of view, he or she comes under the public duty provision, unless that child reverts back to his or her physical gender.[10]

Sex and sexual orientation

The definition of sex for the purposes of the Equality Act is as follows: In relation to the protected characteristic of sex —

(a) a reference to a person who has a particular protected characteristic is a reference to a man or to a woman;

(b) a reference to persons who share a protected characteristic is a reference to persons of the same sex.

(Equality Act, Sections 11(a) and (b))

This definition makes clear that either males or females may have the protected characteristic of sex, and applies to those who have a same sex orientation, such as homosexual males and lesbian females. But the definition does not exclude heterosexuals, who may be discriminated against, such as boys bullying heterosexual girls, or a child feeling disadvantaged, such as in a class dominated by the opposite sex. Equality law would address discrimination in this case, which a school would need to resolve, but the EHRC Technical Guidance would not apply. The Act precludes greater attention being given to one gender against another: all should be treated equally.

Sexual orientation

(1) Sexual orientation means a person's sexual orientation towards —

(a) persons of the same sex,

(b) persons of the opposite sex, or

(c) persons of either sex.

(Equality Act, Section 12(1))

(2) In relation to the protected characteristic of sexual orientation —

(a) a reference to a person who has a particular protected characteristic is a reference to a person who is of a particular sexual orientation;

(b) a reference to persons who share a protected characteristic is a reference to persons who are of the same sexual orientation.

(Equality Act, Section 12(2))

The definition in paragraph (1) above defines what sexual orientation is, which could involve a few or many features that together would make clear a pupil's orientation. However, the evidence would need to be robust enough to satisfy the law, and should not be an intellectual or even an emotionally grounded comment. There would need to be greater evidence of orientation, and not necessarily behavioural. For someone to put their hand up in a charged atmosphere and say, for example, 'I now think I am a homosexual' should be insufficiently robust to justify that person in future being defined as requiring protected characteristic attention.

The second clause makes clear that a characteristic cannot be applied where there is a heterosexual orientation. If a pupil claims to be homosexual but is uncertain, this raises the question of whether that statement is genuine. This could be the case where a child is 'identified' by the representative of an activist organisation as 'gay', and is befriended, then invited to meet others who are 'committed', such as in a homosexual youth group. It should be noted that children classing themselves as orientated towards their own as well as the opposite sex do not have a protected characteristic.

Public Sector Equality Duty (Equality Act 2010, Section 149)

1) A public authority must, in the exercise of its functions, have due regard to the need to –

(a) eliminate discrimination, harassment, victimisation and any other conduct that is prohibited by or under this Act;

(b) advance equality of opportunity between persons who share a relevant protected characteristic and persons who do not share it;

(c) foster good relations between persons who share a relevant protected characteristic and persons who do not share it.

(Equality Act, Section 149)

Clause (a) makes clear there has to be evidence that a school (as a public authority) is aiming at the elimination of discrimination and other 'unlawful conduct', whether it is by teachers or pupils. Clause (b) deals with opportunity, which in the schools setting would mean there is no educational disadvantage. The final clause (c), which requires fostering good relations, addresses issues such as mutual respect.

However, it does not mean intellectual acceptance, such as a teenager who does not accept homosexuality being forced to change his or her mind, although sub-section (5) below could imply the need for re-education. It should mean good relations with those who do not share their behaviour, as illustrated below.

5) Having due regard to the need to foster good relations between persons who share a relevant protected characteristic and persons who do not share it involves having due regard, in particular, to the need to –

(a) tackle prejudice, and

(b) promote understanding.

(6) Compliance with the duties in this section may involve treating some persons more favourably than others; but that is not to be taken as permitting conduct that would otherwise be prohibited by or under this Act.

The PSED also makes clear how a particular protected group should not be shown undue favouritism, but only given essential help to enable equality to be achieved. For example, to take a teenage male pupil who claims to be 'Out' as a transgender person and whose behaviour and other manifestations support this demand, and then require the school to accommodate this by enabling him to use all female toilets, should not be necessary.

Technical Guidance for Schools in England
The Equality and Human Rights Commission has published a Technical Guidance[11] on the Equality Act with the PSED, including 'reasonable adjustments (for disabled persons)' applying from September 1st 2012. Although it is not a legal document, it does carry weight within the judiciary, particularly because of the Commission's government funding,[12] and its guidelines may well be upheld where there is dispute. It is applicable to all kinds of schools, and also affects parents and pupils. The definitions are similar to those used in the Equality Act. For example, the document refers to direct and indirect discrimination (1.15); harassment related to a 'relevant protected characteristic' (1.17), and victimisation (1.20).

The Commission's use of the phrase *positive action* (1.28 and Ch.7) appears to describe the Public Sector Equality Duty:[13] 'to take proportionate steps to help particular groups of pupils to overcome disadvantages that are linked to a protected characteristic'.[14] This phrase is not confined to schools, and the description appears in some police forces.

How 'Positive Action' is interpreted by EHRC is important, since it is the template against which school policy should be judged.

'Positive action' is the term used to describe action that the Act allows schools to take to counter the effects of past or present discrimination experienced by groups of pupils who share a protected characteristic, to meet the particular needs of pupils in such groups, or to facilitate their participation in activities in which participation by members of their group is disproportionately low (7.1).

It is important to note how EHRC bundles together examples of pupils with protected characteristics, such as: 'low achievement of Gypsy and Traveller pupils', with 'high levels of bullying of lesbian, gay and bisexual (LGB) pupils'. There is no particular emphasis on the latter.[15]

It is also interesting how the description of Positive Action includes additional education, facilities or services, to benefit a disadvantaged group (7.3), addressing the needs of pupils in a group who share a people characteristic (7.4). There is incorporated under 7.4 a very significant statement which provides for equality balance:

> It is not about giving preferential treatment to a particular pupil because of a protected characteristic. That is positive discrimination, which is unlawful under the Act in most circumstances.

Public Duty Requirements
The tests to determine whether bodies fulfil their public duty requirements are threefold (7.8), and align with the Government's definition as set out (in italics):[16]

> a. enabling or encouraging persons who share the protected characteristic to overcome or minimise that disadvantage, (*eliminate unlawful discrimination*);
> b. meeting those different needs, (*advance equality of opportunity*);
> c. enabling or encouraging persons who share the protected characteristic to participate in that activity, *(foster good relations)*.

There are two *Basic Requirements* a school has to meet: first, '*that the school must reasonably think that one or more of the three circumstances in which positive action may be taken has arisen*'. Second, '*that the action the school takes must be proportionate to meet the relevant stated aims*' (7.9). The guidance demonstrates flexibility in determining whether pupils with a protected characteristic are meeting the public duty definitions, such as underperformance pointing to an issue, as well as complaints or discrimination claims. An illustration is provided of addressing temporarily or permanently excluded black Caribbean boys (7.10).

The need to take 'proportionate action' (7.11) to meet the relevant aims, points to the balancing of 'any relevant competing factors', taking into account the effect that helping a protected group would have on other groups. A school should ask itself if the proposed steps would achieve the stated aim, which may well be the case. However, it must also examine whether the strategy could inadvertently disadvantage other groups. In this case further alternative routes should be explored, to lessen the likelihood of impacting these other groups unfavourably. (7.12).

The *First Aim* is to overcome or minimise disadvantage (7.13). The Act does not define what 'disadvantage' means, but it includes 'exclusion, rejection, lack of opportunity or choice, and barriers to accessing provision.' It must be proportionate, and so Positive Action could: 'include action to identify possible causes 'and then '(a) target provision at specific disadvantaged groups,' and '(b) aim provision specifically'. This could be provision provided in a different way, times, locations, or just for the disadvantaged group.

The *Second Aim*, to meet different needs (7.16), is to 'target the needs of pupils who share a protected characteristic'. Such needs may be from the past or current discrimination, and they may not be entirely different from the needs of others (7.17). An example is given of Muslim girls having additional cultural issues. The meeting of such needs must be proportionate (7.18), such as 'providing education at a particular time'.

The *Third Aim*, taking action to encourage participation (7.19), is to encourage taking part in an activity where that characteristic is disproportionately low, with adjustments being necessary if this is not the case. Positive Action also means 'encouraging experiences of undertaking the activity and completing it' (7.20). The only limit is 'that it must be a proportionate means of achieving the aim' (7.21).

Suggestions made include the provision of training, or extending times, or changing locations for activities to take place. An illustration is given of girls not undertaking placements with science or technology employers compared with boys. To help change perceptions, an awareness day is arranged, and a tour of a local FE college allows girls to meet apprentices, and meet women in the construction industry.

Implementing and monitoring positive action (7.22) points to the need for an action plan, with specific outcomes, and steps to achieve these, together with assessments of proportionality, and a timetable. Sharing with the targeted pupils having the protected characteristic will assist in identifying needs, also involving parents, and other staff (7.23). The illustration is given of taking learning barriers down from LGB pupils, where a consultation group is run, helped by a local LGB charity. The barriers are identified, with a mentor programme set up. The illustration also suggests running an LGBT history month.[17] The impact of actions needs to be monitored (7.24), as it 'will help the school to make sure that the action continues to be lawful'.

Perverting the law

Protected characteristics are not exclusively about sexual issues, but also include race, religion and belief, disability, age, pregnancy and maternity. Within the schools system the last two are probably least likely to apply, but the broad sweep of responsibilities should be taken into account. An extraordinary emphasis on one characteristic, such that it is exalted above all others, assaults the spirit of the Equality Act, and probably is unlawful. However, the focus of this discussion is upon those protected characteristics that are associated with sexual mores, and how these have been interpreted by activist movements, and in particular Stonewall.

The Act speaks of balance and proportionate action to protect minorities from discrimination, but the focus of activists has been to equate the whole of the Equality Act as a crusade against bullying. This has carried with it overtones that sexual behaviour which is not 'heterosexual' is genetic and innate – as with race. Therefore any criticism, academic or otherwise, is akin to manifesting racial intolerance.

'Bullying' – meaning 'Homophobic Bullying' – and 'Hate Crime', are the twin cries of the activist movement, launched against any and every objection to their beliefs or strategy. The ordinary person would baulk at any injustice and sympathise with those who cry discrimination, and fighting homophobic bullying has pervaded the Christian religious establishment. For example, on 12 May 2014 the Education Division of the Church of England issued guidelines on 'challenging homophobic bullying'.[18] Today, Stonewall is entrenched within the Church of England's educational policy to provide active support in halting this iniquitous practice!

The Oxford English Reference Dictionary[19] defines a bully as: 'A person who uses strength or power to coerce others by fear, persecute or oppress by force or threats, pressure or coerce a person to do something (bullied him into agreement)'. A useful American definition from stopbullying.gov states: 'Bullying is unwanted, aggressive behaviour among school-aged children that involves a real or perceived power imbalance. The behaviour is repeated, or has the potential to be repeated, over time. Both kids who are bullied and who bully others may have serious, lasting problems.'[20] The definition goes on to state that in order to be considered bullying, the behaviour must be aggressive and include an imbalance of power and repetition. It can include teasing or insulting someone.

Wikipedia[21] defines school bullying as: 'An unwelcomed behaviour among school-aged children that involves a real or perceived power imbalance. The behaviour is repeated, or has the potential to be repeated, over time. In order to be considered bullying, the behaviour must be aggressive and include a difference in power: Kids who bully use their physical strength or popularity to control or harm others; repetition: happening more than once or have the potential to happen more than once.'

The UK Government's definition[22] is very similar: 'It is behaviour repeated, intended to hurt someone either physically or emotionally, often aimed at certain groups, e.g. because of race, religion, gender, or sexual orientation, physical assault, teasing, making threats, name calling, cyber bullying.'

To sum up these conventional definitions, true bullying involves unequal power, is aggressive or has that potential, is usually repetitive, and has an intention to hurt or harm someone else emotionally or physically.[23] It is not talking about an issue where the other person may not agree, or the occasional use of terms, which may be critical of someone else's views. A Pakistani child may come into an otherwise all-white class and be called a 'Paki', yet there may be no animosity, but merely recognition the individual has differences of colour and possibly cultural attitudes. In this case, correction is all that is needed. However, if a group of children or individuals deliberately go out of their way to intimidate, that is bullying.

Having therefore defined bullying, we ask what is meant by *homophobic* bullying. The Oxford Reference English Dictionary definition does not refer to 'homophobic bullying', but describes homophobia as those who have an extreme and irrational aversion to homosexuality and homosexual children.[24] Wikipedia considers homophobia as encompassing a range of negative attitudes and feelings

THE SECULARIST SIEGE – WITHIN AND OUT OF SCHOOL

toward homosexuality. It can be expressed as antipathy, contempt, prejudice, aversion, or hatred, may be based on irrational fear, and is sometimes related to religious beliefs.[25] Rivers (2001), and Warwick et. al (2001)[26] have summarised homophobic bullying as occurring when individuals are singled out for their actual or perceived sexual orientation. Rivers highlights verbal abuse – spreading rumours that someone is gay – and physical abuse, including hitting, sexual assault and threatening behaviour.[27]

The importance of correctly defining homophobic bullying is illustrated in research carried out by Akhtar Zobiah in 2011.[28] Her study in a secondary school included exploring what students believed was homophobic bullying. Focus groups' participants did not view phrases such as 'you're so gay' as homophobic bullying, but considered there had to be aggression in its content to meet that criterion.[29] This would, of course, align with the conventional view of bullying as having persistent elements, in contrast to ordinary interaction in the classroom or playground.

Using conventional definitions of bullying, a reasonable person would condemn any kind of bullying; but homophobic bullying, as understood by activist movements, is to do with attitude and opinion. They would therefore consider it is quite legitimate to make allegations of bullying even when someone expresses an opinion calmly and objectively, without hatred or emotional involvement. This is a gross distortion of the English language and reflects a strategy to forward activist campaigns. The manner in which this has been adopted can actually be found within the British police force. In their publication *Protecting lesbian, gay and bisexual people: A practical guide for police forces (2013)*,[30] the police, Crown Prosecution Service and other criminal justice agencies have commonly agreed definitions of homophobic hate crimes and incidents. It is important to note how the adjective 'hate' has been introduced into the definition:

A hate crime is any criminal offence which is perceived, by the victim or any other person, to be motivated by a hostility or prejudice based on a person's sexual orientation or perceived sexual orientation.

A hate incident is any non-crime incident which is perceived, by the victim or any other person, to be motivated by a hostility or prejudice based on a person's sexual orientation or perceived sexual orientation.

In the overall context, it equates with 'homophobia'. Hatred is defined by the Oxford English Reference Dictionary as 'intense dislike or ill will; a hated person or thing'. For Stonewall, any discrimination automatically contains a major emotionally hostile component, equating to hatred. This is absurd, because someone may disagree with a child or student's viewpoint, but that does not mean hatred is involved. The allegedly offended person, under these definitions, need only have a 'perception' that the crime or incident is 'motivated by hostility or prejudice'.

Another illustration of the way language has been distorted is shown in the Equalities and Human Rights Commission's (EHRC) joint publication with Stonewall: *Homophobic hate crimes and hate incidents* (2009). This document sees homophobic bullying and hate crimes as synonymous, and also attempts to create a common understanding between the criminal courts and schools:

> Police and their partners should work with schools and local authorities to tackle homophobic bullying and educate young people about homophobic hate crimes ... also undertake specific work to encourage LGB people to report hate crimes. [31]

Adults or children and young people may actually hold no strong opinions on homosexuality, but should they express opinions felt by another party to be in any way critical, accusations of bullying can quickly follow.

In Stonewall's publication *Homophobic Hate Crime – the Gay British Crime Survey 2013*,[32] which was produced in conjunction with YouGov, there is a consistent merging of 'hate' with 'homophobic', repeatedly referring to 'homophobic hate crimes or incidents'. Stonewall's identification of 'homophobia' with 'hate', with the implication as to how the police should behave, creates a powerful and intimidating pressure. If, for example, a pupil engages in conversation with a staff member who explains the principles of traditional marriage, that child may decide he or she is offended, and even call in the police.

The Norfolk police[33] provide an example of how the Stonewall definition can operate in the public square. The Force refers to homophobic incidents as: 'any incident which is perceived to be homophobic by the victim or any other person'. Their website states that the definition is intentionally wide, and is intended to encourage people to report all such incidents to the police. Conventional definitions of bullying have, therefore, been supplanted by a new interpretation – causing offence. An illustration of this policy was seen when a Norwich Gay Pride March activist attempted, through the Norwich police, to prosecute a pastor whose email post – though neither abusive nor expressing 'hate' – had, he said, caused him 'offence'. It was referred to the CPS as an instance of homophobic bullying, though was not subsequently pursued.[34]

More recently, in May 2014, although not strictly relevant as it did not involve sexual orientation, the same force ordered a poster outside a Norfolk Baptist Church to be removed as inciting hatred, after one person claimed to be 'offended'. The poster had the words: 'If you think there is no God you'd better be right!!' Beneath the words was a picture of flames.[35] It is hard to construe the slogan as in any way abusive or offensive – indeed, had it been so one could justifiably have expected more complaints! Nevertheless, the police logged it as a 'hate incident', leading to the uneasy conclusion that in this day and age Christian beliefs publicly stated could be deemed to be 'hate incidents', leading to police investigation.

The many roles of Ofsted

Ofsted is a crown appointment and reports to Parliament, and has a statutory authority within schools. This includes implementation of the Equality Act 2010 and how it should be interpreted. It has a solemn duty to be impartial, 'to ensure that best practice in equality and human rights is rooted in all aspects of Ofsted's inspection and regulation functions and is based on and supported by a strong evidence base'.[36] On Ofsted's official website, it records its responsibility to 'publish relevant, proportionate information showing compliance... and to set equality objectives'.[37] Any evidence of distortion in its interpretation of the law is disallowed, and a form of corruption.

In 2012 Ofsted published a report *No place for Bullying,* based on a survey to evaluate the effectiveness of actions schools take in order to 'create a positive school culture and to prevent and tackle bullying'.[38] The report's focus was on application rather than research into different kinds of bullying. It gave great attention to 'gay' bullying and disability bullying, and made the assumption that these were a major problem in the context of all other kinds of discrimination.

Prof. John Nolland's paper *Victimisation of Gays and Others in British Schools*,[39] examines some of the available data referred to by the Ofsted report.[40] A significant finding was drawn from the *Longitudinal Study of Young People in England (2008)*,[41] commissioned by the Education Department to inform on future policy.[42] The study broke down the data to explore bullying and asserted that at the starting age of 13–14 years old, bullying experienced by heterosexuals was 38–40%, but for those saying they were LGB it was 53–58%. By age 19–20 the rate was now 2–5%, and for LGBs was 5–9%. This would apparently justify the approach of the Ofsted report that it should give special attention to help LGBs.

However, an additional factor in this study is the relative proportion of bullying compared to the wider school population, which greatly reduces the finding's significance. For example, the study found among boys in the Year 9 group, when bullying was at its worst, 94% takes place in relation to heterosexuals and *just 6%* in relation to LGBs. For girls it was almost identical: 93.6% and 6.4%.[43] To address only LGB bullying would leave nearly 94% of bullying unaddressed.

Dr Nolland points out that whilst there is good data relating to those with LGB orientation or disability, there is a dearth of statistical evidence about other groups. Yet although Ofsted states it has a legal Public Equality Duty to eliminate all discrimination, it has narrowed its focus to LGB and disability, with no research referenced to reducing the vast majority of other kinds of bullying among heterosexuals. Dr Nolland points out: 'Bullying young people for any reason is unacceptable and needs to be addressed with the utmost urgency. But a balanced approach to bullying of LGB young people will place this particular kind of bullying in the context of other kinds of bullying.'[44]

A US bullying prevention programme identifies characteristics identified with conventional bullying,[45] which point to the complexity of personal behaviour, and which can be associated with home life, intelligence, aptitudes and, of course, the wider social environment. The question then has to be asked why Ofsted should distort its bullying report to practically ignore the vast majority of bullying issues. For instance, why are vulnerable groups such as children in care, travellers' children, ethnic minority children and those with special educational needs not addressed? [46] One of Ofsted's exemplar case studies in its report cited amending the curriculum, with training 'informed by external specialist resources such as those produced by Stonewall'.[47] But are Stonewall's resources impartial in view of its highly focussed activist aspirations to normalise sexually aberrant behaviours? The bias of the report points to it concentrating on two particular *Public Sector Equality Duty* components, but that is not stated in its preamble[48] and it has an obvious slant in favour of LGB. The inescapable conclusion is that Ofsted is encouraging unlawful discrimination.

Ofsted's support for *Schools Out,* which campaigns to promote LGB values and practice among schoolchildren, is illustrated in a message of support it sent for LGBT History Month (11/2009). It quotes Sonia Gandhi, Head of Ofsted Equality and Human Rights, who commented:

> We are pleased to share celebrating the contributions and achievements of lesbian, gay, bisexual and transgender people through dedicated events like the LGBT History Month and to combat prejudice and discrimination.

Ofsted also stated it would set up an internal LGBT staff support group *to support our own staff.*[49] One wonders how many support groups have been set up within Ofsted to support the needs of other protected characteristics groups covered under the Equality Act.

Stonewall openly asserts that it is a professional lobbying group, and is 'renowned for its campaigning and lobbying'.[50] Its approach is identical to *Schools Out,* in asserting that LGBTs are discriminated against in the same way as could be the case with disabled people and, in its *Education for All* campaign, Stonewall states it 'works with a wide coalition of groups' to achieve its objectives. The assertions by Stonewall, Schools Out and Ofsted to make 'schools and educational institutions safe places', have common denominators of nurturing children and young people away from heterosexuality into an acceptance that any kind of sexual distortion is not only acceptable but should be welcomed. Ofsted has stooped to the level of an activist movement, and has converted the Equality Act's direct and indirect requirements into a campaign to undermine the traditional family and marriage.

The title of an Ofsted paper published in September 2013 is *Exploring the School's Actions to prevent and tackle homophobic and Transphobic Bullying*.[51] There is no definition, but phrases are used such as: 'how the school meets its statutory duty to prevent all forms of prejudice-based bullying, including homophobia and transphobia'. Ofsted and the activist movement have become synonymous in terms of definitions and interpretations, which makes it difficult for classroom debate, or any other form of teaching which could be perceived by a parent, student or activist representative as showing prejudice and hatred. It is not bullying as would be understood by the general public, who would interpret the phraseology in the conventional meaning – and be fully supportive of Stonewall and others! Ofsted is not to be trusted.

Stonewall's real objectives

In the home page of Stonewall's schools site[52] under the title 'Education for All' is the sentence: 'Find out more about Stonewall's campaign to prevent and tackle homophobic bullying in schools and colleges'. This is Stonewall's consistent strapline. On the page there are sub-headings that cover primary schools, secondary schools, Further Education, Local Authorities, parents and carers, School Champions, Teacher Training, College Champions, Education Champions, Education events, and 'What the law says'.

In its marketing approach, under the site sub-heading 'What the law says', Stonewall creates concern that schools may be breaking the law. 'What the law says: Schools have the duty to prevent and tackle all forms of bullying, including homophobic bullying and they cannot discriminate on grounds of sexual orientation or perceived sexual orientation against a student or teacher.'[53]

It is all about 'What the law says', and 'the duty to prevent and tackle all forms of bullying, including homophobic bullying', and refers to the Public Sector Equality Duty. There is then a reference to *discrimination,* which covers the Equality Act responsibilities generally, and is followed by a reference to the Education and Inspections Act 2006, requiring head teachers, governors and staff '... to prevent all forms of bullying'. Stonewall's consistent message is to use school facilities to stop bullying, because schools can do that, and to protect them from illegal conduct (with its implications for Ofsted inspections). Yet the Equality Act 2010 makes no reference to bullying, or homophobic bullying, but solely to *discrimination*. In other words, homophobic bullying is an *interpretation* of the Act.

The redefinitions already considered enable Stonewall and other activist groups to carry out a campaign that is far more than discrimination, and would be better described as indoctrination. An examination of Stonewall schoolbooks reinforces this opinion. Its *Primary Best Practice Guide* is to help pupils and staff understand homophobic language and bullying, *and shed light on exactly where intervention is needed* (p.5). The message is for children to be aware of the *difference and diversity of family life* (p.10), which can be taken as demeaning heterosexual behaviour and any traditional understanding of the family.

For older pupils, teachers are urged to include in the curriculum interviews with 'lesbian and gay people, exploring in particular some of the discrimination they have faced historically and in the modern day' (p.14). Under 'Celebrating Difference' (p.19), the core objective of the booklet is brought out:

> Primary schools send out a message that it's OK for them not to conform to the norm ... schools that do this create a learning environment where young people feel able to be themselves ... (which) will make them happier, but it will also improve their performance at school.

Stonewall recommends that separation at primary school level can be reinforced *when it involve[s] real gay people who [are] part of the school community* (p.20). Under a separate chapter, *Lesbian, gay and bisexual young people of secondary school age,* it therefore suggests that older LGB pupils be brought into primary schools to talk about *their experiences* (p.21). The approach is assertive, with the underlying message that various kinds of sexual conduct should be the norm among children and within society.

Moving on to Secondary School level is the publication *Supporting*

Lesbian Gay and Bisexual Young People. This has a foreword by Ben Summerskill (former CEO of Stonewall) and contains the sentence: 'Coming to terms with their sexual orientation should be an exciting time for all young people.' It accurately reflects the theme of the booklet, but the overall aim, as rapidly becomes clear, is not just the provision of information, but rather 'indoctrination', teaching children and young people that is perfectly acceptable, and even 'normal' to practise various sexual aberrations.

Stonewall teaches that sexuality is fluid and can change, the implication being that even though someone is 'born' LGBT, there may be no significant manifestation of this orientation during primary school years. But they do acknowledge that *not all boys who don't act like other boys will be gay – though they are more likely to experience homophobic bullying. Similarly, not all 'sporty' girls or girls with short hair will be lesbians* (p.6).

The text appears to say that behaviour and appearance are not critical in determining whether someone has legally recognised characteristics. One presumes that the question Ofsted inspectors would really have to ask teachers is whether a young person consistently engages in the relevant sexual behaviour, or claims to do so. Perhaps Stonewall ambassadors would be brought in to ensure the suspects properly 'come out', so as to avoid the school being criticised in the Ofsted report. But where does this leave the children – because if appearance and behaviour are not the test, what is left?

Gay get over It[54] is described by Stonewall as a pocket sized guide 'designed to help young people challenge their peers' use of homophobic language', and show where they can get further support. It is written in a highly graphic format with short sentences on each page, one of the purposes being to create: *a series of posters that you can put up around school to get the message across and help people 'Get Over It'.* Its style would probably suit young teenagers. The language used is elementary, such as: *All gay means is that you're into people of the same sex. You know that ... and while most of us are grown up enough to be cool about it, some people still use the word 'gay' to mean 'rubbish'. Maybe they don't mean to sound homophobic ... this booklet should help you to help them get over it.*

The theme running throughout Stonewall's educational publications is the immutable nature of LGBT. There is a requirement for schools to provide a protective wall – perhaps better described as a semi-permeable membrane – where homosexuality is exalted and heterosexuality is played down. It is clear that movement of pupils from heterosexual to homosexual orientation is being encouraged, but not the reverse. Although never openly stated, the implication is that some children are genetically different, and it is the duty of teachers and schools to identify and encourage them develop their (homo)sexuality.

This is a serious misinterpretation of the Public Sector Equality Duty. Instead of seeking to ensure equality of educational opportunity for those currently manifesting lesbian or homosexual behaviours, schools are rather being called to attribute the same biological status to sexual orientation as to race, with a duty to reinforce that identity – even though it may, at the time, be unrecognised by the child!

If the principle were applied to other protected characteristics, as statutorily defined, there would be administrative chaos. One may perhaps illustrate the incongruity of Stonewall's approach by analogy with someone suffering a broken leg. Far more than just explaining to other pupils why they must be careful, and not ridicule the sufferer, Stonewall would describe the condition as permanent and something to be praised, explaining that the condition gives the sufferer priority status, and every effort must now be made to ensure there is no change, such as going back to use of two legs!

More seriously, equality legislation clearly emphasises the requirement to avoid discrimination across all groups of protected characteristics, and where assistance is given to one classification it must not bring about inequality to others who do not fit those criteria. A fundamental principle of the Act is the requirement to take proportionate action (para 7.11) that takes into account 'any relevant competing factors', so that helping one protected group, such as LGB, does not discriminate against other groups, including the wider implications for the rest of the school. However, Ofsted's persistent and unrelenting demands for ascendency of one group over another means that however much effort is made by the school to comply, there will continue to be a perceived ambivalence or difference. This then becomes a self-perpetuating problem requiring ever-greater intervention by staff into the school's culture. Then further discrimination occurs elsewhere in order for the school to protect itself from being put into special measures, as the cycle of fear and compliance takes root and grows.

British values

Referring to Ofsted's Trojan Horse report in his parliamentary statement of 9 June 2014,[55] Michael Gove makes the first reference to British values which are to be actively promoted by all schools (Column 266). He also indicated there would be a similar toughening of Independent school standards (C 280), which took place in September 2014, at the same time making it clear that all voluntary-aided faith schools would 'be required to promote those values actively in the future as well' (C284).

A few days later, on 15 June 2014, in an article in the *Daily Mail*,[56] David Cameron linked together the Trojan Horse controversy and the requirement to 'actively promote' British values (paras 1, 5, 6), which are identified in the article's context with SMSC.

In line with this strategy, statutory Regulations released in November the same year aimed to 'strengthen existing requirements', ensuring there be no deviation from the provisions laid down by the Equality Act 2010. More particularly, in the Regulations, respect for other people has the additional clause: *paying particular regard to the protected characteristics set out in the Equality Act 2010* (para 2.5 (vi)). This can only mean that greater proportionate attention has to be given to ensure the minority group of pupils with protected characteristics are not 'disrespected' within the parameters of the law.

This stance was further reinforced by Ofsted's *School Inspection Handbook*,[57] issued in September 2014, which stated:

Schools will focus on pupils' and parents needs – by evaluating the extent to which schools provide an inclusive environment that meets the needs of all pupils, irrespective of age, disability, gender, race, religion or belief, or sexual orientation (para 38 p.13).

While further on, it states, cultural development is shown by the pupils' ...

... interest in exploring, improving, understanding of and showing respect for different faith and cultural diversity, and the extent to which they understand, accept, respect and celebrate diversity, as shown by their tolerance and attitudes towards different religious, ethnic and socio-economic groups in the local, national and global communities (para 9 sub statement 5).

So does the requirement to respect and celebrate diversity also imply participation? It would seem this is indeed so. The original Consultation warned that a failure to address 'homophobia' could lead to the Secretary of State taking regulatory action, and there is no evidence from application of Ofsted policy of any relaxation of this stance. On the contrary, Ofsted has explicitly stated that it will amend its inspection framework to promote British values, and take account of new guidance (Consultation Response para 20 p.8). Because, therefore, 'Gay Rights' might now be perceived as a British value, schools and/ or the Secretary of State may agree with Stonewall and other LGBT organisations that 'homophobia' is any teaching which contradicts their beliefs and agendas.

Two significant sentences within the *Promoting Fundamental British Values* document support this possibility:

Actively promoting the values means challenging opinions or behaviours in school that are contrary to fundamental British values. Attempts to promote systems that undermine fundamental British values would be completely at odds with schools' duty to provide SMSC (Fundamental British Values para 1 p.5).

There could therefore be scrutiny and censorship by Ofsted of Christian views on marriage, the family and its restrained teaching on sexual matters, so as to promote secularist LGBT cultural demands above all others. This, of course, is illegal.

Government counter-extremism strategy

In October 2015 the government unveiled its policy to extend *British Values* to out-of-school activities, where instruction takes place in a semi- or formal environment. The aim of course is to tackle the problem of extremist teaching in Islamic mosques and schools but, as result of equality law, it will extend to include (Christian) Sunday schools, youth groups and other activities where within one week there is at least six hours of teaching. Draconian penalties for non-compliance are proposed, including banning ministers of religion from the instruction of children and young people where their views do not conform to equality and diversity requirements.

Summary of proposals:
Whilst the counter-extremism strategy is to prevent the propagation of any teaching that could lead to indoctrination and commitment to Islamic terrorism, its scope has been widened to incorporate any organisation or individual who publicly contradicts British Values, even though what is said has nothing to do with incitement to terrorism, nor the promotion of extreme right wing political values.

1. Extremism is defined as the vocal or active opposition to fundamental British Values. As framed, publicly expressed opinions or views critical of behaviours falling within the protected characteristics, as defined by law, and causing offence, may be designated hate crimes, meriting police intervention. The proposals are such that they could be used to force the closure of radio or TV stations broadcasting material deemed to contradict any British Value, whether relating to Islam or not.

2. The government's repeated references to sexuality make plain that the counter-extremism strategy will put further pressure on organisations and individuals who are publicly critical of same-sex marriage, and other behaviours contrary to biblical teaching. The intention to further strengthen and extend Ofsted's remit will adversely impact Christian faith schools, limiting their capacity to maintain and teach traditional Christian moral values.

3. The proposed strategy will effectively gag Christian leaders, preventing them from saying anything that might be interpreted as critical of LGBT behaviours, whether quoting from the Bible or expressing personal opinion. Worryingly, because such views fall under the government's definition of 'extremism', steps could be taken through the police and Courts system to ban them, or force attendance on a re-education programme. The same argument could apply to large organisations such as *Christian Concern* and

the *Christian Institute,* because of the 'extremist' nature of their websites.

4. Finally, the Government's mandated restrictions on freedom of speech may well lead in time to the impositions of further limitations, which will inexorably drive the country further along the path to totalitarianism.

What must not be overlooked is the critical role of Ofsted, which, as the statutory body having oversight, has to monitor and judge whether out-of-school teaching complies with *British Values.* Rigorous enforcement of equality law has already established draconian controls over schools and colleges, where priority is (illegally) given to sexuality and gender issues to the exclusion of almost all else. This is plainly unfair, but there seems little prospect of any diminution of Ofsted intervention to redress this imbalance, or of changes in its interpretation of the Equality legislation.

It is then reasonable to assume that out-of-school group supervision will follow a similar direction and rigour. The stated inclusion of church meetings involving children and young people, to monitor whether teaching conforms with what are now defined as *British* Values, will place control of some areas of church doctrine into the hands of the state. Through criminal sanction, the effect will then be to force conformity of Christian doctrine and teaching with secular Marxism.

Conclusion

The LGBT movement despises biblical Christianity, following the teaching of Karl Marx and Engels, who were passionately opposed to monogamy.[58] Over two millennia the Christian faith has been a bastion against totalitarian regimes, and the Church today needs to recognise that the media and government campaigns for the populace to embrace a new morality are just carrying out the mission of radical atheists. It is nothing to do with the clarion cry of 'being born like it' – science and reason refute this claim anyway! Their aim is the abolition of the Christian church as a critical and creative force for good in this country, as one more stage on the journey towards fascist and communist totalitarianism.

Notes

[1] Heiden, Konrad, *The Fuehrer* (Robinson Publishing, London, 1999) p.80

[2] Ibid., p.81

[3] http://people.howstuffworks.com/communism1.htm

[4] www.legislation.gov.uk/ukpga/2010/15/contents Part 2 Ch 1. Protected Characteristics are age, disability, gender reassignment, marriage and civil partnership, pregnancy and maternity, race, religion or belief, sex, sexual orientation.

[5] The actual definition describes direct discrimination as: A person (A) discriminates against another (B) if, because of a protected characteristic, A treats B less favourably than A treats or would treat others.

[6] https://www.gov.uk/discrimination-your-rights/how-you-can-be-discriminated-against
How you can be discriminated against. Discrimination can come in one of the following forms:
(a) direct discrimination – treating someone with a protected characteristic less favourably than others
(b) indirect discrimination – putting rules or arrangements in place that apply to everyone, but that put someone with a protected characteristic at an unfair disadvantage
(c) harassment – unwanted behaviour linked to a protected characteristic that violates someone's dignity or creates an offensive environment for them
(d) victimisation – treating someone unfairly because they've complained about discrimination or harassment
It can be lawful to have specific rules or arrangements in place, as long as they can be justified.

[7] *At school: 'Welcome to the Stonewall Education for All campaign – Stonewall's campaign against homophobic bullying. If you are under 21 please visit our Youth site. If you are someone who works with young people, a parent or a carer, please visit the education for all site.'*
This introduces the Stonewall schools site. Also look at: http://www.stonewall.org.uk/at_school/what_the_law_says/default.asp which is peppered with references to 'homophobic bullying'.

[8] The drive to displace traditional values and exalt the LGBT culture is illustrated by the Yogyakarta Principles developed by a small group of LGBT activists, which has made some headway in the United Nations. http://www.yogyakartaprinciples.org/

[9] *(2) A reference to a transsexual person is a reference to a person who has the protected characteristic of gender reassignment.*
(3) In relation to the protected characteristic of gender reassignment—
(a) a reference to a person who has a particular protected characteristic is a reference to a transsexual person;
(b) a reference to persons who share a protected characteristic is a reference to transsexual persons.

[10] It should be noted that definition (1) could be interpreted as the creation of a person with a protected characteristic that is immutable, but this would read into the Act what is not there. If a pupil decides to no longer change its gender and reverts to a heterosexual position, this takes away the authority for the protected characteristic to be assigned, and treated differently from anybody else.

[11] http://www.equalityhumanrights.com/sites/default/files/publication_pdf/Technical%20 Guidance%20for%20Schools%20in%20England.pdf

[12] https://www.gov.uk/equality-act-2010-guidance#public-sector-equality-duty The Equality and Human Rights Commission is the statutory body established to help eliminate discrimination and reduce inequality.

[13] There is an unusual statement (7.6) that appears to contradict the assumption that *positive action* equates with PSED. It states: *Schools have no duty to take positive action. However, by taking appropriate and proportionate positive action, schools are likely to improve their education and services for pupils, and to overcome barriers for particular groups of pupils ... Also, schools that are subject to the public sector equality duty (schools maintained by a local authority and academies) may wish to consider using positive action to help them to comply with the duty and improve outcomes for particular groups of pupils.* However, this is contradicted by the use of the word 'duty' repeatedly in appropriate contexts, consistently pointing to PSED. Indeed, the very web link refers to PSED.

[14] *1.28* The positive action provisions of the Act permit schools to take proportionate steps to help particular groups of pupils to overcome disadvantages that are linked to a protected characteristic. Where this results in more favourable treatment of pupils with a particular protected characteristic, this is lawful provided that the requirements of the positive action provisions are met. The Act defines the circumstances in which a school may take positive action to overcome disadvantage, to meet different needs or to increase participation of people with a particular protected characteristic.

[15] 7.2 *Positive action might therefore be used to address things such as:*
- *Low participation of girls in certain subjects, resulting in future economic disadvantage*
- *Low achievement of Gypsy and Traveller pupils*
- *High numbers of exclusions of black Caribbean pupils*
- *High levels of bullying of lesbian, gay and bisexual (LGB) pupils*

[16] https://www.gov.uk/government/uploads/system/uploads/attachment_data/file/85019/ equality-duty.pdf There are more detailed descriptions on this site, which provide the cross-over to the Commission's definition.

[17] It is remarkable that after a carefully crafted interpretation of a school's responsibility towards pupils with protected characteristics, the Commission then creates an illustrative scenario, which undermines its professional balance through bringing in organisations that are anything but neutral in their approach!

[18] *'Valuing All God's Children: Guidance for Church of England Schools on Challenging Homophobic Bullying',* 12 May 2014, Report from the Education Division of the Church of England giving recommendations *which should be adopted by schools in combating homophobic bullying.* http://www.churchofengland.org/media/1988293/valuing%20all%20god's%20 children%20web%20final.pdf

[19] Oxford English Reference Dictionary (Oxford University Press, Oxford 2nd. Edit. 1996).

[20] http://www.stopbullying.gov/what-is-bullying/definition

[21] http://en.wikipedia.org/wiki/School_bullying

[22] https://www.gov.uk/bullying-at-school/bullying-a-definition

[23] 'A student is being bullied or victimised when he or she is exposed, repeatedly and

over time, to negative actions on the part of one or more other student.' Olweus D, *Bullying at School: What we know and what we can do* (Blackwell, 1993).

   Rigby and others consider there are just three core identities of bullying: repetition, harm and unequal power. Ken Rigby, *New perspectives on bullying* (London: Jessica Kingsley 2002)

[24] When surveys are undertaken through Stonewall, are the children's claims followed through by teachers to determine whether the 'bullying' is homophobic, or actually is the usual banter of school children which has no sinister depth at all?

[25] http://en.wikipedia.org/wiki/Homophobia

[26] Warwick I et al (2001) Playing it safe: responses of secondary school teachers to LGB pupils, bullying, HIV and AIDS education and Section 28 London Institute of Education.

[27] Ian Rivers (2001) Retrospective reports of school bullying: stability of recall and its implications for research British Journal of Developmental Psychology, 19, 129-141

[28] http://etheses.bham.ac.uk/3157/ Zobiah Aktar (2011) An investigation into homophobic bullying in the education system and the prevalence of homophobic language in a secondary school environment. Ap.Ed^ChildPsy.Dthesis. University of Birmingham

[29] Ibid., p.94/95

[30] Police guide: www.stonewall.org.uk/documents/police_guide_web_final.pdf

[31] http://www.stonewall.org.uk/documents/sexual_orientation_hate_crimes_paper.pdf *Homophobic hate crimes and incidents*, Equalities and Human Rights Commission. Research Summary 38. According to the Introduction, Stonewall was commissioned by the EHRC to write a seminar summary paper, after presenting findings from their Home Office funded *Homophobic Hate Crime: The British Gay Crime Survey 2008,*which was a YouGov online survey of over 1700 LGBs.

[32] http://www.stonewall.org.uk/what_we_do/research_and_policy/9286.asp There are no definitions in this report, which refers, for example, to homophobic harassment, insults or intimidation, but it is reasonable to assume the LGB's interviewed would be asked for their *perception* that whoever was causing offence *was motivated by hostility or prejudice!*

[33] https://www.google.co.uk/#q=Norfolk+police+homophobic+hate+crime

[34] *Christian Watch Newsletter* (August 2013) p.8 Police Interview with Dr A Clifford. Two leaflets (tracts) had been sent by email to the Gay Pride Demo contact address. The police charge was that this was a homophobic incident, having communicated by electronic means something likely to annoy or cause offence. The minister had the option of a £90 on-the-spot fine, or risk proceedings. The police decided that his emails were more than likely to cause offence, and the file was passed to the CPS, who decided not to take any action.

[35] *Daily Mail*, 24 May 2014. http://www.dailymail.co.uk/news/article-2637193/If-think-no-God-better-right-Police-probe-churchs-sign-suggested-non-Christians-burn The report quoted: *'Norfolk Constabulary received a report regarding a poster outside a church in Attleborough which was deemed offensive by the complainant. National guidance required us to investigate the circumstances and the matter has been recorded as a hate incident. Having spoken to the pastor of the church, it has been agreed the poster will be taken down.'*

[36] http://www.Ofsted.gov.uk/resources/single-equality-scheme-2010-13

[37] http://www.Ofsted.gov.uk/about-us/who-we-are-and-what-we-do/public-sector-equality-duty

[38] Ofsted, No Place for Bullying Report (2012) http://www.Ofsted.gov.uk/resources/no-place-for-bullying

[39] www.anglican-mainstream.net/category/gay-activism/ Nolland J (2013) *Victimisation of Gays and Others in British Schools,* Anglican Mainstream, posted 14 November 2013.

[40] Ibid., Ofsted p67

[41] http://www.esds.ac.uk/doc/5545/mrdoc/UKDA/UKDA_Study_5545_Information. htm The study began in 2004 with a sample of 13/13 year olds, whose progress has been monitored subsequently. It is a primary information source for the government to form and appraise policies.

[42] Robinson J P, Espelage L, Rivers I. *Developmental Trends in Peer Victimisation and Emotional Distress in LGB and Heterosexual Youth.* Pediatrics, 2013 pp.423-30.

[43] It is assumed the proportion of boys and girls in the study are 50:50.

[44] Nolland J. ibid., p.3.

[45] http://bullyfree.com/free-resources/facts-about-bullying *Typical Characteristics of Passive or Submissive Students who are Bullied:*

They are generally quiet, cautious, sensitive, and perhaps easily moved to tears.

They are insecure and have little self-confidence (negative self-esteem), perhaps as the result of bullying.

If boys, they are usually physically weaker than their classmates, particularly the bullies, and they do not like to fight.

They have few or no friends, perhaps as a result of bullying.

They may be afraid of getting hurt or hurting themselves.

They find it easier to associate with adults than peers.

Typical Characteristics of Provocative Students who are Bullied:

Only 15 to 20 percent of victims are of this type.

They are often bullied more often and by more peers than passive or submissive victims.

They have tempers and may try to fight back if bullied, but usually without success.

They are restless, clumsy, immature, unfocused, and generally perceived as awkward or tiresome. Some are hyperactive; they may be fidgety, impulsive, or restless and have difficulty concentrating.

They may have reading and writing problems.

They may be disliked by adults because of their often irritating behaviour.

They may try to bully weaker students and therefore may be both victims and bullies.

Some are popular, and some are not. Their popularity may decrease in higher grades, but it never reaches the lowest popularity levels.

[46] education.staffordshire.gov.uk/PupilSupport/Anti-Bullying/TypesBullying/VulnerableGroups/ Those mentioned together with LGB were identified by Staffordshire County Council: *Samuel Learning Net vulnerable group.*

[47] Ibid., p.46/47 (100-102) The direction Ofsted is encouraging is illustrated by this extract from a case study: As part of the campaign against homophobia, staff discussed with pupils the idea that heterosexual people do not need to 'come out as straight', raising the question as to why lesbian, gay or bisexual people are expected to 'come out as gay' rather than just being themselves. This emphasis, in addition to the open, tolerant, safe and inclusive environment in the school means that pupils and staff feel

confident and safe enough to be themselves and to be 'out' in school if they wish. A 'prom couple' recently nominated by the pupils was a same-sex couple. Stonewall had been advising this school.

[48] 'A wide body of research indicates that bullying is a problem for many young people, and that some of this takes place in schools. The aim of this survey was to evaluate the effectiveness of the actions that schools take to create a positive school culture and to prevent and tackle bullying. A large part of the survey focused on pupils' own experiences and understanding of bullying and its effects.' Introductory statement.

[49] http://lgbthistorymonth.org.uk/ofsted-supports-lgbt-history-month/

[50] http://www.stonewall.org.uk/about_us/2532.asp

[51] http://www.schools-out.org.uk/wp-content/files mf/1384363550Ofstedexploringschoolsactionstopreventhomophobicbullying.pdf

[52] http://www.stonewall.org.uk/at_school/education_for_all/default.asp

[53] http://www.stonewall.org.uk/at_school/what_the_law_says/default.asp

[54] http://www.stonewall.org.uk/at_school/education_for_all/quick_links/education_ resources/secondary_school_resources/9307.asp

[55] Extracts from Hansard. Michael Gove. http://www.publications.parliament.uk/pa/cm201415/cmhansrd/cm140609/ debtext/140609-0001.htm#1406095000002 'We need to strengthen our inspection regime even further...' (Column 266) Context is to counter Islamist ideology.

> 'We already require independent schools, academies and free schools to respect British values. Now we will consult on new rules that will strengthen this standard further, requiring all those schools actively to promote British values, and I will ask Ofsted to enforce an equivalent standard on maintained schools through changes to the Ofsted framework.'
>
> 'And we will put the promotion of British values at the heart of what every school has to deliver for children. What we have found was unacceptable, and we will put it right. I commend this statement to the House.'
>
> 'As far as independent schools are concerned we are consulting on toughening independent school standards, as I mentioned to my hon. Friend the Member for Chippenham (Duncan Hames).' (Column 280)
>
> 'Clear requirements apply to all voluntarily aided faith schools. They are, of course, allowed to make provision for appropriate worship and for freedom of conscience, but they must also offer a broad and balanced curriculum, as has always been the case. They must also respect British values, and, as a result of the proposals on which I intend to consult from today, they will always be required to promote those values actively in the future as well.' (Column 284) **Note:** this part of the debate is in the context of faith schools.

[56] Article by David Cameron https://www.gov.uk/government/news/british-values-article-by-david-cameron 'This week there has been a big debate about British values following the Trojan Horse controversy in some Birmingham schools... (para 1) 'The question is: should we actively promote this? (para 5) 'But there are two other reasons why we should promote these values...(para 6)

'Put another way, promoting our values is a key way to economic success...' (para 8)
'The second is social. Our values have a vital role to play in uniting us. They should help to ensure that Britain not only brings together people from different countries, cultures and ethnicities, but also ensures that, together, we build a common home .' (para 9) *Note: there is no reference here to 'equality' although it may be subsumed under 'cultures'.*

'So I believe we need to be *far more muscular in* promoting British values and the institutions that uphold them. That's what a genuinely liberal country does: it believes in certain values and actively promotes them. It says to its citizens: this is what defines us as a society.' (para 10)

'And as we announced this week, we are *changing our approach* further in schools. We are saying *it isn't enough simply to respect these values* in schools – we're saying that teachers should actively promote them. They're *not optional;* they're the core of what it is to live in Britain. '(para 13)

[57] Ofsted School Inspection Handbook 14/9/2014. http://www.ofsted.gov.uk/resources/school-inspection-handbook

[58] Frederick Engels, *Origin of Family, Private Property and State* p. 494-5. Marx, Engels Selected Works. (Progress Publishers, Moscow; Lawrence and Wishurt Ltd, London, 1968).

In an old unpublished manuscript, the work of Marx and myself in 1846, I find the following 'The first division of labour is that between man and woman for child breeding. And today I can add the first antagonism which appears in history coincides with the development of the antagonism between man and woman in monogamian marriage, and the first class oppression with that of the female sex by the male. Monogamy was a great historical advance, but at the same time it inaugurated, along with slavery and private wealth, that epoch, lasting until today, in which every advance is likewise a relative regression, in which the well-being and development of the one group are attained by the misery and repression of the other.

Chapter Six

EDUCATION OR INDOCTRINATION?
An Assessment of CHIPS
(Challenging Homophobia in Primary Schools)
Brian Hadley

"We're coming for your kids"[1]

Introduction

This chapter examines the development, promotion and implementation of CHIPS.[2] It explores the underlying ideology and assumptions, and the pedagogy used with reference to some specific lesson plans and activities. It discusses some of the reactions of parents to the introduction of CHIPS in their children's schools and to similar education schemes in other countries.

The reader is invited to assess to what extent CHIPS *indoctrinates* rather than *educates* the current generation of primary schoolchildren and so revolutionise British society, culture and values.

This chapter only examines CHIPS. Other teaching resources exist which use a similar pedagogy.[3]

What is "CHIPS"?

CHIPS is a teaching resource aimed at children in British primary schools, for use from Reception to Year 6 (ages four to eleven). In essence, it comprises a series of detailed lesson plans, each based on a different children's storybook. The lesson plans include activities, discussion points and songs.[4]

CHIPS aims to change the attitudes and resultant behaviours of children, both while at primary school and beyond. In particular, CHIPS promotes the full acceptance of same-sex lifestyles, behaviours and family structures.

Section 28

Readers may recall that Section 28 of the Local Government Act 1988[5] was introduced because the government of the day was concerned some local authorities were deliberately promoting the acceptability of homosexual practice to schools and youth groups. *Jenny lives with Eric and Martin,*[6] a book aimed at very young children which promoted "gay" parenting was the spark. According to research published by the Christian Institute in 1999, by that time the book's rights were owned by Neal Cavalier-Smith, a publisher who had co-launched a gay pornography company, and a Director of Stonewall. In an interview with *Gay Times* he had observed, "The thing that defines gay men is gay sex. Our aim is to make people feel good about gay sex, and by so doing, to make the world a better place for gay men."[7]

Section 28 prohibited local authorities from committing resources to the promotion of homosexuality in schools or elsewhere. It also made it illegal for them to promote a homosexual lifestyle as a "pretended family relationship". It did not prohibit discussion of homosexual issues or support for pupils who were being bullied. Section 28 was repealed in Scotland in 2000, and in England and Wales in 2003.

CHIPS, and other similar resources, have now emerged. CHIPS promotes what Section 28 specifically prohibited: homosexual practice and family relationship acceptability.

What CHIPS does – it is not "sex education"

CHIPS is *not* about procreation, contraception or the mechanics of intimate sexual behaviours. Likewise, this chapter does not review the numerous sex education resources being deployed in primary schools,[8] sometimes without the knowledge or express consent of parents, for which much research is available.[9]

CHIPS can, however, be regarded as an *enabler* for sex education because it teaches children about intimate same-sex *relationships* rather than the intimate sexual *acts* and *behaviours* which may take place within those relationships. For example, it introduces words such as "lesbian" and "gay" to five-year-olds. This means teachers have to teach very young children what those words *mean*, so priming the children to be receptive to more detailed sexual behaviour teaching later on.

124

CHIPS and the Literacy and Language framework

Under current legislation,[10] primary schools do not have to teach *sex* education but, where they do, they have considerable freedom as to the materials they use. Parents have the right to withdraw their children from sex education lessons.[11] The CHIPS resource explains it can be used as part of the Language and Literacy framework[12] as well as within sex and relationships education (SRE) or personal, social, health and economic education (PSHE). Where used as part of Language and Literacy teaching, parents have no right of withdrawal.

Sustained pressure has been exerted on the Government to make SRE (and PSHE) statutory in all schools. However, during February 2016, the Secretary of State for Education announced the Government would not do so, instead focusing on updating guidance.[13] The legal situation as regards SRE and PSHE as of February 2016 is described in a House of Commons Library briefing paper, which *inter alia* notes the EHRC guidance, updated in June 2014, that schools are *not* required to *promote* same-sex marriage.[14]

The CHIPS lesson plans are based on readily available books which include teaching about *non*-LGBT[15] lifestyle concepts. This offers a way for CHIPS books to be used to develop children's spoken language, reading, writing and vocabulary development. So, where taught as part of the Language and Literacy framework, it is difficult if not impossible for parents to insist their children are withdrawn from any lesson in which CHIPS materials are used. Indeed, the stated intention is that a CHIPS school should implement "a whole-school approach" to LGBT issues, led from the top and involving all staff and all children.

What else does CHIPS do?

CHIPS promotes the acceptance of non-traditional parental relationships and family structures, while downplaying the social structure of society which has prevailed for millennia. The apparent effect is to normalise non-traditional family structures and de-normalise traditional ones.

CHIPS contributes to the normalisation of sexual immorality and the desensitisation of children to it. It inevitably forces the early sexualisation of *all* very young children, e.g. by making teachers explain to five-year-olds what words such as "gay" and "lesbian" *mean*.

What does "sexual immorality" mean nowadays?

A generation or two ago, this question was well understood. Legislation promoted what at the time was considered *best* for society and individuals. However, successive legislative changes, such as no-fault divorce, and the legalisation of abortion and same-sex behaviours, have all helped to shift cultural norms.

The new religion of "Equality", with its own fundamentalist belief system, is the product of decades of secular humanism and cultural relativism. It has its own creed, namely the Equality Act 2010. Perversely, "Equality" provisions inhibit logical and rational discussion of evidence as to whether one lifestyle or family structure may be better for society or individuals than any other. As Charles Moore has observed: "If you believe in big-E Equality, you are not merely saying, as most would, that people should try to make life fairer for all. You are making Equality the all-conquering principle of social organisation and human life. It is like a religion but, unlike actual religions in the West today, it is backed by the full force of law."[16]

So it is necessary to consider how the sexual morality of "Equality" sits with that on which British society has hitherto been structured, namely Christianity.

The established Christian belief about sexual morality is founded on consistent evidence, woven into the Bible from Genesis to Revelation, that sexual intimacy outside one man/one woman, lifelong, faithful marriage, is wrong and not to be encouraged. Other major faiths also hold this view, which has prevailed across societies globally throughout history. It is a definition which accords with nature, with the complementary characteristics of men and women, and with the safe and secure rearing of children. It is what Christians have always believed. It is why Christianity is the principal target of "sexual rights" activists, because it tells people who engage in intimate behaviours (whether opposite-sex or same-sex) outside real marriage that such behaviours are wrong.

CHIPS is an example of how "Equality", seemingly motivated by anti-Christian hatred, is being used to deconstruct established Judaeo-Christian values and especially Christian sexual morality. CHIPS threatens society by weakening the traditional family, usurping parental authority, so increasing State control and increasing the exposure of children to risks of serious physical, mental and psychological harm, all to nudge society to an atheist, cultural Marxist, utopia.

The CHIPS logic seems to be that because *some* children now come from "different" families, *all* children must be taught that all types of family are morally equivalent and that no type is better than, or preferable to, any other. But some children come from families where there is drug or alcohol abuse. So, by CHIPS logic, should not five-year-olds be taught about drugs and alcohol?

CHIPS fails overtly to teach, let alone promote, the established family structure of a married man and woman raising children of which they are each a biological parent (indeed *"King and King"* is the only lesson in the whole of CHIPS where marriage is mentioned: and then only in the context of same-sex "marriage"). Significantly, Department for Education guidance is that "No school, or individual teacher, is under a duty to support, promote or endorse marriage of same sex couples."[17] There is no requirement in National Curriculum science at Key Stage 1 or 2 to teach pupils about same-sex or heterosexual relationships.

So CHIPS appears to be an *attitude and behaviour modification social engineering tool*, promoting the unquestioning acceptance by very young children of LGBT lifestyles.

Of note, although originally conceived as an "LGBT" programme, since early 2015 Educate & Celebrate, the promoters of CHIPS, brand their work as "LGBT+". This change is significant because the number and nature of "sexual orientations" and "gender identities/expressions" being announced by "sexual rights" activists is steadily increasing.[18] Inclusion of the "+" signifies that no sexual orientation, whether known or yet to be described, is outside the scope. Some of these orientations and behaviours may be, or might in future become, illegal or otherwise unacceptable in a civilised society, for example behaviours which involve one person deriving sexual pleasure from the infliction of harm on another person.

"Homophobia"

CHIPS proclaims it is *challenging homophobia in primary schools*. To "challenge homophobia", it is self-evidently necessary to define what "homophobia" is. In spite of "homophobia" being the "H" of CHIPS, CHIPS does not define it.

The Oxford English Dictionary defines a "phobia" as "an extreme or irrational fear of or aversion to something".[19] The *Handbook of Multicultural Counseling Competencies* defines homophobia thus: "In a clinical sense, homophobia is defined as an intense, irrational fear of same sex relationships that becomes overwhelming to the person."[20] So, on that definition, the word "homophobia" stigmatises people who believe in established Christian sexual morality by suggesting they have some sort of mental illness. However, research has concluded that "homophobia" in this clinical sense does not exist.[21]

Psychologist George Weinberg is credited with inventing the word "homophobia" during the 1960s.[22]

Dorothy Riddle, an American-Canadian psychologist, feminist and economic development specialist, devised the "Riddle Homophobia Scale" in 1974. It aims to "explicate the continuum of attitudes toward gays and lesbians and to assess the current and desired institutional culture of an organization or a work place".[23] The Scale classifies attitudes along eight levels from repulsion, pity, tolerance, acceptance, support, admiration, appreciation, through to nurturance. A GLSEN (Gay, Lesbian & Straight Education Network (USA)) resource, *Tackling LGBT Issues in School*, treats all attitudes from levels 1 to 4 as "homophobic levels of attitude".[24] Only attitudes in line with levels 5 to 8 escape this branding. In other words, tolerance or acceptance are not enough to avoid an accusation of "homophobia". The transition from level 4 "homophobic levels of attitude" to level 5 "positive levels of attitude" is widely followed as shown by *Examples of Educational Materials Provided by Advocacy Groups*.[25]

Stonewall has defined it as "the irrational hatred, intolerance, and fear of lesbian, gay and bisexual (LGB) people".[26] But in its new *Getting Started* leaflet for primary schools, Stonewall defines it as "the fear or dislike of someone who identifies as lesbian or gay".[27] This is sophistry: for Stonewall, the dislike *for any reason whatsoever* of someone who so identifies, now amounts to "homophobia". Even Wikipedia seems unable concisely to define "homophobia".[28] So just what is this "homophobia" CHIPS is challenging – among children who have not reached puberty?

Bullying

"Challenging homophobia" is not the same as "challenging homophobic bullying". One stated aim of CHIPS is to address "homophobic bullying". However, the vast majority of school bullying has to do with appearance (e.g. overweight or underweight, wearing glasses or teeth braces, having ragged or "wrong" clothing), academic ability (Mencap has claimed that 82% of those with a "learning disability" are bullied[29]), physical ability/disability and cyberbullying (e.g. "sexting").

Research carried out when Section 28 was being considered for repeal concluded that: "Surveys that claim to show rampant 'homophobic' bullying in schools show nothing of the sort. It may be that in one survey 82% of teachers had heard a pupil call another 'gay' or 'lezzie' but this constitutes childish cruelty in the same way that children use other derogatory terms to insult one another. It does not constitute homophobic bullying."[30]

A Toronto District School Board survey of 100,000 children found only 6% of bullying among 11/12 year-olds was gender-related.[31] The Longitudinal Study of Young People in England tracked more than 8,000 pupils from age 13 to 14 onwards over seven years. It found, for the Year 9 age group, where bullying was at its worst, around 94% was purportedly of *heterosexual* young people and 6% was directed at individuals identifying as lesbian, gay or bisexual.[32] The suggestion is that addressing LGB bullying in isolation ignores 94% of bullying.

The emphasis should always be on the *wrong actions* of the bully and not on the bully's *perceived thoughts or motivations*.[33] That means a good anti-bullying policy needs to concentrate on defining objective, externally-observable behaviours which will be treated as amounting to bullying. Policies should *not* advocate punishment based on perceived motives, intentions, thoughts and beliefs because such a judgemental approach invites teachers to compel children to believe the "right thing", namely to accept without question the worldview of the teacher and school.[34]

All bullying is wrong, whatever the reason for it, and all children deserve to be protected from it simply because they are human beings, quite irrespective of their "sexual orientation" or "gender identity".

A disproportionate emphasis on *homophobic* bullying in primary school anti-bullying measures presents a risk of dividing children up into sub-groups based on self-identification. Could it be that some "sexual rights" activists wish to create a sub-group of "victims" for political purposes? [35]

The activists and the ideology

Ideas from North America typically reach the United Kingdom a few years later. So a study of what "sexual rights" activists have said publicly in Canada and the USA can illuminate the agenda United Kingdom activists are now following.

Writing in the flagship gay publication "The Advocate" in 1995, openly lesbian American author and journalist Patricia Nell Warren stated, "Whoever captures the kids, owns the future." [36]

Robin Perelle, managing editor of the Vancouver edition of the homosexual magazine "Xtra!" ("Canada's Gay and Lesbian News") has written, ". . . the gay rights movement is shifting norms in Canada. And with that comes a message to those who won't evolve: *your outdated morals are no longer acceptable, and we will teach your kids the new norms.*"[37] (emphasis added)

While sexual rights activists usually deny they want to indoctrinate children, Daniel Villarreal, an openly gay American journalist and columnist, has said, in response to the activities of the American NOM (National Organization for Marriage), *"They accuse us of exploiting children and in response we say, 'NOOO! We're not gonna make kids learn about homosexuality, we swear! It's not like we're trying to recruit your children or anything.' But let's face it – that's a lie. We want educators to teach future generations of children to accept queer sexuality. In fact, our very future depends on it."* ... *"Recruiting children? You bet we are."* ... *"Why would we push anti-bullying programs ...unless we wanted to deliberately educate children to accept queer sexuality as normal?"* ... *"I and a lot of other people want to indoctrinate, recruit, teach, and expose children to queer sexuality AND THERE'S NOTHING WRONG WITH THAT."*[38] (emphasis added but capitals as in original)

During March 2015, Canadian children's book author, publisher and "sexual rights" activist S. Bear Bergman, a biological woman who identifies as a man,[39] admitted, "I Have Come to Indoctrinate Your Children Into My LGBTQ Agenda (And I'm Not a Bit Sorry)." Bergman wrote, "I am here to tell you: *All that time I said I wasn't indoctrinating anyone with my beliefs about gay and lesbian and bi and trans and queer people? That was a lie.* All 25 years of my career as an LGBTQ activist … I have been on a consistent campaign of trying to change people's minds about us. *I want to make them like us. That is absolutely my goal. I* want to make your children like people like me and my family, *even if that goes against the way you have interpreted the teachings of your religion.*"[40] (emphasis added)

Why "sexual rights" activists are targeting schools – an insight from America

American Education analyst Candi Cushman has described how and why activists want to capture the hearts and minds of the next generation *and so control the culture of future society*:

> After all, gay activists realize that if they can capture the hearts and minds of the next generation, they will, for all practical purposes, have won the culture war. Problem is, they still find their agenda being blocked by a formidable force – parents and people of faith who don't want their taxpayer-funded schools transformed into indoctrination centers. So they have latched onto a more subtle tactic – infiltrating classrooms under the cover of "anti-bullying" or "safe schools" initiatives.[41]

Cushman goes on to cite numerous examples of how activists have tried to implement this policy in American schools. She explains how organisations such as "Gay, Lesbian and Straight Education Network" and "Parents, Families and Friends of Lesbians and Gays" regard schools as being right at the heart of their "culture war" campaigns. Indeed, the latter's own website states:

> In 2000, PFLAG launched its multi-year *From Our House to the Schoolhouse* safe schools campaign because we recognize that schools are "ground zero" in our efforts to stop homophobia in the classroom and create safe learning environments for all students.[42] (emphasis as in original)

WHAT ARE THEY TEACHING THE CHILDREN?

The organisation is quite open about its aims:

> PFLAG is committed to advancing equality and *full societal affirmation of LGBTQ people* through its threefold mission of support, education, and advocacy.[43] (emphasis added)

Why "sexual rights" activists are targeting schools – an insight from Australia

Purporting to be an anti-bullying programme, the agenda of "Safe Schools Coalition Australia" has been publicly stated by the coordinator of "Safe Schools Coalition Victoria", Roz Ward,[44] to be nothing of the sort:

> Safe Schools Coalition is about supporting gender and sexual diversity. Not about celebrating diversity. Not about stopping bullying. It is about gender and sexual diversity. About same-sex attracted. About being transgender. About being lesbian, gay, bisexual – say the words – transgender, intersex. Not just "Be nice to everyone. Everyone's great."[45]

Indeed, speaking at the March 2015 Melbourne Conference on Marxism, Roz Ward said:

> Marxism offers both the hope and the strategy needed to create a world where human sexuality, gender and how we relate to our bodies can blossom in extraordinarily new and amazing ways that we can only try to imagine today, because Marxism has a theory of social change.[46]

Other commentators in Australia have produced evidence that the ideology motivating "Safe Schools Coalition Australia" is indeed Marxism.[47]

Why "sexual rights" activists are targeting schools – insights from the creator and publishers of CHIPS

The creator of CHIPS is Andrew Moffat, an openly gay assistant head teacher. According to a newspaper report,[48] he resigned from Chilwell Croft Academy, a Birmingham primary school, during December 2013, because of a dispute "which mainly involved Muslim parents" who complained they did not want their children learning "that it's OK to be homosexual". Moffat was quoted in that report as saying some Christian parents had also complained.

The CEO and founder of Educate & Celebrate, publisher and promoter of CHIPS, is Elly Barnes, an open lesbian[49] and top of the Independent on Sunday's Pink List 2011.[50] She stopped teaching music in December 2012 to focus on "Educate & Celebrate". Since September 2012, she has been the LGBT schools advisor for Birmingham City Council. She has been appointed schools advisor to Durham City Council,[51] and has worked for LGBT History Month Schools OUT. She has described her career in the national media.[52] Elly Barnes has said:

> We are currently rolling out the resource to all primary schools across the UK *to achieve our ultimate goal of making all our schools LGBT friendly* [53] (emphasis added).
>
> I ask teachers to think about the lesson they're teaching tomorrow and how they can expand it to include an LGBT element, *and to do that for every lesson* [54] (emphasis added).
>
> As teachers, we can and should attempt to *break patterns of heteronormativity and gender-normative approaches.*[55]

In this article, she also describes a headteacher telling her, "*We are giving them the counter arguments to what they hear at home.*" One CHIPS lesson plan tells teachers to, "*Remind the children they are changing the world – they are making sure every child knows that in our school you can be who you want to be and no one will judge you for being different*" [56] (emphasis added).

To summarise: Every school, every lesson, break the traditional family structure and male/female distinctions, usurp parental rights and change the world.

Andrew Moffat, originator of the CHIPS lesson plans, now behind "Equalities Primary", says, referring to his work at Parkfield Primary School, Birmingham: "The key thing we hope to achieve is for our students to want to live in a diverse Britain and *our school's promotion of diversity will give us the agency* to help our students see all the good that can come from living in harmony with people different to us."[57] (emphasis added) "We can't be simply telling children that their beliefs are wrong or unacceptable; we have to be delivering a curriculum that enables children to understand the benefits that exist in a society where diversity and difference are celebrated. Furthermore, *we need our children to want to be part of that society, and we have to sell it to them; that desire may not come naturally by itself.*"[58] (emphasis added)

In other words, Moffat acknowledges the desire is *not natural*, so children have to be *persuaded* to accept it.

The cover picture of CHIPS version 4 offers evidence that LGBT lifestyle promotion underlies the CHIPS agenda.[59] Version 4 was published in September 2014, at the commencement of the 2014/15 school year. It featured images of 17 CHIPS books on its cover. The cover page was changed by February 2015 to show just five of the most overtly pro-LGBT CHIPS books, namely: *And tango makes three*, *Mommy, Mama and ME*, *Dad David, Baba Chris and ME*, *King and King* and *This Day in June*.

So as the smokescreen of "challenging homophobia" and "anti-homophobic bullying" is blown away, the true ideology underlying projects such as CHIPS is revealed as nothing less than anti-Christian, anti-capitalist, anti-family, Cultural Marxism.[60]

The CHIPS timeline – its origins and history
CHIPS can be traced back to the controversial "No Outsiders" project, which involved fifteen schools across England. It ran from 2006 to 2008.[61]

The project stopped after a media outcry, as the TES explains:

It all started … with a conference run by Exeter University, one of the organisers of the project along with Sunderland University and the Institute of Education in London. Exeter hosted an event titled "Queering Primary Education", which was not representative of the No Outsiders project, but featured people from the team. The event was aimed at academics and designed to explore the limits around discussing homosexuality in primary schools. This involved debates on some deliberately provocative subjects, including whether it should be taboo to mention that sex is pleasurable. Notes for the event mentioned the No Outsiders project, stating: "The danger of accusations of the corruption of innocent children, particularly in the context of the worldwide media attention the project has received, has led team members to *make repeated claims that this project is not about sex or desire – and that it is therefore not about bodies. Yet, at a very significant level, that is exactly what it is about,* and to deny this may have significant negative implications for children and young people" [62] (emphasis added).

"No Outsiders" was supported by the Economic and Social Research Council (ESRC). ESRC have published a supporting catalogue of papers [63] and the full research report on their website. [64]

The overall CHIPS timeline is:

2006 to 2008 – the "No Outsiders" project.

2007 – Moffat writes *Challenging Homophobia in Primary Schools: An Early Years Resource.* [65]

2007 – original version of CHIPS published by Hounslow Healthy Schools.

2008 – CHIPS published by Coventry Healthy Schools.

2010 – CHIPS published by Birmingham City Council and sent to all their primary schools.

2012 – second version of CHIPS published on Birmingham City Council website.

2013 – third version published by Educate & Celebrate on their website.

2014 (September) – fourth version launched, in line with the Educate & Celebrate's stated policy of releasing an updated version of CHIPS once a year "to keep abreast of availability of texts and promote new LGBT-inclusive books" (presumably to coincide with the start of the school year in September).

2015 (January) – fourth version reissued, with revised front cover.

2015 (August) – CHIPS evolves into "PRIDE in Early Years Education" and "PRIDE in Primary Education" ("PIPE"). [66] Approximately half of the books used in CHIPS are used in PIPE. PIPE and CHIPS share a similar pedagogy.

2016 – CHIPS lesson plans (11 plans) available on the Birmingham City Council website.

In 2016, Educate & Celebrate describe themselves as "an Ofsted recognised teacher training and resource programme that gives staff, students, parents and governors the confidence and strategies to implement an LGBT+Inclusive curriculum to successfully eradicate homophobia, biphobia and transphobia from our schools and communities."[67]

During June 2015, Andrew Moffat established his own organisation, "Equalities Primary", and related website.[68] This offers CHIPS-style lesson plans.[69] His book includes 35 lesson plans, one for each of the 35 LGBT+ books (five for each of the seven primary school years). Equalities Primary also offers training and consultancy.

Additional activities
"Educate & Celebrate"
Having published and promoted CHIPS since 2010, Educate & Celebrate are now publishing and promoting their PRIDE in Education and related resources. A detailed evaluation of these is beyond the scope of this chapter. However, it is worth noting Educate & Celebrate are offering:

– Training for teachers and staff, including 1 day CPD events, both open course and INSET.

– Training of "Educate & Celebrate Co-ordinators" to work within schools and organisations. A "Train the Trainer" programme commenced during the academic year 2014-15 in which a member of the school staff is: "trained up as an Educate & Celebrate coordinator (ECCO) whose role it is to embed good practice and to at a later [time] disseminate the learning to neighbouring schools in their community once they have made their own school LGBT+Friendly".[70]

– Consultancy, including enabling schools and organisations to become "Educate and Celebrate" best practice centres. This means implementing a whole-school five-point plan focusing on "training, policy, curriculum, community and the environment engaging all stakeholders including students, staff, parents, governors... As well as supporting all students and teachers within the school, LGBT+ display is made visible throughout the school in classrooms, corridors and the library with welcome messages at reception. This positive message is emphasised in assemblies and lessons and through participation in LGBT+ events and campaigns lead by the schools Pride Youth Network or school council."[71]

– Sale of supporting books.

– Promoting events such as their Edu-cake and Cel-a-bake school cookery competitions.

– Supporting LGBT History Month activities.

CHIPS – the books, the teaching, messaging and lesson plans
Each CHIPS version 4 lesson plan is based on an LGBT-friendly book. Each of the 21 books is widely available via the internet, although they can be procured as part of the CHIPS package.

Each lesson plan is a ready-to-use lesson on one side of A4 – a gift for a busy primary school teacher. The plans typically include whole-class teaching, teacher-led and student-led activities, and songs. As well as recordings of each song with vocals, each is typically offered with a backing track, lyrics, chords and actions for whole-class performance.

In CHIPS lessons, children:

– learn about lesbian and gay parenting (Reception lesson based on the book "Mommy, Mama and ME",[72] Year 1 lesson "Picnic in the Park",[73] Year 2 lesson "The great big book of families",[74] Year 5 lesson "Dad David, Baba Chris and ME"[75]);

– waltz around the playground or classroom singing "Take my hand, my Princess Boy" to each of their classmates (Year 2 activity, while singing the song "My Princess Boy"[76] which promotes transgenderism);

– dress up in opposite sex clothing[77] (Year 2 activity, also based on "My Princess Boy"[78]). Activities include wearing different combinations of clothes, with the children applauding each other, designing a dress for Princess Boy and thinking about what a Prince Girl might like to wear;

– are taught what "sexual orientation" and "gender reassignment" mean (Year 3 activity on "This is our house",[79] using the protected characteristics in the Equality Act 2010);

– learn about gay adoption (Year 3 lesson, based on "And tango makes three"[80]);

– act out gay wedding ceremonies – with two princes standing at the front, getting "married" (role play activity in Year 4 lesson plan, based on the book "King and King"[81] which promotes same-sex marriage: the lesson plan says the setting is a pretend church – but same-sex wedding ceremonies in churches are not generally legal!);

– are taught that same-sex marriage is absolutely fine (Year 4 lesson plan "King and King"[82]: "Would we say these two people can get married but these two people can't? Of course not! What do we think in our school about gay people getting married (we say it's ok!))";

– learn to demand their "rights" (Year 5 CHIPS song[83]: "Nobody will harm or shame us, Nobody will take our rights");

– search the internet for pictures of gay people (Year 5 lesson "Dad David, Baba Chris and ME"[84]);

– are introduced to transgenderism and transvestism (Year 6 lesson covering cross-dressing, transvestism and transgender behaviours, based on the book "10,000 dresses"[85]);

– are taught what happens on Gay Pride marches and why they should take part (Year 6 activity and song based on the book "This day in June".[86]) *"This day in June"* explicitly promotes LGBT lifestyles, using few words but lavish illustrations representative of "Gay Pride" marches. It both draws together the previous twenty lessons and promotes LGBT culture, so encouraging Year 6 children (10- and 11-year-olds) to embrace acceptance of LGBT culture and encourage participation at Gay Pride events.

CHIPS – the pedagogy: "usualising" and "actualising"
The CHIPS pedagogy centres on "usualising" and "actualising".[87] These words are not found in a typical dictionary. Sue Sanders, an LGBT activist linked with "Schools OUT", "LGBT History Month" and "The

Classroom", developed the pedagogy.[88]

Usualising

According to the Elly Barnes website, Educate & Celebrate was commissioned to write and create lesson plans for "The Classroom"[89], "an accessible website for teachers to download a range of resources to make Lesbian, Gay, Bisexual, Trans people visible in education."[90] The page goes on to explain: "All the lessons are LGBT+Inclusive and present the effective methodology of "Usualising" which enables teachers to be confident practitioners in their own subject areas by making our learners aware of the everyday existence of LGBT+people." The Classroom website explains:

> When we usualise something, we acclimatise people to its presence, and take away the threat of difference which creates fear and discrimination. Usualising in schools has more to do with familiarizing learners with a subject's everyday occurrence or existence rather than an in-depth understanding of the subject... In the context of the Classroom "usualising" occurs when a teacher *references* Lesbian, Gay or Bisexual sexual orientation *without inviting further comment.*[91] (italics as on website)

Actualising

Usualising "acclimatises children to the existence of something (e.g. LGBT people). This prepares children to be taught in more detail about those lives later on."[92] This second stage is termed "actualising" which "involves lessons with specific objectives that include a greater understanding of LGBT identities, and their impact on people and culture."[93] The stated intention is to make these real in the minds of the children. As The Classroom website goes on to explain:"Once pupils are habituated to something (LGBT life) they can then study it without distraction. Actualising describes and disseminates subjects that usualising has made an acceptable part of reality."[94]

Educate & Celebrate summarise "usualising" and "actualising" in this way: "'Usualising' makes our learners aware of the everyday existence of LGBT people by referencing LGBT people in our lessons; this leads to 'Actualising' where having established a new language we can then make LGBT people real by, for example, having a discussion on LGBT rights."[95]

So, CHIPS lessons "usualise" children to LGBT ideas and culture. This means teachers just talk about them, without making any comment, so they become "usual" in the minds of the children. Later on, teachers talk about real LGBT people to "actualise" these ideas and culture, to make them real, in the minds of the "usualised" children. No debate as to the rights and wrongs of LGBT lifestyles is allowed.

The CHIPS pedagogy therefore sets out to do something very different from imparting factual information on which children can form their own opinions (e.g. the serious health risks associated with LGBT behaviours) or teaching critical thinking. Rather, it aims to manipulate a child's worldview through subtle emotional conditioning.

Education – or indoctrination?
The focus is on feelings not rational logic. CHIPS uses numerous heart-warming stories about loveable, cute and cuddly animals (e.g. the rabbits in *Rabbityness*, penguins in *And tango makes three* and cats and kittens in *The Whisperer*) to plant and entrench ideas about "difference" and homosexuality.

The lesson plans centre on making children focus on the *feelings* of the animals and fictional characters at the expense of rational logic (e.g. foxes and chickens in *Nanny Fox*, ducks and crocodiles in *The Odd Egg*).

Certain words describing abstract concepts appear at high frequency in the CHIPS resource lesson plans. A study of their frequency of occurrence is helpful in appreciating their significance in the CHIPS "emotional conditioning" process (see Table below).

CHIPS resource lesson plans – analysis of word use (excludes the Introduction)

CHIPS lesson plan	Year	'No Outsiders'	'Different'/ 'Difference'/ 'differences'	'Proud'/ 'Pride'	'Feel'/ 'Feels'/ 'Feelings'/ 'Felt'
"Red rockets and rainbow jelly", "The artist who painted a blue horse", "Mommy, Mama and ME"	Reception		40		9
"Elmer", "The Odd Egg", "Picnic in the Park"	Year 1	2	34	13	20
"Rabittyness", "The great big book of families", "My Princess Boy"	Year 2	3	23		12
"This is our house", "Nanny Fox", "And tango makes three"	Year 3	2	15		12
"The Hueys in the new jumper", "The story of Ferdinand", "King and King"	Year 4	1	21		22
"We are all born free", "Dad David, Baba Chris and ME", "The Whisperer"	Year 5	2	9		11
"William's Doll", "10,000 dresses", "This day in June"	Year 6	4	6	19	7
	Totals	**14**	**148**	**32**	**93**

CHIPS uses concepts of "acceptance", "no outsiders" and no "difference" to mould the minds of very young children, teaching them to form opinions and make decisions on the basis of their *emotions* and *feelings* rather than *rational logic*.

Songs

Back in 1951, philosopher and educationalist Bertrand Russell observed that:

> The social psychologists of the future will have a number of classes of school children on whom they will try different methods of producing an unshakeable conviction that snow is black. Various results will soon be arrived at. First, that the influence of home is obstructive. Second, that not much can be done unless indoctrination begins before the age of ten. Third, *that verses set to music and repeatedly intoned are very effective.*[96]

Elly Barnes has stated part of the thinking behind CHIPS is to link books and music "under a broad diversity umbrella" so children "learn to accept differences".[97]

Songs used in CHIPS, with vocals, lyrics and background music are available for download.[98] Examples include: "My Princess Boy", a song[99] in waltz time to which Year 2 children (age 6/7) dance and swap partners.[100] Lyrics include *Take my hand my Princess Boy, Now dance with me* and *Come and play my Princess Boy.* The phrase "Princess Boy" is repeated 12 times in the song. Children sing the song to each other as they dance and change partners (*"a different partner every time"*). This means "Princess Boy" will have been said boy to boy, boy to girl, girl to boy, girl to girl, *"until everyone has danced with everybody else".* Does not participation in this song risk both disrupting the normal development of a child's understanding of "boy" and "girl" and arousing an interest in transgender and transvestite behaviour?

There is "Elmer"[101] in which children are invited to put hands between other children's legs "for extra fun" when walking around, singing a song, playing at elephant trunks holding tails (class activity in Year 1 song based on the book "Elmer".[102]) What are girls and boys supposed to think when other children put hands on or near their genital areas?

Peer pressure

Throughout the lesson plans and activities, children are required to conform to the ideas being taught. Each child is taught "No Outsiders in our School!"

Another technique is the use of older children to influence younger children. For example, in the Year 6 lesson based on the book *William's Doll*, Year 6 children go into Reception to "model boys playing with dolls and girls playing with trains". The lesson plan tells teachers to "Remind the children they are changing the world – they are making sure every child knows that in our school you can be who you want to be and no one will judge you for being different."[103]

Is it right to force older children to "model" (i.e. to "peer teach") very young children to play with toys traditionally associated with the opposite sex?

"Love" – but what kind of "love"?

CHIPS talks a lot about love, especially love between parents and parents' love for children. But it doesn't mention the different *types* of "love", let alone how they are experienced. It doesn't teach that sexual "love" is different from affection "love" or caring "love".

In *The Four Loves*, C. S. Lewis eloquently distinguishes between affection, friendship, erotic love and charity, and explores how these different types of love are expressed. For example, he contrasts "The love which moves a man to work and plan and save for the future wellbeing of his family…" and the love "which sends a lonely or frightened child to its mother's arms."[104] Ignoring Lewis's powerful truths, CHIPS teaches very simply that, "Gay is when two people who are the same gender love each other."[105]

The teaching of "love" in CHIPS is particularly dangerous where it blurs the differences between strong non-sexual affinity between two good friends and romantic love/arousal expressed sexually. There is a risk that two primary school boys (or girls) who like each other, play and spend a lot of time together, start to think they are gay (or lesbian) because they confuse good friendship with romantic "love". For CHIPS to fail to explain the many meanings of "love" and how they can be expressed is a serious omission. Is there not a risk that CHIPS could expose children to increased risk of abuse by others who may claim to "love" them affectionately or give them "love" gifts, but in reality want to "love" them sexually?

Is CHIPS intended to destroy a child's natural sense of shame? How is a child to distinguish between sexual desire "love" and affection "love" and friendship "love" if CHIPS teaching has confused his or her understanding of the word "love"?

Case study – the "Love has no labels" video

"Love has no labels"[106] exhibits what might be termed "love confusion". It features a street scene in which onlookers view the X-ray skeletons of actors dancing, embracing and kissing back-projected onto a screen. Each pair then emerges from opposite sides of the screen. Onlookers' reactions are cut into the video.

After two lesbians emerge, with the slogan "love has no gender" displayed on the screen, two apparently homosexual men emerge with a small child and kiss in front of the screen, also back-dropped "love has no gender". Other couples assert love has no race, disability, age or religion. Two sisters are shown. In an accompanying behind the scenes video, the participants tell their stories.[107]

Some Educate & Celebrate primary schools are using "Love has no labels". For example:

Howletch Lane Primary School, Peterlee, Co Durham

Year 6 children from this 450-pupil school have uploaded their voiceover of the original video.[108] Their comments suggest "love confusion" in that they display no awareness of the *differences* between the various types of love in the video:

(as the lesbians appear): *"We think the audience are applauding because the women are proud of who they are."*

(as the two "gay" men and their child are shown): *"We think these men are either boyfriend or husband and the child is their son. We think that the crowd accepts this family."*

"Love has no rules. Anyone can love anyone no matter what."

"Love has no right or wrong. You cannot change who you are."

The school is active in various LGBT promotion activities. For example, the Year 6 blog[109] reveals participation in the Educate &

Celebrate "Edu-cake and Cel-a-bake Rainbow Bake Off" competition. They were primary school winners with their "Non-homophobic Heaven" cake, having reached the final with their "Anti-bullying week" cake.[110]

However, in its January 2016 School report, Ofsted assessed the school's "Overall effectiveness" as "Requires improvement" (previously "Good"). "Effectiveness of leadership and management", "Quality of teaching, learning and assessment", "Outcomes for pupils" and "Early years provision" were all assessed as "Requires Improvement". Only "Personal development, behaviour and welfare" was assessed as "Good".[111]

Murrayfield Community Primary School, Ipswich, Suffolk

As at January 2016, the School had 392 pupils.[112] Its logo features a rainbow motif. In a recent school newsletter, the Interim Executive Headteacher explains:

> The school has agreed a partnership with Educate and Celebrate to engage in a year long programme to tackle discrimination with particular regards to LGBT+ (Lesbian, Gay, Bisexual, Trans+ issues). This is part funded through the Department for Education. Our staff have received their first training session and we will be working on a 5 point plan to create an enlightened and educated environment where everyone can feel safe to be themselves without fear of discrimination. As part of that programme we have launched this week with a special assembly where we viewed a short video "Love has no labels".[113]

He describes how, "a school Educate and Celebrate Co-ordinator has been appointed" and that, "We will be developing a zero tolerance of discrimination in any form, highlighted by our equality pledge". This pledge requires that, "Everyone must respect each other's age, disabilities, gender, race, religion, gender identity and sexual orientation ... Everyone *must welcome and celebrate all others in the school*." [114] (emphasis added).

The school was inspected by Ofsted in September 2015.[115] Its overall effectiveness was judged "Inadequate". Two years earlier, it was judged "Requires improvement".[116] During December 2015, the Secretary of

State approved the application of the Local Authority to dissolve the Governing Body and replace it with an Interim Executive Board (IEB).[117]

CHIPS – an examination of some of its underlying beliefs and messaging

An inflated view of the percentage of LGBT people in the population

In a presentation created for use in staff training and assemblies, Educate & Celebrate assert: "1 in every 10 people are LGBT: How many people could be LGBT in this room?"[118] However, recent UK Government statistics state: "1.6% of United Kingdom adults identify their sexual identity as lesbian, gay or bisexual."[119]

The "1 in 10" suggestion can be traced back to the work of Kinsey, published in 1948.[120] That work was uncovered as unreliable as far back as 1981.[121] In 2003, Kempling, a Canadian educationalist and psychologist, stated:

> Kinsey asked his subjects if they had participated in any homosexual activity in the past three years (1945-1947). Incredibly, 26% of Kinsey's 5,300 subjects were male prison inmates including sex offenders (Pomeroy, 1972). Other subjects were recruited from less than neutral locations, such as gay bars in Chicago. Kinsey simply did not use a representative sample. His statistics were not valid in 1948, and are certainly not so 50 years later.[122]

In 1994, American academic and social critic Camille Paglia wrote scathingly about Kinsey's fraudulent 10% finding and its service to the homosexual movement:

> As a teacher of twenty-three years, most of which were spent in art schools, I have been struck by the rarity, not the frequency of homosexuality... The 10 percent figure, servilely repeated by the media, was pure propaganda, and it made me, as a scholar, despise gay activists for their unscrupulous disregard for the truth.[123]

So why, in 2016, does Educate & Celebrate still claim "10%"?

"LGBT+" people are "born that way" and can't change

CHIPS asserts that primary school children can be lesbian, gay, bisexual or trans. The implication is that children are "born that way" and cannot change. However, in a similar Educate & Celebrate presentation accessed in 2015, the corresponding slide also stated: "Anyone could be LGBT and it can change within your life."[124]

The work of Reisman has shown how the Kinsey reports of 1948 and 1953, suggesting that people are sexual beings from birth, were deeply flawed and unreliable.[125] There is a substantial body of evidence that people are not "born gay"[126] but rather develop same-sex attraction and same-sex behaviours as a consequence of unpredictable life events[127] experienced as they grow up.

In 2014, the Royal College of Psychiatrists adjusted its position, explaining that it now considers "sexual orientation is determined by a combination of biological and postnatal environmental factors".[128] This is very significant. "It implies that if a child does not encounter such postnatal life experiences, he/she will grow up heterosexual."[129]

The evidence seems to be that sexual orientation can change,[130] spontaneously or with therapeutic support[131] and/or over time.[132] The Royal College says, "It is not the case that sexual orientation is immutable or might not vary to some extent in a person's life".[133]

According to the 2014 ONS Integrated Household Survey, "The likelihood of an adult identifying as lesbian, gay or bisexual decreased with age. Around 2.6% of adults aged 16 to 24 years identified themselves as lesbian, gay or bisexual. This decreased to 0.6% of adults aged 65 and over."[134]

Confirmation of "can change" is elegantly described by Jeffrey Satinover in "The Trojan Couch" in which he evaluates the work of Laumann:

Laumann[135] is universally recognized as definitive. Since its publication, numerous large-scale epidemiologic surveys, conducted in all the English-speaking and many other industrialized nations, have repeatedly confirmed and strengthened its findings. One of the major points of the Laumann study, which the authors themselves did not expect, is that "homosexuality" as a fixed trait scarcely even seems to exist.

"[E]stimating a single number for the prevalence of homosexuality is a futile exercise," Laumann declares in the first paragraph of an entire chapter devoted to the subject. It is futile not because of bias, underreporting, methodological difficulties, or complexities of behavior, but "because it presupposes assumptions that are patently false: that homosexuality is a uniform attribute across individuals, that it is stable over time, and that it can be easily measured." All the evidence points to the fact that homosexuality is not a "stable trait." Furthermore, the authors found to their surprise that its instability over the course of life was one-directional: declining, and very significantly so. Homosexuality tended spontaneously to "convert" into heterosexuality as a cohort of individuals aged, and this was true for both men and women – the pull of the normative, as it were.

So striking and unexpected was this finding that it led researchers all over the world in subsequent years to see if it was really true. Their research involved hundreds of thousands of people and strongly confirmed Laumann.[136]

In other words, not only is it the case that people "can change" as regards sexual orientation, they *do* change....

Further objections

CHIPS interferes with early child development
"Five year olds need to be taught that gay men, lesbian women, bisexual and trans people exist" – This assertion is made on the first line on page 5 of the Introduction of the CHIPS resource but, by so doing, CHIPS risks disruption of the normal process of sexual identity development at its most sensitive stages.

   Standard child psychology is that a child is not a miniature adult and gender awareness develops in three stages:
1. Gender identity (at about age 3, a boy knows he is a boy).
2. Gender stability (at about age 4, a boy knows he will grow up to be a man).
3. Gender permanence (by age 6 or 7 at the latest, a boy knows he cannot become a girl even if he wears a dress).[137]

CHIPS interferes with the natural processes of psychological development

CHIPS starts to deconstruct the true meaning of "male" and "female" as being a person's biological sex by planting the idea in young children's minds that they can create for themselves any gender and sexuality they wish – *and that's OK*. For example, in the Year 6 CHIPS lesson *William's Doll,* children are told, "You can be who you want to be".[138]

Early sexualisation has been identified as a risk factor for later development of same-sex attraction and same-sex behaviours.[139] So, perversely, under the guise of "challenging homophobia", could CHIPS trigger gender identity confusion ("gender dysphoria") in children? Could CHIPS-exposed children be at increased risk of sexual exploitation by adults or older children?

CHIPS does not acknowledge negative aspects of LGBT lifestyles and culture

There is substantial evidence that LGBT lifestyles and culture present elevated risks to health.[140] In its analysis of 2014 STI/HIV diagnoses, Public Health England have reported substantial variation in the distribution of the most commonly diagnosed STIs by gender and sexual orientation. In particular, that:

> Men who have sex with men (MSM) accounted for 81% of syphilis and 52% of gonorrhoea diagnoses.

They also reported that,

> Of particular concern is the continuing rise in STI diagnoses, especially of syphilis and gonorrhoea, among MSM, which may be due to ongoing high levels of unsafe sex. Furthermore, serosorting, the practice of engaging in condomless sex with partners believed to be of the same HIV status, increases the risk of infection with STIs, hepatitis B and C, and sexually transmissible enteric infections like Shigella spp. For those who are HIV negative, serosorting increases the risk of HIV seroconversion as 16% of MSM are unaware of their infection.[141]

Should CHIPS be promoting to very young children lifestyles and behaviours which could result in significantly elevated health risks?

CHIPS disguises its intent

The introduction to the CHIPS resource states, "We are not teaching about sex, we are merely teaching children that LGBT people exist and that it's okay."[142] It is a fact that people who identify as "LGBT" exist. However, "It's okay" is an opinion which could be interpreted either as "it's okay for LGBT people to exist" or "LGBT behaviours are morally acceptable".

Further, by repeatedly teaching that same-sex and opposite-sex relationships are morally equivalent (by referring only to "love" and "caring"), is not CHIPS priming young children to believe that homosexual and heterosexual intimate acts are morally equivalent?

The biological reality is that only a man and a woman can produce a child *of which each is a biological parent*. No gay or lesbian relationship can do that.

CHIPS goes against The Universal Declaration of Human Rights (UDHR)

CHIPS tries to redefine the word "family". It teaches that because *some* families nowadays come in all sorts of shapes and types (two mums, two dads, single mum, etc.), therefore *all* sorts of shapes and types of family structure are suitable for bringing up children and of equal inherent moral worth. This logical fallacy is reinforced by making children think about how they would *feel* if they came from a non-traditional family background.

The UDHR states that not "everyone" but only "men and women" (even clearer in the original French text which states "man" and "woman" in the singular[143]) "have the right to marry and to found a family". This family, based on marriage between a man and a woman, is called "the natural and fundamental group unit of society". It is this "family" that is recognised even by the UN Convention on the Rights of the Child as "the natural environment for the growth and well-being of all its members and particularly children".[144]

CHIPS goes against parents as primary educators of their children

CHIPS teaches its own morality, without any regard for children's cultural or religious backgrounds or the wishes of their parents. Parents have the primary responsibility for the education and upbringing of their children.

Because CHIPS focuses on feelings rather than logic or a child's long-term best interests, CHIPS primes children to develop ideas and behaviours hostile to their parents' religion or beliefs. For example, the lesson based on the book *We are all born free* [145] focuses entirely on rights with no reference to related obligations, and *King and King* [146] promotes same-sex marriage.

But Article 26(3) of the Universal Declaration of Human Rights specifically gives parents, "a prior right to choose the kind of education that shall be given to their children".[147]

Parents rightly expect primary schools to be teaching reading, writing, mathematics and related academic subjects. Very few parents would wish their child's primary school to be a place for Orwellian indoctrination into the State's preferred belief system.

Moreover, such indoctrination runs contrary to the principles of good social cohesion. Because CHIPS cuts across parent-child relationships, its ideology can be wildly at variance with the culture and values of the community in which a particular school is located. This seems to have been the case in Birmingham (see below).

CHIPS plays down traditional family structures
CHIPS imposes the notion that opposite-sex marriage is irrelevant, let alone a desirable or preferable structure in which to raise a family, by using books which make minimal or no reference to "marriage", "husband" or "wife".

Indeed, the word "marriage" only occurs in the CHIPS resource four times and all of these are in the *King and King* lesson, which promotes same-sex "marriage". Put another way, *the only discussion of marriage in the whole CHIPS resource is in the context of same-sex marriage.* The benefits to children and families of opposite-sex marriage are simply ignored.

CHIPS says that all that matters in parenting is "love"
"Love" and "caring" for a child are certainly necessary for good parenting. However, the evidence is that a child needs to experience the

different *kinds* of relationship offered by a father and a mother. How can "two dads" support a "daughter" experiencing her first menstrual cycle?

Research published in 2012 by sociologist Mark Regnerus[148] into eight different family structures using a nationally representative random sample (the New Family Structures Study), found a number of negative outcomes were associated with having a parent who is or has been in a same-sex relationship, compared with having two married biological parents. The original findings attracted criticism[149] but were nonetheless strengthened in a follow-up paper published later that year.[150]

Research by Paul Sullins published during February 2015 showed:

Children with same-sex parents in the United States suffer twice as many emotional problems as do children with opposite-sex parents, and four times the emotional problems of children raised by their own joint biological parents. Since no same-sex partners can be joint biological parents, such families cannot, by definition, achieve the aggregate level of child benefit that is the case in (non-adoptive) opposite-sex intact marriages.[151]

Discussing the Sullins research, Regnerus stated:

Results reveal that, on eight out of twelve psychometric measures, the risk of clinical emotional problems, developmental problems, or use of mental health treatment services is nearly double among those with same-sex parents when contrasted with children of opposite-sex parents. The estimate of serious child emotional problems in children with same-sex parents is 17%, compared with 7% among opposite-sex parents, after adjusting for age, race, gender, and parent's education and income. Rates of ADHD were higher as well – 15.5% compared to 7.1%. The same is true for learning disabilities: 14.1% vs. 8%.[152]

CHIPS definitions of "gay" and "lesbian", "bi", "trans" – and "love"

The CHIPS resource states:

Before delivering the lesson plans it is a good idea for the School to identify a definition for everyone to use to define the terms 'gay' and 'lesbian', 'bi', 'trans'. Andrew suggests using: "When a man loves a man or when a woman loves a woman. Some families have a Mum and a Dad, and some families have a Mum and a Mum or a Dad and a Dad." A definition of 'bi' could be when a man loves men and women equally and vice versa. Trans could be, "a girl who feels happier living and identifying as a boy, or a boy who feels happier living and identifying as a girl".[153]

As noted earlier, CHIPS does not explain that "love" in this context includes expression through sexual behaviours.

CHIPS and legislation

The Equality Act 2010 requires non-discrimination against *people* with protected characteristics. It does not require the promotion of ideologies linked to those characteristics.[154]

Rather than stating that gay and lesbian relationships exist and that same-sex "marriage" is legal, CHIPS promotes gay and lesbian relationships, same-sex "marriage" and certain LGBT behaviours as morally acceptable. As already noted, some religions and belief systems hold strongly opposing views.

However, Educate & Celebrate have been using the Equality Act 2010 and Ofsted guidance to promote CHIPS. The evident suggestion is that schools *do* have to promote LGBT lifestyles because sexual orientation and gender reassignment are protected characteristics under the Act.

The application of the Equality Act 2010 to the education sector is discussed in detail elsewhere in this book (see Chapter 5).

CHIPS in schools

Where it is being taught

CHIPS is being used in scores of primary schools across England, especially in Birmingham and County Durham. In Birmingham, the plan has been to introduce it into all 36 primary schools by 2018.

According to their latest newsletter (December 2015), Educate & Celebrate have delivered "in-house LGBT+Inclusive training to staff, support staff, departments, leadership teams, parents and governors in over 100 children's centres, nurseries, primary schools, secondary schools, colleges and universities across the UK, reaching 1000s of teachers and students".[155] They acknowledge funding from the Government has helped. Some 60 Educate & Celebrate schools took part in sponsored LGBT anti-bullying week events held during November 2015.

During Autumn 2015, almost 30 schools (not all primary) from Birmingham, London, Hampshire, Essex, East Sussex, Suffolk, Kent, Rutland and Co. Durham took part in the Educate & Celebrate Edu-cake & Cel-a-bake Great Rainbow Bake-off competition.[156]

Birmingham City Council support

The Council continues to actively promote CHIPS to primary schools.[157] It specifically endorses PRIDE in Primary Education.[158]

Additionally, it enables its employees, teachers and schools to access the Educate & Celebrate programme and training for free. This includes booking a date for whole staff training in a school, registering for the 12-month Educate & Celebrate Best Practice Programme, enabling the school to become "an Educate & Celebrate school" and enabling staff to attend a one-day CPD course.[159]

Parents' reactions to the introduction of CHIPS

The introduction of CHIPS into some 35 Birmingham primary schools has caused division and precipitated strong adverse parental reactions.

In April 2014, the assistant headteacher at Chilwell Croft Academy, Andrew Moffat (the author of CHIPS), resigned. CHIPS had been introduced without prior discussion with parents, some of whom had principled objections to the CHIPS materials being taught to their children.[160]

At 480-pupil Welford Primary School, which introduced CHIPS during 2014 in the wake of the "Trojan Horse" affair, parents protested robustly to the headteacher over its introduction.[161]

During November 2014, parents presented a petition against the introduction of CHIPS to Birmingham City Council, filmed by ITV News Central. Concerns raised included age-inappropriateness and the undermining of parental rights to explain these issues to their children when they are mature enough. In the film, a parent explains "...seven-year-old, five-year-old, it's just not appropriate, and I think by bringing it into school it's taking away our parental right of introducing it when the child is mature enough and when the parent deems fit enough".[162]

In March 2015, Clifton Primary School parents launched a petition against the introduction of CHIPS.[163] Three consultation meetings had been held. Parents' concerns included going against religious beliefs and age-inappropriateness.[164]

During December 2014, the "Birmingham Parent Association" launched an online petition. Addressed to the Secretary of State for Education and the Leader of Birmingham City Council, the petition's demands included:

1. An immediate end to the teaching of CHIPS and similar themes and topics to our children.

2. Our children be protected from teaching and materials which are inappropriate, having regard to their age, religious and cultural background.

By the time it was closed in December 2015, the petition had attracted 5,363 signatories and 1,568 detailed expressions of objection.[165]

In his new book, Moffat states that in his current school he shows the books being used to parents in advance, commenting that parents are not objecting to the books once they see them.[166] Perhaps parents are simply relieved not to find illustrations and descriptions of sexual acts. But it seems he does not show the *lesson plans* to parents, meaning parents are unaware how the books are actually used in classes.

CHIPS and State funding

During October 2014, the Government Equalities Office, Department for Education, Nicky Morgan (Secretary of State for Education at the time) and Jo Swinson (Minister for Women and Equalities at the time), announced the Government was establishing a £2 million "Homophobic, Biphobic and Transphobic (HBT) Challenge Fund" to tackle HBT bullying in schools. It invited interested organisations to apply for funding.[167]

During March 2015, the eight successful organisations and their funding allocations were announced. Educate & Celebrate were awarded £214,048 "to train staff in 60 schools, giving them confidence and strategies to address HBT language and bullying and promote inclusiveness throughout the school environment and the curriculum".[168]

On 11 August 2015, Elly Barnes announced the funding, "will train all teachers in selected schools on appropriate language and how to build inclusive lessons across the curriculum. There will also be dedicated school co-ordinators working to embed good practice throughout each school. An online web resource will also be available from September".[169]

What's happening now and what's happening next?

In North America, "Gay Straight Alliances" (GSAs) have become established in schools. According to the GSA website, a GSA, "is a student-run club, typically in a high school or middle school, which provides a safe place for students to meet, support each other, talk about issues related to sexual orientation and gender identity and expression, and work to end homophobia and transphobia".[170]

Peter Sprigg explains, "Their introduction in American schools has proved controversial as it has become evident the real agenda is the promotion of homosexual behaviours to vulnerable teenagers."[171]

Educate & Celebrate are now promoting "PRIDE Youth Networks" in schools.[172] These appear similar to GSAs. The stated intention is to enable young people, with help from a staff member, to, "mobilise and initiate campaigns, raise awareness, increase visibility, hold celebrations, talk about their own experiences of sexual orientation and gender identity, engage with students, staff, parents, governors and take part in local and national events".

During March 2016, Educate & Celebrate published detailed guidance on how to set up and operate a PRIDE Youth Network Guidance, including "how to overcome resistance".[173] The target appears to be secondary schools. However, secondary school pupils will have attended primary schools where they may have been "usualised" and "actualised" to accept same-sex behaviours and lifestyles.

Will PRIDE Youth Networks provide opportunities for vulnerable teenagers to experiment?

Gender mainstreaming

In essence, "gender mainstreaming" is an agenda to deconstruct all difference between male and female, denying the reality of biological difference. It goes much further than equality of men and women. It is the aim of gender mainstreaming artificially to create a diverse range of genders, each of which has equal value and equal rights, by deconstructing the "binary hierarchical gender order".[174] Put another way, notwithstanding the sex of your body, "you can be whatever gender you wish to be".

Sexualisation of children is part of the gender mainstreaming agenda. As German author and sociologist Gabriele Kuby explains:

> Gender theory says our sexual orientation is the main criterion for our identity. The main value by which this is promoted is freedom. Our hyper-individualized society claims that we have freedom to choose our sex, whether we are man or woman, and it is our freedom to choose our sexual orientation. Society must not only tolerate but positively accept any kind of sexual orientation. But in fact, heterosexuality is the natural condition of our human existence, and more than 97 percent of the population of this earth is heterosexual and has an instinctive rejection of homosexuality. The people who push the gender agenda around the world of course have to start with very young children and teach them that any kind of sexual orientation is equally valid.[175]

It is evident how programmes such as CHIPS sit within the gender mainstreaming agenda. Kuby observes that, "Deconstruction of gender identity through 'diversity education' and dissolution of 'gender stereotypes' is an irresponsible experiment on defenceless children."[176]

"Gender neutral" uniforms

During May 2015, Educate & Celebrate joined the campaign to introduce gender neutral uniforms in schools. For example, Barnes is reported as telling the Boarding Schools Association: "If it's all right for a girl to wear trousers, why should a boy not be allowed to wear a skirt. We should be giving them the option."[177]

In January 2016, Brighton College (an 11 to 18 school) became the first UK school to introduce a gender-neutral uniform policy, allowing

WHAT ARE THEY TEACHING THE CHILDREN?

all pupils to choose between wearing trousers or a skirt and a shirt or a blouse.[178]

Transgenderism

The Tavistock and Portman NHS Trust, the UK's only centre specialising in gender issues in under 18s, said that, in total, the number of under 11s referred to the unit has risen from 19 in 2009/10 to 77 in 2014/15, more than quadrupling over those five years. The Trust said referrals over the period included 47 children aged five or under, and two children just three years old.[179]

At Maldon Primary School, Essex, where CHIPS implementation began in 2014, a pupil aged seven "transitioned" during 2015 from male to female.[180]

Melanie Phillips has observed that:

Gender politics is all about subjective feelings. It has nothing to do with fairness or equality. It embodies instead an extreme egalitarianism which holds that any evidence of difference is a form of prejudice.

She adds,

We can all predict what will happen. Gender fluidity will be actively promoted as just another lifestyle choice. Under the commendable guise of stopping the minute number of transgender children being bullied, the rest of the class will be bullied into accepting the prescribed orthodoxy — that gender is mutable, and any differentiation in value between behaviour or attitudes is bigoted and prohibited. *The intention is to break down children's sense of what sex they are and also wipe from their minds any notion of gender norms.*[181] (emphasis added)

Propaganda

The United States Holocaust Memorial Museum, Washington D.C., website offers this definition:

Propaganda is biased information designed to shape public opinion and behavior. Modern propaganda draws upon techniques and strategies used in advertising, public relations, communications, and mass psychology. It simplifies complicated issues or ideology for popular consumption, is always biased, and is geared to achieving a particular end. Propaganda generally employs symbols, whether in written, musical, or visual forms, and plays upon and channels complex human emotions towards a desired goal. It is often employed by governmental and private organizations to promote their causes and institutions and denigrate their opponents. Propaganda functions as just one weapon in the arsenal of mass persuasion. The real danger of propaganda lies when competing voices are silenced – and unchecked, propaganda can have negative consequences.[182]

Successful propaganda relies on the application of powerful marketing techniques such as "desensitisation", "jamming" and "conversion". Marketeer Paul Rondeau has researched how sexual rights activists have used these techniques step-by-step to deconstruct the sexual morality of established Judaeo-Christian societies.[183] Activists have applied these techniques with much success, using the homosexual agenda promotion strategy prescribed by Kirk and Madsen in *After the Ball*.[184]

Does CHIPS teaching match this definition of propaganda?

The road to totalitarianism – suppression of free speech

Fichte laid it down that education should aim at destroying free will so that after pupils are thus schooled they will be incapable throughout the rest of their lives of thinking or acting otherwise than as their school masters would have wished.

So wrote Bertrand Russell 65 years ago. As well as being a philosopher, he worked extensively on the education of young children, viewing the use of the education system as the most influential modern propaganda technique.[185]

Journalist Dennis Prager has commented how, "Those indoctrinated by leftist thinking become largely incapable of making accurate moral judgments."[186]

Is CHIPS (and similar programmes) part of an agenda to deconstruct foundational Christian belief about marriage and family life, to suppress the expression of that belief and so facilitate the onset of totalitarian, atheist government?

Conclusion

The prevailing culture is fast becoming one of grievance and victimisation, leading to special privileges being given to those who feel aggrieved or victimised. Government ministers talk much about combating "extremism", sometimes conflating traditional views, for example about Christian sexual morality, with "extremism". Such conflation must be either intentional or incompetent. Does the Government really wish to destabilise society by fermenting anti-Christian hatred? What is wrong with traditional Christian morality?

Moreover, does not such a culture play into the hands of those who wish to promote only one worldview and silence any opposition – those who seek to usher in an era of totalitarianism?

During the marriage redefinition Parliamentary process, the Government was keen to dismiss some concerns as "myths". For example:

MYTH: Teachers will have to promote same-sex marriage to pupils in sex and relationships education.

REALITY: This is not true. No teacher will be required to promote or endorse views which go against their beliefs. As with any other area of the curriculum teachers will of course be required to teach the factual position, that under the law marriage can be between opposite-sex couples and same-sex couples. There are many areas within teaching, particularly within faith schools, where this type of issue already arises and where subjects such as divorce are taught with sensitivity. The guidance governing these issues is the same guidance that will govern how same-sex marriage in the classroom will be approached. *Sex and relationships education is categorically not about the promotion of a particular sexual orientation – that would be inappropriate teaching.*[187] (emphasis added)

But CHIPS is about the promotion of LGBT sexual orientations. So, by the Government's own measure, is it "inappropriate teaching"?

Notes

[1] Patricia Nell Warren, *The Advocate*, 1995, cited in *The Great Gay Deception* (Michael Brown)
http://www.charismamag.com/spirit/devotionals/daily-breakthroughs?view=article&id=19734:the-great-gaydeception&catid=1559, accessed 8 March 2016.

[2] Although the version 4 launch announcement is no longer on the Educate & Celebrate website, it is available at *'CHIPS' Challenging Homophobia in Primary Schools*, The SchoolBus education Blog, http://theschoolbusblog.net/2014/10/02/chips-challenging-homophobia-in-primary-schools/, accessed 29 February 2016.

[3] For example, the Stonewall Education Guide *Including Different Families*, 2010, includes lesson plans and activities for use in primary schools,
https://www.stonewall.org.uk/sites/default/files/including_different_families_lo.pdf,
accessed 7 March 2016. 'Equalities Primary' have had CHIPS-style lesson plans available on their website, http://www.equalitiesprimary.com/, since autumn 2015. During January 2016, *No Outsiders in Our School: Teaching the Equality Act in Primary Schools*, written by the founder of Equalities Primary, Andrew Moffat, was published. This includes 35 CHIPS-style lesson plans. Since January 2016, Birmingham City Council has had a booklet of 11 CHIPS-style lessons ("Challenging Homophobia in Primary Schools" by Andrew Moffat, created 11 January 2016) available for download from its website,
http://www.birmingham.gov.uk/cs/Satellite?c=Page&childpagename=
Children%2FPageLayout&cid=1223336569886&pagename=
BCC%2FCommon%2FWrapper%2FInlineWrapper, accessed 9 March 2016.
Out For Our Children promotes LGBT resources and books for children aged 0 to 3,
http://www.outforourchildren.org.uk/childrens-books/, accessed 29 March 2016.

[4] Over the summer of 2015, the publishers, Educate & Celebrate, replaced CHIPS with their "PRIDE in Education" resources. CHIPS (especially volume 4, first published at the commencement of the 2014/15 school year) may well remain in use for some time. Accordingly, unless stated otherwise, in this chapter "CHIPS" means "CHIPS volume 4, March 2015 version". This 32-page volume includes 21 lesson plans. It is downloadable from
http://www.ellybarnes.com/wp-content/uploads/2014/07/chips-march-2015.pdf,
accessed 18 March 2016.

[5] Section 28 of the Local Government Act 1988 stated:
(1) A local authority shall not -
(a) intentionally promote homosexuality or publish material with the intention of promoting homosexuality;
(b) promote the teaching in any maintained school of the acceptability of homosexuality as a pretended family relationship.

[6] Bösche S, *Jenny lives with Eric and Martin* (Gay Men's Press, 1983).

[7] Quoted in *Bankrolling Gay Proselytism: The case for extending Section 28*, The Christian Institute, November 1999,
http://www.christian.org.uk/wp-content/downloads/bankrolling-gay-roselytism.html,
accessed 4 March 2016.

[8] Sex education is non-compulsory at primary school level. Although all schools are

required to have a sex education policy, for primary schools this can simply be that they do not cover sex education topics.

[9] For an insight into the nature of these resources, see *Too much, too young: Exposing primary school sex education materials*, Christian Institute, 2011, http://www.christian.org.uk/ wp-content/downloads/toomuchtooyoung_lordsed_sept11_web.pdf, accessed 7 March 2016.

[10] Education Act 1996, Section 403 Sex education: manner of provision

(1) The governing body and head teacher shall take such steps as are reasonably practicable to secure that where sex education is given to any registered pupils at a maintained school, it is given in such a manner as to

encourage those pupils to have due regard to moral considerations and the value of family life.

(1A) The Secretary of State must issue guidance designed to secure that when sex education is given to registered pupils at maintained schools—

(a) they learn the nature of marriage and its importance for family life and the bringing up of children, and

(b) they are protected from teaching and materials which are inappropriate having regard to the age and the religious and cultural background of the pupils concerned.

(1B) In discharging their functions under subsection (1) governing bodies and head teachers must have regard to the Secretary of State's guidance.

[11] Education Act 1996, Section 405 Exemption from sex education. "If the parent of any pupil in attendance at a maintained school requests that he may be wholly or partly excused from receiving sex education at the school, the pupil shall, except so far as such education is comprised in the National Curriculum, be so excused accordingly until the request is withdrawn."

[12] The national curriculum in England: Framework document, Department for Education, July 2013, Section 6, https://www.gov.uk/government/uploads/system/uploads/ attachment_data/file/210969/NC_framework_document_-_FINAL.pdf, accessed 7 March 2016.

[13] Letter from Nicky Morgan to Neil Carmichael MP, Chair of Education Select Committee, House of Commons, 10 February 2016, http://www.parliament.uk/documents/commons-committees/Education/ Letter-from-the-Secretary-of-State-to-the-Committee-on-statutory-status-for-PSHE. pdf, accessed 30 March 2016.

[14] Robert Long *Sex and Relationships Education in Schools (England),* House of Commons Library, Briefing Paper Number 06103, 17 February 2016, http://researchbriefings.files.parliament.uk/documents/SN06103/SN06103.pdf, accessed 30 March 2016.

[15] LGBT: lesbian, gay, bisexual and transgender.

[16] Charles Moore, 'This Equality obsession is mad, bad and very dangerous,' *Daily Telegraph*, 1 February 2013, http://www.telegraph.co.uk/women/womens-politics/9842384/This-Equality-obsession-is-mad-bad-and-very-dangerous.html, accessed 8 March 2016.

[17] Department for Education, *The Equality Act 2010 and schools, Departmental advice for school leaders, school staff, governing bodies and local authorities*, May 2014,

paragraph 3.27, https://www.gov.uk/government/uploads/system/uploads/attachment_data/file/315587/Equality_Act_Advice_Final.pdf, accessed 6 April 2016.

[18] For example, having previously asked users to identify themselves as male or female or 'nothing', from February 2014 Facebook offered a choice from 58 sexual orientations. *Here's a List of 58 Gender Options for Facebook Users*, ABC News, http://abcnews.go.com/blogs/headlines/2014/02/heres-a-list-of-58-gender-options-for-facebook-users/, published 13 February 2014, accessed 7 March 2016. From early 2015, it allowed users to type whatever they wished into the gender field, effectively offering an infinite choice. *Facebook Finally Stops Trying To Restrict What Gender You Can Choose*, Gizmodo, http://gizmodo.com/facebook-finally-stops-trying-to-restrict-what-gender-y-1688236317, posted 26 February 2015, accessed 7 March 2016.

[19] Definition of *phobia* in English, http://www.oxforddictionaries.com/definition/english/phobia, accessed 10 March 2016.

[20] *Handbook of Multicultural Counseling Competencies*, edited by Jennifer A. Erickson Cornish, Barry A. Schreier, Lavita I. Nadkarni, Lynett Henderson Metzger, Emil R. Rodolfa (Wiley, 2010) p.298.

[21] *Disgust, Not Fear, Drives Homophobia, Say UA Psychologists*, University of Arkansas, News release, 7 June 2002, http://news.uark.edu/articles/9587/disgust-not-fear-drives-homophobia-say-ua-psychologists, accessed 21 March 2016.

[22] According to *Definitions: Homophobia, Heterosexism, and Sexual Prejudice*, http://psc.dss.ucdavis.edu/rainbow/html/prej_defn.html, accessed 7 March 2016, "Weinberg used homophobia to label heterosexuals' dread of being in close quarters with homosexuals as well as homosexuals' self loathing. The word first appeared in print in 1969 and was subsequently discussed at length in Weinberg's 1972 book, *Society and the Healthy Homosexual*."

[23] *Riddle Scale*, https://en.wikipedia.org/wiki/Riddle_scale#cite_note-7, accessed 7 March 2016.

[24] *Tackling LGBT Issues in School*, A Resource Module edited by Leif Mitchell & Meredith Startz (GLSEN Connecticut, Third edition, 2007) p.56, http://www.glsen.org/sites/default/files/GLSEN%20CT%20Tackling%20LGBT%20Issues%20In%20Schools.pdf, accessed 7 March 2016.

[25] *Examples of Educational Materials Provided by Advocacy Groups*, Focus on the Family, 2014, http://media.focusonthefamily.com/true-tolerance/pdf/concerningclassroommaterials.pdf, p.10, accessed 7 March 2016.

[26] Referenced on *What is biphobia?* The Bisexual Index, http://www.bisexualindex.org.uk/index.php/biphobia, accessed 7 March 2016.

[27] *Getting Started: A toolkit for preventing and tackling homophobic, biphobic and transphobic bullying in primary schools*, Stonewall, published 17 February 2016, page 3, http://www.stonewall.org.uk/sites/default/files/getting_started_toolkit_-_primary.pdf accessed 7 March 2016.

[28] *Homosexuality*, Wikipedia, https://en.wikipedia.org/wiki/Homophobia, accessed 7 March 2016.

[29] *Disablist bullying is wrecking children's lives says Mencap*, posted 18 June 2007, https://www.mencap.org.uk/node/7000, accessed 9 March 2016.

[30] *Bankrolling Gay Proselytism: The case for extending Section 28*, The Christian Institute, 1999, pages 33 and 36, http://www.christian.org.uk/wp-content/downloads/bankrolling-gay-proselytism.pdf, accessed 7 March 2016.

[31] *2006 Student Census, Grades 7-12: System Overview*, Toronto District School Board Research Report 07/08 – 1 October 2007, http://www.tdsb.on.ca/Portals/0/aboutus/research/2006studentcensussystemoverview1.pdf, accessed 9 March 2016.

[32] *Longitudinal Study of Young People in England*, UK Data Service, https://discover.ukdataservice.ac.uk/series/?sn=2000030, accessed 9 March 2016.

[33] *Fast facts and Talking Pts on Bullying in Schools*, Focus on the Family, updated 25 July 2014, http://media.focusonthefamily.com/true-tolerance/pdf/FastFactsonbullying-schools.pdf, accessed 10 March 2016.

[34] Although written from an American perspective, further guidance on differences between 'good' and 'bad' policies can be found in *Anti-Bullying Policy Yardstick*, ADF, http://media.focusonthefamily.com/true-tolerance/pdf/AntiBullyingPolicyYardstick.pdf, accessed 17 March 2016.

[35] *Coddle U. vs. Strengthen U.: Which is best for students in the era of diversity?* Jonathan Haidt, http://heterodoxacademy.org/wp-content/uploads/2015/11/haidt.transcript-of-Coddle-U-lecture.pdf, accessed 31 March 2016. Although based on American High School experience, his observations concerning the merits of 'viewpoint diversity' are relevant.

[36] Cited in *The Great Gay Deception*, Michael Brown, http://www.charismamag.com/spirit/devotionals/daily-breakthroughs?view=article&id=19734:the-great-gay-deception&catid=1559, accessed 8 March 2016.

[37] *Left behind*, published in *Xtra!*, 20 October 2011, cited in *The Push is On! Canadian, U.S. Public Schools Continue to Promote Homosexuality*, Lee Duigon, http://chalcedon.edu/research/articles/the-push-is-on-canadian-u-s-public-schools-continue-to-promote-homosexuality/#_edn6, accessed 8 March 2016.

[38] *Can We Please Just Start Admitting That We Do Actually Want To Indoctrinate Kids?* Queerty, published 12 May 2011, http://www.queerty.com/can-we-please-just-start-admitting-that-we-do-actually-want-to-indoctrinate-kids-20110512/, accessed 4 March 2016.

[39] *Just A Big Guy With A Fun Sense Of Sin*, posted 20 September 2011, http://sbearbergman.dreamwidth.org/16530.htmlhttp://bearsir.livejournal.com/380711.html, accessed 4 March 2016.

[40] *I Have Come to Indoctrinate Your Children Into My LGBTQ Agenda (And I'm Not a Bit Sorry)*, HuffPost Queer Voices, published 7 March 2015, http://www.huffingtonpost.com/s-bear-bergman/i-have-come-to-indoctrinate-your-children-lgtbq_b_6795152.html, accessed 4 March 2016.

[41] Candi Cushman, *Parents beware: "Anti-bullying" initiatives are gay activists' latest tools of choice for sneaking homosexuality lessons into classrooms*, CitizenLink, June/July 2010, pages 10-13, http://media.citizenlink.com/truetolerance/p9_June_Jul_Citizen_10_antibullying.pdf, accessed 10 March 2016.

[42] *Safe Schools & Youth: A PFLAG Priority*, http://community.pflag.org/page.aspx?pid=358, accessed 10 March 2016.

[43] *About PFLAG*, http://community.pflag.org/page.aspx?pid=191, accessed 10 March 2016.

[44] 'Aussie 'safe schools' leader admits program is about gay activism, not bullying', *LifeSiteNews,* 18 March 2016, https://www.lifesitenews.com/news/watch-aussie-safe-schools-leader-admits-program-is-about-gay-activism-not-b, accessed 24 March 2016.

[45] *'Safe Schools' is not about bullying, organiser admits!*, uploaded 17 March 2016,

https://www.youtube.com/watch?v=daQCF8CyHhs, accessed 24 March 2016. For a view of the ideology and people behind Safe Schools, see *Safe Schools Coalition*, uploaded by JamFaze to YouTube 9 March 2016, https://www.youtube.com/watch?v=vtvIO6jNKco, accessed 24 March 2016.

[46] Roz Ward, *The role of the left in the struggle for LGBTI rights*, Melbourne Marxism Conference, March 2015, full talk downloadable at http://marxismconference.org/index.php/previous-highlights/audio-archives/item/1310-The-role-of-the-left-in-the-struggle-for-LGBTI-rights.html, accessed 4 March 2016. For comment on this talk, see *Safer schools or a radical Marxist sexual revolution?* Pat Byrne, posted on Online Opinion 19 February 2016 at http://www.onlineopinion.com.au/view.asp?article=18033&page=0, accessed 24 March 2016.

[47] See also *Dumb, Sodomy and the Cash*, Merve Bendle, published on Quadrant online, 2 March 2016, https://quadrant.org.au/opinion/qed/2016/03/dumb-sodomy-cash/, accessed 24 March 2016.

[48] 'Gay teacher who writes books challenging homophobia has resigned after parents complained they did not want him to teach their children,' *Mail Online*, 7 April 2014, http://www.dailymail.co.uk/news/article-2598231/Gay-teacher-writes-books-challenging-homophobia-resigned-parents-complained-did-not-want-teach-children.html, accessed 10 March 2016.

[49] *GaydarRadio Heroes & Heroines*, GaydarRadio, uploaded 23 January 2012, https://www.youtube.com/watch?v=afQCcJGmMmM, accessed 10 March 2016.

[50] 'The IoS Pink List 2011,' *Independent on Sunday*, http://www.independent.co.uk/news/people/news/the-ios-pink-list-2011-2374595.html, accessed 10 March 2016.

[51] 'Special advisor to tackle homophobia and transphobia in schools', Durham County Council, published 1 October 2014, http://www.durham.gov.uk/article/4914/Special-advisor-to-tackle-homophobia-and-transphobia-in-schools, accessed 18 March 2016.

[52] 'How I built a career in LGBT education', Elly Barnes interviewed by Emily Drabble, *The Guardian*, 17 February 2013, http://www.theguardian.com/teacher-network/teacher-blog/2013/feb/17/lgbt-education-career-why-i-became-a-teacher#comment-21419851, accessed 10 March 2016.

[53] *'Educate and Celebrate' welcomes volume 4 of 'Challenging Homophobia in Primary Schools' or 'CHIPS'*, posted 29 September 2014, at http://www.ellybarnes.com/2014/09/educate-and-celebrate-welcomes-volume-4-of-challenging-homophobia-in-primary-schools-or-chips/, last accessed 12 April 2015, since removed. Note that "LGBT friendly" means "no criticism or resistance to the promotion of pro-LGBT ideology is permitted", way beyond "challenging 'homophobia'" or "combating 'homophobic' bullying".

[54] 'How I built a career in LGBT education', Elly Barnes, *The Guardian*, published 17 February 2013, http://www.theguardian.com/teacher-network/teacher-blog/2013/feb/17/lgbt-education-career-why-i-became-a-teacher, accessed 10 March 2016.

[55] 'Primary Geography', Elly Barnes, Spring 2016 edition, The Geographical Association. Also published at http://www.educateandcelebrate.org/wp-content/uploads/2016/01/PG_Spring_2016_BARNES.pdf, accessed 27 February 2016.

[56] Student-led activity whole class, Year 6 CHIPS lesson plan, based on "William's Doll", http://www.ellybarnes.com/wp-content/uploads/2014/07/Williams-Doll-Lesson-Plan.jpg, accessed 10 March 2016.

[57] 'Why literature is a vital tool for teaching students about equality', Farzana Khan,

TES, 11 January 2016, https://www.tes.com/news/school-news/breaking-views/why-literature-a-vital-tool-teaching-students-about-equality, accessed 10 March 2016.

[58] Andrew Moffat, *No outsiders in our school: Teaching the Equality Act in Primary Schools* (Speechmark, 2016) http://www.speechmark.net/shop/no-outsiders-our-school-teaching-equality-act-primary-schools, p.3. The book also demonstrates how he is shifting the focus from primarily promoting the LGBT+ agenda (Educate & Celebrate) to promoting the LGBT+ agenda as a part of 'teaching the Equality Act' (Equalities Primary).

[59] http://www.ellybarnes.com/wp-content/uploads/2013/03/CHIPS-update-June-2014.pdf, accessed 27 February 2016.

[60] For a one-page introduction, see *Political Correctness/Cultural Marxism* at DiscoveringtheNetworks.org, http://www.discoverthenetworks.org/viewSubCategory.asp?id=552, accessed 31 March 2016. For a more detailed introduction, see *A Guide for the Perplexed: A brief history of political correctness and its origins*, Cartes A. Jouer, http://pamelageller.com/2012/09/a-brief-history-of-political-correctness-and-its-origins.html/, accessed 31 March 2016. Also see *The Origins of Political Correctness*, Bill Lund, 5 February 2000, http://www.academia.org/the-origins-of-political-correctness/, accessed 31 March 2016.

[61] *No Outsiders press*, University of Sunderland archive of 50 press reports referring to the No Outsiders project, http://projects.sunderland.ac.uk/archived/ell-nooutsiders/news/no-outsiders-press/index.html, accessed 29 March 2016. The project was led by Elizabeth Atkinson and Renée DePalma at the University of Sunderland, in collaboration with researchers at the University of Exeter and the Institute of Education (University of London). According to http://coruna.academia.edu/Ren%C3%A9eDePalma, since September 2010 Renée DePalma has been a member of the Faculty of Education Sciences at Universidade da Coruña where *"her research and teaching has focused on equalities and social justice in terms of race, ethnicity, language, sexuality and gender. She is mainly interested in the social construction of marginalization within and beyond schools, ways in which success and failure are co-constructed in institutional settings, and the design of counter-hegemonic institutional contexts and classroom practices."*

[62] 'Gay education in primaries climbs back into the closet', *TES* report by Madeleine Brettingham, 17 October 2008, https://www.tes.com/article.aspx?storycode=6003864, accessed 10 March 2016. This report also includes a timeline of significant 'Homosexuality and the Classroom' events from1974 to 2008.

[63] *No Outsiders: Researching approaches to sexualities equality in primary schools* (ESRC, 2009), http://www.researchcatalogue.esrc.ac.uk/grants/RES-062-23-0095/read, accessed 10 March 2016.

[64] Elizabeth Atkinson, et al (2009). *No Outsiders: Researching approaches to sexualities equality in primary schools: Full Research Report ESRC End of Award Report, RES-062-23-0095. Swindon: ESRC*, http://www.researchcatalogue.esrc.ac.uk/grants/RES-062-23-0095/outputs/read/372d939e-02e9-4d7d-b51e-06c936147b4c, accessed 10 March 2016.

[65] Andrew Moffat, *Challenging Homophobia in Primary Schools: An Early Years Resource*, 2007, located at http://csapps.norfolk.gov.uk/csshared/ecourier2/fileoutput.asp?id=12015, accessed 31 March 2016.

[66] *LGBT+Inclusive Resources, PRIDE in Early Years Education, PRIDE in Primary Education, PRIDE in Secondary Education, PRIDE Youth networks, PRIDE in Higher Education, PRIDE in Further Education, PRIDE in Organisations* (Educate

& Celebrate), http://www.educateandcelebrate.org/resources/, accessed 5 April 2016.
[67] 'Welcome to Issue 8 of LGBT+Education Today', *Educate and Celebrate Newsletter 8*, http://us3.campaign-archive1.com/?u=4ff9f66854547b55eca6ccc75&id=bcd13112eb, accessed 3 March 2016.
[68] http://www.equalitiesprimary.com/home.html, accessed 7 March 2016.
[69] http://www.equalitiesprimary.com/equalities-lesson-plans.html accessed 7 March 2016.
[70] *Tackling homophobic, biphobic and transphobic bullying in schools in the UK*, The SHM Foundation (an organisation working with Educate & Celebrate, SHM Productions Ltd and Goldsmiths University of London Department of Education since March 2015), http://shmfoundation.org/?page_id=22978, accessed 5 April 2016.
[71] Ibid.
[72] http://www.ellybarnes.com/wp-content/uploads/2014/07/chips-march-2015.pdf, p.13.
[73] Ibid., p.16.
[74] Ibid., p.18.
[75] Ibid., p.27.
[76] *My Princess Boy*, http://www.ellybarnes.com/wp-content/uploads/2014/10/MY-PRINCESS-BOY-lyrics-chords-and-actions.pdf, accessed 18 March 2016.
[77] Cross-dressing at a young age is a known risk factor for subsequent development of transgenderism. For example, Walt Heyer describes at first hand the effects of being cross-dressed by his grandmother from age 4, *Stand4Truth: The Truth About Real People and Homosexuality*, https://www.youtube.com/watch?v=m-3hNPY_P00 starting at 32:17, uploaded 9 November 2015, accessed 18 March 2016.
[78] http://www.ellybarnes.com/wp-content/uploads/2014/07/chips-march-2015.pdf, p.19.
[79] Ibid., p.20.
[80] Ibid., p.22. Based on a story of two male penguins who live as a couple and eventually adopt a chick.
[81] Ibid., p.25. In this story, the queen insists her son, the prince, gets married, but after meeting every princess in the land he decides that it's a prince he'd really like to marry. The queen is delighted. In the real world, of course, Royal families are extremely interested in having their own biological offspring to continue the bloodline.
[82] http://www.ellybarnes.com/wp-content/uploads/2014/07/chips-march-2015.pdf, p.25.
[83] *We're all born free*, http://www.ellybarnes.com/wp-content/uploads/2014/10/WE-ARE-ALL-BORN-FREE-lyrics-and-actions.pdf, accessed 18 March 2016.
[84] Ibid., p.27.
[85] Ibid., p.30.
[86] Ibid., p.31.
[87] Usualising and actualising: see http://the-classroom.org.uk/how-to-do-it/usualising-and-actualising/, accessed 24 March 2016.
[88] Sue Sanders, *Write4Children, Books 4 all Kids: Usualising the lives of LGBT people through children's books*, (Winchester University Press, June 2013) Vol IV, Issue II, pages 130 to 136, http://www.winchester.ac.uk/academicdepartments/EnglishCreativeWritingandAmericanStudies/Documents/w4cJune2013Diversity.pdf, accessed 31 March 2016. Sanders claims credit on page 136.
[89] *The Classroom* website, http://the-classroom.org.uk/, accessed 31 March 2016.
[90] Elly Barnes, *LGBT+Inclusive Lesson plans*, http://www.ellybarnes.com/birmingham-the-classroom-lessons/, accessed 31 March 2016.

[91] *Method 1: Usualising*, The Classroom, http://the-classroom.org.uk/how-to-do-it/usualising-and-actualising/method-1-usualising/, accessed 31 March 2016.

[92] *Method 2: Actualising*, The Classroom, http://the-classroom.org.uk/how-to-do-it/usualising-and-actualising/method-2-actualising/, accessed 31 March 2016.

[93] Ibid.

[94] *Method 2: Actualising*, The Classroom, http://the-classroom.org.uk/how-to-do-it/usualising-and-actualising/method-2-actualising/, accessed 31 March 2016.

[95] Elly Barnes, Educate & Celebrate, *Government and School Policy presentation*, slide 13, accessed 21 April 2015, since removed but text accessible at http://documents.mx/education/government-and-school-policy-presentation.html as at 31 March 2016.

[96] Bertrand Russell, *The Impact of Science on Society* (Columbia Press, 1951) p.40.

[97] Tris Reid-Smith, 'Can karaoke cure kids of anti-gay attitudes?' *GayStarFamily*, 9 July 2014, http://www.gaystarnews.com/article/can-karaoke-cure-kids-anti-gay-attitudes090714/#gs.xWa4XUA, accessed 18 March 2016.

[98] http://www.educateandcelebrate.org/resources/, accessed 18 March 2016.

[99] *My Princess Boy*, song, http://www.ellybarnes.com/wp-content/uploads/2014/10/My-Princess-Boy-with-vocals.mp3, accessed 18 March 2016.

[100] *My Princess Boy*, lyrics and instructions, dated 6 October 2014, http://www.ellybarnes.com/wp-content/uploads/2014/10/MY-PRINCESS-BOY-lyrics-chords-and-actions.pdf, accessed 18 March 2016.

[101] *Elmer*, song, http://www.ellybarnes.com/wp-content/uploads/2014/10/Elmer-with-vocals-.mp3, accessed 18 March 2016.

[102] *Elmer*, lyrics and instructions, http://www.ellybarnes.com/wp-content/uploads/2014/10/ELMER-THE-ELEPHANT-lyrics-and-chords.pdf, accessed 18 March 2016.

[103] CHIPS lesson plan, *William's Doll*, http://www.ellybarnes.com/wp-content/uploads/2014/07/Williams-Doll-Lesson-Plan.jpg, accessed 18 March 2016.

[104] C. S. Lewis, *The Four Loves* (Harcourt, Brace, N.Y.,1960).

[105] *CHIPS volume 4 resource*, http://www.ellybarnes.com/wp-content/uploads/2014/07/chips-march-2015.pdf, page 22, accessed 18 March 2016.

[106] *Love Has No Labels, Diversity & Inclusion*, uploaded by Ad Council 3 March 2015, over 56,700,00 views, https://www.youtube.com/watch?v=PnDgZuGIhHs, accessed 3 March 2016.

[107] *Love Has No Labels - Behind the Scenes, Diversity & Inclusion*, uploaded by Ad Council 21 April 2015, https://www.youtube.com/watch?v=IExCqC79UBw, accessed 3 March 2016.

[108] *Howletch Primary Love has no labels*, uploaded 4 December 2015, https://www.youtube.com/watch?v=2Xpk99NapRc, accessed 27 February 2016.

[109] *The Rainbow Bake Off Final - Primary Winners!!*, uploaded 13 February 2016, http://howletchblog.weebly.com/year-6-blog/the-rainbow-bake-off-final-primary-winners, accessed 18 March 2016.

[110] *You have to see these incredible LGBTI-themed cakes baked by school pupils*, GayStarFamily, 13 February 2016, http://www.gaystarnews.com/article/you-have-to-see-these-incredible-lgbti-themed-cakes-baked-by-school-pupils/, accessed 18 March 2016.

[111] *School Report, Howletch Lane Primary School, 12-13 January 2016*, Ofsted, published 3 February 2016, http://reports.ofsted.gov.uk/inspection-reports/find-inspection-report/

provider/ELS/114198, accessed 5 April 2016.

[112] *School and College Performance Tables*, Department for Education, School Details last update 21 Jan 2016, http://www.education.gov.uk/cgi-bin/schools/performance/school.pl?urn=124649, accessed 11 March 2016.

[113] *Murrayfield School Newsletter, 16 November 2015, Term 2, Issue 2*, https://primarysite-prod-sorted.s3.amazonaws.com/murrayfield-community-primary/UploadedDocument/ba8c0e6d19d34e2ebb2f2fa53fd2372f/151116-newsletter-16-nov.pdf, accessed 27 February 2016.

[114] *Murrayfield Community Primary School Website*, Equality, http://www.murrayfieldprimary.co.uk/equality-pledge/, accessed 27 February 2016.

[115] *School report, Murrayfield Community Primary School, 24 September 2015*, Ofsted, published 30 November 2015, https://primarysite-prod-sorted.s3.amazonaws.com/murrayfield-community-primary/UploadedDocument/b90aee2611f94736bb3a9af1e74b90d3/final-ofsted-report-sept-2015.pdf, accessed 11 March 2016.

[116] *School report, Murrayfield Community Primary School, 19 September 2013*, Ofsted, published 11 October 2013, http://reports.ofsted.gov.uk/provider/files/2273217/urn/124649.pdf, accessed 11 March 2016.

[117] *Murrayfield Community Primary School Website*, Governors, http://www.murrayfieldprimary.co.uk/governors/, accessed 11 March 2016.

[118] Elly Barnes, *Staff Training presentation*, created 18 January 2016, last modified 1 February 2016, http://www.educateandcelebrate.org/wp-content/uploads/woocommerce_uploads/2016/02/EC-Staff-Training-and-Assemblies.ppt, slide 23, accessed 21 March 2016. "This powerpoint is an excellent resource for covering the information that will allow teachers and staff to introduce young people to LGBT+ history and how to make schools LGBT+Friendly."

[119] *Integrated Household Survey, January to December 2014: Experimental Statistics*, Office for National Statistics, released 1 October 2015, http://webarchive.nationalarchives.gov.uk/20160105160709/http://www.ons.gov.uk/ons/dcp171778_418136.pdf, accessed 18 March 2016. "The IHS is the largest social survey undertaken by the Office for National Statistics (ONS). It provides estimates from approximately 325,000 individual respondents – the biggest pool of UK social survey data apart from the census."

[120] Kinsey et al, *Sexual Behavior in the Human Male*, 1948 and *Sexual Behavior in the Human Female*, 1953.

[121] See, for example, Judith Reisman, PhD, *Kinsey and the Homosexual Revolution*, c. 1997, http://www.sweetliberty.org/issues/bless/kinsey.htm#.VwQT9UnmqM8, accessed 5 April 2016.

[122] Chris Kempling, *Sexual Orientation Curricula: Implications for Educators*, 2003, http://www.dijg.de/english/sexual-orientation-school-educators/,accessed, accessed 7 April 2016.

[123] C. Paglia, *Vamps and Tramps: new essays*, 1994, p.73-74.

[124] *Introduction to LGBT+Inclusion assembly powerpoint, LGBT History Month presentation by Elly Barnes*, Educate & Celebrate, slide 7, downloaded from www.ellybarnes.com/resources on 21 April 2015 but since removed.

[125] Judith Reisman, PhD, *Kinsey: Crimes and Consequences: The Red Queen & The Grand Scheme* (Institute for Media Education, Fourth Edition, print and digital, 2012), downloadable in its entirety at http://www.drjudithreisman.com/archives/2014/01/kinsey_crimes_c.html, accessed 6 April 2016.

[126] *What do the experts say*, http://www.nooneisborngay.com/experts-say.html, accessed 22 March 2016.

[127] *So Why are Some People (2% of U.S.) Homosexual?* http://www.nooneisborngay.com/root-causes-of-ssa.html, accessed 22 March 2016.

[128] *Royal College of Psychiatrists' statement on sexual orientation*, Position Statement PS02/2014, April 2014, http://www.rcpsych.ac.uk/pdf/PS02_2014.pdf, accessed 21 March 2016.

[129] *Psychiatrists in climb-down on 'born gay' claim*, Core Issues Trust Press Release, 3 June 2014, http://us2.campaign-archive1.com/?u=bed173cc9adfcad1e0e442a35&id=cbf1acb3e2&e=134f1da7d9, accessed 22 March 2016.

[130] Dr N E Whitehead, PhD, *My Genes Made Me Do It! A scientific look at Sexual Orientation*, 290 pages, 3rd edition, July 2014 New Zealand, http://www.mygenes.co.nz/index.html, in particular Chapter 12 *Can sexual orientation change?* http://www.mygenes.co.nz/PDFs/Ch12.pdf.

[131] *Is Change Really Possible?* http://www.peoplecanchange.com/, accessed 22 March 2016.

[132] *Men and Women Who Have Experienced Authentic Change in Sexual Orientation Through Therapy that Works!* http://voices-of-change.org/our-stories.html, accessed 22 March 2016.

[133] *Royal College of Psychiatrists' statement on sexual orientation*, Position Statement PS02/2014, April 2014, http://www.rcpsych.ac.uk/pdf/PS02_2014.pdf, accessed 21 March 2016.

[134] *Integrated Household Survey, January to December 2014: Experimental Statistics*, Office for National Statistics, released 1 October 2015, http://webarchive.nationalarchives.gov.uk/20160105160709/http://www.ons.gov.uk/ons/dcp171778_418136.pdf, accessed 18 March 2016.

[135] E.O. Laumann, J.H. Gagnon, R.T. Michael, S. Michaels, *The social organization of sexuality: Sexual practices in the United States.* (University of Chicago Press; 1994)

[136] Jeffrey B. Satinover, M.D., Ph.D., *The "Trojan Couch": How the Mental Health Associations Misrepresent Science*, National Association for Research and Therapy of Homosexuality, created 28 February 2007, modified 21 January 2009, http://factsaboutyouth.com/wp-content/uploads/TheTrojanCouchSatinover.pdf, page 11.

[137] *Child psychiatrist testifies on SB48 before California Legislature*, Dr. Miriam Grossman, an expert in child development, https://www.youtube.com/watch?v=eTglqQFkbGY, uploaded 6 April 2011 in which she indicates the incidence of a child feeling 'trapped in the wrong body' is about 8 in 100,000.

[138] CHIPS lesson plan, *William's Doll*, http://www.ellybarnes.com/wp-content/uploads/2014/07/Williams-Doll-Lesson-Plan.jpg, accessed 18 March 2016.

[139] *So Why are Some People (2% of U.S.) Homosexual?*, http://www.nooneisborngay.com/root-causes-of-ssa.html, accessed 6 April 2016.

[140] See e.g. Chris Kempling, *Sexual Orientation Curricula: Implications for Educators*, 2003, http://www.dijg.de/english/sexual-orientation-school-educators/,accessed, accessed 7 April 2016. This outlines evidence pertaining to Promiscuity and High Risk Behaviours, Relationship Instability and Attitudes towards Monogamy, and Suicide Risk.

[141] Public Health England *Infection Report Vol 9 No. 22, Sexually transmitted infections and chlamydia screening in England 2014, Advanced Access report* published 23 June

2015, https://www.gov.uk/government/uploads/system/uploads/attachment_data/file/437433/hpr2215_STI_NCSP_v6.pdf, accessed 6 April 2016.

[142] CHIPS version 4 resource, page 6, http://www.ellybarnes.com/wp-content/uploads/2014/07/chips-march-2015.pdf, accessed 18 March 2016.

[143] *La Déclaration universelle des droits de l'homme*, United Nations, adopted 10 December 1948, http://www.un.org/fr/universal-declaration-human-rights/index.html, accessed 8 March 2016.

[144] *The United Nations Convention on the Rights of the Child*, United Nations, 1989, Preamble, p.3, http://www.unicef.org.uk/Documents/Publication-pdfs/UNCRC_PRESS200910web.pdf, accessed 8 March 2016.

[145] CHIPS version 4 resource, p.26, http://www.ellybarnes.com/wp-content/uploads/2014/07/chips-march-2015.pdf, accessed 18 March 2016.

[146] CHIPS version 4 resource, p.25, http://www.ellybarnes.com/wp-content/uploads/2014/07/chips-march-2015.pdf, accessed 18 March 2016.

[147] *The Universal Declaration of Human Rights*, http://www.un.org/en/universal-declaration-human-rights/index.html, accessed 22 March 2016.

[148] *How different are the adult children of parents who have same-sex relationships? Findings from the New Family Structures Study*, M. Regnerus, Social Science Research, Volume 41, Issue 4, July 2012, Pages 752–770, http://www.ncbi.nlm.nih.gov/pubmed/23017845, accessed 22 March 2016.

[149] The criticisms are addressed in *Mark Regnerus and the Storm over the New Family Structures Study*, Matthew J Franck, Public Discourse, 30 October 2012, http://www.thepublicdiscourse.com/2012/10/6784/, and *The Vindication of Mark Regnerus*, Matthew J Franck, Public Discourse, 31 October 2012, http://www.thepublicdiscourse.com/2012/10/6786/, both accessed 22 March 2016.

[150] Mark Regnerus, *Parental same-sex relationships, family instability, and subsequent life outcomes for adult children: Answering critics of the new family structures study with additional analyses*, Social Science Research, Volume 41, Issue 6, November 2012, Pages 1367–1377, http://www.ncbi.nlm.nih.gov/pubmed/23017960, accessed 22 March 2016.

[151] D. Paul Sullins, 'Emotional Problems among Children with Same-sex Parents: Difference by Definition,' *British Journal of Education, Society & Behavioural Science*, ISSN: 2278-0998,Vol. 7, Issue. 2, February 2015, http://papers.ssrn.com/sol3/papers.cfm?abstract_id=2500537, accessed 22 March 2016. It analyzed 512 children of same-sex parents, drawn from a pool of over 207,000 respondents who participated in the (US) National Health Interview Survey (NHIS) at some point between 1997 and 2013.

[152] Mark Regnerus, *New Research on Same-Sex Households Reveals Kids Do Best With Mom and Dad*, Public Discourse, 10 February 2015, http://www.thepublicdiscourse.com/2015/02/14417/?utm_source=The+Witherspoon+Institute&utm_campaign=7b2f618205-RSS_EMAIL_CAMPAIGN&utm_medium=email&utm_term=0_15ce6af37b-7b2f618205-84102557, accessed 30 March 2016.

[153] CHIPS version 4 resource, page 9, http://www.ellybarnes.com/wp-content/uploads/2014/07/chips-march-2015.pdf, accessed 18 March 2016.

[154] Equality Act 2010, http://www.legislation.gov.uk/ukpga/2010/15/contents, accessed 18 March 2016.

[155] *Welcome to Issue 8 of LGBT+Education Today*, Educate & Celebrate, posted 15 December 2015,

http://us3.campaign-archive1.com/?u=4ff9f66854547b55eca6ccc75&id=bcd13112eb, accessed 22 March 2016.

[156] http://www.educateandcelebrate.org/great-rainbow-bake-off/, accessed 22 March 2016.

[157] *LGBT+Inclusion: The Educate & Celebrate Programme*, http://www.birmingham.gov.uk/cs/Satellite/educate&celebrate?packedargs=website%3D4&rendermode=live, accessed 4 March 2016.

[158] *PRIDE in Primary Education*, http://www.birmingham.gov.uk/cs/Satellite?c=Page&childpagename=Schools%2FPageLayout&cid=1223493683312&pagename=BCC%2FCommon%2FWrapper%2FInlineWrapper, accessed 4 March 2016.

[159] *Training and Policy*, Birmingham City Council, http://www.birmingham.gov.uk/cs/Satellite?c=Page&childpagename=Schools%2FPageLayout&cid=1223493831640&pagename=BCC%2FCommon%2FWrapper%2FInlineWrapper, accessed 8 March 2016.

[160] 'Gay teacher who writes books challenging homophobia has resigned after parents complained they did not want him to teach their children,' *Daily Mail Online*, published 6 April 2014, http://www.dailymail.co.uk/news/article-2598231/Gay-teacher-writes-books-challenging-homophobia-resigned-parents-complained-did-not-want-teach-children.html, accessed 3 March 2016.

[161] 'Police called after reports of disorder at 'Trojan horse' school in Birmingham, Parents allegedly involved in confrontation with headteacher at Welford primary school,' *The Guardian*, published 3 October 2014, http://www.theguardian.com/education/2014/oct/03/birmingham-police-trojan-horse-welford-primary-school-parents-headteacher, accessed 3 March 2016.

[162] *Homophobic crimes recorded on the rise in the Midlands*, http://www.itv.com/news/central/2014-11-26/violent-homophobic-crimes-recorded-on-the-rise-in-the-midlands/, (eighth video clip), published 26 November 2014, accessed 3 March 2016.

[163] 'Parents launch petition to stop homosexuality being taught at a Balsall Heath primary school,' *Birmingham Mail*, published 12 March 2015, http://www.birminghammail.co.uk/news/midlands-news/parents-launch-petition-stop-homosexuality-8824612, accessed 3 March 2016.

[164] 'Primary School to Teach LGBT Issues,' *The Asian today*, published 13 March 2015, http://www.theasiantoday.com/index.php/2015/03/13/primary-school-to-teach-lgbt-issues/, accessed 3 March 2016.

[165] *Stop Sexualisation and Indoctrination in State Primary Schools*, petition by the Birmingham Parent Association, change.org, https://www.change.org/p/secretary-of-state-for-education-and-leader-of-birmingham-city-council-stop-sexualisation-and-indoctrination-in-state-primary-schools?recruiter=133219255&utm_campaign=signature_receipt&utm_medium=email&utm_source=share_petition, accessed 3 March 2016.

[166] Andrew Moffat, *No Outsiders in Our School: Teaching the Equality Act in Primary Schools* (Speechmark, London, 2016).

[167] £2 million fund to tackle homophobic bullying in schools,

https://www.gov.uk/government/news/2-million-fund-to-tackle-homophobic-bullying-in-schools, first published 29 October 2014.

[168] *Awards announced from £2 million homophobic bullying fund,* https://www.gov.uk/government/news/awards-announced-from-2-million-homophobic-bullying-fund, first published 24 March 2015.

[169] *Government Equalities Office Press Release,* http://www.educateandcelebrate.org/dedicated-services-designed-to-eradicate-homophobic-biphobic-and-transphobic-bullying-from-the-classroom-to-the-playground-are-up-and-running-in-midlands/, accessed 3 March 2016.

[170] *What is a GSA?,* GSA Network, https://gsanetwork.org/resources/building-your-gsa/what-gsa, accessed 18 March 2016.

[171] Peter Sprigg, *Homosexuality in Your Child's School* (Family Research Council, 2006) http://downloads.frc.org/EF/EF06K26.pdf, accessed 21 March 2016. This leaflet exposes some of the strategies implemented by pro-homosexual activists in American schools to undermine established teaching on sexual morality, including GSA's, "anti-discrimination" policies, pro-homosexual special events and meetings treatment for "discrimination". It seems Educate & Celebrate are trying to apply the same strategies in British schools.

[172] *PRIDE Youth Networks,* http://www.ellybarnes.com/youth-pride-networks-2/, accessed 4 March 2016.

[173] *PRIDE Youth Network Guidance,* Educate & Celebrate, 2016, http://www.educateandcelebrate.org/product/pride-youth-network-guidance/, accessed 18 March 2016.

[174] Genderbüro, *Gender Manifesto, A call for critical reflection on Gender-oriented capacity building and consultancy,* http://www.gender.de/manifest/GenderManifesto_engl.pdf, accessed 6 April 2016.

[175] Gabriele Kuby, *The Global Sexual Revolution and the Assault on Freedom and Family,* Catholic World report, 8 September 2014, http://www.catholicworldreport.com/Item/3357/the_global_sexual_revolution_and_the_assault_on_freedom_and_family.aspx, accessed 23 March 2016.

[176] Gabriele Kuby, *The Global Sexual Revolution: destruction of freedom in the name of freedom* (LifeSite, first published in English 2015). For further information about the book, see *Gabriele Kuby's The Global Sexual Revolution: a must-read book in defence of the family,* 15 December 2015, https://www.lifesitenews.com/news/sociologist-praised-by-pope-benedict-lays-out-evils-of-the-sexual-revolutio, accessed 3 March 2016.

[177] 'Britain's boarding schools told to adopt 'gender neutral' uniform policies to avoid discrimination against LGBT pupils,' *The Independent,* 6 May 2015, http://www.independent.co.uk/news/education/education-news/britains-boarding-schools-told-to-adopt-gender-neutral-uniform-policies-to-avoid-discrimination-10229946.html, accessed 27 February 2016.

[178] 'Brighton College scraps uniform code for transgender pupils,' *BBC News,* 20 January 2016, http://www.bbc.co.uk/news/uk-england-sussex-35362368, accessed 8 March 2016.

[179] 'Rise in child transgender referrals, The number of children referred to the NHS as a result of transgender feelings and confusion about their gender has quadrupled in five years, new figures show,' *Daily Telegraph,* 7 April 2015, http://www.telegraph.co.uk/news/health/news/11519603/Rise-in-child-transgender-referrals.html, accessed 3 March 2015.

[180] 'From Blake to Jessie: a 7-year-old's transgender story, The number of primary school children referred to the NHS with transgender feelings has quadrupled in five years. But do teachers know how to help them?', *The Guardian*, Teachers Network, 2 June 2015, http://www.theguardian.com/teacher-network/2015/jun/02/from-blake-to-jessie-a-7-year-olds-transgender-story, accessed 3 March 2016.

[181] Melanie Phillips, 'It's dangerous and wrong to tell all children they're 'gender fluid': What started as a baffling skirmish on the wilder shores of victim culture has now turned into something more menacing,' *The Spectator,* 30 January 2016, http://www.spectator.co.uk/2016/01/its-dangerous-and-wrong-to-tell-all-children-theyre-gender-fluid/, accessed 8 March 2016.

[182] *What is Propaganda?,* United States Holocaust Memorial Museum, Washington D.C., https://www.ushmm.org/propaganda/resources/, accessed 8 March 2016.

[183] Paul E. Rondeau *Selling Homosexuality to America*, Regent University Law Review (Vol 14:2002, pages 443 to 485). Available online at https://www.regent.edu/acad/schlaw/student_life/studentorgs/lawreview/docs/issues/v14n2/Vol.%2014,%20No.%20 2,%208%20Rondeau.pdf, accessed 18 March 2016.

[184] Marshall Kirk and Hunter Madsen, *After the Ball: How America Will Conquer Its Fear and Hatred of Gays in the 90s*, (Doubleday, NY, 1989). For an up-to-date and succinct analysis of *After the Ball*, see Daniel V. Runyon, *Gay Marriage Considerations: A Review of After the Ball* (Saltbox Press, Michigan, 2015).

[185] Bertrand Russell, *The Impact of Science on Society* (Columbia Press, 1951) p.61.

[186] www.brainyquote.com/quotes/quotes/d/dennisprag649317.html, accessed 2 March 2016.

[187] *Myths about equal marriage – setting out the truth*, HM Government, https://www.gov.uk/government/uploads/system/uploads/attachment_data/file/212542/Mythbuster.pdf, accessed 30 March 2016.

Chapter Seven

INDOCTRINATION IN SCIENTISM:
The British Educational Establishment's Response to Intelligent Design
Dr Alastair Noble

Our concern ... is whether a secular indoctrination process is at work in British and European society, programming people against religious belief and, if so, whether education is an accomplice in this.

> – Terence Copley in the Preface to
> *Indoctrination, Education and God*, SPCK 2005

I discovered Intelligent Design (ID), or at least its modern manifestation, about a decade ago. It came about as a result of two lectures I attended. The first of these, in Glasgow in 2004, was given by Professor Phillip Johnson, former law clerk to the Chief Justice of the US Supreme Court and Law Professor at the University of California in Berkeley. He described how, on a year's sabbatical in London in 1988, he encountered in the same bookstore two books about evolution: Richard Dawkins's *The Blind Watchmaker*[1] and Michael Denton's *Evolution – A Theory in Crisis*.[2] He was intrigued that evolution could be the subject of such diametrically opposed treatments, and spent a good part of his year examining the subject closely. From a position of unquestioning acceptance of Darwinian evolution, he came to the conclusion, as a lawyer, that the evidence for it would not stand up in court. He describes his findings in his book *Darwin on Trial*.[3]

His lecture in Glasgow was the first time I had heard such a devastating yet non-religious critique of evolution. Johnson explained that evolution, as popularly understood, is not sustained by the scientific evidence, but by a prior commitment to the philosophy of naturalism.[4] Although I had been a science student, researcher and teacher for forty years, I had never appreciated that, in the area of origins, science is not neutral, but is underpinned by a philosophical commitment, which rules out the existence of any intelligence beyond nature. Mind you, I should have seen that, because several scientists have been honest enough to admit it. Richard Lewontin, Professor of Biology at Harvard, for example, could hardly be more explicit:

> It is not that the methods and institutions of science somehow compel us to accept a material explanation of the phenomenal world, but, on the contrary, that we are forced by our a priori adherence to material causes to create an apparatus of investigation and a set of concepts that produce material explanations, no matter how counter-intuitive, no matter how mystifying to the uninitiated. Moreover, that materialism is absolute, for we cannot allow a divine foot in the door.[5]

Now at one level you have to admire that degree of honesty, but at another it is quite shocking. What he is saying is that scientific conclusions are not ultimately based on the empirical evidence but on a philosophy – variously described as materialism or naturalism – which excludes any explanation that goes beyond natural processes.

The second lecture I attended was in Cambridge in 2005. It was given by American geologist and Cambridge-trained philosopher of science, Dr Stephen Meyer. He was describing his work on DNA and in particular what conclusions can be drawn from its information content carried in the coded sequences of its base pairs.[6] I had often marvelled at the chemical beauty of the DNA molecule with its double helix and base pair units embedded within its structure. What I had never heard before, and what in retrospect is blindingly obvious, is that the sequence of the base pairs carries real genetic information. In fact it is in digital code, rather like a computer but much more sophisticated. Little wonder Bill Gates described DNA as 'like a computer program but far, far more advanced than any software ever created'.[7]

Meyer's argument was that it is not only legitimate for a scientist to ask about the origin of that information, but also that it is entirely scientific to make an inference to the best explanation. To do that it is necessary to draw on our knowledge of processes currently in operation, which are known to produce the result observed. In all our experience, functional information, such as is found in print, film or computer software, arises only from the activity of intelligent mind. Hence the best explanation for the origin of the information carried in DNA is that it is the product of intelligence.

I could hardly believe my eyes and ears. Here, from scientific data, not religious or philosophical considerations, was clear evidence of a supreme intelligence behind nature, written all over DNA. It was, in fact, evidence of Intelligent Design. For me it was a *eureka* moment!

I was to discover later that the evidence of design in nature is extensive. It can be inferred, for example, from the 'fine tuning of the universe' for life,[8] from the improbability of generating randomly the complex macromolecules required for life,[9] and from the irreducible complexity of biological systems.[10]

And I had forgotten that the great pioneers of Western science, like Galileo, Copernicus, Newton, Kepler, Faraday, Clerk Maxwell and Kelvin did their science in the belief that the universe is designed, rational and, therefore, intelligible. The perception by these pioneers of 'Intelligent Design' in the universe is what gave us Western science in the first place.

How then have we arrived at a position where the scientific community argues that there is no evidence of design in Nature? It seems the answer is by applying the philosophy of naturalism[11] to science in a way that constrains its explanatory power and only allows merely physical or natural causes.

Science and Scientism

At the beginning of 2016, John Cleese tweeted that he would 'like 2016 to be the year when people remembered that science is a method of investigation, and NOT a belief system'.[12] That pretty much sums up the difference between science and scientism.

Peter Atkins, Professor of Physical Chemistry at Oxford and Fellow of Lincoln College, takes a rather higher view of science than Cleese. In his book,[13] in which he explores 'the great questions of existence', he claims:

> The scientific method can shed light on every and any concept, even those that have troubled humans since the earliest stirrings of consciousness and continue to do so today.

Interestingly, science doesn't seem to have shed much light on consciousness or on a host of other human experiences. But I have heard Atkins go further than that. On Radio 4's *Today* programme, I once heard him assert that there is, in principle, no aspect of human experience that science cannot explain. Actually, this much-exaggerated claim proved an embarrassment to some of his fellow atheists who were only too aware of experiences such as love, beauty and creativity which are not readily amenable to any kind of scientific explanation.

It is the Atkins view of science which produces scientism – the conviction that scientific explanations trump all others and alone can offer ultimate explanations. Scientism becomes what John Cleese calls 'a belief system'. Science has, of course, massively extended our understanding of the universe and of nature, and has brought immense benefits to all of us. But science has its limits and its downsides. It is salutary to remember that the science which gave us antibiotics also gave us atom bombs.

Scientism[14] has arisen because science has been manipulated to promote a worldview which insists that any explanation beyond 'natural processes' cannot be considered. It is the view that science can offer a natural explanation for everything in life. It is essentially the philosophy of naturalism into which the scientific data is made to fit. Michael Shermer, the historian of science, puts a positive spin on the word 'scientism' and describes it as:

> … a scientific worldview that encompasses natural explanations for all phenomena, eschews supernatural and paranormal speculations, and embraces empiricism and reason as the twin pillars of a philosophy of life appropriate for an Age of Science.[15]

Science, on the other hand, should be the uninhibited exploration of the natural world and the search for explanations, which are consistent with all the evidence, even if those point to intelligence beyond nature. It is important to note that intelligence as we know it is an immaterial phenomenon, yet it operates within the natural order. There should be no reason in principle why science cannot recognise the evidence for an intelligence which comes from beyond nature, yet operates within it. It is just too easy to dismiss this as the supernaturalism which belongs to religion. The much-repeated appeal in scientific explanations to 'natural processes' clearly includes the operation of immaterial human intelligence, otherwise science or any other intellectual pursuit would be impossible. It is not unreasonable, therefore, to infer in the operation of nature the presence of a supreme intelligence.

Scientism is ultimately self-defeating because it is not open to all of reality. It is constrained in its interpretation of scientific data by its underlying commitment to naturalism. Its conclusions about origins fly in the face of reality. Mind, consciousness[16] and the information carried in the DNA[17] of all living things point to immaterial realities which, though they operate in the natural world, are not explicable by purely natural processes. Scientism will not allow you to infer from phenomena such as these that the universe has an intelligent cause but, creed-like, insists on the highly improbable and counter-intuitive conclusions that universes can come into existence out of nothing[18] and that life emerges by blind, purposeless forces; or as Lord Rees, the Astronomer Royal, opined recently, by a massive 'fluke'[19] – not, it has to be said, the most scientific of conclusions and certainly not one which is consistent with our experience of the biochemical world. To prefer the 'fluke theory' to the design theory is a measure of how far contemporary origins science has drifted from reality.

Now all of this might not matter overmuch if it remained purely an issue of intellectual debate about the nature and limits of science. But scientism has become a popular belief. A significant proportion of the population of Britain would subscribe to the view that scientific explanations make God unnecessary. He is not needed any more, apparently. Science has explained everything. If you are inclined to think this is an exaggeration, you should look at the recent survey of belief in Britain which found, among other things, that a third of British adults do not believe in God and 46% of 18–24 year olds deny the existence of any greater spiritual power.[20]

Of course, people are entitled to believe what they wish. But much more sinister is a recent set of instructions from the Department for Education limiting the discussion of origins in science lessons.[21] What is at stake now is whether our children in school should learn science and its methods or be indoctrinated with scientism.

The new approach to Origins Science
– make challenging the consensus 'illegal'

It was Kirsty Wark, the presenter of BBC's *Newsnight*, who raised the question in the broadcast of 24th April 2014. The subject being discussed was the alleged Islamisation of some Birmingham schools and, among other things, the claim that 'Creationism' was being taught in science lessons. Given the scale of the alleged abuses, this sounded like the least of their difficulties. Nonetheless, on this point, to a member of the Muslim Council of Great Britain, Kirsty exploded, 'but that's illegal'. Now I don't know what was happening in Birmingham schools, but strictly speaking, teaching 'Creationism' is not illegal – not yet anyway. The guidance from the Department for Education to schools is that Creationism is not to be considered as science, but if it is raised in science lessons it should be discussed sensitively.[22] That is quite different from 'illegal'.

However, in recent years the discussion of Intelligent Design in school science lessons has become the subject of Government guidance to schools. In essence this guidance to schools and teachers by the Department for Education in several publications contains the following elements:

1. Intelligent Design and 'Creationism' are not to be regarded as science and must not form any part of science education. These subjects are apparently legitimate within Religious Education and related studies. However, this frequently repeated mantra consistently fails to describe the important difference between Intelligent Design and Creationism.

2. Any explanation or theory which holds that 'natural biological processes' cannot account for the history, diversity and complexity of life on earth and therefore rejects the scientific theory of evolution cannot

be permitted in science classes. This effectively makes 'naturalism' or 'materialism' the exclusive and obligatory basis for all explanations in biological science and, in effect, imposes a narrow philosophical position on the study of origins.

3. It is conceded, though, that if students raise questions about Creationism and Intelligent Design, teachers should deal with them sensitively, pointing out, of course, that the official line is that this is not science because they challenge accepted evolutionary theory. (In the case of Intelligent Design, this is not necessarily the case as some aspects of evolution could be designed. What Intelligent Design challenges is the random nature of Neo-Darwinism.)

Some of this is said to be necessary in order to prevent religious extremism invading science lessons, which is not, so far as I am aware, a significant problem in the UK. It has also been a response to representations from bodies such as the British Humanist Society and the Scottish Secular Society. Officers of the latter body recently wrote to the Cabinet Secretary for Education in the Scottish Government to ask that 'Creationism and intelligent design are expressly prohibited from schools outside of RME (Religious and Moral Education) classes'.[23]

The impact of all this, however, is that any open and informed discussion of 'creation' or 'Intelligent Design' is effectively outlawed. It is important to note that these two propositions are not the same. Unlike 'Creationism', Intelligent Design does not depend on religious texts but argues from scientific data – an inconvenient truth which is simply ignored by the secular zealots in the Department for Education. Curiously, in attempting to combat perceived religious extremism, the Government is adopting an equally extreme and quasi-religious position with regard to science education, which flies in the face of the understanding of science we have inherited over five centuries of scientific endeavour.

It is also interesting that some of the advice from the Department for Education appears in documentation relating to the funding of schools and academies. The implication is brutally clear: teach Intelligent Design and you lose your funding. The legalities hardly matter in that context. It is hard to imagine a position which is more detrimental to proper investigation in science and to the unfettered discussion of ultimate questions which will arise in the minds of students, particularly when exploring the origins of the universe and of life. It is, in fact, a form of intellectual fascism.

The ferocity with which this position is adopted was seen dramatically in an incident which involved Professor Michael Reiss, a biologist and Professor of Science Education at the Institute of Education, University of London, as well as the Royal Society's Honorary Director of Education. Speaking at a conference of teachers in 2008,[24] he said that if issues of Intelligent Design and Creationism arose in science classes, teachers should discuss these matters sensitively, taking account of the pupils' backgrounds and the religious convictions of their families, and pointing out that the scientific consensus does not accept them.

You might think this was an entirely reasonable and professional approach to classroom discussion, but the furore which followed, particularly from the distinguished fellows of the Royal Society, including some Nobel Prize winners, was astonishing. Professor Reiss was accused of 'bringing science into disrepute' and giving credibility to 'non-scientific' or 'pseudo-scientific' propositions. He was eventually forced to resign from his post at the Royal Society, an outcome which even Richard Dawkins said made him feel 'squeamish'. I should think so, especially given that the motto of the Royal Society is 'Nullius in Verba' which roughly translated from the Latin means 'take no-one's word for it' or, more recognisably, 'be open to objective enquiry, not dogmatic assertion'.

The irony of all this is that Professor Reiss is committed to an evolutionary model of origins. His offence was to be broadminded enough to discuss alternative positions raised by students, an approach, curiously, which is within the guidelines issued by the Department for Education. It makes you wonder if freedom of speech and enquiry is on its last legs in Britain.

The Government's position on what can or cannot be taught about science is also probably in violation of the European Convention of Human Rights (ECHR), which gives parents the right to have their children educated 'in line with their philosophical and religious beliefs'.[25] In this connection, it is worth remembering that all Christians, Jews and Muslims, by definition, are 'creationist', in a broad sense. 'Creationist' has become a term of abuse, largely because it is generally taken to mean a position based on what is perceived as a rigid and literalist interpretation of Bible passages. In reality, scientism challenges the historic Judeo-Christian worldview – of a designed and rational universe – which has built our society, and regarding which we have, until now, enjoyed freedom of enquiry and expression.

Equally seriously, what the Government is proposing is an affront to the scientific method. Scientists have always understood their task to be the unfettered investigation of nature without imposed dogmas, and to be able to challenge any scientific hypothesis if the evidence merits it. In the area of origins, the scientific evidence certainly merits a re-think of naturalistic Darwinian evolution, as a recent paper in *Nature* highlighted.[26]

What the Government is in danger of doing is encouraging science students to think that scientific theories, particularly about origins, cannot be challenged and must be accepted without criticism. I hope the secularists blush when they realise what they are doing. The examples in recent history of countries in which the Government told its citizens what to think are not reassuring.

So is quasi-legal protection of scientific dogma from uncomfortable enquiry the way to advance our understanding? If scientism is imposed on education as proposed, science becomes merely the search for strands of evidence which are consistent with the already agreed worldview that there is nothing beyond the material. And that inevitably leads to atheism, which is, of course, a faith position – the very thing you are not supposed to mix with science.

Is this how Britain and the West achieved the stunning successes of modern science? Is this how scientific matters and their implications are to be discussed? Clearly nothing arouses the passions of the ideologues quite like the mention of 'creation' or 'Intelligent Design'. Better to ban them, apparently, than to have to confront, in the case of Intelligent Design, the obvious design implications of the scientific data.

What we are witnessing in our schools and universities is not really a commitment to science, but rather a dogmatic adherence to the unproven and unproveable propositions of naturalism.

Lessons from the American experience

The situation we have arrived at has parallels with developments in the United States. In 2004, a case supported by the American Civil Liberties Union (ACLU) was brought against the School Board in the town of Dover, Pennsylvania. The background was that the Board wanted high school students taking biology classes to be informed that there were positions about origins other than Darwinian evolution, including Intelligent Design, and that if they wished to study these, they could find books on them in the school library.

This may seem innocuous enough and consistent with good educational practice. But the furore raised by the liberal and scientific establishments led to a major court case against the School Board, in which the defendants lost and Intelligent Design was judged to be unscientific. It was claimed essentially that Intelligent Design introduced religion into science and was therefore unconstitutional. This was an interesting outcome in that one belief system – naturalism, which implies atheism – was apparently constitutional; but another – Intelligent Design, which implies theism – was unconstitutional.

The really intriguing thing, though, is that Judge Jones, a non-scientist, came to the astonishing conclusion that while 'Intelligent Design may well be true, a proposition on which the court takes no position, it is not science'.[27] Maybe we should not have expected too much scientific insight from a judge, especially when his judgement was taken, almost verbatim, from the ACLU submission. However, the unambiguous conclusion to draw from his judgment is that science is no longer to be considered a search for the truth about origins.

If there is a Designer behind the universe, then, on the basis of Judge Jones's judgment, science is unable to detect or even infer his presence. So much the worse for science, I suggest. You might recast Judge Jones's ruling on the explanatory power of naturalistic science on origins as, 'science may well be wrong, a proposition on which the court takes no position, but it is definitely not intelligent design'.

It is of interest that the American Senate had addressed some of the implications of open enquiry in science in 2001 with the Santorum Amendment[28] which said simply that, 'it is the sense of the Senate that (1) good science education should prepare students to distinguish the

184

data or testable theories of science from philosophical or religious claims that are made in the name of science; and (2) where biological evolution is taught, the curriculum should help students to understand why this subject generates so much continuing controversy and should prepare the students to be informed participants in public discussions regarding the subject'. Essentially, this amendment from Senator Santorum merely acknowledged the existence of disagreements and controversies over scientific theories, especially biological evolution, and supported the conclusion that science education would be more effective if it prepared students to understand these controversies.[29] It contained no provisions for implementation or enforcement.

The Amendment passed, in a slightly amended form, with a huge bipartisan majority of 91-8.[30] The late Senator Edward Kennedy urged all the Senators to vote for the amendment because, as he put it, 'we want children to be able to talk about different concepts and do it intelligently with the best information before them'. That seems to be exactly what we should do, but which the guidance of the British Department for Education severely restricts. However, the Santorum Amendment, not unexpectedly, became a source of considerable controversy and some backtracking because of its perceived anti-evolution tone.

This all seems part of a not-so-subtle campaign to impose materialistic thinking on scientific debate in schools and elsewhere, to the exclusion of other considerations. For example, only a few miles from where I live, two head teachers have recently been removed from post because of the distribution to pupils of literature which makes reference to evolution and creation.[31] More recently, a physics teacher in an East of Scotland School was under press scrutiny for suggesting to senior pupils that scientific theories about origins are subject to a degree of uncertainty.[32] Recently, the Scottish Secular Society sought, under the Freedom of Information Act, to elicit information, among other things, about whether 'creationists' are infiltrating our schools.[33] The results were deeply underwhelming.

Of course, I am not in a position to defend all the actions of others and I recognise that people can act unwisely in the pursuit of personal or professional goals. I am also clear that 'Creationism' as popularly understood is not the same as 'Intelligent Design', and I have written about that elsewhere.[34] But the determined and sometimes mindless opposition to any suggestion of the possibility that we are here as the result of an intelligent cause, as opposed to blind materialistic forces, borders on the irrational and certainly does not sit easily with proper scientific enquiry and freedom of expression.

Science and origins

The scientific study of origins falls into the category of historical science, where the everyday methods of experimental laboratory science don't so readily apply. It is not possible to repeat the events of long ago and so scientists often have to make 'an inference to the best explanation' of the evidence available to them – an approach which significantly distinguishes historical science from much experimental science.

This is precisely the approach Darwin took when theorising about the origin and development of life. It is also the approach taken by the proponents of Intelligent Design who argue that there is clear evidence in nature and life of pre-existing mind.[35]

Now that is a highly controversial proposition. But Intelligent Design proponents are clear that this is not primarily a religious position, but one which is clearly inferred from the evidence. That evidence, as we have seen, includes the fine-tuning of universal constants, the specified complexity of living systems, and the information content of the genome. The latter is the most persuasive, in that all our experience teaches us that functional information, such as that digitally coded in DNA, always arises from intelligent mind. As Henry Quastler, the pioneering information theorist observed, 'information habitually arises from conscious activity'.[36]

But the scientific consensus is aggressively opposed to this obvious conclusion. And in its concerted opposition to what many would feel is blindingly obvious, it consistently makes two critical errors.

Firstly, contemporary science defines itself in a way which excludes any non-material explanation of origins. This is not a scientific finding, but an assumed position which places a massive constraint on origins science, and rules out the rather obvious conclusion that our universe shows evidence of intelligent mind. Professor Steven Weinberg, a Nobel Prize winner, is unambiguous about this. The goal of science, he argues, is 'to find explanations of natural phenomena that are purely naturalistic'.[37] Clearly, if that is the starting point, the end point is predictable. Interestingly, the perception of intelligent causation of the universe was held, to varying degrees, by a significant number of eminent scientists including, for example, Isaac Newton and Albert Einstein.[38]

While Professor Richard Dawkins will freely admit that he has no idea about the origin of life,[39] or the universe for that matter, Professor Laurence Krauss argues that a 'universe from nothing' is a feasible scientific position.[40] This is where the materialist agenda gets you, in spite of the whole cause and effect structure of the universe and the rational analysis of data, which is the foundation of scientific thought. The naturalistic philosophy, which now dominates science, leads to breathtaking absurdity, as well as the suppression of legitimate debate.

The second error in origins science is equally irrational. It is the confusion of process with agency. It goes like this: if we can explain how certain processes might have operated, we can dispense with any designing agency. So if we propose, say, an 'RNA-world' as a precursor to the DNA world, and find some chemical evidence of the possibility (actually, such a scenario is by no means certain), then we have proved that no intelligence is at work behind the process.

A striking example of this approach was when Craig Venter's team managed to synthesise active DNA in the laboratory by copying the known sequences of base pairs in real DNA.[41] A leading scientist, when interviewed on Radio 4's *Today* programme, hailed this as conclusive proof that DNA could arise naturally without any intelligent agent at work, somehow missing the point that the highly intelligent scientists who worked with Venter took some fifteen years to assemble their synthetic DNA.

Professor John Lennox exposes this fallacy by pointing out that there are two ways to understand a Ford motor car.[42] You can describe it in terms of the laws of engineering, combustion and motion, or you can explain it through the original agency of Henry Ford and the hundreds of design engineers who have subsequently worked for the company. These are clearly not mutually exclusive positions.

A designing intelligence behind the universe is entirely consistent with the laws and processes which have got us to this point in our existence.

That is the position of Intelligent Design, which does not suffer from the two critical errors which beset contemporary origins science.

It is just a pity and, more seriously, also an affront to academic and public debate, that these matters cannot be discussed dispassionately in schools, universities and the public arena. It makes you wonder if there really is an ulterior motive. Why not just debate where the evidence leads to and drop the need for Government interference? Nothing, it seems, must be allowed to unsettle the brittle protectorate of secularism.

Teaching evolution

Any discussion about origins quickly becomes a debate about evolution. In a recent discussion in a high school, a representative of the Humanist Society in Scotland, who had become increasingly frustrated with my arguments about Intelligent Design, shouted, as a kind of last resort, 'But do you believe in evolution?' It didn't seem to help when I explained to him that scientific theories like evolution are not things you believe in. You either accept the theory or doubt it according to the extent to which it is consistent with the evidence.

Of course, evolution is always taught as 'a fact', a status which, strictly speaking, you should not apply to any scientific theory. Science advances by trial and error. All scientific theories are tentative and capable of being revised in the light of experience. Some theories are much better attested than others, but no scientific proposition can ever be the last word on the subject.

Proponents of evolution, and indeed the officials of the Department for Education, seem to forget this, and are now effectively protecting evolutionary theory with the force of law. Guidance to teachers contains comments like 'any theory which holds that natural biological processes cannot account for the history, diversity and complexity of life on earth and therefore rejects the scientific theory of evolution' cannot be permitted in science classes. Alternative propositions are not to be tolerated. This is a very peculiar position for any scientific theory to get into, and you begin to suspect that a scientific theory is really in trouble when it needs Government persuasion to keep it afloat.

And there is another problem with 'evolution'. It is a very slippery word which has several meanings, including adaptation, common descent of all life forms from simple precursors, and the generation of complex life via a completely unguided process of 'natural selection acting on random variations', described in the words of Professor Richard Dawkins as 'the blind watchmaker thesis'.[43] These are very different propositions.

The evidence for adaptation is largely uncontroversial. However, the evidence for common descent and the development of complex life forms from simple ones is much more sparse and ambiguous. The evidence for the 'blind watchmaker thesis' is open to vigorous scientific and philosophical dispute. To present 'evolution' broadly as 'a fact' without distinguishing between its various claims is to mislead students and deny them the opportunity to understand the often tentative nature of scientific theories, and of biological evolution in particular.

Scientists and authors who are critical of key aspects of modern evolutionary theory based on scientific data include, 'The Altenburg 16',[44] Jerry Fodor,[45] Michael Denton,[46] Stephen Meyer,[47] Michael Behe,[48] Lee Spetner,[49] and David Swift.[50] Some, such as the late Stephen J Gould,[51] Lynn Margulis,[52] James Shapiro,[53] while accepting the main proposition of evolution, have disputed that the proposed mechanism of natural selection acting on random mutations is sufficient for the task. Certain iconic arguments for evolution such as 'the tree of life' and 'junk DNA' have recently been called into question,[54] and in the latter case been overturned.[55] The growing body of doubt about Darwin cannot be ignored and should be part of progressive science education. Only ideologues dismiss it.

Among the astonishing statements in the writings of the above dissenters is this one from James Shapiro:

> In the context of ideological debates about evolution, this insistence on randomness and accident is not surprising. It springs from a determination in the 19th and 20th centuries by biologists to reject the role of a supernatural agent in religious accounts of how diverse living organisms originated. While that determination fits with the naturalistic boundaries of science, the continued insistence on the random nature of genetic change by evolutionists should be surprising for one simple reason: empirical studies…[56] [have shown otherwise – my summary].

This is an astonishing admission by a highly respected professor of biochemistry and molecular biology. He is saying quite explicitly that biologists have been blind to what the data shows because of their presuppositions. That is pretty much what I am trying to say in this chapter.

In this connection it is noteworthy that, in a public lecture entitled 'Darwin on Trial' at the University of California, Irvine, Professor Phillip Johnson argued that 'ambiguous terminology, faulty assumptions, and questionable rules of reasoning have transformed a theory which explains minor evolutionary change into a dogmatic naturalistic religion.'[57]

You can be sure that the growing body of evidence against the all-pervasive theory of evolution will not be considered. And here is what children won't be told about evolution:

1. Evolution has no explanation for the origin of life in the first place. Saying evolution doesn't deal with that, while implying it does, just highlights its deficiency.

2. Random mutation and natural selection cannot explain the synthesis of the hundreds of complex bio-molecules, like proteins, which are necessary for life.[58] Strictly speaking, natural selection doesn't kick in until life gets started.

3. The mechanism of evolution – natural selection acting on random mutation – has been shown to be unequal to the task of creating new organisms.[59]

4. The 'junk DNA' hypothesis, an integral part of the teaching of evolution, has now been abandoned in light of recent work on the human genome.[60]

5. The much-vaunted 'tree of life' is being increasingly shown to be highly speculative and at odds with the evidence.[61]

6. The fossil record is not consistent with the numerous slight successive changes required by evolution, as Charles Darwin himself recognised.[62]

7. Evolution is completely unable to explain the existence of the complex genetic information carried by every living cell in its DNA.[63]

8. Evolution has no explanation for mind and consciousness, other than that it is an accidental by-product of chemistry and physics.[64]

Any other scientific hypothesis with such glaring deficiencies would certainly not be taught as 'fact' in schools.

But the second problem is that, behind all this, there are now, as Philip Johnson has pointed out, two definitions of science.[65] The first is the popular definition, which insists science can only deal with natural processes and, for example, cannot contemplate any explanation about origins which suggests a non-material explanation such as 'mind before matter'. The older and more honest definition is that science goes where the evidence leads and does not rule out any possible explanation before it is given due consideration.

It is clear, then, that evolution is based on the first definition. It is essentially materialistic dogma, not science. It persists for ideological reasons, despite the evidence.

So what is being taught in schools is the secular, humanistic, naturalistic worldview, which rules out any possibility of design in nature, even before the evidence is considered. It is, in fact, a form of secular indoctrination.

The scientific study of origins is unlike any other because it has to consider the possibility of deliberate design in nature. That is why Intelligent Design should also be considered in any scientific study of origins.

The origin of life
There is a further issue. If we do not know how life began in the first place, how can we assert with any certainty, as Neo-Darwinism does, that we know how life developed? In the absence of a credible explanation for how life began, any theory about its development must surely remain tentative at best. It is a bit like extolling the structural safety of a skyscraper without having any idea about the nature of its foundations.

It is not as if the origin of life can be ignored. To say that, strictly speaking, Darwinism doesn't deal with the origin of life is disingenuous and avoids the issue. Any factors at work in life's origin – intelligent mind for example – are likely to continue to be involved in its development.

Glib answers don't help either. Some months ago, a scientist on Radio 4's *Today* programme, commenting on the possible presence of water on Mars, asserted, 'Life is not a miracle, but a cosmic infection'.[66]

Great soundbite, but palpable nonsense based more on wishful thinking than empirical evidence.

The scientific consensus about the possibility of life on Mars, or elsewhere in the galaxy for that matter, goes like this: There is some evidence of water on Mars, so there is a good chance life existed there. Of course you need a few other elements thrown in, like carbon, nitrogen and probably oxygen, and some miscellaneous salts. But, hey, as the man said, life is a 'cosmic infection'. It is bound to happen.

Professor Stephen Hawking is pretty much on board with this. 'We believe life arose spontaneously',[67] he asserted recently, so the matter is settled. Not by the evidence but by the sheer unacceptability of the alternative of an intelligent agent. Mainstream science can't handle that, so the consensus sticks with the philosophy of naturalism – only natural causes can ever be allowed in science. Incidentally, that must mean the natural world itself has a natural cause, a route that leads you eventually to philosophical incoherence. But no matter, keep asserting the position and it gets accepted.

However, the irreducible complexity of many biological systems and the sophisticated information content of living cells are monumental obstacles to the accepted explanation of their origin through chance and necessity, and point to deliberate design. If that is so, the blind, purposeless proposition of contemporary Darwinism becomes untenable. In this connection, the recent film *The Information Enigma*[68] from Seattle's Discovery Institute is highly relevant.

Interestingly, in Radio 4's *Today* programme on 6 March 2004, Sir David Attenborough said, 'The problem Darwin never solved was how one inorganic molecule became a living one. We're still struggling with that one.' That is the kind of honesty science needs, even though it is less apparent in some of his nature programmes. And in the film *Expelled*,[69] Richard Dawkins, in an interview with Ben Stein, unwittingly appears to support Intelligent Design by admitting that the intricacies of cellular biology could lead us to detect the existence of a 'higher intelligence' or 'designer' (his words). So why wouldn't we want to explore that with students?

It is high time we stopped indoctrinating pupils with the philosophy of naturalism dressed up as the scientific consensus. We should do what all honest scientists do, which is to go where the evidence leads. As has been observed, it takes years of indoctrination to miss the obvious signs of design in nature.

Scientific controversies and science education

In all of this, the fundamental issue is whether, in scientific work and in science education, it is permissible to ask the ultimate questions about the origin of the universe, the origin of life and the origin of our consciousness. Why can't science address these issues? If the evidence points, as it does, to an intelligent cause for the universe, why is that ruled out of scientific discourse? Must scientific enquiry be constrained by naturalistic considerations? If so, why? And if science is unequal to the task of exploring origins objectively, why doesn't it just abandon the field and say that it can't cope with the obvious, but non-materialistic conclusions the universe thrusts on us?

It is obvious that 'natural biological processes' are extensive and offer adequate explanations for many aspects of living things. However, there are features of life which call for explanations which go beyond purely 'natural processes', such as the origin of such processes themselves, the evidence for design in nature, and the emergence of genetic information and conscious life.

Ironically, Intelligent Design is the position which gave rise to modern science in the first place, because it provided a basis for the conviction that rational and systematic investigation of nature is a reliable and productive pursuit. The Neo-Darwinian position that life and the universe, including conscious thought, are the result of blind and purposeless processes provides little confidence to believe that our investigations and conclusions have any validity or truth. Students should be aware of this.

My argument is that it is completely inappropriate for Government to accord to any scientific theory the status of a protected position, which cannot be challenged on the basis of the empirical evidence. This stifles debate, closes off legitimate areas of research, intimidates teachers in pursuing questions raised by pupils in science classes, and gives students a wholly false view of the methods of science. How are teachers expected to respond to the inevitable questions from pupils in science about 'creation' and 'Intelligent Design' and the limitations of evolutionary theory? By telling them that such discussion is off limits? Such a position, advocated by Government, is a form of intellectual intolerance unworthy of a country which values academic freedom and encourages critical enquiry, especially in science education.

I am most certainly not arguing that biblical literalism or any other religious position should be imposed on science lessons, but current Government advice excludes legitimate discussion in science of the ultimate questions posed by the evidence about the origin of the universe and the development of life. This includes the obviously non-material features of living things, such as genetic information, sentience, mind and consciousness. To claim that naturalistic and random processes have explained all this is as absurd as it is inaccurate. It is important to note that, while scientific data is neutral, some theories and interpretations imposed on it may not necessarily be so.

I agree that evolution should be taught in schools. However, it should be presented objectively, indicating the evidence for and against the theory, as well as its limitations. Pupils should also be made aware that 'evolution' has several meanings.

The proposition that a scientific theory, such as evolution, should be given protected status and be beyond criticism is a complete denial of the scientific method. The nature of science is to constantly challenge scientific propositions and modify them in the light of experience. It is also the case that science frequently advances when the consensus is challenged in the light of fresh evidence. All scientific theories are tentative and should not be beyond challenge, no matter how well established. It is also extremely poor practice to teach school students that the scientific consensus must be accepted without question, that no controversy exists when it plainly does, and that dissent must be suppressed.

It is especially noteworthy that the world-renowned philosopher and atheist Thomas Nagel subtitled his recent book 'Mind and Cosmos, Why the Neo-Darwinian conception of Nature is almost certainly false'.[70] His argument is that Neo-Darwinism cannot begin to explain mind and consciousness – both immaterial phenomena – and is therefore incapable of providing a credible explanation of origins. Intelligent Design does not suffer from that disadvantage as it is prepared to countenance that there is evidence in nature of intelligent mind. Students need to be aware of these debates. The kind of guidance issued by the Department for Education would completely stifle this legitimate discourse.

Interestingly, Nagel, although he is an atheist, concedes the validity of Intelligent Design as a scientific proposition worthy of serious consideration.[71] His comment on this emphasises the intellectual arrogance of limiting debate on the origin and development of life:

> Even though writers like Michael Behe and Stephen Meyer are motivated in part by their religious beliefs, the empirical arguments they offer against the likelihood that the origin of life and its evolutionary history can be fully explained by physics and chemistry are of great interest in themselves.

> Another sceptic, David Berlinski,[72] has brought out these problems vividly without reference to the design inference. Even if one is not drawn to the alternative of an explanation by the actions of a designer, the problems that these iconoclasts pose for the orthodox scientific consensus should be taken seriously. They do not deserve the scorn with which they are commonly met. It is manifestly unfair.[73]

The claim that the introduction of Intelligent Design into science lessons will confuse students is disingenuous. What will certainly confuse students is to demonstrate how scientific advances are made through painstaking research, sustained intellectual effort and hard work, and then claim that the vastly more complex structures of life arose by random naturalistic processes. This is not just counter-intuitive, but completely at odds with the cause and effect structure of the world. To brainwash our young people into accepting such contradictory positions is wholly reprehensible.

What is to be done?

At the very least we need to be aware of what is being done in our name in schools, both in science and across the curriculum. Terence Copley's comment about education being complicit in the secular indoctrination of young people, at the head of this chapter, is both important and ominous.

If we cannot persuade legislators and educationists that the rights and beliefs of parents are being disregarded, particularly in the area of the science of origins, then we need to find other ways of ensuring that our young people remain open-minded and hear the argument from design. If schools won't do it, homes and churches should.

But the signs are not encouraging. A recent survey in the US found that although pastors included issues of science and faith in a sermon at least once a year, only 1% of youth workers thought this area was relevant to their young people.[74]

So there is a double whammy for you. Our young people are exposed to a thoroughly secularised education system for a minimum of fifteen years of their life, and their youth pastors don't think these matters are important enough to include in their teaching programme.

Why is it that, when our society is descending into dark, meaningless, secular confusion, the church is largely asleep? And when it is aroused to the problem, its leaders just mumble feebly that they are sure there is no conflict between science and faith and offer 'theistic evolution' as a solution, without apparently realising the absurdity of the Creator guiding an unguided process. Of course, there should not be any conflict between faith and science, but there certainly is a massive conflict between Darwin and Design.

It is time to wake up, before we lose the next generation of our young people to secular indoctrination. In truth, the battle may already be lost.

Notes

[1] Richard Dawkins, *The Blind Watchmaker* (Penguin Books, 1986).

[2] Michael Denton, *Evolution: A Theory in Crisis* (Adler & Adler, 1986); see also by the same author, *Evolution: Still a Theory in Crisis* (Discovery Institute Press, 2016).

[3] Phillip E Johnson, *Darwin on Trial* (IVP, 1991 and subsequent editions).

[4] For a treatment of Naturalism see e.g. James W Sire, *The Universe Next Door*, The Silence of Finite Space, chap 4, (IVP 2004).

[5] New York Review of Books, 9 January 1997, in a review of Carl Sagan's book, T*he Demon Haunted World: Science as a Candle in the Dark*, quoted by John Lennox in *God's Undertaker, Has Science Buried God?* (Lion, 2009) p.36.

[6] Stephen C Meyer, *Signature in the Cell* (HarperOne, 2009).

[7] Bill Gates, *The Road Ahead*, p188,

[8] See e.g. Paul Davies in *The Goldilocks Enigma* (Penguin, 2007).

[9] David Swift, *Evolution under the Microscope,* chap 7 (Leighton, 2002).

[10] Michael Behe, *Darwin's Black Box,* (Simon and Schuster, 1996).

[11] See e.g. *The Nature of Nature – Examining the Role of Naturalism in Science*, ed. Gordon, Dembski et all (ISI Books,2011).

[12] See @JohnCleese, 3 January, 2016

[13] Peter Atkins, *On Being* (OUP, 2011) p. 7.

[14] The Collins English Dictionary gives one meaning of scientism as *'the uncritical application of scientific or quasi-scientific methods to inappropriate fields of study or investigation'*

[15] Michael Shermer, 'The Shamans of Scientism', *Scientific American*, June 2002, quoted in Dennis Sewell, *The Political Gene* (Picador, 2009) p.227

[16] See, for example, Thomas Nagel, *'Mind & Cosmos, Why the materialist Neo-Darwinian Conception of Nature is almost Certainly False'* (Oxford University Press, 2012).

[17] See ref 6

[18] See e.g. L Krauss, *A Universe from Nothing*, (Simon and Schuster, 2012).

[19] Lord Rees, *Daily Telegraph*, 8 January 2015

[20] Yougov.co.uk/new/2015/02/12

[21] See the School and Early Years Finance (England) Regulations 2014, Department for Education

[22] See DCSF (2007) guidance on Creationism and intelligent design. Available at www.teachernet.gov.uk/docbank/index.cfm?id=11890) and can now be found at http://webarchive.nationalarchives.gov.uk/20071204131026/http://www.teachernet.gov.uk/docbank/index.cfm?id=11890.

[23] See e.g. Petition 01530 to the Scottish Parliament, 2014, and associated papers

[24] Michael Reiss: Students must be allowed to raise doubts, *www.theguardian.com › Science › Evolution*, 11 Sep 2008

[25] ECHR, Article 2 of the First Protocol.

[26] *Nature*, Comment, 8 October 2013, K Laland et al.

[27] *Kitzmiller v. Dover Area School District et al.* (2005)

[28] For a discussion of the implications of the Santorum Amendment see Phillip E Johnson, *The Right Questions* (IVP, 2002) chap 1, 'Biology and Liberal Freedom'

[29] Ibid, p31

[30] The Santorum Amendment won overwhelming bipartisan support in the United States Senate. In fact, Sen. Ted Kennedy enthusiastically endorsed the Amendment on the Senate floor. Others voting in favour of the Amendment included Sen. Hillary Clinton, Sen. Joe Biden, Sen. Barbara Boxer, Sen. Harry Reid, Senator John McCain, and Senator Sam Brownback. See *Congressional Record,* June 13, 2001, p. S6153. The Amendment became the source of continuing controversy.

[31] See e.g. www.bbc.co.uk/news/uk-scotland-glasgow-west-24077924

[32] See e.g. http://www.heraldscotland.com/news/home-news/calls-for-probe-into-creationist-physics-teacher.22287215

[33] See www.scottishsecularsociety.com and their Facebook page for details

[34] See my article on www.c4id.org.uk on ID and Creationism under *An Introduction to ID, section* 14, and also in my booklet of the same title, available for www.c4id.org.uk

[35] See ref 6

[36] Quastler, *The Emergence of Biological Information*, p16

[37] Steven Weinberg, *To Explain the World*, (Allen Lane, 2015) p. 14.

[38] See e.g. Walter Issacson, 'Einstein's God' in *Einstein, His Life and Universe*, (Simon and Schuster, 2007) chap 17.

[39] See interview in the DVD *Expelled- No Intelligence Allowed*, NPN Videos, Swindon.

[40] Laurence Krauss, *A Universe from Nothing* (Atria Books, 2012).

[41] See e.g. http://www.ted.com/talks/craig_venter_unveils_synthetic_life.html

[42] See John C Lennox, *God's Undertaker – has Science buried God?* (Lion, 2009) p.45.

[43] See ref 1

[44] Susan Mazur, *The Altenburg 16, An Expose of the Evolution Industry* (Scoop Media, 2009). *See also The Paradigm Shifters,* by the same author (Caswell Books, 2015).

[45] Jerry Fodor et al, *'What Darwin got Wrong'* (Farrar, Straus and Giroux, 2010).

[46] See ref 2

[47] See ref 5

[48] See ref 10

[49] Lee Spetner, *The Evolution Revolution*, (Judaica Press, 2014).

[50] See ref 9

[51] See e.g. Stephen J Gould and Niles Eldredge, 'Punctuated Equilibria: The Tempo and Mode of Evolution Reconsidered', *Paleobiology 3,* 1977, 115-51.

[52] Mann, C (1991). "Lynn Margulis: Science's Unruly Earth Mother". *Science 252* (5004): 378–381. *doi:10.1126/science.252.5004.378. PMID 17740930.*

[53] James A Shapiro, *Evolution, A from the 21st Century* (FT Press, 2011).

[54] See e.g. Stephen C Meyer in *'Darwin's Doubt'* (HarperOne, 2013) chap 6.

[55] See e.g. *news.bbc.co.uk/2/hi/science/nature/4940654.stm.*

[56] James A Shapiro, *Evolution, A from the 21st Century*, (FT Press, 2011) p.2.

[57] Published on 10 July 2014 at *https://www.youtube.com/watch?v=emrBRLZ_JbE*

[58] See e.g. David Swift, ref 9, chap 7.

[59] See e.g. Michael Behe, *The Edge of Evolution*, (Free Press, 2007).

[60] See Wells, *The Myth of Junk DNA* (Discovery Institute Press, 2011).

[61] See e.g. Dembski and Wells, *The Design of Life*, (The Foundation for Thought and Ethics, 2008) chap 5.

[62] See Stephen Meyer, *Darwin's Doubt* (HarperOne, 2012).

[63] See Stephen Meyer, *Signature in the Cell* (HarperOne 2009).

[64] See ref 16

[65] Philip Johnson, lecture in Newcastle, 2004.
[66] In *Today*, BBC Radio 4, 29.09.15
[67] *Daily Telegraph*, 21 June 2015.
[68] https://www.youtube.com/watch?v=aA-FcnLsF1g
[69] Available from NPN Videos, Swindon
[70] Thomas Nagel, *Mind & Cosmos, Why the materialist Neo-Darwinian Conception of Nature is almost Certainly False* (Oxford University press, 2012).
[71] Ibid p.10.
[72] David Berlinski, *'On the Origins of Life'*, Commentary , 2006, reprinted in *'The Deniable Darwin and other essays,* (Discovery Institute Press, 2009).
[73] See ref 70 above, p.10
[74] John G West, *Are Young People Losing their Faith because of Science*, (Discovery Institute, Seattle, 2014)

Chapter Eight

ARE CHRISTIAN ASSEMBLIES STILL RELEVANT?
Robert S. Harris

Background to the question

It may seem that the question of the legal requirement of a collective act of daily Christian worship in schools[1] (referred to as "collective Christian worship") in England and Wales is one of narrow interest and minor relevance. I attempt to show how this strand of our school culture is a vitally significant part of what happens at school, and is of great relevance to the opportunities afforded to children during their formative years in education.

To some, this legal requirement produces lukewarm reactions or plain indifference. There are also others whose mission is to create a utopian world of their own composition in which all expressions of religion in public life are eradicated. Their advocates claim that this is for the good of all humanity, and will ensure a more free, tolerant and inclusive world.

What kind of society is generated by this utopian formula? Two examples suffice.

The aims of the National Secular Society (NSS) as stated in its *Secular Charter*,[2] include the disestablishment of the Church of England, the abolition of both State-funded religious schools[3] and all religious charities,[4] and the removal of free speech protections.[5]

The British Humanist Association (BHA) sets out to promote humanism[6] and, like the NSS, judges reason to be in direct conflict with religious beliefs that are deemed superstition. The BHA wants the law around collective Christian worship to be repealed and replaced by a requirement for inclusive assemblies that promote the spiritual, moral, social and cultural development of all pupils.

Its resources for inclusive assemblies[7] include considering good news about human achievements which can inspire students. Children may also be asked, "What sort of person do you want to be? Kind/ unkind? Trustworthy and respected/dishonest and disliked?" and, "What would you like to be remembered for towards the end of your life?" All these questions serve as essential educational tools but they fall short of addressing the spiritual development of pupils, being focused instead on self-development.

The BHA Resources include a Calendar of "Days to Remember" marking a long list of dates of birth and death of philosophers, social activists and other reformers; there are also dates marked for World Press Freedom Day and International Day for the Abolition of Slavery, among other observances. It is unclear how these commemorations contain anything "spiritual", though they might well promote awareness of moral issues. In fact, the humanist tradition rejects belief in a spiritual reality altogether.[8]

Before examining the purposes of Christian assemblies and what the law provides, it seems necessary to consider some wider social issues that underpin the identity of our society. After all, the law as it stands was produced by those who not merely believed in Christianity but saw it as the prism through which our nation and its peoples were to live and make sense of their lives. Even if one is sceptical, uneasy or indifferent about the modern day relevance of whether this history has any contemporary application, two issues demand attention.

First, what is our national identity built upon? Our answer to this question will determine our beliefs about the education ethos that shapes our schools, hence the need or not of a daily act of Christian worship. This becomes vitally important to all, especially parents and all those in the teaching profession.

A second issue is the growing demands from some very vocal quarters who argue that since a large proportion of the population is no longer Christian, this supposed reality must bear directly into the law of the education system. Yet government assertions from senior ministers assure us that Britain is still a Christian country,[9] though this has been strongly denied.[10] The components used to decide whether the country is "Christian" or not brings in view a range of interrelated factors including demographics, practice of religion, church attendance, self-designation and the guiding values of our wider culture, laws, history and heritage.

In a politically correct climate of multiculturalism and inclusion, a growing range of media and public figures appear to be increasing the pressure on legislators to drastically intervene with the goal of limiting the religious freedoms traditionally enjoyed by our schools. Some have gone to extremes in recommending the abolition of faith schools altogether.[11] Were this to materialise, it would seriously weaken the Christian bedrock upon which this country has developed, and still, in many ways, stands. It would restrict the full workings of a healthy democracy by removing a fundamental right of parental authority and freedom – namely, the legal right of parents to choose a religious education for their children – replacing it with State control over parental freedoms.

As issues of Islamist teachings in schools become a daily subject of news reports and national commentary, the government has increased pressure on Ofsted to investigate schools suspected of promoting extremism, typically where intolerance and misogyny are, among other things, being peddled. It is right to challenge attitudes which, for example, treat women in a less than equal manner or when attitudes towards certain social or religious groups are designed to harbour actual hatred. But such focus is misplaced and becomes dangerously conflated when this drive to uproot extremism is directed to law-abiding Christian schools.[12]

At the heart of a Christian education (with provision for Christian collective worship) is the powerful idea of a self-sacrificial love for others and devotion to God. Much of what Christianity is about involves how we serve others measured against Christ's example. One of the two greatest commandments is to "love your neighbour as yourself", the practice of which should lead to developing moral responsibility. Harbouring real hatred for certain groups of people – an intrinsic feature of extremism - is therefore the very antithesis of Christianity.[13] Practice of forgiveness, which sits at the centre of Christian living,[14] makes tolerance possible. It is the spirit of reconciliation, naturally generated by a mentality of selfless love, that acts as a protection against extremist agendas.

As so often happens now, a preference for and advocacy of certain lifestyle values rooted in Christian teaching is often labelled with kneejerk speed as "intolerant", with an implication that it promotes or feeds into actual "extremism". This is at best a naive, or at worst, a hostile reaction founded not on reasoned observation of the facts but driven by its own brand of hatred for people of faith. This hatred sometimes hides behind apparently benign labels of "diversity" and "inclusion".

The *raison d'être* of Christian faith schools is to present the faith and its principles to pupils.[15] This should be distinguished from "indoctrination", in which there is evidently a difficulty or impossibility to consider alternative views and opinions different from one's own. We should stress that to hold staunchly to a religious worldview is no more partial than views held by humanists, whose beliefs are resiliently defended by their advocates. It is a non-negotiable facet of humanist belief to reject belief in God and the afterlife, but our society seems not to label this as "closed-mindedness", although it is held with equal strength of conviction to that of a Christian's beliefs. The fact that this is so seems to tell us something about how certain stereotypical ideas about religious people are defined by opinion-formers who are dismissive of Christianity.

The hostility of militant atheists (including humanists and all others with a similar endgame) who challenge the right of Christian schools to exist, see their cause as not only "progressive" but relevant to everyone, irrespective of the differing range of opinions that make up notions of education. Eliminating Christian schools in the interests of creating a secular society is to make a sham of diversity in education and the practice of tolerance in our wider culture. It also presumes a supreme moral authority is invested in the State over matters of religion and its transmission.

A State that chooses to restrict or close down faith schools has exceeded its democratic remit. It also would impoverish the education system by providing a "one size fits all" approach. Parents hold the prerogative to transmit their values and religious traditions to their children, and so we would enter dangerous waters if the State (through law and policy) usurped the role of parents. One protection, and indeed litmus test of a free society, is the extent of freedom enjoyed in the exercise of religion (and speech in general), including also the freedom of families to live out their values without State restrictions or bans.

State intervention in matters of Christian education, and Christianity in general, ought not to lead to legal bans, especially when seen against the backdrop of centuries of struggle for religious freedom. The value of a democracy is retained when liberties are protected; acts of abolition or prohibition serve in their various ways only to stifle the will of communities in whose name democracy is said to exist.

A key strand of how this wider debate about religion in education is taking place, and in what the media dubbed the "Trojan horse" scandal, is how schools deemed to be under the sway of radicalisation have rightly intensified government concerns about the welfare of children. A test of "British Values" has now become the State's litmus test, intended as a tool to demonstrate integration and, as far as schools are concerned, whether they are preparing children for modern life. What is deemed to constitute British values has become a highly controversial question that is by no means straightforward, at least not in its interpretation and application. The question of "British Values" is treated as a topic of its own in several other chapters so I will not consider this further.

Humanist campaigners want religious faith to be confined to the private sphere of the home, and for every public manifestation of religion to be eradicated in the interests of "tolerance". But what is tolerance if it is not living alongside difference – those with different opinions, beliefs and values? Humanists as well as others who preach messages of inclusion and tolerance must, if they are to remain credible, allow room for religious education and cannot be selective in what it is they claim to tolerate.

The humanist or secular aspiration is that all schools should be secular, with religion only being given an airing as an academic subject because education cannot be weighted in favour of views deemed biased and partial. But to present Christianity as a faith and lifestyle worthy of preference and consideration to pupils during the course of their schooling is no more partial than the humanist ethos that treats all religious faith sceptically, often with outright hostility when it is believed to clash with shifts in modern lifestyles.

Questions of national identity

It is non-contentious that the bedrock of our national institutions and history is inherently Christian. The place held by Christianity in England is not simply constitutional veneer just because the Head of State is the Supreme Governor of the established church. In the 2001 Census, 71% of the population of England and Wales described themselves as "Christian". In the 2011 Census, this figure dropped to 59%, still a clear majority. Since 2011, the much smaller population samples used in polls and some studies seem to demonstrate a further decline in the affiliation of Christian identity amongst the population of England and Wales. According to the British Social Attitudes Survey, between 1983 and 2014, those describing themselves as having no religion in England and Wales increased from over 30% to just under 50%.[16]

The 2011 Census statistics are treated by militant atheists as evidence of how our country is losing its Christian allegiance and identity. T. S. Eliot put the issue eloquently when he said: "A society has not ceased to be Christian until it has become positively something else." When Baroness Cox considered this insight of Eliot into national identity, during a parliamentary debate on Christian teaching in schools in 1988, she concluded: "As a nation we have not yet declared ourselves to be something else."[17] Her comments will not, of course, be an evaluation everyone would readily hold to.

Certainly, the decline in those describing themselves as "Christian" provokes a number of questions: whether people have actually shifted in their identities, or whether people who believe their lifestyle is not suggestive of the Christian faith have been prompted to rethink this identity question and so identify themselves in a way better aligning with their own religious beliefs or entire lack of them.

The question of how many of this 59% actually practise Christianity would seem to open up more questions than it would probably answer; certainly attempting to address such a loaded question in any sufficient way moves beyond the boundaries of this current enquiry. Yet a majority of the population in the last Census chose to identify as "Christian", as opposed to that of another world religion. Hypothetically, even if we could find a way of discovering objectively the degree to which religious practice formed part of this 59%, ensuring a stricter test, a lower demographic of people professing actual Christian religious practice would not render those "not practising" as invalidating the figure. For many people, strict Christian religious practice does not feature at the centre of their life and their commitment. If it exists, it can fluctuate over the course of time. Nevertheless such people choose to align themselves broadly with the values and ethos of Christianity. If nothing else, this strand of the "non-practising Christian" demographic still demonstrates a chosen cultural identity rooted in and informed by Christian values.[18]

Reports of declining church attendance figures are often used as a barometer test to suggest how many Christians exist. However, this spurious measurement wrongly implies certain narrow, questionable assumptions: that all people attending church services actually designate themselves as "Christian"; that all those who designate themselves as "Christian" automatically attend church. The argument is not helped by the fact that virtually all reported figures in the national press routinely draw on attendance at Anglican churches, excluding other denominations.

When the 1944 Education Act (a key piece of legislation) was passed, the social and moral consensus was unambiguously Christian in character. In debates about religion or social attitudes, contemporary pundits often remind us how our society is distinguished from its antecedents in the area of belief and practice. At the very least, until the major social shifts of the 1960s, our society held a clear semblance of Christian identity and morals. The reference points serving to guide and inform individuals, the education system, our public institutions and lawmakers drew their meaning and purpose broadly from a Christian template. The basic understanding upon which society functioned was that it all converged, in terms of authority and values, in the religion of Christianity, based on the Judeo-Christian messages of the Bible.

Purposes of school assemblies

The assembling of the whole school on regular days is symbolic of a community. Young minds are given a glimpse of what it means to be part of a bigger society. Whereas a class of a few dozen children might draw parallels to the gathering of a big family or to a village, the entire school population of pupils and teaching staff becomes more characteristic of a small town. The assembly becomes a kind of microcosm of the wider world, suggesting a unity among the different age groups but also, with the teachers present, it represents the presence of authority and boundaries. Children thus enter into a communal gathering and experience that goes well beyond the numerical limits of their home life.

The assembling of all or most of the school pupils and staff at regular intervals is a practice with a long tradition in our country. But it is more than mere tradition. It is noteworthy that, in recent years, the law has provided some freedom to schools as to the patterns of their assemblies according to specific groupings – seen, for example, in relation to age groups.[19]

What about the purposes or messages conveyed at such gatherings? These fall into two broad areas. First, announcements may be given about school activities, prizes, examinations, parent evenings and a range of other news items specific to the day to day functioning of a school. Second, messages of a moral, spiritual and educational character may be conveyed.

For the Christian assembly, there are two broad strands traditionally forming part of the occasion, which may overlap with one another, so should not be viewed as entirely separate activities: (a) the worship dimension, and (b) the moral, spiritual, educational or reflective part.

Worship dimension
The "worship" component typically involves communal singing of Christian hymns or songs, and communal prayers. Hymn singing is taken by most people, certainly in popular culture, as the exclusive or main expression of what makes up Christian "worship". In reality, for practising Christians at least, actual worship is not reserved to any one specific act, which is somehow capable of separation from other activities. Worship intentionally permeates every activity and impacts every commitment of the believer. Worship of God engages and impinges upon all the emotions, desires, decisions, thoughts, aspirations, plans, gestures, actions and relationships of a person.

Christian worship is, first and foremost, a reverential love of God, centred on the teachings of Christ, who as a Person of the Trinity is the divine incarnation. Christianity is, among other things, a call or invitation to know and live according to the divine will as revealed by the Bible's teachings; and to worship God, in place of all things such as money or possessions and the lust for sex and power. It involves both the private and public aspects of the believer's life, since the devotion characterising the life of a Christian potentially permeates all dimensions of daily living.

Having considered this wider definition, we would be easily forgiven for wondering how such a life-defining feature can be understood by children. As worship contains a personal dimension (even while it is expressed communally), those being asked to participate in it are being provided with an opportunity to engage, through their hearts, with its meaning for their lives. It therefore does not ultimately depend on cognitive faculties, but the state of the inner heart and the relationship one has with the Creator. Children are, therefore, as part of their wider education and development, being *introduced* to Christian worship.

In the parliamentary debates of 1944, one peer seemed to successfully resolve this question by clearly distinguishing the faculty of cognition from an act of worship. He explained that while devotion depends on theological beliefs, religion for both children and adults in ordinary life is "devotional rather than theological". He argued that, in general, religious practice for people is illustrated by worship, for example, by the saying of prayers. Therefore, practice is not characterised by "engaging in reading manuals of theology or reciting Creeds." [20]

On this note, we may conclude that for children to be asked to engage in an act of worship for the narrower purposes of a school assembly, it is their "devotion", more than or instead of cognition (depending on age), that is being called into play. Whereas the full range of cognitive faculties becomes progressively apparent with the emergence of adulthood, devotion of the heart is not limited by the strictures of age.

In anticipation of the Education Reform Bill that was to revisit the issue of collective Christian worship after some forty years since Parliament last addressed the issue, Baroness Cox, during a Lords debate she initiated, lamented those schools that failed to uphold the legal requirement to hold an act of collective worship:

> What is happening in too many of our schools is not only a failure to comply with the law – though that is serious enough – but also a failure to provide young people with a spiritual experience of

worship and with an opportunity to become familiar with some of the most precious expressions of Christian faith which are part of this country's heritage, with the scriptures and with prayers and hymns, which have been the spiritual resource of incalculable value for countless people in times past and present.[21]

In her speech, Baroness Cox went on to speak of the "dreadful betrayal" suffered by children. She also highlighted the opportunities and lifelong benefits children receive from participating in acts of school worship, regardless of whether they actually recognise the value of the worship itself.[22] She said:

Even if young people do not appreciate the experience of worship while they are at school, it provides them with an opportunity to become familiar with some of the deepest expressions of the human spirit and for those to enter into the minds and hearts to be available as a resource in times of need later in life. Anyone who has contact with people who are *in extremis* is aware of how often they find comfort in the prayers, hymns and psalms learnt, sometimes reluctantly, in childhood. To deny young people the opportunity to become familiar with these spiritual resources is to leave them bereft indeed.[23]

What is at stake for the next generation was summed up clearly in a 1977 parliamentary debate. Lord Blake warned of the consequences when children are denied a general knowledge of Christianity during their education. Although he was not referring to "Christian worship" specifically, his warning still seems apt. The danger, he believed, was that a "generation will grow up which has not forgotten, but which has never even known, what Christianity is about and has never had an opportunity to know. I am not pressing for evangelism or for indoctrination; I am pressing for knowledge... What in my view would be a real tragedy would be an education which, by apathy, omission or neglect, deprived the coming generation of one of the most important aspects of human existence."[24]

Moral, spiritual, educational or reflective purposes

The moral, spiritual, educational or reflective strand includes messages about moral conduct and our place in the world, and the perspectives, attitudes, imperatives and ideals we are encouraged or urged to develop, adopt and integrate into our identity, as well as the broader religious messages we are invited to consider in the New Testament Gospels and other books of the Bible.

Some underlying principles here are: that there is a larger purpose underlying life that extends beyond the materiality and transience that comes to define life when the spiritual is excluded; that we are accountable to the God who created us; and that in learning to selflessly love others it then becomes possible to forgive those who have inflicted injustices upon us.

The spiritual, moral, social and cultural development of pupils already forms part of the law,[25] so this merits more than a cursory look at how the spiritual needs of pupils are being met. "Education", both as an idea and practice, is understood in this chapter to include, alongside academic attainment and physical education, development in all these key areas, enabling one's full humanity to be realised.

How is Christian doctrine to be treated during a school assembly? It suffices to say that children should never feel compelled to accept any religious belief. The Christian faith cannot be forced upon others; it is not just that this would be counter-productive and wrong, but totally meaningless. Christian faith starts voluntarily in the heart, free from external pressure, but can be facilitated by others, in that someone has introduced a person to the Christian message. As pupils approach their adulthood, they will have the opportunity to choose whether they can own, as their own, the Christian values and beliefs they had presented to them at school.

Objectors express concern about any religious belief being offered to children, beyond the merely academic. They judge that to hold religious beliefs is to promote indoctrination and close minds to alternatives. However, those defining themselves as "humanists" or "atheists" have fixed their mind on their own life path (rejecting religion as an alternative), but they have conveniently refrained from judging their stance as indicative of a "closed mind"!

The belief that "killing is always wrong" is a settled view held by many humanists and is not treated as symptomatic of a closed mind. Similarly, it is an intentionally skewed concept to suggest of people holding Christian beliefs that they have closed minds *by virtue of* their beliefs. The pertinent and crucial distinction is that holding to Christian beliefs demonstrates a settled rather than closed mind.

If a Christian religious ethos is maintained at school, the Christian faith will be presented not merely academically but given a special emphasis or priority over other world religions or beliefs in terms of how people are called to live. The "slantedness" of this school ethos is no more partial than a secular ethos that treats religious belief and faith sceptically, if not with hostility. Depending on the teachers in question, such religious scepticism may be promoted, held as an end in itself, and deemed to fall outside of intelligent, critical and respectable thinking.

It seems necessary to briefly illustrate something of the nature of moral rules or beliefs taught within secular education.

There is the primary rule that "killing is wrong". If we are to ensure society is held together and protected against social disorder or outright anarchy, the moral rule against killing cannot be optional and is not considered as such in the ordinary course of daily life in peacetime. Rather, society's adherence to respect for human life makes the establishment of an ordered and safe society possible.

We are also taught to treat others as we would like to be treated. Likewise, if absolutely everyone were not to treat others with the due attention with which they would wish to be treated, a total moral breakdown would follow; acts of giving or care would cease and it would be quite literally, "each man for himself" on a grand scale.

How dependent is the smooth moral functioning of society on the presence of Christian values? Even when people are not professing Christians, the Golden Rule, to treat others as one wants to be treated, has sufficiently permeated our culture through the social and cultural impact of Christianity, so it no longer depends on acts of service performed by practising Christians alone. This Golden Rule is present in the religious traditions of the world, but if schools are not to become moral blank slates, their moral foundations require connections to external reference points of authority. The Christian Bible provides, and has been the source of, such authority. By seeing morality through the prism of Christianity, the test as to whether our actions are moral is neither based on pragmatism nor the fluctuating whims of personal choice.

In contrast, when humanism acts as the foundation of moral messages in the school context, the moral authority supporting such ideas exists in a moral vacuum. The advocates of such messages can only appeal to themselves, the school's authority, or because "that's the best method humans have invented to live in cooperation". This inevitably implies an uneasy conclusion: if the universal moral standards by which we live are the result of social evolution, then belief in the existence of intrinsic goodness or intrinsic evil is a fallacy. By contrast, a Christian explanation for the "why" behind moral imperatives is found in the Bible's Judeo-Christian teachings: the origin of the moral law is found in the Creator, as the supreme law-giver.

What Does the Law Provide?

The law covering the Christian dimension of school assemblies is found mainly in two pieces of UK legislation, the Education Act of 1944 and the Education Reform Act of 1988. Human rights law relating to parental rights is also considered. The overview and critique offered should not be treated as exhaustive.

Education Act 1944

Sometimes known as the Butler Act, the 1944 Act was introduced by Rab Butler, then President of the Board of Education, in the wartime Churchill government. It was seen and is still considered a major legal landmark in the history of education. It replaced all previous education law. As Sir Michael Barber, former government education adviser and author of *The Making of the 1944 Education Act* has explained, the new law meant: "Anglicans and Catholics would be able to determine the nature of the school's daily act of worship."[26]

Regarding the requirement for an act of daily worship, section 25 (1) of the Act stipulates:

> The school day in every county[27] school and in every voluntary[28] school shall begin with collective worship on the part of all the pupils in attendance at the school, and the arrangements made therefor shall

provide for a single act of worship attended by all such pupils....

All schools in England are expected to comply with the law unless exempted from doing so.[29]

The Act never specified that the act of collective worship had to be "Christian". It may be thought this omission was testimony of the fact that Britain was confident enough of its national identity and there was no need to state what was all too plain. However, during the 1944 parliamentary debates, in response to the Bishop of Chichester's strong concerns about the Bill failing to stipulate that it was "Christian" worship (and "Christian" instruction)[30] with which the proposed Bill was concerned, the Earl of Selborne on behalf of the government, attempted to offer assurance, when he stated:

> that it is the intention of the Government and of the Bill that ... the corporate act of worship shall be an act of Christian worship ...[31]

The Earl of Selborne explained that the omission of the word "Christian" with regards to Christian "worship" (and "religious instruction")[32] was partly out of concern that legal action could follow in the courts over questions of what constituted the Christian faith.[33] The Bishop of Chichester's concerns over this omission arose partly from fears that Paganism, as a religion, held the potential to act effectively as a substitute for Christianity.[34]

The problem of "worship" taking on a character other than Christian was highlighted in Parliament in 1988 when the law was being reviewed (see below).

As part of the wider parliamentary debates of 1944, Lord Quickswood observed that it was "a time of great religious crisis" and issued grave warnings of how movements like Nazism and Fascism had "in one form or another" already "spread everywhere". He explained that such movements were characterised by a "widespread tendency to substitute the worship of man for the worship of God".[35] (In fact, two weeks later, the Bishop of Chichester warned of the paganism of "modern religion", at the heart of which is a "worship of the State", as illustrated by Nazi Germany.)[36]

Lord Quickswood was prophetic to contemplate a time when he feared hostility to Christianity from education ministers or local education authorities could be driven by what he believed was an already existing tendency to substitute man for God. He feared the proposed Bill failed to offer the necessary protection for the "religious life of the people" in the face of an anti-Christian "movement of opinion" in which a "conception of human perfection [was put] in place of the worship of God".[37]

The modern secular education system, having removed so much of the living expression of the Christian faith from the school ethos, certainly fulfils this prophecy. The humanistic principle of appealing to the wisdom of human 'perfection' now seems to sit at the heart of much of the education system, with its perilous promotion of sex as a leisure activity, freed from the boundaries of marital commitment and procreation. Put differently, humanism recognises the existence of no higher moral authority than that of man. It is not so much that divine moral authority is open to different and diverse meanings. Rather, humanism rejects the existence of a divine law-giver; it is man who creates codes of morality, according to perceived needs and changing preferences. To the extent that such morality is open to review and amendment over the course of time, as shaped by rapid shifts in public opinion, any such moral codes are built on the relativism that reflects the transience of human desires.

Viscount Samuel, who was Jewish and had served as Home Secretary and also as leader of the Liberal Party, articulated this view in the 1944 debates, when he warned:

> there can be no doubt that the troubles of the world are due more than to any other thing to the rebirth of paganism and to the absence of any agreed moral standards.[38]

Alongside the Christian dimension of the new legal order, the Act enshrined tolerance in our law so that parents, whether for religious or other reasons, could withdraw their children from collective Christian worship.[39]

Education Reform Act 1988
In 1944, when the Bishop of Chichester warned that "Governments and circumstances change"[40] – hence the need not to leave the law open to chance – he was far-sighted enough to contemplate a time when society might abandon Christianity. His foresight was to be validated when, in

1988, acts of worship in some schools were, according to Baroness Cox, being "transmuted into a multi-faith celebration of shared values."[41] This development was also said to have been commended by the government of the day.[42]

The 1988 Act clearly stipulates that the act of worship had to be "wholly or mainly of a broadly Christian character."[43] This means that it must reflect the "broad traditions of Christian belief without being distinctive of any particular Christian denomination."[44] This broad dimension was designed to safeguard against any one Christian tradition or denomination being accorded undue weight. It is in the school's discretion how "broadly Christian" is understood and applied.[45]

Section 6 (1) states that "all pupils in attendance at a maintained school shall on each school day take part in an act of collective worship." A distinction has been suggested between "corporate worship" and "collective worship" performed in schools. The former occurs within faith communities and is characterised by a "*body* of believers bound together by their shared commitment."[46] The latter involves a collection of individuals "representing diversity of beliefs. What they do when they come together for such worship is therefore subject to wide variation."[47]

We may add here several additional points. The pupils in question may or may not have yet formed their own religious beliefs. It should never be assumed that children are incapable of forming religious beliefs and an identity co-existing with such beliefs. Clearly, as children mature with age, we can rightly expect greater levels of autonomy.

It should be stated that there is an apparent tension between two realities. On the one hand the law requires pupils to take part in worship, while on the other we ought to recognise the personal freedom implicit in this experience. Two helpful analogies have been provided by Brenda Watson to illustrate how this apparent dichotomy need not be problematic. People attending a concert are provided the "opportunity to have a musical experience, but it does not ensure it, for the response remains individual and free; providing mathematics lessons opens up for pupils the possibility of their becoming mathematically literate, but it cannot guarantee it."[48]

Since any expression or act of Christian "worship" is, by its nature, voluntary, what can we make of the mandatory aspect of what the law requires? It has been argued that it is "important indeed to acknowledge that whether or not it is worship for any one person depends on their own free choice. The 1988 legislation did not make this clear enough." [49] Certainly, the law could have been better worded.

The most recent non-statutory guidance from the Department for Education on collective worship is Circular 1/94.[50] It states that in collective worship the aim should be to "provide the opportunity for pupils to worship God, to consider spiritual and moral issues and to explore their own beliefs", and, "encourage participation and response, whether through active involvement in the presentation of worship or through listening to and joining in the worship offered; and to develop community spirit, promote a common ethos and shared values, and reinforce positive attitudes."[51] This nuanced guidance is certainly an improvement on the wording of the legislation.

How did this 1988 legislation treat children from non-Christian families? The Act provided legal exemptions from collective Christian worship for some or all of the school pupils.[52] Schools are also able to holds acts of collective worship reflecting non-Christian religions.[53]

Human rights law

It is noteworthy that the 1944 and 1988 Acts recognised the crucial role of parents in the upbringing of their children, namely, when choices about religion or belief were at play. A guarantee of parental freedom was thus created, ensuring the cultural and/or religious life of the child's home not be in conflict with the religious ethos or practice upheld by a school.[54]

The parental freedoms provided by the 1944 Act were to evolve several years later into a broader legal principle of the parental right to choose a school whose religious or philosophical ethos aligns with their own beliefs. Article 2 of the Protocol to the Convention for the Protection of Human Rights and Fundamental Freedoms (signed in 1950), the *Right to Education*, states:

No person shall be denied the right to education. In the exercise of any functions which it assumes in relation to education and to teaching, the State shall respect the right of parents to ensure such education and teaching in conformity with their own religious and philosophical convictions.

The Convention, building on the 1948 UN Declaration of Human Rights, was drafted in response to the totalitarian regimes of Eastern Europe, but also in view of the horrific violations of human rights and abuses in political power that defined the Fascist and Nazi regimes. The Convention exists to promote, among other goals, human rights, the rule of law, freedom and democracy.

Article 2 was enshrined into the 1998 Human Rights Act.[55] So, when State authorities exercise their functions within the sphere of education, parental rights (choices) about the religious or philosophical education of their children must be respected by the State.

Is the requirement of collective Christian worship legally protected in any way by Article 2? In other words, if the State repealed the daily act of Christian worship, is there any conflict with the "respect" owed by the State to not breach parental rights, as contained in Article 2? Relevant here are those parents who would want their children to be able to continue participating in collective Christian worship at school.

The Article makes no mention of worship or specific religious practices but merely refers to "education and teaching" provided by schools, which parents can choose, so that it conforms to or reflects their own beliefs; or as the Article puts it, "their own religious and philosophical convictions". So the scope of Article 2 is adequately broad to cover the question of "worship" when it refers to the State's "exercise of any functions which it assumes in relation to education and to teaching." "Worship" already forms part of the spiritual and moral development of pupils, so there can be no doubt that this legal requirement clearly fits within the sphere of education covered by Article 2.

With the support of Article 2, combined with the "free school" reforms championed by Michael Gove, it is arguable that the State would be unable or at least open to legal challenge in preventing schools from offering collective Christian worship. Such provision would be a test of both "free schools" and parental rights being respected by State authorities.

Is Legal Reform Needed?
Two non-government reports, addressing legal questions pertaining to the Christian dimension of assemblies, deserve special mention.

In *A New Settlement: Religion and Belief in Schools*,[56] the authors recommend the abolition of the requirement for an act of collective Christian worship in school, and that decisions about the "form and character" of assemblies should be left to school governors.[57]

The report was jointly written by Charles Clarke, former Education Secretary (2002–2004) and Linda Woodhead, a Professor of Sociology of Religion, with input from, among others, Andrew Copson, Chief Executive of the British Humanist Association. The recommendation for abolition is said to be "formed on the basis of relevant recent research".[58] Part of the evidence is to cite trends, suggesting the national Christian demographic is in decline.[59] But whatever is made of such trends, the "Christian" demographic is still the largest. It therefore seems there is no compelling reason, other than a dislike of, or hostility to, Christianity, to use and/or interpret such apparent evidence as a basis for removing the Christian ethos of schools. The authors state:

> ... issues around the place of religion in schools are not going away. Indeed they are rising up the political and educational agenda as it becomes clear that the way in which religion is being dealt with in schools is not meeting the needs of our time."[60]

Such belief about the "needs" of pupils not being met is too wide sweeping and presumes superficially that the place of Christianity in schools – including acts of Christian worship – provides no benefits in helping to develop and promote the "spiritual" aspects of their potential. It also leads to a situation where, were the Christian faith element of education to be removed entirely, nothing concrete is proposed to replace the "spiritual" component of education.

The report did propose that schools would need a strategy for promoting the spiritual, moral, social and cultural aspects, where "school community assemblies" would form an "important part of that strategy".[61] Yet the question remains: in addition to RE, how is the "spiritual" development of pupils to be promoted?[62]

The report asserts somewhat vaguely the need for a "healthy and up-to-date framework which reflects modern religious and educational life and practices."[63] As to what specific "modern" practices will replace the status quo, we are not told.

A proposal for a daily "period of reflection" is suggested, though it is stressed how this would "stimulate significant debate with difficulties of definition and interpretation in practice".[64] The report recommends leaving decisions about assembly to school governors and stresses how national demographic trends show how Christianity holds less influence, alongside the growing emergence of other groups (religious and non-religious). It then uses the data of this pluralist demographic to argue for the Christian assembly to be replaced with content reflecting a framework of "modern religious and educational life and practices". This unclear notion suggests an appeal would at the least be made to religious content from other faiths that make up the nation's minorities. But we are left without any clues about how this "modern" framework would satisfy the spiritual development of pupils.

Four legal options are examined in the report.[65]

First, to maintain the current law, guidance and formal arrangements, but to "treat it as a dead letter", because it is "effectively unenforced and probably unenforceable". It is further claimed that to maintain the current legal requirement for an act of worship will do nothing to alter the national demographic decline in religious practice. This attitude of resignation can only help lead to a self-fulfilling prophecy and to reinforce further the apparent status quo of decline in religious practice.

Second, to maintain the current law, guidance and formal arrangements and to "force" schools to abide by the law, which would "highlight clashes of conscience and belief". The authors are concerned at the damaging effect this would have on some schools. The problem with this straw man argument is that no school teacher or head, for the purposes of a Christian assembly, should ever feel obliged or compelled to act in a way that contravenes their beliefs and conscience. It is already an established practice in many schools to recruit external ministers to oversee acts of Christian worship, so ultimately it does not depend on the religious beliefs of the staff. This "outsourcing" seems to be the best and most workable solution that resolves both conscience issues and potential staff shortages within schools.

Third, a statutory requirement should be maintained for "some form of assembly which would promote spiritual, moral, social and cultural development".

Fourth, the current legal requirement for an act of Christian worship should be abolished, with the issue left to governors and school heads to decide what is "appropriate for the particular circumstances of their own school, subject to non-statutory government guidance and inspection by Ofsted".

Clarke and Woodhead consider the best choice lies between the third and fourth options, though they ultimately favour option four, complete abolition.

Another report, *Living With Difference: Community, Diversity and the Common Good*[66] was produced by the Commission on Religion and Belief in British Public Life.[67] It was chaired by Baroness Butler-Sloss, former President of the Family Division of the High Court of England and Wales; its Patrons included Sir Iqbal Sacranie, formerly Secretary General of the Muslim Council of Britain; Lord Williams, former Archbishop of Canterbury; Lord Woolf, formerly Lord Chief Justice of England and Wales; and Professor Lord Parekh, Emeritus Professor of Political Philosophy. The twenty-member group of commissioners included Andrew Copson of the British Humanist Association and Lord Harries, former Bishop of Oxford.

It recommends the repeal of the legal requirement to hold acts of collective Christian worship and calls for the Westminster Government and devolved administrations across the UK, to issue:

> ... new guidelines building on current best practice for inclusive assemblies and times for reflection that draw upon a range of sources, that are appropriate for pupils and staff of all religions and beliefs, and that will contribute to their spiritual, moral, social and cultural development."[68]

What seems inevitable is that "inclusive assemblies and times for reflection that draw upon a range of sources" would generate a controversial assortment of ideas. As (rightly) feared by the Clarke and Woodhead report, the controversies flowing from changes in this area of the law, "tend to generate far more heat than light and can be quite divisive".[69]

The Butler-Sloss Commission applauded a joint initiative in Scotland between the Humanist Society Scotland and the Church of Scotland to work together for an inclusive "time for reflection". The Commission saw this arrangement as exemplary for all of the UK and, "would build on the good practice of holding inclusive assemblies that already exists in many schools but remains technically unlawful".[70]

Two points stand out as particularly striking. First, the unlawful practice of "inclusive" assemblies is being commended. Second, the vague and ill-defined recommendation of "inclusive" times for reflection is problematic. It seems to have the potential for an indiscriminate and piecemeal mix of religious and other references (note the "range of sources" stated by the report).

It should be clarified here that we are not talking about "religious education" in which pupils are being educated in their knowledge and understanding of the world religions; this is already covered by RE as an academic subject. Instead, the occasion is the school assembly and the proposal is to urge pupils to "reflect" in an "inclusive" manner in relation, it seems, to a variety of religious beliefs and ideas. In which way does this free-floating nexus of references serve to "promote" the spiritual development of pupils? The report provides no obvious answers of its own, but the idea seems to be that in merely reflecting on the inspiring ideas drawn from the religious and humanist beliefs of the world, the spiritual needs of pupils will be served.

Conclusion

The law on collective worship provides opportunities for pupils to be introduced to an experience of Christian worship, whether this involves hymns, reflections on Bible messages or the saying of prayers. These spiritual resources have provided generations of school children with personal support they can depend on for the rest of their lives. This relevance exists alongside the pertinent moral messages conveyed at Christian assemblies which form part of the spiritual, moral, social and cultural development of pupils.

The Christian message of self-sacrificial love for others and devotion to God serves to develop attitudes of moral responsibility and service to others, all of which facilitates integration into society, a clear antidote to extremism.

The majority Christian affiliation of England and Wales still adequately merits keeping the legal requirement of Christian worship in schools.

Therefore, in view of these many benefits, the proposals to abolish the Christian assembly are considered a regressive step. Furthermore, the idea of "inclusive" assemblies is vague, ill-conceived and demonstrates nothing that meets the spiritual needs of pupils.

The recruitment of ministers from outside the school to oversee worship resolves those concerns over possible clashes of belief and conscience of teaching staff. Parents hold the right of withdrawal; this continuing provision guarantees tolerance of families who hold a religious or philosophical ethos other than Christian.

Notes

[1] This is known in Scotland as "religious observance".

[2] http://www.secularism.org.uk/secularcharter.html (Accessed 14 March 2016)

[3] One goal of the Charter contemplates a future when: "Religion plays no role in State-funded education, whether through religious affiliation of schools, curriculum setting, organised worship, religious instruction, pupil selection or employment practices." For religion to play no part in employment practices, this would mean, among other things, churches not being permitted to recruit staff on the basis of belief and practice. (www.secularism.org.uk/secularcharter.html). Although not stated in the Charter, the ultimate logical goal would be to abolish private religious schools because they too, would violate the humanist goal of creating a society based on reason, which in humanism stands in sharp opposition to the "superstition" of religion.

[4] The Charter states: "The State does not engage in, fund or promote religious activities or practices."

[5] The Charter campaigns for a secular State where the State "does not express religious beliefs or preferences". As part of its campaign to promote LGBT issues, all dissenting voices (in education, employment, social and all printed media etc.) in support of family life premised on heterosexuality are automatically treated as falling foul of equality, labelled as hate speech; the goal is to have the State criminalise free speech in this area.

[6] See the "What we do" section of its website: www.humanism.org.uk/about/ (accessed 14 March 2016)

[7] See the BHA briefing, "Ideas for Inclusive Assemblies" described as "Resources for education".
http://humanismforschools.org.uk/guidance/inclusive-assemblies/ (Accessed 14 March 2016)

[8] It seems "spiritual" is being treated in a subjective and vague manner to include any type of story or object of reflection that has the potential to inspire.

[9] "David Cameron declares: 'Britain is still a Christian country'," *Daily Telegraph*, 5 April 2015; Eric Pickles, Community Secretary, "Britain still a Christian nation – get over it", *Guardian*, 6 April 2014; Nicky Morgan, as Education Secretary, stated the "fact that the religious traditions in Great Britain are, in the main, Christian while taking account of the teaching and practices of the other principal religions represented in Great Britain." "Faith groups back move to protect religious education freedom", Department for Education, 28 December 2015. Her words mirror what is stated in the Education Reform Act 1988; see section 8 (3).

[10] See the *Daily Telegraph* Letter signed by more than fifty high profile signatories (20 April 2014).

[11] "Faith Schools are divisive. Let's get rid of them", Alice Thompson, *The Times*, 6 June 2014, p. 25; "Atheists and Anglicans could unite against intolerance," Matt Ridley, *The Times*, 24 July 2014. Ridley is a Peer and Patron of the British Humanist Association (one of twenty parliamentarians). He advocates the abolition of faith schools and describes Anglicanism as a "mild and attenuated form of the faith virus." As to the ultimate goal, he wrote: "rationalists no longer expect to get rid of religion altogether by explaining life and matter: they aim only to tame it instead, and to protect children from it." His words offer a clear hint of the humanist endgame that seeks to "protect" children raised

on religious faith in the home; his openness brings to light what is less commonly said in public by humanists. Even the Butler-Sloss Commission (considered below) proposed to shift to the margins the very existence of faith schools, when it recommended that UK governments should "expect publicly funded schools to be open for the provision of religion- or belief-specific teaching and worship on the school premises outside of the timetable for those who request it and wish to participate; this would be in line with the autonomy of young people and their human right to freedom of religion or belief." (p. 38) This somewhat convolutedly worded proposal effectively commends the abolition of publicly-funded faith schools, with the provision for children to take part in what it describes as religion or "belief-specific teaching and worship" on school premises, but outside of school hours. This rationale is premised on the idea that the parental right to choose for their children the religious ethos in which they are educated must be removed. It also removes the authority and primary guardianship parents hold over their children, and thereby reconstitutes one aspect of the traditional family model.

[12] Jewish schools, too, have been placed under the critical spotlight of Ofsted inquiries.

[13] Matthew 22:37–39.

[14] Luke 11:4.

[15] This should work alongside the teaching of the world religions, an essential subject in any education.

[16] See the discussion in the Report of the Commission on Religion and Belief in British Public Life (chapter 2). This report is considered further below.

[17] HL Debates, Christian Teaching in Schools, 26 February 1988, Vol 493, col 1455.

[18] The practice of the Christian faith is expressed by people at differing levels of commitment and so it would be problematic to designate a test of religious practice. One measurement might, it seems, be based on self-reporting so that people are asked whether they are "practising". But again, we would be left with the question of whether the subjectivity of such reports sufficiently satisfies what it means to "practise". On this finer question, there appears to be no data. It is also unclear who would be qualified to draw up such a test to decide what factors would require inclusion and exclusion.

[19] In the 1944 Education Act, local education authorities were permitted to waive the requirement of the entire school meeting together for worship, if they believed limits to school space made a collective gathering impracticable (section 25 (1)). The Education Reform Act 1988 enacted further change which still applies: acts of collective worship are now either done for all of the school pupils assembled, or for pupils in different age groups or according to "different school groups"; see section 6 (2).

[20] HL Debates, 21 June 1944, vol 132, cc 349-350, Lord Quickswood in Committee Stage.

[21] HL Debates, Christian Teaching in Schools, 26 February 1988, vol 493, cc 1455-1456.

[22] This seems to be a weighty argument, showing how that in retaining the current law, it is not only about transmitting the Christian heritage of this country; this argument could suggest nostalgia or sentimentality for the nation's past. Rather, it is about offering life-enhancing and life-giving resource opportunities to pupils, which have stood the test of time for generations past.

[23] HL Debates, Christian Teaching in Schools, 26 February 1988, vol 493, cc 1455-1456.

[24] Official Report, 18 May 1977, col 713.

[25] The Education Reform Act 1988 (section 1) made it a duty on the Secretary of State for Education, schools and LEAs to exercise their functions (as regards religious education, religious worship and the National Curriculum) in a way that promotes the

"spiritual, moral, cultural, mental and physical development of pupils". In 1992, when Ofsted, the national school inspectorate, was established by the Education (Schools) Act, it became a requirement that HM Inspector of Schools (a newly created post) had to be "informed of the spiritual, moral, social and cultural development of pupils." See section 2 (d). See also the Education Act 1993, section 259. Religious worship in schools of a religious character must be inspected by Ofsted; (Education Act 2005, section 48). See Ofsted's "Inspecting Faith Schools: Briefing for Section 5 Inspection", Reference no: 100142, April 2014.

[26] See his summary article, "Rab Butler's 1944 Act brings free secondary education for all", 17 January 2014. www.bbc.co.uk/schoolreport/25751787.

[27] County schools are now known as "community" schools.

[28] Voluntary schools are now known as "faith" schools.

[29] For details see Circular 1/94, Department of Education, pp 22-25 (1994). For Wales, see Circular 10/94, Welsh Office Education Department (1994).

[30] 'Religious instruction', then a feature of education law but distinct from 'religious worship', was later replaced by the now familiar "religious education" (RE).

[31] Education Bill, Committee of the House, HL Debates, 21 June 1944, vol 132, col 366.

[32] See section 25 (2).

[33] HL Debates, 21 June 1944, vol 132, col 367.

[34] HL Debates, 21 June 1944, vol 132, col 362.

[35] HL Debates, 6 June 1944, vol 132, col 66.

[36] HL Debates, 21 June 1944, vol 132, col 362.

[37] Read Lord Quickswood's full range of arguments (HL Debates, 6 June 1944, vol 132, cc 59-67).

[38] He went on to illustrate his argument by seeing politics and economics as "means only, and not ends; they have to have their ends set for them by the moral law, and in our European civilization it is the ideas embodied in the Christian ethic which can alone supply that moral law. It is right, therefore, that the system of British education, subject to due provision for conscientious objection [parental right of withdrawal], should give full recognition to that fact and effective application to that principle." HL Debates, 6 June 1944, vol 132, col 28.

[39] See section 25 (4). The Earl of Selborne acknowledged during the Committee stage "that where there is a large number of Jewish children a syllabus based on the Old Testament only should be prepared for them, and they should be given the opportunity of Jewish worship..." HL Debates, 21 June 1944, vol 132, col 366. This same right is now found in the Education Reform Act 1988, section 9 (3).

[40] HL Debates, 21 June 1944, vol 132, col 363.

[41] HL Debates, 16 May 1988, vol 497, col 12.

[42] Ibid.

[43] Section 7 (1).

[44] Section 7 (2).

[45] See the Department of Education, Circular 1/94, especially para. 63.

[46] Cited by Brenda Watson, *The Effective Teaching of Religious Education* (Longman: London, 1993) p. 159. Emphasis original.

[47] Ibid.

[48] Ibid.

[49] Ibid.

[50] *Religious Education and Collective Worship* (1994). www.gov.uk/government/uploads/system/uploads/attachment_data/file/281929/Collective_worship_in_schools.pdf (Accessed 14 March 2016).

[51] Para. 50.

[52] See sections 7 (6) and 12.

[53] Section 7 (6) (b). See also circular 1/94, especially paragraphs 77-80.

[54] A complicating factor is how there is the potential for the rights of children, as opposed to parents, to be given primary consideration. Consider the UN Convention on the Rights of the Child: "States Parties shall assure to the child who is capable of forming his or her own views the right to express those views freely in all matters affecting the child, the views of the child being given due weight in accordance with the age and maturity of the child." (Article 12) Sixth form pupils can already excuse themselves from collective worship; see the Education and Inspections Act 2006, section 55.

[55] Part II, The First Protocol.

[56] The pamphlet (published June 2015) "arises from the research and debate carried out by the Westminster Faith Debates and the Religion and Society Research Programme." p. 5. The debates were funded by the Arts and Humanities Research Council, the Economic and Social Research Council and Lancaster University. www.faithdebates.org.uk

[57] p. 27.

[58] p. 63.

[59] While acknowledging the 2011 Census figure that identifies 59% of England and Wales as "Christian", the authors place great weight on research suggesting that these shifts towards "greater religious diversity" and "a higher proportion of religiously unaffiliated people, are likely to continue." p.16.

[60] p. 7.

[61] pp. 63-64.

[62] Treating religion academically (rather than spiritually) already forms part of the basic curriculum. As the publication points out, one of the reasons RE did not form part of the National Curriculum, when it was introduced by the Education Act 1988, was out of concern that the right of withdrawal from RE, enshrined by the 1944 Education Act, ought not to apply to any aspect of the National Curriculum. (pp 12-13).

[63] p. 22.

[64] p. 25.

[65] See section 4, pp. 20-27.

[66] It was funded by, among others, the Joseph Rowntree Charitable Trust and the Open Society Foundation. Published by the Woolf Institute, Cambridge, 7 December 2015.

[67] The Commission was convened by the Woolf Institute in 2013 and, "promotes the multidisciplinary study of relationships between Christians, Jews and Muslims." The Commission's purpose is, "to consider the place and role of religion and belief in contemporary Britain, to consider the significance of emerging trends and identities, and to make recommendations for public life and policy. Its premise is that in a rapidly changing diverse society everyone is affected, whatever their private views on religion and belief, by how public policy and public institutions respond to social change." p.6.

[68] p. 37.

[69] p. 25.

[70] p. 34.

Chapter Nine

HUMAN RIGHTS: THE RISE OF THE ALL POWERFUL STATE?

Edmund Matyjaszek

It is one of the ironies of the present day that legislation that emerged from the most terrible war in the history of the last century – legislation designed to prevent repetition of the persecution of a race or minority – should now trouble so many with its unforeseen propensity to stifle one of the basic freedoms that war was fought to defend – freedom of speech.

The most ironic aspect is that increasingly – in employment, in education, in public pronouncements – it is the expression of Christian belief that is in danger of being criminalised. Recent examples include: where Christian belief is held to be "divisive" (House of Lords, February 2016);[1] where emphasis on teaching of Christianity in a Christian Free School is held not to "prepare (students) well for life in modern Britain" (Ofsted Report Durham Free School January 19th 2015);[2] where according to a Head of Safeguarding at a College in 2015, belief is fine but "if you speak out loud you might be breaking the law"[3] and where the expression of opinion among colleagues regarding the value of mother and father parents over same-sex parents by a magistrate led to his being reprimanded and recommended for "equality training" and now removed from the bench by the Minister for Justice.[4]

This is by no stretch of the imagination at the same level as the worldwide persecution of Christians, now acknowledged the most persecuted faith in the world today (Pew Research Centre report 2015);[5] nor what the EU and the US Congress among other bodies now call "genocide" by ISIS in Syria/Iraq in the Middle East. It does however share a common element – it is Christians and Christian belief that is now subject almost without comment to public opprobrium and condemnation.

How has this situation arisen, where what is still formally the established religion of the state can make those who espouse its tenets subject to legal penalties? And what happened not just to freedom of speech but freedom of worship – what President Roosevelt in a speech of 1941 called "The Four Freedoms", which we will revisit shortly – "the freedom of every person to worship God in his own way, everywhere in the world."[6]

It is a curious state of affairs. But the steps are clear if seen through the long lens of history – and the resolution equally at hand. The issue has arisen in legal form in the UK as a result of the 2010 Equality Act and its creation of a new legal protection – not just of the person but of "characteristics". This is new in English Law. The roots of the original protection of the person lie deep in English Law and Constitutional Development. Essentially it is a long and noble tale of the assertion of the rights of the individual against arbitrary power. The successful defence of this against its most serious onslaught in modern times by the Nazi tyranny led to its codification by the victorious allies in 1948, in what became the Universal Declaration of Human Rights. This led to subsequent legislation round the world. In the UK in particular, with the Human Rights Act of 1998 and the amalgamation and compositing of post-war legislation on different "minority" or sectional rights into the Equality Act of 2010, this process took a very definite form. But the clear and unambiguous definition of Universal Human Rights in 1948 began to be merged with a "historicist" or "sociological" view of "minorities" oppressed by social development. Inspired in many ways by the struggle of colonies after the war to liberate themselves from control by imperial powers such as Britain, France and the Netherlands, the "liberation" of these groups became the pressing task of all "progressive" governments. This has led to the current situation where it is no longer the individual alone who is protected, but the group he or she belongs to, and the "characteristics" of that group. The consequence is that any examination of these "characteristics" that does not accord to them the inviolate status accorded to the person, brings the opprobrium of the law.

Everyone is equal, but Equality Act "protected characteristics" have, in the words of the Statutory Instrument enforcing the active promotion of British Values in schools in September 2014,[7] to be shown "particular regard". All men are equal, but "protected characteristics" are more equal than others. This creation of a hierarchy of "rights" is the very nub of the problem we now face and is in direct contradiction to the universality of the original "Human Rights". Where this confusion arose; how it evolved; and what its implications and dangers are is the subject of this chapter.

Dieu et Mon Droit – the roots of human rights

England – and I will be examining in particular English legal development of the idea and rights of the person – has a very particular history in this regard. The origin and guiding light of all Western human rights is the concept of the person. This is founded on the biblical view we encounter in the Book of Genesis: that all persons are created in the image of God, believers being redeemed by Christ, as expounded by St Paul: "There is neither Jew nor Greek, there is neither bond nor free, there is neither male nor female: for ye are all one in Christ Jesus."[8] This gave dignity to each individual. It is inherent in the very incarnation of Christ, which identifies Jesus as *both* human, born of a Galilean Jewish mother called Mary, *and* divine – the Son of God. This claim marks out Christianity from all other religions, whether they have deities or not, as well as its fellow "religions of the book" Judaism and Islam, in that it attributes a unique and divine status to Jesus. In turn, his "taking flesh" accords to the human person, already made in the image of God, an extraordinary dignity.

The theology of this need not trouble us; it is the juridical consequence of the status of the human person that flows from it. England is an unusual country in its formation. The "English", the product of invasions by Angles, Saxons and Jutes that occurred in the main in the 5th and 6th centuries, saw themselves as separate from the Britons, Celts, and Romans, as well as from later Viking invaders in the 8th and 9th centuries. But an often overlooked aspect of this is that from the 7th century, long before the country was subsequently united as a political entity by the descendants of King Alfred in the 9th and 10th centuries, it was already being governed as a single entity for religious purposes.

It was a spiritual kingdom before it became a physical one.

This came as a result of the processes of conversion of the "rude" English by a roughly twin process from North and South composed of Irish/Celtic missionaries based at Iona and then Lindisfarne; and the advent of Roman missionaries (sent by Pope Gregory the Great), who landed in Thanet in Kent in 597.

There were two crucial meetings or conferences ("synods", from the Greek, meaning "brought together"). The first was in Whitby in 664 and made the Roman pattern of Easter and of Church governance (parishes, bishops, pope) run throughout the lands of the English, comprising the seven kingdoms known as the heptarchy: Wessex, Sussex, Kent, Essex, East Anglia, Mercia, Northumbria (roughly contiguous, if one adds modern Cornwall and the Isle of Wight, with England to this day). But it was the second and lesser known Synod at Hertford in 673 that created the first "English institution", by bringing bishops from these heptarchy kingdoms, either in person or by proxy, to agree a common set of canons or rules for the church. This meant quite simply that through the kingdoms of the "English" the same writ of church governance, church law, liturgical practice, language and sacramental dispensation ran irrespective of political or regional power.

As F W Stenton writes in the classic *Oxford History of England*, [9]

> Collectively these canons … were put out by a body which represented the entire church of the English peoples … the whole English church acknowledged a single archbishop and was capable of united action. The synod of Hertford was the first occasion on which that unity found practical expression.

In effect England was an ecclesial entity before it became a physical kingdom. It existed as a spiritual reality before it had any governmental or administrative existence. Not enough examination of the importance or effect of this has been carried out. But that is not the concern of this chapter. The critical thing is that from the beginning of the English "kingdoms" that became the kingdom of "England" – Offa, a full century later king of Mercia, was the first to refer to himself as *Rex Anglorum* or King of the English, and it awaited the 10th century before the term "England" became a recognised and repeated juridical and documented expression – their shared and common spiritual identity was intact and has remained so.

The law, learning, and liturgy of the church were there from the beginning, from the 7th century. It was in this context that English Law developed. The recognition of the unique and inviolate status of the human person as seen in the Bible was the bedrock of all English Law on the "person". That legal understanding of the status of the person is crucial to the development of later Human Rights Law.

In fact, historically, there were only two "subjects" of English law: person or property. Ideas or practices were never given an equivalent legal status. It is the recent and novel attribution of quasi-legal existence to "characteristics" of a group that is at the root of the current problems of Human Rights Law. But that is to leap ahead.

From the point of view of human rights, the Christian concept of the human person was the central juridical fact. A child of God, endowed with rights and dignities, and able to be saved by the sacrifice of Christ the Son of God and therefore due respect from his or her fellow human beings. This is still today the view of the person under Human Rights Law. As we shall shortly see, it was in defence of this idea of the person or individual that the Allies fought World War II, and in that same spirit founded the United Nations that first codified Human Rights.

The formation of the constitutional means of conducting government and administration with this concept or idea is, of course, the story in many ways of English History. The words used at various times are critical to illuminate this central point. The first major point where it becomes a settled term of the law of the land, and is still on our statute books, is in Magna Carta in 1215.

No Freeman shall be taken or imprisoned, or be disseised of his Freehold, or Liberties, or free Customs, or be outlawed, or exiled, or any other wise destroyed; nor will We condemn him, but by lawful judgment of his Peers, or by the Law of the land. We will sell to no man, we will not deny or defer to any man either Justice or Right.[10]

The evolution and extension of the franchise in Parliament, from Bishop and noble to knight, to "burgher", to merchant, to property holder, to individual, and finally to women as well as men in later times, is a familiar story. But it all flows from this one central idea – the inviolate dignity of the human person as a child of God.

The clash of this idea with temporal power has of course illuminated English History as no other. The internal battle to establish individual rights, traceable from Magna Carta through the Civil War to the Chartists and the Suffragettes, is mirrored externally in defence of the realm against foreign aggressors, whether Spanish, French, German or whatever. The idea has remained the same: the individual – be it person or country – can and should govern him or herself and consent to governance only by act of will and free compliance – never forced and never suborned.

As early as the 15th century, for instance in the work of Sir John Fortescue, Chief Justice of the King's Bench of England and author of *De laudibus legum Angliæ (Commendation of the Laws of England)*,[11] the concept of a Limited and not Absolute Monarchy and the role of the Common Law, was being explored. His writings became enormously influential, and formed much of early "constitutional" thinking. The clash between king and government found its formative expression in the Civil War of the 17th century and the triumph of Parliament. This of course was in contradistinction to the developing absolute monarchies of Europe – seen in Charles V, Louis XIII, and the Tsars of Russia – and gave the English such a strong sense of identity. This issue of free consent of the governed is the central issue of English History and has given rise to that most characteristic of English institutions, Parliament. It is of course the central issue of Christian scripture, from the fatal choice made in the Garden of Eden to the injunction in Deuteronomy 30:19, "I have set before you life or death; therefore choose...."[12]

This freedom to choose could well be at the root of the ancient term by which England was known – the *"Dowry of Mary"* – first encountered in documentary form in Richard II's reign in 1399.[13] Deriving from the Latin "dos" meaning "gift", it denotes a legal concept for the portion of land or estate set apart for a woman's – usually a widow's – use alone. Dower house comes from the same term. (What we know now as the "dowry" of a bride is a later, though allied, development.) The underlying idea is that England is set apart as the special domain of the mother of Jesus. This has direct associations with the ancient and now revived pilgrimage site of Walsingham (it is the Annunciation or Angel's greeting to which Mary gave her consent that is particularly honoured there). Fifteenth century documents about Walsingham speak of England as:

> To be called in every realme and regyon
> The holy lande, Oure Ladyes dowre [14]

If the maid of Nazareth had the right to choose whether or not to respond to the invitation of the angel, then there would be complete consonance in that kingdom, seen in ancient tradition as "belonging" to her, as being the place that above all others upholds the freedom of the individual and the right to choose. Unproveable, but an indication of the spiritual reality underlying England's history and, perhaps, purpose.

Whatever one's assessment, it is undeniable that throughout English Constitutional development this concept of the dignity of the human person is crucial, and was then "exported" from these shores to America. It is interesting that the Pilgrim Fathers of 1620 were fleeing religious persecution and tyranny in search of another land where they could practise their religion without fear. In many ways Christians in present day England feel subject to similar repression, with increasing restriction of freedom of expression, so that there is an unhappy contemporary echo and parallel with the Pilgrim Fathers of old.

These were the founding principles of the idea of the "person" in English Law, revolving around the central idea of choice, of the exercise of the human will, of the freedom to choose. It is now vital to turn and examine the evidence for this in documentary and legal form, and how it led, after World War II, to the UDHR of 1948.

A new world

On the twin pillars of English Constitutional development and American republican independence (itself a product of the search for freedom by initially the Pilgrim and then the Founding Fathers) are to be found the antecedents of modern Human Rights Law, together with the later developments of the French Revolution and the "Rights of Man".

The Bill of Rights is the first full formulation of this. It was passed on 16 December 1689. It also sets out — or, in the view of its drafters, restates — certain constitutional requirements of the Crown to seek the consent of the people, as represented in Parliament.

This Bill of Rights, along with Magna Carta 1215, the Petition of Right 1628, the Habeas Corpus Act 1679 and the Parliament Acts 1911 and 1949, are deemed as some of the basic documents of the uncodified British constitution. The Bill of Rights 1689 was one of the inspirations for the United States Bill of Rights.

In America however, the matter took on, with its written constitution, a more formal and explicit nature, as stated in the American Declaration of Independence, drafted by Thomas Jefferson:

IN CONGRESS, July 4, 1776

The unanimous Declaration of the thirteen united States of America,

When in the Course of human events, it becomes necessary for one people to dissolve the political bands which have connected them with another, and to assume among the powers of the earth, the separate and equal station to which the Laws of Nature and of Nature's God entitle them, a decent respect to the opinions of mankind requires that they should declare the causes which impel them to the separation.

We hold these truths to be self-evident, that all men are created equal, that they are endowed by their Creator with certain unalienable Rights, that among these are Life, Liberty and the pursuit of Happiness....[15]

This then played out in very significant measure throughout the 19th and 20th centuries, particularly in the arena of race and slavery, and increasingly in the rights of women.

I want to focus in particular on one area of campaigning and legislation: the abolition of slavery, as this shows the intimate link between the equality of all in Christ as earlier scripture quotations show, and the nature of the statement "All men are created equal."[16]

The original impetus for the abolition of slavery came from Pennsylvania Quakers; and then from English Christians, in particular Thomas Clarkson. William Wilberforce, an evangelical convert, was recruited as the Parliamentary "agent" for the Abolition of the Slave Trade Society, whose first Chairman was Granville Sharp, an Anglican who was deeply affected by an encounter with a runaway young slave in London's docklands, who came to the surgery of Sharp's brother, a doctor, having been pistol-whipped by his slave master. It was Sharpe's tireless efforts in case after case in the English Courts that led to the Lord Mansfield judgment of 1772, that established slavery had no place in English Law. All this stemmed entirely from their Christian convictions.

This was emphasised by another key figure in this story: Abraham Lincoln, whose second inauguration speech in March 1865 left no doubt as to its Christian content and inspiration.

> The Almighty has His own purposes. "Woe unto the world because of offenses; for it must needs be that offenses come, but woe to that man by whom the offense cometh." If we shall suppose that American slavery is one of those offenses which, in the providence of God, must needs come, but which, having continued through His appointed time, He now wills to remove, and that He gives to both North and South this terrible war as the woe due to those by whom the offense came, shall we discern therein any departure from those divine attributes which the believers in a living God always ascribe to Him? Fondly do we hope, fervently do we pray, that this mighty scourge of war may speedily pass away. Yet, if God wills that it continue until all the wealth piled by the bondsman's two hundred and fifty years of unrequited toil shall be sunk, and until every drop of blood drawn with the lash shall be paid by another drawn with the sword, as was said three thousand years ago, so still it must be said "the judgments of the Lord are true and righteous altogether."
>
> With malice toward none, with charity for all, with firmness in the right as God gives us to see the right, let us strive on to finish the work we are in, to bind up the nation's wounds, to care for him who shall have borne the battle and for his widow and his orphan....[17]

The references or quotations range widely over scripture, and encompass among others the books of Genesis, Psalms, Matthew, Luke and the Letter of St James.

In the later Civil Rights movement this inspiration continued. To listen to, or read, the words of Rev Martin Luther King, a Baptist Minister, is to hear again this echo of the fundamental concept of what, for lack of a better phrase, can be called the English-speaking view of what a human being is: a child of God of infinite and absolute worth and not able to be subject to the will of any, other than his creator, without derogation and damage to his or her being or dignity.

Nowhere is this clearer than in his famous speech in 1963 to the 250,000 who "Marched on Washington".[18]

> "So even though we face the difficulties of today and tomorrow I still have a dream. It is a dream deeply rooted in the American dream.
>
> I have a dream that one day this nation will rise up and live out the true meaning of its creed: 'We hold these truths to be self-evident; that all men are created equal.'
>
> I have a dream that one day on the red hills of Georgia the sons of former slaves and the sons of former slave owners will be able to sit together at the table of brotherhood.
>
> And when this happens, when we allow freedom to ring, when we let it ring from every village and hamlet, from every state and every city, we will be able to speed up that day when all of God's children, black men and white men, Jews and Gentiles, Protestants and Catholics, will be able to join hands and sing in the words of the old Negro spiritual, 'Free at last! Free at last! Thank God almighty, we're free at last!'"

Psalms, Isaiah, Amos are among the many sources for quotes or references. Martin Luther King takes his place with Jefferson and Lincoln as those who both mould and embody the spirit of American democracy and freedom.

The survival of Christian civilisation

We have slightly leapt ahead in our narrative, but the above sets the scene and spirit for what then became the specific historical context that gave rise to codified laws of Human Rights, set down most explicitly in the UDHR of 1948. What framed and formed this was the cataclysm of World War II.

In January 1933 Hitler came to power as Chancellor in Germany. In March of the same year a new President of the United States was sworn in, and in his inauguration speech spoke very clearly in similar biblical tones:

So, first of all, let me assert my firm belief that the only thing we have to fear is ... fear itself.

The money changers have fled from their high seats in the temple of our civilization. We may now restore that temple to the ancient truths.[19]

It has been noted by many historians that the Nazis represented something more than just a political party, one example of which is the Cambridge University Press *History of Germany* that drew explicitly on Naval Intelligence reports of the Admiralty during World War II. It described the Nazi party as:

... a great movement of the mind and soul of the German people, and not merely a new political party amongst many rival parties. It sought to transcend all the deep divisions of tribe and class, of religious and political creeds, amongst Germans, and to unite them in fanatical trust both in the mission and future of their country and in the God-given infallible personality of the leader, Hitler.[20]

More recent authorities, for instance Michael Burleigh in his book, *The Third Reich, A New History*, published in 2000, expands on this, describing,

... these political movements (Fascism, Nazism, Communism) as by-products of an absence of religion ...where ideologies akin to Christian heresies of redemption in the here and now had fused with post-Enlightenment doctrines of social transformation. Political religions were emphatically "this worldly", partly to distinguish them from a supposedly obsolescent Christianity, whose values they sought to replace...[21]

It was clear then in the framework of World War II, which gave rise to our modern Human Rights legislation, that the contest was one between competing ideologies or world views. The insights of Burleigh and other historians into the essentially non-material appeal of the tyrannies and tyrants of the 20th century invites the question: what was opposed to them? This brings us straight to the two leaders of what, post war, came to be known as the "Free World". It is hard now to understand the degree to which political debate in the first half of the 20th century was conducted in remorselessly economic terms – capitalism versus communism – and yet the language in which the war was fought on both sides was framed in spiritual and religious terms. But when one looks back at the formative influences of the "West's" views of freedom, particularly in England and America, and at the language of the leaders – Churchill and Roosevelt – in wartime, it is clear this was the mental and spiritual framework within which they worked – and one entirely and explicitly Christian. Let us examine it in detail.

To start with, at the outbreak of war, when Churchill was First Lord of the Admiralty, he broadcast on September 3rd 1939 as follows:

> This is not a question of fighting for Danzig or fighting for Poland. We are fighting to save the whole world from the pestilence of Nazi tyranny and in defence of all that is most sacred to man ... It is a war, viewed in its inherent quality, to establish on impregnable rocks, the rights of the individual, and it is a war to establish and revive the stature of man.[22]

The key phrase is of course, "the rights of the individual". Subsequently, in his first radio broadcast as Prime Minister in May 1940, he spoke as follows:

> Side by side, the British and French peoples have advanced to rescue not only Europe but mankind from the foulest and most soul-destroying tyranny which has ever darkened and stained the pages of history. Behind them – behind us – behind the Armies and Fleets of Britain and France – gather a group of shattered States and bludgeoned races: the Czechs, the Poles, the Norwegians, the Danes, the Dutch, the Belgians – upon all of whom the long night of barbarism will descend, unbroken even by a star of hope, unless we conquer, as conquer we must; as conquer we shall. Today is Trinity Sunday. Centuries ago words were written to be a call and a spur to the faithful servants of Truth and Justice: "Arm yourselves, and be ye men of valour, and be in readiness for the conflict; for it is better for us to perish in battle than to look upon the outrage of our nation and our altar. As the Will of God is in Heaven, even so let it do."[23]

The last sentence is a direct quotation from the Apocrypha – 1 Maccabees.

The star of hope needs no explanation in biblical terms, be it that over Bethlehem or the Bright Star of the Morning of St John's Revelation.[24]

As Prime Minister from May 1940, he spoke of the New World and the Old (respectively America and Europe) in terms of both Testaments of the Bible; of blood, toil, tears and sweat, echoing the Garden of Gethsemane. He invoked prayer and providence through all his speeches, but especially in 1940; and nothing is more explicit than when Britain stood alone in June of that year:

> What General Weygand called the Battle of France is over. The Battle of Britain is about to begin. Upon this battle depends the survival of Christian civilisation. Upon it depends our own British life, and the long continuity of our institutions....[25]

Then again, on 14 July after the sinking of the French Fleet at harbour in Oran, to keep it out of German hands, a tough and remorseless decision that jolted the world, Churchill broadcast:

> And now it has come to us to stand alone in the breach, and face the worst that the tyrant's might and enmity can do. Bearing ourselves humbly before God, but conscious that we serve an unfolding purpose, we are ready to defend our native land against the invasion by which it is threatened. We are fighting by ourselves alone; but we are not fighting for ourselves alone. Here in this strong City of Refuge which enshrines the title-deeds of human progress and is of deep consequence to Christian civilization; here, girt about by the seas and oceans where the Navy reigns; shielded from above by the prowess and devotion of our airmen – we await undismayed the impending assault.[26]

In similar vein, on the eve of expected invasion on 11 September, he broadcast again:

> Therefore we must regard the next week or so as a very important period in our history. It ranks with the days when the Spanish Armada was approaching the Channel, and Drake was finishing his game of bowls; or when Nelson stood between us and Napoleon's Grand Army at Boulogne. We have read all about this in the history books; but what is happening now is on a far greater scale and of far more

consequence to the life and future of the world and its civilisation than those brave old days of the past.

Every man and woman will therefore prepare himself to do his duty, whatever it may be, with special pride and care.

It is with devout but sure confidence that I say: Let God defend the Right.[27]

When Churchill and Roosevelt and their Ministers met mid-Atlantic in 1941, they framed a document that was the direct ancestor of the UN's later Human Rights charter.

The Atlantic Charter was a policy statement issued on 14 August 1941, that in effect set out the Allied goals for the post-war world. Drafted and first agreed by Churchill and Roosevelt, all the Allies of World War II later confirmed it. The Charter stated the ideal goals of the war: no territorial aggrandizement; no territorial changes made against the wishes of the people, self-determination; restoration of self-government to those deprived of it; reduction of trade restrictions; global cooperation to secure better economic and social conditions for all; freedom from fear and want; freedom of the seas; and abandonment of the use of force, as well as disarmament of aggressor nations.[28]

In the Declaration by the United Nations of 1 January 1942, the Allies pledged adherence to this Charter's principles. This is the beginning of the United Nations as we know it today. As has been rightly said, the Atlantic Charter set goals for the post-war world and inspired many of the international agreements that shaped the world thereafter, none perhaps more important than the Universal Declaration of Human Rights (UDHR) in 1948.

When America did enter the war after the attack on Pearl Harbor by Japan in December 1941, Roosevelt's words, as Churchill's, make clear the spiritual and moral dimension in which the struggle was undertaken:

And in the difficult hours of this day—through dark days that may be yet to come—we will know that the vast majority of the members of the human race are on our side. Many of them are fighting with us. All of them are praying for us. But, in representing our cause, we represent theirs as well—our hope and their hope for liberty under God.[29]

In this he was only being faithful to the words and spirit of the Founding Fathers and to Lincoln himself.

The world declares

We must now turn to the stream of legislation and statement that emerged from this conflict, and to the United Nations to which it gave birth.

The UDHR of 1948 is unequivocal and inspiring.[30] It is cut from the same "rock" so to speak as the speeches of wartime, and of anti-slavery and freedom. Eleanor Roosevelt, the widow of Roosevelt who died in 1945, had much influence in its framing.

After it was ratified by a sufficient number of individual nations, the Bill took on the force of international law. Article 1 makes the core principle clear:

> All human beings are born free and equal in dignity and rights. They are endowed with reason and conscience and should act towards one another in a spirit of brotherhood.

However, this does suggest the question: if all men are brothers, who is their common father?

And what has happened, that in our current time we find this very legislation turned against the tenets and doctrines, and the persons of the faith, who gave it form? The result being those who maintain Christian and biblical faith and morality are now harried with accusations of discrimination, bigotry, and causing offence? There are three stages in this development that we shall focus on:

1. The main post-war legislation in English Law relating to non-discrimination, subsequently gathered together in the Equality Act 2010, with its new concept of "protected characteristics".

2. The ideology that lay behind this legislative development as caught in the words of Prime Minister Tony Blair quoted below, whose government passed the Human Rights Act 1998 and the major legislation later consolidated in the Equality Act 2010.

3. The idea of "Fundamental British Values" that emerged in 2014 in education regulations, and originated from a perceived need to combat Islamic jihadist activity.

Enactment over the post war years of laws in the spirit of the UDHR proceeded on issues of race, disability, gender, age and sexual orientation, to ensure, as the UDHR states, "that human rights be protected by the rule of law".[31] They can be summarised in this heading from the Equality Act of 2010.

> A new Equality Act came into force on 1 October 2010. The Equality Act brings together over 116 separate pieces of legislation into one single Act. Combined, they make up a new Act that provides a legal framework to protect the rights of individuals and advance equality of opportunity for all.
>
> The Act simplifies, strengthens and harmonises the current legislation to provide Britain with a new discrimination law which protects individuals from unfair treatment and promotes a fair and more equal society.[32]

The Act sets out 9 "Protected Characteristics" that are intended to encapsulate the various aspects of earlier human rights legislation: Age; Disability; Gender reassignment; Marriage and civil partnership; Pregnancy and maternity; Race; Religion and belief; Sex; Sexual orientation.[33] The Act makes it unlawful to discriminate against people with a "protected characteristic".

So far so good. Except, how can "Religion" be a characteristic? Is it not a free choice? Are you born with a religion? What use is our free will if that is the case? And although sexual orientation may or may not be a fact of nature, is sexual practice the same?

Age, race, ethnicity, pregnancy, gender – all these may be facts of nature. But is the *practice* of a faith or of a sexuality to be accorded the same legal protection as the *person*? That is the nub of the problem. And the matter becomes further bedevilled when the group with a "protected characteristic" becomes protected too. That is what has happened, by way of example, with two groups – Muslims, and Gays. And that is where Christians start becoming the objects of legal disapproval, for they cannot share the view of Muhammad as a prophet – but in disagreeing, does this mean they "discriminate" against Muslims? And in the condemnation of homosexual practices as abominations in the sight of God, are they "discriminating" against gays? Certainly, this is what the words "Islamophobia" and "Homophobia" suggest.

To understand how this almost criminalising of Christian belief has happened, we must examine where the status of the individual person, fought for and protected in English Law, began to be the property of groups, and then in turn the property of that group's beliefs or behaviours.

The scene is the Labour Party Conference of 1999; Tony Blair is addressing his third conference as Prime Minister; his party's majority is the greatest any party has held since 1906. It is an hour of triumph.

Today at the frontier of the new Millennium I set out for you how, as a nation, we renew British strength and confidence for the 21st century; and how, as a party reborn, we make it a century of progressive politics.... A New Britain ... liberated from the forces of conservatism ... to create a model 21st century nation, based not on privilege, class or background, but on the equal worth of all. And New Labour, confident at having modernised itself ... now the new progressive force in British politics ... can modernise the nation, sweep away those forces of conservatism to set the people free ... The cause we have fought for, these 100 years, is no longer simply our cause of social justice. It is the nation's only hope of salvation.[34]

He goes on to itemise those being "set free" from the "old order" – "women, and black and Asian talent ... inner city kids ... where multiculturalism is ... something to celebrate."

Note how much religious – and specifically New Testament – language lies beneath a disturbing division of the world into Manichaean halves – "progressive" versus "conservative"; "modernise" versus "privilege"; "new" versus "old order".

New Labour, apparently picking up Our Lord's encomium to Simon Peter, having been converted or "modernised", can now go and strengthen the brethren or, in this instance, "modernise" the nation. The "devil" of the old order is still there; but the new party of "salvation" will sweep away his old ways and "set the people free".

"It is us, the new radicals, the Labour Party modernised, that must undertake this historic mission."[35] Yes, today is the acceptable day of salvation.

So to disagree with someone about what they think or do, because you may hold other ideas about, in these examples, the role of sexuality in life, or the rights of religious believers to compel others to agree with them under threat of force, has come to mean that you wish to hate or oppress that person, or the "group" to which they are deemed to belong.

Any distinction between sin and sinner, between person and practice, between an idea and the individual who holds it, is eliminated. You are on one side or other of an unbridgeable gulf. You are either "progressive" or not – either a sheep in the flock of New Labour's pastures, or a goat on the way to bigotry or worse. It is the very language of the New Testament that is prayed in, but with the result of division and exclusion in regard to Christians in public life, unless they sign up for: "The cause we have fought for ... this historic mission." [36]

The triumph of New Labour is not a victory for one political party against another. Oh no. Nothing so trivial or base. It is salvation itself. The nation's only hope. How then could there be another hope, that of Christians in their Lord? No. Christians are on the wrong side of History. They must be "swept away".

Of course, this is not a new phenomenon, unique to New Labour. Nor is it a party political issue. Later governments, Coalition or Conservative, have continued this process of criminalising Christian belief. Michael Burleigh had it summarised well, and his words quoted earlier, re-phrased, fit this new phenomenon well:

> ... these political movements ... by-products of an absence of religion ... where ideologies akin to Christian heresies of redemption in the here and now fused with post-Enlightenment doctrines of social transformation.... [37]

It does not matter where on the political spectrum you locate this; all that is important is that you base good and evil on something or someone, some chosen group, some specific "characteristics", rather than on conduct and actions. It is a denial of the moral nature of man and the reality of his choice. And it always hates and resists religion, for that would call it to account at the bar of an authority higher than itself. This is what is happening *in our time* with Christianity; admittedly so far mildly in England (but let us not forget various Christians denominations have been outlawed and persecuted in England in the past), but savagely and horribly in other countries round the globe.

So if therefore gays have been discriminated against – of which there can be little doubt historically – and form with "women, and black and Asian talent" those "held back" and "kept down" by the old order; and if all good rests in their "salvation" … then anyone raising questions about the felicity or not of homosexual conduct must be aligned with that "old order" from which the nation is to be "saved".

It therefore follows that any belief or ideas about the nature and purpose of human sexuality, if such views "discriminate" against homosexual sex, and do not accept its validity as a practice, must be a product not of an alternative and valid system of thought or belief, but be the result of a problem or aberrancy, or sickness. Christians then become branded as suffering from a "condition", which must be dealt with. This is exactly the case with the magistrate sent for "re-education" as to his view that a child is best brought up by its natural parents, father and mother.[38]

This is the sequence of thought that has led to the accusation against the Christian community of being "homophobic". A similar sequence of thought brings the accusation of being "Islamophobic", where to disagree with the views of a "minority", in this case Muslims, is to discriminate against their very persons. The "protected characteristics" of the group put their views or practices beyond examination or review. Any voice raised in dissent must be punished or suppressed. Debate ceases. An orthodoxy of silence prevails. Freedom of speech disappears.

The Christian Church must expect for a long time to suffer accusations of bigotry and intolerance. It will be denounced as disrupting social cohesion and promoting division, seen most clearly in its exclusive and selective schools policy. It will be charged with conspiring to hold back the progressive cause of "salvation". It will be told it must "keep up to date"; to adapt to changed social circumstances or be obsolete. History has moved on. As a recent Prime Minister David Cameron said, Christians have only one choice: "Get with the programme".[39]

For we are not dealing here with straightforward politics, but rather an ersatz religion that has transferred to public life its religious terminology and thought. Hence the increasing bitterness of the denunciations of religion from certain political quarters. The one thing an ersatz believer hates above all is the real thing. It is in a way a compliment: for at least

Christians are recognised as a body that will not yield to this new way of thinking. And this fuels the vitriol of the antagonism.

Let us move forward to the final and third element of our modern dilemma. The earlier protection accorded Muslims, as objects of discrimination, changed with the emergence of British jihadists in 2005, and even more so with the scandal of fundamentalist infiltration of schools in Birmingham, in what became known as the "Trojan Horse" affair.

The fact that indoctrination into extreme Islamist views was taking place, and that tactics of fear and bullying were prevalent, led the then Education Secretary Michael Gove to frame in June 2014 what has become a most interesting set of principles. Entitled "Fundamental British Values" (FBV), their active promotion was set down as required in all schools. The Statutory Instrument outlining them lays a duty on schools to:

> (a) actively promote the fundamental British values of democracy, the rule of law, individual liberty, and mutual respect and tolerance of those with different faiths and beliefs

> (b) (vi) encourage respect for other people, paying particular regard to the protected characteristics set out in the Equality Act 2010(a).[40]

It is highly interesting that there is no definition of equality in either the UDHR or the Equality Act 2010. The statement in the UDHR of "brotherhood" (and we would add sisterhood) is only logical if there is a common father. That was never a problem to those who helped form the English Constitution, for to them we all enjoyed the common Fatherhood of God. But omit that foundational idea and you have a slight problem.

The difficulties increased when the Department of Education sought to clarify how these FBV were to be implemented. An inherent flaw in the Equality Act is that it conflates characteristics of nature (age, gender, race, disability) with those of choice or practice – especially as relating respectively to sexual and religious practice, which are entirely dependent on choice. It sets them on a collision course with one another. When you have different and superficially opposing "protected characteristics" – such as faith and sexual orientation – and both are "protected" under the law, who is then to rank one above the other when they conflict?

There was a consultation on FBV in the summer of 2014. Many raised the problem of reconciling freedom of speech and worship with the need to promote FBV – with its link to the Equality Act. This is what the Department said:

> There was considerable opposition in the consultation responses but this was founded on two misconceptions that the proposed revision – that is FBV – would require schools to promote other religions and have a negative impact on religious freedoms, and that they would require schools to promote the protected characteristics and extend equality requirements. The proposed standard does not have this effect, rather it requires respect for other people, including those of different faiths.[41]

The vital distinction is between persons and their beliefs or practices. We can disagree with someone's belief and culture. That is individual liberty. But their persons are sacred: not their thoughts, beliefs or cultures. However, the government continues to switch between persons and practices, and this is the source of much current confusion.

Several legal disputes in relation to this have been tested in the courts. In a recent case, a firm of bakers in Northern Ireland (Ashers Bakery) were asked to bake a cake for a gay wedding, with a slogan supporting same sex marriage. They refused on the grounds they were Christian and the message went against their faith. They had no problem baking the cake: it was the message to go onto it they objected to. They were found to have discriminated on the grounds of sexual orientation.[42]

Such a ruling demonstrates exactly the contradictions inherent in the Equality Act. But then this elicited a most interesting analysis from a well-known gay campaigner, Peter Tatchell. He takes up the very point made in this chapter, namely the difference between "person" and "practice"; to put it another way, between an individual and an idea. Upon that distinction and its observance will turn the preservation of our liberties. Tatchell wrote in 2016:

> Like most gay and equality campaigners, I initially condemned the Christian-run Ashers Bakery in Belfast over its refusal to produce a cake with a pro-gay marriage slogan for a gay customer, Gareth Lee. I supported his legal claim against Ashers and the subsequent

verdict – the bakery was found guilty of discrimination last year. Now, two days before the case goes to appeal, I have changed my mind. Much as I wish to defend the gay community, I also want to defend freedom of conscience, expression and religion.

The judge concluded that service providers are required to facilitate any "lawful" message, even if they have a conscientious objection. This raises the question: should Muslim printers be obliged to publish cartoons of Mohammed? Or Jewish ones publish the words of a Holocaust denier? Or gay bakers accept orders for cakes with homophobic slurs? If the Ashers verdict stands... it would leave businesses unable to refuse to decorate cakes or print posters with bigoted messages.

In my view, it is an infringement of freedom to require businesses to aid the promotion of ideas to which they conscientiously object. Discrimination against people should be unlawful, but not against ideas.[43]

That is consistent with the theory of human rights.

All human beings bear the image of God who created them. That biblical belief has been the bedrock of our laws and our liberty. To make one group or its "characteristics" higher than another is to negate that equality. That is the challenge Christians – indeed the country – face. For if honestly held differences about human action and conduct cannot be debated because that "discriminates" against a person, or a group, and the state enforces this by penalising anyone who disagrees, we are seeing the "Rise of the All Powerful State". In defending our right to proclaim the message of Christ, we will find we are fighting not just for ourselves, but for the freedom of all.

Notes
[1] House of Lords, 5 February 2016, www.pressreader.com/uk/the-church-of-england/20160205. House of Lords expressed concern that they consider Christianity's exclusive truth claim 'divisive'.
[2] Of Durham Free School: "The curriculum does not help students to understand fundamental British values or prepare them well for life in modern Britain. For example, until very recently the religious studies curriculum was too narrow and did not give students enough opportunities to learn about different faiths and beliefs". Ofsted Report published 19 January 2015. See, *https://www.theyworkforyou.com/debates/?id=2015-01-27a.830.0*

[3] Polly Harrow, Head of Safeguarding, Kirklees College, Huddersfield, W Yorkshire, speaking on *BBC Radio 4's Today Programme*, 18 September 2015. On being asked whether a "Muslim who believes that homosexuality is wrong should be accepted", Ms Harrow replied: "If that's what you think and that's what you believe and you want to hold it in your head, that is your business and your right but bear in mind that if you speak it out loud you might be breaking that law".

[4] Magistrate Mr Richard Page "told colleagues behind closed doors during an adoption case that he thought it would be better for a child to be brought up in a traditional family rather than by a gay couple". www.dailymail.co.uk/news/article-2914951 See also, http://judicialconduct.judiciary.gov.uk/wp-content/uploads/2016/03/JCIO-press-statement-removal-Mr-Richard-Page-JP.pdf

[5] "Religious Persecution and Discrimination against Christians and Members of Other Religions." *Pew Research Center, Religion & Public Life*, 26 February 2015.

[6] F.D. Roosevelt, 'The Four Freedoms', delivered 6 January 1941 http://www.americanrhetoric.com/speeches/fdrthefourfreedoms.htm

[7] (the Proprietor) "actively promotes the fundamental British values of democracy, the rule of law, individual liberty, and mutual respect and tolerance of those with different faiths and beliefs... (vi) encourage respect for other people, paying particular regard to the protected characteristics set out in the Equality Act 2010(a)" *The Education (Independent School Standards) (England) (Amendment) Regulations,* 29 September 2014 www.legislation.gov.uk/uksi/2014/2374/regulation/made

[8] In his Letter to the Galatians 3:28

[9] F.M. Stenton, *The Oxford History of England, Anglo Saxon England,* 3rd Edition (Oxford University Press, 1971) p. 133

[10] Magna Carta 1215, Clause 39. Only three clauses of Magna Carta still remain on the statute book in England and Wales. These clauses concern 1) the freedom of the English Church; 2) the "ancient liberties" of the City of London (clause 13 in the 1215 charter, clause 9 in the 1297 statute); and 3) a right to due legal process (clauses 39 and 40 in the 1215 charter, clause 29 in the 1297 statute).

[11] Sir John Fortescue (c.1394-1479) Chief Justice of the King's Bench 1442-1460. Author of *de Laudibus legum Angliae (Commendation of the Laws of England)*, published c.1468-1471.

[12] "I call heaven and earth to record this day that I have set before you life and death, blessing and cursing: therefore choose life, that both thou and thy seed may live." Deuteronomy 30:19

[13] www.rcsouthwark.co.uk/dowry_walsingham.html At the same time (1399) Thomas Arundel, Archbishop of Canterbury, wrote to his suffragan bishops: "The contemplation of the great mystery of the Incarnation has drawn all Christian nations to venerate her from whom came the first beginnings of our redemption. But we English, being the servants of her special inheritance and her own dowry, as we are commonly called, ought to surpass others in the fervour of our praises and devotions."

[14] From the Pynson Ballad printed by Richard Pynson, later printer to King Henry VII c.1495 www.walsinghamanglicanarchives.org.uk/pynsonballad.htm
'O Englonde, great cause thou haste glad for to be, Compared to the londe of promys syon, Thou atteynest my grace to stande in that degre Through this gloryous Ladyes supportacyon, To be called in every realme and regyon The holy lande, Oure Ladyes

dowre; Thus arte thou named of olde antyquyte.'

[15] United States Declaration of Independence, In Congress, July 4th, 1776, Preamble.

[16] Ibid.

[17] United States President Abraham Lincoln's Second Inaugural Address on March 4th, 1865.

[18] Martin Luther King Jr, speech delivered at the Lincoln Memorial on 28th August 1963

[19] President Franklin D Roosevelt's Inaugural Address, 4 March 1933.

[20] *A Short History of Germany 1815-1945* (Cambridge University Press, 1959) p. 189

[21] Michael Burleigh, *The Third Reich: A New History* (Pan Books, Reprints Edition, July 2001) p.10.

[22] Winston S. Churchill, First Lord of the Admiralty: Parliament, 3 September 1939.

[23] Winston S. Churchill, Prime Minister: BBC Radio Broadcast, 19 May 1940.

[24] See 1 Maccabees 3:58-60; Revelation 22:16

[25] Winston S. Churchill, "Their Finest Hour", speech to Parliament, then BBC Radio Broadcast 18 June 1940.

[26] Winston S. Churchill, "The War of the Unknown Warriors", BBC Radio Broadcast, 14 July 1940.

[27] Winston S. Churchill, "Every Man To His Post", BBC Radio Broadcast, 11 September 1940.

[28] The Atlantic Charter, https://history.state.gov/milestones/1937-1945/atlantic-conf The Atlantic Charter was a joint declaration released by U.S. President Franklin D. Roosevelt and British Prime Minister Winston Churchill on 14 August 1941.

[29] President Franklin D Roosevelt's Address from the Oval Room at the White House, 9th December 1941.

[30] http://www.un.org/en/universal-declaration-human-rights/

[31] Preamble, Universal Declaration of Human Rights (UDHR) 1948.

[32] Introduction to the Equality Act 2010. http://www.legislation.gov.uk/ukpga/2010/15/content

[33] Equality Act 2010, Part 2, Chapter 1 Protected characteristics. http://www.legislation.gov.uk/ukpga/2010/15/content

[34] Speech by Prime Minister Tony Blair at the Labour Party Conference, 28 September 1999. http://news.bbc.co.uk/1/hi/uk_politics/460029.stm

[35] Ibid.

[36] Ibid.

[37] See note 21 above.

[38] See endnote 4 above.

[39] Prime Minister David Cameron, Prime Minister's Questions, November 21st 2012

[40] Department for Education "Proposed New Independent School Standards," 27 November 2014, para. 8 https://www.gov.uk/government/uploads/system/uploads/attachment_data/file/380017/SMSC_consultation_response.pdf

[41] https://www.gov.uk/government/news/consultation-on-promoting-british-values-in-school

[42] Ashers Bakery of Belfast, Northern Ireland were found guilty of discrimination by Judge Isobel Brownlie at Belfast County Court, 19 May 2015 www.irishtimes.com/news/crime-and-law/ashers-bakery-found-guilty-of-discrimination-1.2218032

[43] Peter Tatchell, *The Guardian*, 1 February 2016, www.theguardian.com/commentisfree/2016/feb/01

Chapter Ten

BRITISH VALUES: A PANDORA'S BOX? THE SYMPTOMS

Dr Christopher Shell

'British values' – an overview

As we watch anti-intellectual political correctness and taboo threaten contemporary UK education, we need to note at the outset three points about this popular buzzword phrase.

First, it is based on an *inaccurate world-view* if it suggests *either* that 'British values' have always (or even for a long time) been as they are today[1] – they haven't; *or* that being 'British' (rather than simply 'beneficial') must be a mark of merit; *or* both.

'British values' is an unclear phrase because it denies the elephant in the room. The values our older citizens grew up with (pre-c.1963) are often *opposed to* today's values. 'British values' has no clear meaning unless the slate of pre-1963 memory be wiped clean Soviet-style. The values of (say) 1955,[2] which the world often, for good or ill, associates with Britain, are certainly opposed to post-1963 values. The former include gentlemanliness/ladylikeness; duty/service; fair play; stiff-upper-lip stoicism; precision; insularity (an Englishman's home is his castle); a Christian basis. The latter are secular[3] and revolve round individual 'liberty', plus 'none of the above'. A very stark difference. So which of the two constitutes 'British values'? Both, maybe. But in that case we can't speak of 'British values' at all without further qualification.

Why 'British' anyway? Actually, the values highlighted in UK schools from 2014 (democracy, rule of law, individual liberty, tolerance/mutual respect) aren't exclusively British; while just being 'British' is obviously neutral. What matters is that values be good or beneficial. This we can measure statistically by outcomes (health, happiness, etc.[4]), which is a far more profitable and less jingoistic approach. Now, the existence of two competing sets of British values wouldn't matter if they performed equally well. But if they don't, then the need to pursue *good* (not necessarily *British*) values just becomes more acute.

Secondly, the term 'British values' is a *slogan*, and the world of slogans is not the world of reasoned thought. Unfortunately, it also belongs to a *family* of phrases or slogans (we deal with 29 of these in Section B below) which typically have four things in common that we need to be on the lookout for. They are *too short and simple*: so short that they often even appear without the grammatical object that they require (thereby rendering themselves meaningless in one stroke). There is therefore a *Trojan Horse tendency*: it looks like the minimum possible (only the part that is innocuous, unexceptionable and welcome) is being disclosed; while the maximum possible is being hidden or 'smuggled in under cover'. Such phrases are nevertheless *uttered as though their meaning were obvious*: like a mantra, or a presupposition that must not be questioned. In practice, however, the obvious meaning is often avoided in favour of some *private meaning* (the Humpty-Dumpty or Orwellian tendency).

Thirdly, it can be an imposed *ideology* – and ideologies do not bow to research-findings: private interests are the master that they serve. The decision about what things are and are not British values was made for us and imposed on us by a small number of people (David Cameron, Michael Gove, Nick Clegg) as though already written in stone.

This last point looks to be an explanation for the first two, which would both be puzzling otherwise. Why not start from the world-view known to produce far superior results (A)? And why express things in slogans, which are bound to be simplistic and therefore inaccurate (B)? Well, if the adopted world-view, however statistically catastrophic, is a means to an end; and if the slogans can serve as Trojan horses 'innocuously' importing that same end – then it'll be 'worth it' (C).

We will look at these three aspects in turn. Our analysis of the first two concerns the symptoms, and the third matter – diagnosis – follows in Chapter 11.

(A) Which values are better? By how much?[5]

1% can, rightly, be big news. For example, a 1% drop in interest rates, inflation, or church attendance. But when comparing the Christian-majority and secular-majority regimes, a 400%+ worsening under secularism is (as is apparent from the following, had it ever been doubted) *normal*.

Recorded crime

From 500,000 recorded offences in 1955 to a peak of 6 million (scaled in 1987 and 2004/5)[6] is a *900% rise*. This occurred even in a period when things previously illegal (abortion, homosexual practice) became legal. Such a rise is too huge to be explained mainly by more scrupulous recording. For the give-away is that the crime graph of massive worsening between c.1963 and c.1983 (followed sometimes, but alas *only* sometimes, by a plateau) is replicated in all the statistics below.

Abortion[7]

In England and Wales, there were 23,641 'abortions' in the 8 months of 1968 that followed legalisation. That equates to around 35,000 in 12 months. But now the annual figure hovers around 200,000,[8] which constitutes an approximate *500% rise*. In fact, the rise is much larger: both because legalisation everywhere brings normalisation and unarguably brought a precipitate rise after 1967 in this instance; and also because the available figure for 1962 (covering women seen by a hospital only, which is all the evidence we have) is 14,600.[9]

Divorce[10]

Divorces per year per 1,000 married people were 1.9 in 1958, rising to 5.9 in 1971, after new 1969 legislation came into force.[11] In 2003 the rate had risen to 14.0 (a *640% rise*); after which came a drop in marriages.[12] Again: legalise, and you normalise. Regular churchgoers (as opposed to those who tick 'Christian' in a survey) are massively less likely to divorce than the norm.[13] (This is an especially clear illustration of our contention that the key fault-line is people's attitude to historic and not cultural Christianity on the one hand and to the sexual revolution on the other: a phenomenon's connection to the sexual revolution conceptually and/

or chronologically will regularly be enough evidence for us to prophesy successfully its failure or harmful fruits. Other research points to the same conclusion. Thus, Mark Regnerus discovered in 2014[14] that same-sex-marriage-supporting Christians were far closer to non-Christians than to other Christians in their beliefs on abortion, pornography, polyamory, no-strings sex, marital infidelity, and cohabitation.[15])

Cohabitation[16]

Of single women pre-marriage, 1-2% cohabited in the 1950s, rising to 70% in 1993 (followed by a drop in marriage itself).[17] A *3400% rise* at least. Cohabitees (similarly to singles) are 50% above non-cohabitees in post-marital separation or divorce; 130% above in smoking in pregnancy; 900% above in serial relationships and 250% in concurrent; 300% above in 'abortions'; and 60% above in anxiety, neurosis and depression. 52% of cohabitees (as against 8% of married couples) split before a child is 5:[18] a *550% rise*.

Extramarital births

The 2-5% rate which remained fairly constant between 1750 and the 1950s (slightly higher only in the early 1800s and wartimes) has become around 50% today: a *900% rise*.[19]

Under–16s[20]

Under-16s at birth control clinics[21]

Under-16s had no such experience in the 1950s; the figure of 8,000 attending in 1975 rose to 92,000 in 2003 – after which came the abortifacient Morning After Pill, which could be obtained direct from chemists. The rise since the 1950s, therefore, was infinite; but even since 1975 there was a *1050% rise*.

Under-16 intercourse[22]

The percentage of girls having 'under-age' sex rose from 5% (1955-64) to 38% (2008): a *660% rise*. When it comes to girls *and* boys, Channel 4's *The Joy of Teen Sex* (2011) and *Times of India* (26.9.2010) both quoted research (though the reliability of this figure is perhaps open to question) that the average had become 3 partners before turning 16. Intercourse under 16 leads to a sixfold chance of subsequently having

2+ sexual partners in a given year.

Under-16 pregnancies

These rose from 0.03% (1955) to 0.51% (present day): a *1600% rise*.

Child abuse

Secularists have championed the rise of 'alternative families' (those where at least one parent is no longer present). One common type is mother plus father-substitute (stepfather/boyfriend/'uncle'). The risk of child abuse sees a *500% rise* with this latter family-type. But in the 1980s alone, such 'alternative families' saw a 95% rise from 17% to 33%.[23] We should join the dots.

Domestic violence

For domestic violence against women, this picture is replicated.[24] A related category here is boyfriend violence: fully a third of teenage girls have suffered this particular inevitable downside of a superficially feminist culture's actual promotion of close intimate relationships that lack lifelong commitment.[25]

Clerical abuse

The John Jay Report into the appalling American Catholic abuse[26] reveals the following findings.

– The sharp spike in the graph of abuse precisely between the 1960s and the early 1980s – which is the same as what we see in care-home/children's-home abuse, and in so many of the areas we are presently discussing – was not coincidental: it shows that social/attitude change (the sexual revolution) was to blame.

– Boston, a (or the) centre of liberalism, and therefore of revisionist culturally-conformist 'Christianity', was predictably the centre of abuse too.

– Secular abuse proportionally far outnumbers abuse at priests' hands; abuse in US schools has sometimes been calculated to be up to 100 times worse than that by priests, with around 9.5% of students being targets at some point.[27]

– 83% of the abuse (yet only 1-2% of the population) was homosexual.

STDs[28]

In the 1950s, there were essentially 2 STDs: gonorrhoea and syphilis, both treatable by antibiotics. Both remain scourges – more so since newly evolved strains are frighteningly antibiotic-resistant. But there are also some 30 new STDs (and since they began 'from nothing', we record an *infinite percentage rise*): especially chlamydia (1976-), HIV and HIV/AIDS (1981-), herpes (1981-), HPV, with 40 strains of its own (1985-). Each, unsurprisingly, broke out irrevocably shortly after the sexual revolution; though counter-intuitively this did not lead to backtracking on either promiscuity or homosexuality, only to (sporadically relevant) emphasis on contraception. What happened next? STIs,[29] having already increased sixfold in Britain between 1951 and 1986,[30] doubled in the 1990s alone (*more* among teenagers, who were fed the normalising message). Of the USA's 'sexually active' teenage girls (around half), 40% had an STI in 2008.[31] The pattern of formerly rarer sexual practices such as anal and oral intercourse becoming more widespread and causing disease is seen not just in the case of HIV/AIDS but also in that of HPV (linked to a significant rise in throat cancer). The time-honoured sequence runs: 'liberalise', ignoring what the Christians are saying; then, before long, be forced to deal with 'freedom's' fallout.

Drugs

As with STIs, there were essentially just two in the earlier 1950s: tobacco and alcohol. Both still remain scourges, though smoking-reduction efforts have seen significant success. But with regard to use of other stimulants we have since the 1950s seen *an almost infinite percentage rise*. At times this has been especially precipitate. UK cannabis users rose 88% in the 1990s (40,194 to 75,986); cocaine users rose 500% (from 0.6 to 3.0% of the population between 1996 and 2008/9); and heroin use rose 100% every four years in the 1990s.[32] Drug use is also correlated with youth suicide.[33]

Pornography

In the last half-century, pornography in family shops has seen an *infinite percentage rise* – and to a high level. Pornography as a whole will have risen over 99% between the 1948 Kinsey Report and the rise of the internet; and then *again* by a similar percentage since. Internet pornography is the classic example of secularists' inaccurate (and therefore pragmatically failing) world-view allowing them to make 'liberal' policies that don't foresee likely consequences (nor know human nature itself), only to have to pick up the pieces afterwards. How many Christians wanted satellite/internet pornography in the UK? The immature take decisions and cause mess; but why is it not the mature that we are being expected to follow?

Pornography's consequences are unpleasant. Teenagers who often see sexual content on TV (i.e., a vastly increasing number) are far more likely to become pregnant as teenagers.[34] Teenage viewers of pornography show a greater likelihood of being lonely and/or depressed.[35] And pornography increases marital infidelity by over 300%.[36] This last figure will have risen further with the outbreak of infidelity sites such as Ashley Madison, which unbelievably are publicly advertised,[37] again because the mature are far from power.

Obscenity on stage and screen
In the UK we have seen an *infinite percentage rise* over the period since the removal of the Lord Chamberlain's powers (Theatres Act, 1968) and Professor Bernard Williams's 1970s Committee on Obscenity and Film Censorship. As for swearing in the mass media, once again we have seen an *infinite percentage rise*. A lesson from such rises is that the level can easily remain at 0% for very long periods. The US Parents Television Council found swearing to have increased by 70% between 2005 and 2010,[38] just when UK audiences got *Big Brother*, Gordon Ramsay's and Jamie Oliver's cookery shows, and *The Apprentice*, and obscene language became so commonplace as often to pass without notice.

Depression
In the 'me'-decades after the sexual revolution, there was already by 1988 a *900% rise* in rates of depression compared with World War II![39] The main factor could therefore be whether or not the sexual revolution influenced people's formative years. By 2007 1 in 4 people in England were expected to experience a mental health problem each year.[40] Worryingly, 'mental illness' (which Christians would have expected to

rise given transitory sexual relationships) is being treated as inescapable rather than as being a result of harmful norms.[41]

Other negative trends post-1955

Some accompanying 'me'-generation trends include: pollution; money-worship; isolation within the community,[42] not knowing one's neighbours any more; abstraction and navel-gazing in the arts.

Positive trends post-1955

Equally welcome to Christian and to secularist have been: an increase in overt affection; life-expectancy increase; technological and medical advances; an increase in efficiency and often also in hard work; clean air; smoking reduction; absence of World Wars; fewer war-casualties.

Some possible objections to the above analysis

'We're happier now than in 1955.'

In fact, the opposite is true. In 1957, 52% of those polled were 'very happy'; in 2005, 36%.[43] If individual 'liberty' has therefore reduced happiness, what has been the point? Similarly, in relation to the hard-won right of women to work, a recent Gallup poll found that 56% of US mothers with children under 18 would be happier at home looking after their children.[44] There will also be scepticism about whether a 'have it all' desire and/or lifestyle is either healthy; necessary in an era of time-saving devices; a dream that is possible to achieve; beneficial to others; or remotely enjoyable. Gain that is not *net* gain amounts to loss.

Moreover, religious involvement and marriage are regularly the two best predictors of a 'very happy' state. The link of marriage with *health* is now a well-known finding.[45] Its link with *happiness* is equally well established.[46] Those with highest levels of church attendance (or equivalent) are happiest:[47] obviously those with a ready-made community or 'parish' are happier. Church attendance also has clear benefits for children.[48] (The religion-health link is less straightforward since, for example, secular Sweden has much better health and life-expectancy than most parts of religious Africa.)

Such obvious findings always make headlines every time a new study appears. But why, given that there is 'nothing new' in them? Maybe the answer is that they contradict media orthodoxy. Similarly, every time that homosexuals are again found to comprise 1-2% of the population[49], this makes headlines, as though findings (except those of Kinsey, who encouraged child-abuse among his non-random sample) had ever been different. It just conflicts with the false media 'normality', one of whose most telling results was that in a 2011 Gallup poll Americans believed on average that 25% of the population was gay or lesbian![50]

'All these statistics are "correlated" with the rise of secularism, not "caused" by it.'

Again, untrue. They *constitute* part of what secularism *consists in*. The changes happened because secularists pressed for law changes. Anyway, secularists must admit *most* of life isn't 'A-causes-B': rather, *all* simultaneous factors in our environments affect us somehow ('chaos theory') in a complex causative web. Most of all, obviously, the *immediate* factors: norms promulgated by authority figures (government, law, media), and/or adopted by the families and peer-groups that so greatly influence us.

Yet if we discern causation within suspiciously constant correlation, isn't that like saying ice cream causes rape? No. First, obviously ice cream and rape are part of a fully causative pattern: hot weather's the parent; ice-cream and rape are offspring. Second, there's no conceptual overlap between ice cream and rape, unlike with our proposed causes and effects (e.g., pornography and infidelity intrinsically overlap as ideas). Third, *if,* say, homosexuality and non-marital ties don't help 'cause' promiscuity, that doesn't *help* if they are unfailingly connected.

'These changes are good changes.'

Divorce is often rated[51] the most stressful experience other than bereavement (and occasionally moving house).[52] So which changes are good? Teen STDs? The spread of pornography? Increased drugs? Teen/pre-teen sexualisation? Loss of ability to form lasting/marital unions, because transience is presented as normal and so becomes an early-formed habit? Pre-birth killing?

WHAT ARE THEY TEACHING THE CHILDREN?

'We're in a different world now.'
This is the classic circular argument, and for that reason invalid. To the extent that the world is different in ways relevant to our present discussion, it's largely these secularist changes and initiatives that *made* it so. The world is often what we make it, so there is all the less excuse to be passive or disengaged.

'We can't turn back the clock.'
This is a strange objection. Whoever *either* said that we could *or* necessarily wanted to? (For the philosophical error that this objection contains, see the next paragraph.) The issue is not about historical periods at all (not a single person can be produced who thinks, for example, that Churchill could *actually* return as Prime Minister), but rather about era-neutral, nation-neutral social policies. And we can implement whichever social policy has the best track-record in producing health, happiness, educational success, etc.. Some (not historical specialists) generalise on the unexamined naïve basis that *everything* in, for example, the Victorian age or the 1950s was bad. Yet even by the law of averages, a given era will be better than one's own 50% of the time. Given increased education (though in fact several newspapers reported on 24th February 2016 that today's B in Maths would have been an E in 1960), one may *hope* for this to drop to (say) 30%. But all of that is *a priori* hypothesising. How come we would need to hypothesise *a priori* at all about what might or 'ought' to be the case, when we *already know* what is the case since the actual statistics are already in our possession?

Secularism is exposed here for treating unfashionability as the unforgivable sin, rather than a matter of indifference. In fact, to be unfashionable is to be capable of independent thought: the intelligent don't just follow the crowd. C S Lewis called the intellectual fallacy that modern/fashionable is best 'chronological snobbery', following G K Chesterton who marvelled at those who think the clock or the century (as opposed to the facts) can determine what's likely to be true![53]

'Many of these things increased mainly because they were legalised (or the laws were 'relaxed'), so people no longer had to avoid doing them.'
First, I agree. Second, that means that things long agreed to be bad began

262

to happen more frequently. Third, sometimes things are made legal only because hard pressed law enforcers prefer a quiet life – *however bad* the acts in question may be. Fourth, when prominent voices (government, media, parents, teachers) seem not to care about standards, their charges lose motivation (and 'covering') to uphold those standards. Fifth, people found that they could indulge their lower nature by bending the laws, especially the abortion law. The mental state factor in the legislation was found to be conveniently vague and infinitely flexible – and wasn't even generally checked out. Thus it became unheard of to refuse a request or referral for abortion; and this remained the case even when it was often pointed out that the mental state of those who considered abortion, but went ahead with the pregnancy, was (unsurprisingly!) a lot better on average than that of those who did not go ahead, thus proving the mental health clause to be incoherent.[54] Sixth, legalisation obviously brings normalisation, together with a perceived seal of approval.

'We're a multicultural nation now.'

Yes, and we always have been; but today the expectation is that we will give higher *proportional* regard to minority cultures (UK Christians make up 58%[55] of the population, other religions less than 5% each). Yet all the 'religions' which have become large international communities still agree with Christianity in rejecting the tenets of secularism. No one voted for it, and it would be voted out on its own merits if there were not any effort put into presenting it as the only game in town.

'Secularists are more this-worldly, so have more of a social conscience.'

No: the Barna Group's 2006 survey[56] found that Christians give twice as much to charity as the average non-believer, a figure which rises to 7.5 times as much when church-based giving is included.

'Statistics aren't everything.'

This is true, but it does not follow that they are 'nothing'! Far from that, they are the best we have when asking what reality is actually like, and they are where government and businesses (and all of us) go for accurate information. Not only can no alternative to statistics be proposed (we discuss below the severe limitations of anecdotal evidence), but they are the feature of any argument that is most likely to be unanswerable. Again, how do we know that those most vociferous in objecting to statistics are not merely reacting to the unwelcome exposure of a reality they dislike? Finally, those who would wager that the truth is the opposite to what statistics indicate should bear in mind that even where statistics are inaccurate (and they are generally our most or only reliable indicator) they may as easily be inaccurate in an unwelcome direction as in a welcome one.

'The particular statistics quoted above are selective.'
Quite the reverse. It is not controversial to say that government statistics on abortion or divorce etc. are accurate down to the last unit: there are no alternative sources of information. And to anyone who tries to argue that media swearing or pornography *wasn't* at less than 1% of present levels just 50 years ago, one could only wish luck.

'Statistics are one thing; but the interpretation of statistics is another thing.'
There are several points to be made here:
– Don't try to make this a false either/or dichotomy. Clearly both are important, because we always need both context and a rounded understanding.
– 'Facts are nothing, interpretation is everything' is incoherent: what are you interpreting unless the raw data? And that point further shows that the raw data is *prior*: it's already there *before* any interpretation.
– Also, facts are a great deal less deniable and less open to questioning than is interpretation: a further reason to prioritise them.
– Appeal to 'interpretation' can be a way of trying to escape unwelcome statistics. That is dishonest.
– If the raw statistic is highly damning in one direction, 'interpretation' is not going to make matters point in the other direction.

'These statistical conclusions are not true of the people I know.'
Yet again, examination of this assertion exposes a series of logical fallacies:
– How do you know that your neighbours, family or friends were not among the people surveyed? Large-scale is not *opposed to* small-scale

(let alone inferior!) but rather includes it.

– Anecdotal evidence isn't non-statistical, but merely operates on a much smaller scale. To base an argument on anecdote is therefore numerically a very regressive step.

– It would obviously be wrong to say small-scale findings are as good as large-scale. Yet this assertion presupposes something even less defensible: that *extremely* small-scale findings are *better than* large-scale studies.

– The circle of your acquaintances is a non-random sample. They will in many cases be more than averagely similar to you.

– It is obviously incorrect that the views of non-researchers should be given as much weight as the time-consuming labours and independently verifiable findings of researchers – let alone *more* weight.

'People may judge historical eras good/bad for psychological reasons.'
– That is undoubtedly true. *But* normally people 'judge' their own formative years to be best. Yet here the reverse appears true, for I am taking the period for the most malign shift in prevailing UK philosophy to be approximately 1963-83; yet I was born in 1966.

– Nor does the present case have anything to do with the other cliché: things are getting worse and worse. Plateauing after c.1983 fits uncomfortably with that theory.

– The 400% minimum increases in harmful things are in most instances claimed on the basis of the only available statistics, *which are not questioned*. Psychology is therefore irrelevant here. It is rare to find even 100% changes in a single area in so short a period; but 400%+ change in multiple areas will be agreed to be extraordinary.

– If we have a tendency to give psychological explanations for things, that may just be our personal bent. Psychological theories need to be weighed against other competing theories to see how they measure up, by comparison, against the facts.

Conclusion on which values are better
The emperor has no clothes. Comparing Christian and secularist cultures shows that the latter quickly produces at least 400% deterioration in both values and outcomes.

All it takes to effect change is for different norms to be broadcast ('ideally' on the back of a media and/or education monopoly) and adopted before the young are sufficiently critical or experienced. As when sex-education took off in earnest circa 1967, neither mentioning marriage (by far the most common option both then and for generations past!) nor apologising for portraying extramarital and multiple sexual relationships as normal.[57] A society where *by far* the most typical marriage-length was lifelong then changed so enormously and quickly that cohabitation, failure to marry, and marriage lengths under 10 years all suddenly skyrocketed. Things like 'teenage pregnancy' (which Christians couldn't see anything wrong with, provided the girl in question was married[58]) were suddenly regarded as worse than fornication or adultery;[59] yet juvenile pregnancy is automatically increased by juvenile sex increasing,[60] and it was the revolutionaries who increased the latter by treating it (inaccurately) as normal and inevitable.

These universally attested and huge statistical discrepancies between Christian-majority regime and secular-majority regime show either the extreme excellence of the Christian option;[61] or the extreme harmfulness of the secularist option[62] – with which the sexual revolution[63] is virtually coterminous and synonymous; or both. But for those who say that we are now stuck with the way things 'are' – well, the secularists didn't say that in 1963, and neither should we. They fought for change, and we should learn from their example. If we (a) are happy to tolerate a massive shift for the worse, and (b) simultaneously do not try to produce a shift for the better, then we are doing two separate nonsensical things. In that scenario, we would not only be content for much better to change to much worse,[64] but also not be especially concerned to expend effort to achieve the opposite result. Logically, such an attitude would be either ignorant, malicious, uncaring ... or any combination of these.

(B) Slogans and buzzwords – and what they hide: an A to Z

Abortion (and/or termination)
This word cannot coherently be used without an object. To abort is to cut short. Things are often cut short, and such a description in itself is morally neutral. But the utterly central issue being avoided here is *what*

is getting 'cut short'. To put it another way:
(1) What is being 'aborted'? Answer: a life.
(2) *Whose* life? Answer: a human's.
(3) Can I hazard why those two centrally important facts were bypassed in the choice of the term 'abortion'? Answer: no.

The term 'abortion' is a misnomer for further reasons too. It hides the all-important dimension of intent; and it masquerades as 'medical procedure' and as something akin to an inevitable biological reality. In fact, *deliberate* ending of a baby's life has nothing to do with natural unintended 'abortion', which is miscarriage. To use such a term is dishonestly to portray this unnaturally invasive process as natural and unavoidable. And the word 'termination' is disingenuous for similar reasons because a *birth* is the standard way that a pregnancy is terminated – not its *opposite*, a death.

Affirming and/or inclusive

'Affirming Catholicism' was born on 6th September 1990, with a service at St Alban's, Holborn. Again, the ungrammatical *absolute* (object-less) use of a participle/adjective looks suspicious:
(1) It will be assumed that everyone knows (or should know) what this puzzling absolute usage means;
(2) It will mean adherence to an entire package, of which in reality one might 'affirm' some bits and reject others;
(3) The more questionable bits will be smuggled in by virtue of having one thing in common with the less questionable bits: namely that (as is the case with everything else in creation) it's possible to affirm them. (But is it always advisable?) For example, today, it is assumed that to 'affirm' the rights of the disabled is also to 'affirm' the agendas of LGBT activists: such is the perspective of the UK group Inclusive Church.[65] This is both logically in error and even insulting, because disability is unexceptionable and often inborn; but homosexual behaviour (like smoking) can often be the result of weakness or immature experimentation (or, not infrequently, molestation) becoming ingrained. So where's the point of comparison?

Belief and faith

(1) Both these words are all too vague when used in an *absolute* way

with no object. They are over-abstract, unlike, e.g., 'God' or 'Jesus'.

(2) If they combine together Christian, Jewish, Muslim and Hindu belief-systems, they produce a mutually self-contradictory mass. However, the benefit of this amalgamation to the secularist is that Christians can also be investigated when any non-Christian 'faith organisation' does something questionable: after all, Christians belong to the same 'faith' category.

(3) The use of 'belief' to target religion is disingenuous. Each of us believes many things. Equally, we have 'faith' in many people and organisations, from doctors to Virgin Atlantic. There is nothing 'religious' about that.

(4) The two words are widely imagined to derive from Christian roots; but actually a large and distorting change has taken place in between, since our *two* words are just the *one* (*pistis*) in the New Testament. We cannot therefore claim that our present usage is true to the New Testament.

(5) *Pistis* is never used of believing things that are less than likely to be true. It is used of believing and trusting those people, whose reality is unquestioned, who have proven themselves trustworthy.

(6) *Pistis* and its verb *pisteuo* are relational and not purely cognitive words – as shown by prepositions that follow them: *eis* ('into'), *epi* (sometimes translated 'on').

Bigot

If a 'bigot' (like the virtually interchangeable slang terms 'fundamentalist' and 'Bible-basher') is someone who makes swift, stereotyping, debate-bypassing, negative judgements, then users of the word 'bigot' are, by definition, themselves prime candidates for similar designation. So the word becomes self-defeating: to utter it is to be guilty of not only bigotry, but hypocrisy as well.

Change

How can change be *essentially* good? Election candidates' mantra 'change' is the false idea that anything at all would be better than the present regime; but others of us can slip into the same error. Obviously, change in and of itself is *neutral*. Beneficial change is good; harmful change is bad.

Choice (and women)

'Choice' is a common slogan in pro-abortion, sex-education, and drug-education circles. As commonly used, it is incoherent, being based on a series of unquestioned and false assumptions that lead to apparently self-serving decisions:

– In order to choose, you must know what the options are – otherwise you have not been given a proper choice. An example: the one thing that gives the most *accurate* understanding of a pregnancy is a real-time 3D scan of an unborn child; and that is the one thing standardly withheld at abortion clinics! Is this really just 'a blob of tissue', 'a product of conception', 'a bunch of cells'? Aren't we all? And what do you take us for?

– This is especially true of 'choices' that are presented to young people. By definition, the younger you are, the less knowledge you will have of available options. So to withhold the full facts removes all possibility of real 'choice'.

– In relation to 'abortion', 'choice' obviously is not a synonym for 'the choice to kill one's own son or daughter before they are born'! This is light years from the dictionary definition. Nor is this a choice made by 'women' (who are in any case a diverse not a monolithic group), but rather by a *subgroup* of women heavily circumscribed by age, historical circumstances and the existing norms of their subculture and peer-group.

– Even if (improbably) it *were* a synonym for that, 'choice' would be a very unsuitable word to use for any action that *deprives* another not merely of one choice but, at a stroke, of every possible lifetime choice.

– It is inescapable that 'choice'/'mistake' is today often used for instances where the rational has lost out to the emotional: cases of weak will and of animal passion. But this is an abuse of language. 'Choice'/'mistake' implies a decision made on the rational assessment of known facts.

– There are unarguably some occasions when it's better not to know what the choices are,[66] nor to be presented with options. For example, would Mother Teresa's life have been better had she learnt when young that she could choose between various 'recreational' drugs, or even none at all?

– If a teenager announces he's bedding his girlfriend, that's a choice, but a *good* choice? It takes no effort to submit to primitive instincts; but it undoubtedly requires character-building effort to say 'no' to them.

Which is more admirable?

– Frequently people say they should have a choice to do something that, as free agents, they *already* have a choice to do. What they mean is that they want a *legal* choice to do something society has rated morally questionable.

In sum, therefore, the word 'choice' is neutral. It is good to choose good things, bad to choose bad things.

Consent

Once again, this word is currently used highly selectively.

– The second and seventh points of the above section 'Choice' are again relevant. Two teenagers, for example, may need little encouragement to 'consent', but how is that admirable?

– Moreover, you cannot 'consent' to what you don't know. How are they, at such a young age, in a position to know any short-term or long-term consequences, physical or emotional?

– That 'consent' can legitimise behaviour is a strange idea. For example, a man and woman 'consenting' to sleep together will not stop their spouses justifiably objecting intensely.

– Is the non-consent of parents towards their children sleeping with a given person irrelevant? We would benefit from asking how cultures where parental authority is strong compare in health and success to cultures where it is weak.[67]

– The notion of 'consent' becomes incoherent in light of the possible conflict between an individual's rational and short-term pleasure loving natures. Both are equally real. For example, what if a young person looks at the previous drunken night's partner and finds that their whole life story has now been irrevocably rewritten for the sake of someone who, in the cold light of day, they would not look at twice? Did (or do) they really consent? Does their 'better' self ever consent to this kind of behaviour? This confusion comes from abandoning the boundaries that a marriage-culture established for the very purposes of (a) civilising men (and they have something to aim for only if they are not permitted to have their cake and eat it[68]) and (b) the flourishing and proper maturation and character formation of all.

Creationism

This is the perfect Trojan Horse. Ostensibly it means a view opposed to evolution, involving special, separate, individual creation of different species so that they are not all part of one gigantic family tree.[69] But the word 'creationism' actually *looks like* it just means the widespread view that the universe was created, as opposed to existing without a creator. Because the word is so well suited to that second meaning, those who have a mind to do so can conflate the two meanings together and so give the covert or overt impression that all believers in a creator (and 'creator' is a term often synonymous with 'God') are anti-evolution and anti-intellectual. When you have found a Trojan Horse word as effective as that, you stick with it!

Democracy

Democracy is clearly superior to many other polities, but that does not take away the flaws in the concept.

– It is conceded that the UK is actually a *'parliamentary* democracy'. That is true. However, does one 5-yearly vote that almost always sways nothing (and one period of jury service) mean that you 'rule'?

– Yet what is a 'parliamentary democracy'? Only a small percentage of us live in marginal constituencies. Even then, we have 2 or 3 realistically possible 'representatives'. There's no guarantee we will especially prefer, nor even admire, any particular candidate.

– MPs voted in are then subject both to whips and to party manifestos, which are package deals that may well include parts the voter is opposed to.

– The body of MPs in its entirety falls some way short of socially mirroring national diversity.[70]

– If democracy means everyone's views are to be treated equally, then obviously we all know different amounts about different things; we would expect at least that executive voting powers should be limited to areas where people have more knowledge. Otherwise, for example, I end up having just as much say on astrophysics questions, in my ignorance, as does a professor of that subject. It follows that any just democracy will be part-meritocracy.

Diversity

Diversity, in the sense of 'difference', is obviously neutral. If there are two people, of whom one is a mobile phone stealer and the other a non-mobile phone stealer, they collectively exhibit poles-apart diversity. But why would anyone consider that to be good?

Equality

So-called 'equal marriage' (for a more detailed analysis of same-sex marriage, see Chapter 11) is a good example of the deliberate abuse and misapplication of the over-used terms 'equal' and 'equality'. The perceived rights of just one particular vocal minority were without explanation equated to equality for all, just as Pride festivals celebrate rainbow-like diversity *in general*: gay advocacy becomes the one overarching issue. But equality was not present here. In the revised understanding of marriage, adults were privileged over children; pairs over other groupings; a tiny-minority perspective over the vast majority internationally and historically. The latter soon found themselves discriminated against even before the new Bill became law. The upholders of the *existing* law[71] (unlike the revisionists) were, in the shape of the organization Christian Concern, banned from holding events at the Law Society and at the government-owned QEII Conference Centre.[72]

Extremism

Obviously, there is nothing intrinsically wrong with being extreme. The greatest experts on any matter are rarely mainstream and very often 'extreme' in their views. But they will also be closer to the truth. The idea that the extreme is somehow wrong can only be held in a society that values conformity above all else, so implying that might is right and debate beside the point. It is a scenario where the first victim is truth. But the situation is worse, because *who* has the right to state which things should be conformed to in the first place? *They* were not conforming, since they were stating the principles afresh with a view that *others* should conform to them. Such a system is first about power, second about conformity; but when is it about truth?

Freedom

Where freedom is a fetish, all kinds of bad results and unhappiness can result. So-called personal freedom is greatest where abortion and divorce are highest. That does not make the freedom a false freedom. It does mean that (1) freedom is only sometimes a good thing (depending on what it is freedom *from*, and what it is freedom *for*); (2) 'freedom', being another single word, is another ill-thought-through simplification; (3) no consideration has been given to the idea that boundaries and discipline are necessary for flourishing and for happiness.[73]

Fundamentalism, Islamism

These words are etymologically confused. How can 'Islamist' describe people utterly different from actual adherents of Islam? That is the exact opposite of its natural meaning. Such misapplication would be bad enough in any word – but this one was a *deliberate* coinage. And the term 'fundamentalist'[74] makes a nonsense of the entire Augustinian maxim 'in essentials unity, in non-essentials liberty, in all things charity'. For surely the *fundamentals* of a world view, as opposed to the non-fundamentals, are the bits that adherents ought especially to hold to; and it is precisely holding to these fundamentals that makes them rightly be classified as adherents of that world view in the first place. So how is it possible to reject those fundamentals and still somehow be classified as adherents?

Good disagreement

There are several major flaws in this concept, which has been central to recent Shared Conversations on homosexuality within the Church of England.

First, if everyone presupposes that views will remain polarised, there is no need to investigate whether evidence matches one's own preferences (and the chances of evidence matching anyone's *preferences* are never great!). That breaks the cardinal rule of debate. A conclusion comes at the end: least of all at the start.

Second, there is no requirement to be familiar with evidence before stating one's 'views'/'conclusions'. Take the Church of England discussions on homosexuality. Generally, in scholarly discussion, the more startling the statistic, the more central it will be to the investigation.

Not so here, however. There is no apparent expectation (and little evidence) that anyone knows the startling statistical discrepancies between typical heterosexual and homosexual rates of promiscuity, indulgence in risky sexual practices, STIs, and life expectancy. Nor any expectation of familiarity with the exegetical discussions of two millennia.

Third, it is impossible that an opinion-graph with peaks at both poles yet no reading in the middle (i.e., the very reverse of normal distribution) represents honest reading of the evidence. Such a graph accurately plots polarised ideologies and preferences as opposed to evidenced conclusions. But ideology is not evidence-based: it is the enemy and opposite of scholarship.

Fourth, the homosexual issue is getting preferential treatment if it is the only issue where people are granted the luxury of 'good disagreement'. Whereas if it is *not* the only such issue, then a free-for-all beckons, since it would seem unfair and illogical to exclude *any* issue.

Fifth, it is a strange issue to select for such preferential treatment. There are plenty of controversial issues in theology and exegesis, but through two millennia it has scarcely been noticed that this is one of them: the Scriptures seem plain and forthright. Even when this is finally 'noticed', the timing and location of this development suggest that social conformity is the driver.

Homophobia[75]

This word[76] is etymologically confused, since it literally means 'fear of that which is the same'. The same as what, one asks? It is dishonest in at least three ways:

– No-one can actually produce people who fear homosexuals or homosexuality.

– The similarity to 'arachnophobia' or 'claustrophobia' wrongly suggests a technical psychological term.

– No-one can produce an individual who has been clinically diagnosed to have this condition.

A further problem is that hatred is normally implied by this word. Yet 'phobia' does not mean 'hatred': it means 'fear'. And today hatred is inferred every time someone is rationally opposed to *even one thing connected with* homosexuals or homosexuality; even where that opposition is based on well-evidenced facts (as for example concerning comparative rates of promiscuity, of STIs, of life-expectancy, etc.). But scientific findings are just that: observation-based and ideologically neutral. They have nothing to do with emotion.

The word, like 'bigot' and others, is also used as a convenient conversation-stopper as soon as the science gets inconvenient.

Homosexual and Heterosexual

The fact that they look so similar is precisely the point. This recently-chosen pairing of words is designed to give the message that these are two precisely equal, and equally good, alternatives.

Law, rule of law

If there is no obligation for law to match reality, then law itself can be a Trojan Horse. Some examples:

– *Anything* can be voted into law. For example, green can be voted red.[77]

– There can be ever-present motives (for example, an MP's wish to ensure re-election) to vote untrue things into law.

– Abortion votes (walks into a lobby!) can't reconstitute biological reality.

– MPs are *not expert* on most issues, yet as part of their job are still expected to vote. Many votes will therefore be made in ignorance.

– Untrue things are beginning to creep into law. A few examples:

- The terms 'Progenitor A' and 'Progenitor B' have now replaced 'Mother' and 'Father' on Spanish birth certificates.

- Non-parents are beginning to appear in parents' place on *birth* certificates – but once the factual bedrock that everyone has two parents, one male and one female, is forsaken, how do you select from available candidates with their competing claims? And why restrict the number to two?

- Non-biological genders on birth-certificates have now existed for a while in many European and Asian countries.

– Most would agree that it is clearly worse to steal a husband than a car; but that is not the position in law! The law therefore seems opposed to both good sense and good morality.

WHAT ARE THEY TEACHING THE CHILDREN?

– Since 20th May 2008, UK law has said that a child does not need a father. That is wrong in at least four ways. It is the reverse of reality: they *have* a father, and that fundamental biology precedes any issue of need. Also, the statistics are very stark in showing that having or not having a father is perhaps the biggest factor in determining how their lives are likely to turn out.[78] So far from not needing a father, a father is the very thing they *most* need. Third, the proposal is a lazy father's charter. Fourth, the innovators claim to be equality supporters!

– In separation/divorce, the law actually sides with the divider (likely to be the more selfish) and *not* with the peacemaker (likely to be the more mature). If they want two different outcomes, division is the outcome that they get. How negative! The idea (which doesn't sound obviously true) is presumably that being forced to remain married is *worse* than being forced to become divorced. In comparison of these two options, the compulsions on either side cancel each other out, leaving the two states 'marriage' and 'divorce', of which incredibly the *latter* is then judged preferable. Nor is it explained why it is fine to abandon a spouse but not to abandon children. If that is put forward as the unargued assumption, it should be no surprise if people act according to it.

– It may be argued that the UK law provides far greater financial incentives for couples to live apart than to live together.[79]

Left-wing and right-wing

If politics were conducted by truth-seekers, it is unlikely in the extreme that they would find that on any given issue the evidence pointed to just *two* alternatives – let alone that it would point to two alternatives that were typically *poles apart*! For example, do all capitalists have traditional views on the family? Or are they all in favour of guns? Or of fat cats? No: the stereotype is of an all-or-nothing package, but the reality is far different. So the rhetoric of left-wing and right-wing is perhaps likelier to be a social mechanism of peer-groups, indicating who is in and out, included and excluded. A better perspective is Tom Wright's, at the Fulcrum launch on 5th November 2003: 'A bird needs two wings, but its fulcrum, its point of balance, is its body.'.

Literal and metaphorical

Tony Blair[80] asks that sacred texts now be read metaphorically, not literally. As many as eighteen problems within this very brief proposal come to mind.

– It is a generalisation; and the larger the generalisation, the less likely it is to be true. I thought only 'fundamentalists' spoke unthinkingly of 'the Bible' or 'the Koran' as an undifferentiated unity. Yet 'the Bible' alone (from Greek *ta biblia*: meaning plural 'books') is a multi-author library of 66 books (73 for Catholics).

– These books cover 10 to 20 genres of literature. It would be dogmatic and highly inaccurate to claim that all of these were metaphorical genres. Very few are.

– The New Testament (the more central portion for Christians) has 27 books: all either letters (including circulated homilies) or narratives about recent events. It would therefore be eccentric to take either of *those* two genres as *not* making literal claims. After all, do we generally contact letter-writers or biographers to see which bits they intended 'literally'? No: 'literal' is just the default that applies unless there is good reason for it not to.

– The New Testament, when describing the indescribable, naturally uses extended similes (which are not metaphors): parables of what the kingdom of heaven is *like*; visions that look *like* something. But these text-portions are demarcated clearly – even to a child – within the overall literal narrative.

– One of the 66 (or 73) books in the Bible is genuinely metaphorical: the Song of Songs. But that's less than 1% of the Bible, and the more-than-99% that is in non-metaphorical genres is far more typical. To state that 'the Bible' is more metaphorical than literal is to substitute unscholarly personal preference for the facts of literary genre.

– Sometimes, of course, only 'metaphorical' language is strong and glorious enough to convey the intended meaning. But here, far from obscuring or muddying the literal/basic meaning, metaphors are hand-picked to correspond to it, serve it, and emphasise it. It is the literal meaning that determines that only a tiny proportion of possible metaphors will be *appropriate*. To get as close as possible to the reality, one sometimes has to say (for example) that God is 'a sun'[81] rather than just

radiant – because that is stronger and more vivid, therefore more accurate.
– So you cannot dream up a metaphor until you *first* understand the literal meaning. 'Literal' interpretation[82] is not merely one of many equal kinds of interpretation from which we can cull one understanding – let alone cull our private personal preference! It is the foundation for all the others (typological, allegorical, prescriptive, etc.), which can simultaneously coexist.

– Mr Blair's approach presents literal truth and 'metaphorical truth' as the only two possibilities. This makes two errors. First, like those people who say 'there are different kinds of truth', it sees fit to apply the *same* central word 'truth' to at least two quite *distinct* realities. This can only cause confusion. Therefore, a clear thinker would use a different word on the second occasion, to avoid that confusion.

– And second, on this line of thought the ever-present possibility of *falsehood* is excluded. But infinitely more things are false than are true: for every single particular true fact, there are very many (in fact, an infinite number) that are untrue.[83] And if nothing is false, everything is 'true'; but if everything is true, nothing is true.

– By wrongly treating 'metaphorical' as being the *opposite* of literal, thereby excluding the latter, Mr Blair is apparently saying that all we know about the sacred text is that it is not saying what it appears to be saying.

– One of many problems with that is that we then cannot tell *which* of the billions of things it doesn't appear to be saying is the one that it actually 'is' saying.

– Mr Blair's solution here is even stranger. Which meaning to choose? Why, the one that's *opposite* to the literal or natural. If, for example, the text disapproves of homosexual practice, then just read it 'metaphorically', and you can soon get the meaning you want.

– Why would the very thing that a culture-bound reader two millennia later does not wish to be literally false miraculously turn out to be the correct 'metaphorically true' interpretation?

– It is not at all clear that anything *so* untrue as to be *literally* false could manage to *be* 'metaphorically true'.

– The literal and the metaphorical are not polar opposites: they sometimes exist along a single sliding-scale. Nouns refer to concrete objects; but when we come to verbs, who is to say how 'literally' accurate a given verb is?[84]

– The whole idea of 'metaphorically true' (as opposed to 'metaphor', which is understandable) is incoherent. Who is to decide, and by what criteria, which things are 'metaphorically true'?

– It does seem that this new suggested 'interpretation' has been hand-picked by Mr Blair, the reader. But if 'Labour' or 'Catholic' can mean anything that the individual wishes, then so can any text.[85] The biblical writers would be amazed to discover that they were 21st century liberals all along.

– Slippery (or 'political'?) use of language can then increase. Metaphors are embraced for being *not* strictly true, harder to pin down, less precise. Claims to factual truth, however well supported by evidence, are sidelined.

What a knotty rigmarole. Why not just jettison the text, and admit: *'La Bible, c'est moi!'*?

Love

It is often complained that people who oppose same-sex marriage are blocking love, and different people may 'love' someone of the same gender, just as they may love someone of a different gender. But again this raises problems:

– Everyone knows we don't 'love' just one person. We love parents, children, friends, self, pets, (if Christian) enemies, etc..

– We don't, and can't, marry everyone we love!

And if, as is frequently said, *'God is love'*[86] is the be-all and end-all of the Bible, then several things logically follow:

– It is also a mere millionth of the text. That means colossal over-simplification and selectivity are imposing themselves. With selectivity comes both inaccuracy and ideology.

– What is meant by 'love' has to be defined. It clearly doesn't mean 'indulgence'; and why should it 'obediently' mean just exactly what we would like it to mean? Its meaning is for lexicographers and exegetes to determine more objectively.

– Even if this principle settles ethical questions, it doesn't touch on cosmological or historical questions.

– How does one determine which principles are the central ones in 'the Bible'? 'Show your working', in other words.

– Why do the proponents of such a view reject much of what was written even by the same author (John), let alone by other biblical authors? Clearly their principle of selection is congeniality; but obviously congenial doesn't equal 'true'. And (worse) if they emphasise only the bits they already agreed with anyway, why bother 'using' a sacred text of which they are arbiter? Simpler, one would have thought, to jettison the text and enunciate their own alternative philosophy.

Progressive and reactionary

It is hard to imagine a more ideological word than 'progressive'. People will certainly disagree about what counts as *being* progress (one person's 'progress' is another's 'regress'); but which of them, then, has the authority to dictate 'orthodoxy' in this matter? The only hope here is to consult maximally objective data and evaluate claims to progress in this way. Once we do that, we find, for example, that the 'progressive' sexual revolution is in fact regressive by all kinds of statistical measures.[87]

Further, merely to classify people with the same preferred ideology as oneself as 'progressive' and those who disagree as 'regressive' is inaccurate, simplistic, and insulting: nothing less than an attempt to sidestep debate while also aiming to silence those who question one's own ideology. The claim is sometimes made, by those who hold to a grand teleological narrative, that one can be 'on the right side of history'. But history is quite massively complex; nor does it move in straight lines; nor does it culminate 'now'. Consequently, we cannot speak of a 'right side of history'; still less assume that everyone must agree with one's own grand imposed narrative – or else they need to 'get with the programme'![88] This too is a kind of 'might is right': discerning trajectories in history and making sure one jumps ship where necessary in order always to end up on the 'winning' side. Thought should be given instead to whether that 'side' is actually *in the right* in terms of its measurable effects, whether or not it is currently 'winning' in (media-influenced) public opinion.

'Reactionary', the most favoured term of abuse in this scenario, implies the present age is always (not sometimes) right, is infallible; and that the only reason people question it is a psychological one: nostalgia! Both claims are incorrect.

Relationship, loving/stable relationship
This word is very vague, and constitutes a useful Trojan Horse. Any two entities share *some* relationship. If the idea is that all relationships involve *two* people, that is false. If it is that the sexual/non-sexual dimension is indifferent, that is false, since sex is a matter of significance.[89] If the idea is that 'loving' means 'sexual', that is false too. And if it is that typically 'stable' non-marital sexual types of relationship exist, then that is statistically quite false too[90], as is too rarely explained.

Religion
Protestants and Pentecostals often dismiss or despise what they term 'religion'; in this, they are in line with Barth, Bonhoeffer, and others from the earlier 20th century. There are certainly several reasons not to have an essentially positive view of this word, whatever merits it may have:
– 'Religion' is not just a vague word but is *quintessentially* vague.[91]
– 'Religion' (whatever it may mean) is not what Christians are concerned with. They are concerned with reality, relationship, life.
– 'Religion' is highly marginal (or, depending on translation, absent) in the New Testament. James 1.27 – but where else?
– Its etymology ('bound' or 'tied to') isn't necessarily promising – though of course obligations can often be healthy.
– One cannot generalise about such internally and collectively diverse phenomena as Christianity, Judaism, Islam, Hinduism etc. under this (or any) one head. Some of the disparate things thoughtlessly classified together as 'religions' are more mythology, some more world-view/ philosophy, some more ritual, some more history, some more spirituality or lifestyle, and so on.
– Using 'religion' as the overarching category has anti-education effects such as have recently been produced in schools and colleges: the widespread view that Jesus was essentially a figure of 'religion', and therefore didn't exist.[92]
– The popularity of the word 'religion' among secularists, compared to the indifference to it shown by Christians, shows that secularists have

not grasped where Christians are coming from.

– Recent court-cases have hinged on 'deeply-held religious views'. That is incoherent in at least three ways. First, however 'deeply' you 'hold' something, it becomes no truer purely on the basis of conviction. What is the *evidence*? Second, 'deeply-held' suggests *emotional* attachment, but what about Christians who prioritise rational/logical grounding? Third, 'religious view' is incoherent, because any 'view' held should be on the basis of evidence alone.

Rights

Few will question whether it is good to assign people legal rights: no further ground is required for these beyond human dignity. Yet beyond this, the concept of 'rights' is often problematic. Five points:

– Whereas (for example) the life of an unborn baby exists tangibly and unarguably, rights don't. Yet they are often held to loom *larger than* the tangible and unarguable!

– Since the existence of a right is legally and not scientifically determined, we cannot expect full agreement on any list of human rights.

– However, we can agree that none can be exercised without the most fundamental: the right to life.

– Appeal to rights can sometimes be the recourse of the immature, who prefer them to responsibilities.

– Framing the homosexual debate in terms of 'gay rights' brings the inevitable comparison with civil rights and black activism. But the latter movements are quite different in that they concern an inborn/basic characteristic (pigmentation).

Scripture, tradition and reason

The conveniently plural Anglican approach to truth (derived from the Anglican Richard Hooker) can at worst allow people to emphasise or de-emphasise different parts of this traditional 'tripod' (or, indeed, Experience instead) in order to arrive at their preferred conclusion. The dangers that attend all slogans are especially prevalent in this case; rather than restating the principle, both the three (or four) concepts themselves and the relationship between them need further clarification.

Thus, the oldest and most authentic *tradition* is very regularly that found in Scripture anyway: the two categories strongly overlap. But even where it is not, nothing is true *by virtue of* being traditional – only by virtue of being accurate. Then again, neither is anything true *by virtue of* being in *Scripture*, since every truth in Scripture (as in every book or library) was *already* true on other grounds before being written down. Being written down could not make it any more or less true. And if its wholesale truth is just taken on trust, evidence has been abandoned as a criterion, so we have moved beyond legitimate debate. *Experience* ranges from being highly authoritative (where 'experience' means the world as it really is, empirically discovered, and not as one might wish it to be) to not authoritative at all (where 'experience' means what is important to the private world and interests of one individual). *Reason*, however, is embraced by truth-seekers. To find truth is to examine and research what's in the world, in documents, and in experience (this is the scientific method), and to analyse that data rationally.

Sex

It is obviously impossible to be either in favour of 'sex' or against it: because it is not one unitary phenomenon. In terms of value, it encompasses every level from the heights to the depths. Accordingly, 'anti-sex' is an incoherent Trojan horse accusation that makes out that if one is anti one manifestation of sex, one 'must' therefore be anti all of them.

Tolerance

Tolerance has been included as a core British Value after mysteriously taking centre stage in the 1980s.[93] It is a good Trojan Horse because intolerance is so bad. But it is incoherent:
– It undercuts itself: tolerance prevents tolerance. For if tolerance becomes the chief virtue, then I can do whatever I want, and people will be *forced* (which is not very tolerant) to tolerate that.
– Tolerance is amoral, because it includes tolerating what is wrong.
– The word 'tolerance' is vague and meaningless (perhaps deliberately vague), something that the unnatural lack of a grammatical object accentuates. For to tolerate *everything* is to be in favour of everything (or perhaps nothing) – and is therefore impossible.

As remarked by the writer Dorothy L Sayers,[94] tolerance is otherwise known as despair because, 'It believes in nothing, cares for nothing, seeks to know nothing, interferes with nothing, enjoys nothing, hates nothing, finds purpose in nothing, lives for nothing, and remains alive because there is nothing for which it will die.'

A far stronger option than mere tolerance is *love*. Acclaimed as the chief fruit of the Spirit,[95] it is active, and is far more gladly received. After all, what would anyone prefer to hear: 'I tolerate you' or 'I love you'?

View/position

Everyone has a view/position on most topics. But some of these are the result of research, and others are nothing better than pure ideology, wishful thinking or a selfishly-preferred scenario. This is the *main* divide: between truth-seekers and ideologues. Yet, unbelievably, people often ask 'What is your view/take/position/opinion on this?', when they would be far better asking, 'What is the evidence?'

In fact, it is best not to speak of having a personal 'view' (as though *everything* were just a matter of opinion!) *over and above the publicly-available evidence that already exists.* Where the evidence is clear *and* where it isn't, our 'view' should still be one and the same thing as the evidence – so why speak about 'views' at all?

In a debate, people expect a (dogmatic) conservative to be pitted against a (dogmatic) radical, so fail to realise that being a conservative (on every possible issue?) or a radical (in everything?) are both untenable positions: two of many possible dogmatic/ideological (and therefore untenable) positions. E.g.: ever-diplomatic, ever-maverick, ever-pessimistic, purely pious, purely fashion-led.

Nor, when it comes to truth-seeking, is the main divide between Christians and non-Christians: there are many Christian ideologues too. For example, some may be tempted to believe the promises of heaven, acceptance, etc., because they are pleasant, rather than on the basis of being convinced of their truth.

Failure to identify evidence-vs-ideology as the central issue also bedevils media discussions and debates. The observable datum that there *are* often *precisely two* main views on things, which are *poles apart*, is highly significant. Even in cases where there were precisely two *honest* views of anything, the evidence could never point only to the two poles to the exclusion of middle ground. We can only conclude that very often the two views in question are none other than the ideological, wishful-thinking one and the evidenced one. But these could scarcely be less equal to one another from a scholarly point of view. Despite that, media discussions get framed[96] in terms of this ongoing 'debate', and presuppose that 'this one will run and run'. (So what was the point?) There will be soundbites; no close cross-questioning. Defeat is impossible, so cherished irrational ideologies can live on. Also, the choice of two debate-partners determines where the central ground 'is'; so ideologues can, by clever choice of debate-partners, move that perceived centre-ground in their preferred direction.[97]

In truth-seeking we don't know what we will find; but it often won't fit our expectations and will *rarely* fit our wishes. Now we will no doubt sometimes come to provisional conclusions that are conservative,[98] or radical, or anything else. But that isn't because we ourselves are ideologically conservative or radical, but simply because that is where the *evidence* led *this time*.

In conclusion, the only possible position is to be an open-minded truth-seeker. But there is no blank slate here: we already possess prior provisional conclusions from our previous investigations and those of other truth-seekers.

We proceed in Chapter 11 to the third and final part of our argument: Section (C). The burden of this section is to demonstrate that we can best understand what is going on if we see the events of the last fifty years in terms of a battle between truth-seeking and selfish, unevidenced ideology.

Notes

[1] Or even perhaps that it is possible to amalgamate into one the present secular values and recently-abandoned Christian values – it isn't.

[2] For good or ill, 'British' c.1955 has a strong tint of 'English': they are equivalent in W Golding, *Lord of the Flies* (Faber, London, 1954) chapters 12, 2 respectively.

[3] On the secularization process, see (historically) C G Brown, *The Death of Christian Britain: Understanding Secularisation 1800-2000* (Routledge, Abingdon & New York, NY, [2001] 2nd edition 2009); M Eberstadt, *How The West Really Lost God: A New Theory of Secularization* (Templeton Press, West Conshohocken, 2013); A Haydon & Sir E Leigh (edd.), *The Nation That Forgot God* (Gracewing, Leominster, [2009] 2nd edition 2016).

[4] See p.260.

[5] We must privilege statistical surveys which: (a) have large samples; (b) are most long-term (often also being the most up-to-date is important); (c) have the most random samples; (d) are most representative or typical in their results. Most of all we should privilege meta-analyses: studies which combine previous research into one. Sometimes data from the USA and other countries will be relevant to the UK, particularly as closely-related countries follow one another in their social innovations.

[6] Statistics: Office of National Statistics.

[7] This is a problematic term: see pp.266-7.

[8] Statistics: Department of Health.

[9] The Royal College of Obstetricians and Gynaecologists gave this figure for the number of women treated in hospital for the consequences of criminal abortions in 1962 in its paper 'Legalised Abortion' [1966] British Medical Journal 1.4. It repudiated the inaccurate figures between 50,000 and 250,000 that were sometimes bandied around – as they were that very year by the architect of the Act, David Steel: 'probably between 40,000 and 200,000 a year' (*Hansard* 5th series Vol. 7, Col. 1071, 22.7.1966). Scandalously, David Steel had not learnt any better even by 2007: on Channel 4 News 25.10.2007 he opined that the present 193,000 annual abortions in England and Wales were probably roughly the same as before legislation. In the USA, Dr Bernard Nathanson admitted hugely inflating the actual abortion figures in the run-up to the passing of Roe vs Wade: see B N Nathanson with R N Ostling, *Aborting America* (Doubleday, Garden City, NY, 1979) p.193.

[10] See E S Williams, *The Great Divorce Controversy* (Belmont House, Sutton, 2000).

[11] The release of Germaine Greer's *The Female Eunuch* (Harper Perennial, New York, NY & London, [1970] 2006) coincided with this new laxer legislation. Engelbert Humperdinck's song *Release Me*, dating from 1966, had helped pave the way with its superficially logical but actually nonsensical and selfish lyrics.

[12] Statistics: Office of National Statistics.

[13] B R E Wright, *Christians Are Hate-Filled Hypocrites...And Other Lies You've Been Told* (Bethany House, Bloomington, MN, 2010) pp.132-5; S Feldhahn, *The Good News about Marriage: Debunking Discouraging Myths about Marriage and Divorce* (Multnomah, Portland, OR, 2014). Feldhahn's research also exposes the '50% divorce rate' in the USA as a myth: rather, 20-25% of first-time marriages break down even within this most 'liberal' of cultures. One can only guess at the motives of those who promulgated the myth; but one clue is that the myth has been *used* to 'prove' that marriage

is dying in the modern world. There are two errors here. First, it would have been the legal changes pushed for by the revolutionaries that *caused* the weakening of marriage within the culture; so they cannot complain about something they themselves caused. And second, it is not the institution of marriage that is problematic (despite claims made even by Christian organs: see *Church Times* leader 7.6.2013), since, if it were, the fallout from this would be found in every one of the very many cultures where that institution is found. But it is not: quite the reverse: marriage is consistently correlated with increased health and happiness (see first Objection below). So the problem must lie within particular cultures and their foundational philosophies and laws.

[14] www.thepublicdiscourse.com/2014/08/13667/.

[15] Cf. C Vicari, *Distortion: How The New Christian Left Is Twisting The Gospel And Damaging The Faith* (FrontLine, Lake Mary, FL, 2014). Therefore, to normalise the sexual revolution in UK schoolteaching at the expense of Christian principles is, incredibly, to force a high-achieving social group to learn at the feet of under-achievers (and, in some cases, criminals)!

[16] See the summary of evidence from mainstream sources in E S Williams, *Cohabitation Or Marriage?* (Belmont House, Sutton, 1997). Though at times only a single gender may have been researched, by definition the figures will be much the same for both genders. Note that the flight from marriage has also led to the downgrading of the marital title Mrs, so that we are now in freefall via Ms to Mx. Introducing the title 'Ms' does not provide equality of the sexes, since the system that combines 'Mr'/'Master' and 'Mrs'/ 'Miss' has just as much equality. But only the latter system allows marriage to be something of significance *at all*! – and every wedding photo tells us it is in fact something of *great* significance. C Ash, *Married for God* (IVP, Nottingham, 2007) analyses the ways that marriage is better than cohabitation. Something even more important than school-entry and house-buying shouldn't receive much less planning.

[17] Statistics: General Household Survey.

[18] This last finding was the work of Harry Benson of the Bristol Community Family Trust. See, for example, thefamilywatch.org/doc/doc.0087.es.pdf.

[19] www.familysearch.org/learn/wiki/en/Illegitimacy_in_England.

[20] See E S Williams, *Lessons in Depravity* (Belmont House, Sutton, 2003) appendix.

[21] Statistics: Government Statistical Service Contraceptive Bulletins.

[22] Statistics: National Surveys of Sexual Behaviour.

[23] See R Whelan, *Broken Homes and Battered Children* (Family Education Trust, Oxford, 1994). The findings from the USA are similar. The Fourth (and, to date, most recent) National Incidence Study of Child Abuse and Neglect (NIS-4), covering the years 2004-9, found that children living with a single parent and no partner were 5 times more likely to suffer sexual abuse than the average; those living with a step-family 8-9 times likelier; and those living with a single parent and partner 20 times likelier. One often hears that most sexual abuse takes place 'in the home'. An accurate picture will be given only if it is specified *what sort of* home.

[24] A single mother is estimated to be 30 times more likely to suffer domestic violence than is a married mother: see the tables and research cited at ozconservative.blogspot. co.uk/2014/07 (1.7.2014).

[25] See *Guardian* 1.9.2009: joint research of NSPCC and Bristol University.

[26] John Jay College of Criminal Justice, *The Nature and Scope of the Problem of Sexual Abuse of Minors by Catholic Priests and Deacons in the United States* (US Conference of

Catholic Bishops, 2004). It may be wondered whether anything can exceed the victims' misery; but endlessly repetitive playing out of abuse cases in the media might well do so. Given that on past form this would be judged extremely likely to take place were abuse cases made public, it may well be that the policy of secrecy had at least some sense behind it; which is more than can be said for the removal of offending priests to some further post. Yet even that may have been to prevent the inevitable and interminable media scandal and 'revelations' that would be caused by a complete removal from office. We make the point in the text that the overwhelming peak period of church-based abuse entirely overlaps with that of care-home / children's-home abuse, on which see B Corby *et al.*, *Public Inquiries into Abuse of Children in Residential Care* (Jessica Kingsley, London, 2001); an updated synthesis will clearly be needed in light of more recent developments.

[27] C Shakeshaft, *Educator Sexual Misconduct* (US Department of Education, 2004).

[28] See E S Williams, *Lessons in Depravity*, pp.317-18.

[29] The term 'STDs' refers to the different diseases, and 'STIs' to the individual cases where a person is infected by any of these.

[30] Public Health Laboratory Service Communicable Disease Surveillance Centre, 'Sexually Transmitted Disease in Britain, 1985-6' [1989] Genitourinary Medicine 65.

[31] As calculated by the US Centers for Disease Control and Prevention, 2008.

[32] Statistics: Department of Health and Home Office Drugs Division.

[33] L Appleby *et al.*, 'Suicide by Children and Young People in England' [2016] Manchester University research paper.

[34] A Chandra *et al.*, 'Does Watching Sex on Television Predict Teenage Pregnancy?' [2008] Pediatrics 122.5.

[35] V C Yoder *et al.*, 'Internet Pornography and Loneliness: An Association?' [2005] Sexual Addiction and Compulsivity 12.1.

[36] S Stack *et al.*, 'Adult Social Bonds and Use of Internet Pornography' [2004] Social Science Quarterly 85.1. See too the research of S Perry and C Schleifer from the 2006-14 General Social Survey (risk doubled for men and tripled for women): www.sciencemag.org/news/2016/08/divorce-rates-double-when-people-start-watching-porn. Incidentally, is not the term 'porn' too friendly, cosy and lacking in seriousness (like 'E' for ecstasy tablets) for something that is no friend of ours?

[37] Here we touch on the disconnect between the Christian and non-Christian outlooks. The existence of infidelity-promoting organisations like Ashley Madison – let alone their public advertisement – strikes a Christian as beyond belief. When in 2008 Google underwent a court-case with the Christian Institute because they would not accept the CI's pop-up ads concerning abortion facts, Google were lodging their objection while simultaneously openly allowing infidelity advertisements of this kind! There are several similar examples. Christians would instinctively class the spread of sexual-phone-line advertisements in national newspapers as a kind of cancer, and wonder why other people could not see that pattern. Likewise, a Christian who read that Prince Charles or Sarah Ferguson had had significant sexual experience before marriage would fear for the future union of each, as both the habit of transience and strong extramarital ties that could interfere with a marriage would have already taken root. But all the discussion was instead about 'compatibility'. In the Christian perspective, unresolved flaws in individuals and societies (more than 'incompatibility') will be a key predictor of marriage breakdown. The best theory, the most accurate world view, is the one that can make the best predictions.

[38] D Rowles, Trade News 10.11.2010 (on www.pajiba.com).

[39] M Seligman in J Buie, '"Me" Decades Generate Depression: Individualism Erodes Commitment to Others' [1988] APA Monitor 19.18. The then-leader of the Liberal Party, Nick Clegg, showed an unimpressive inability in joined-up thinking in his dual evangelism for cannabis and for attention to mental health problems (to which cannabis is a significant contributor!): see dailymail.co.uk/news/article-3058298/Heard-joined-thinking-Cleggy-ANDREW-PIERCE-stories-spin-doctors-DON'T-want-read.html.

[40] S McManus et al. (edd.), *Adult Psychiatric Morbidity in England 2007* (NHS Information Centre for Health and Social Care, 2009).

[41] B O'Neill, www.spiked-online.com 18.2.2016.

[42] The purported 'housing crisis' would vanish if the average household were a bit less unnaturally small in number – as it is for immigrants from more traditional (and often healthier) cultures. When we speak of cultural differences, we also ought not to ignore the possibility that it is more a case of culture vs lack of culture, especially where rich histories of thousands of years contrast with the abandonment of all history before 1963. Abandonment of the community that comes with church gatherings and parishes will inevitably bring an impoverishment and severe diminution of national culture in its train.

[43] UK Happiness Formula Survey 2005 compares the two years. The USA Pew Research Center's 'Are We Happy Yet?' survey had similar findings. The UK Office of National Statistics has since 2012 issued an annual report 'Measuring National Wellbeing' on levels of wellbeing and happiness – but results have constantly been uninteresting and relatively unchanged, as the vast majority of people seem to put their happiness level at 7 or 8 out of 10 (a level that does not quite count as 'very happy').

[44] www.gallup.com 7.10.2015.

[45] T F Robles et al., 'Marital Quality and Health: A Meta-Analytic Review' [2014] Psychological Bulletin 140.1.

[46] S Grover & J F Helliwell, *How's Life At Home?* (Working Paper 20794. National Bureau of Economic Research, 2014). See too Louise Kirk, 'We Should Listen To This Judge. Marriage Means Happiness' (Conservative Woman 24.2.2016). The judge in question, Sir Paul Coleridge, best known for being forced to resign for championing marriage, has devoted himself to laying out the rational and financial case for married/ family life. In this he follows in the tradition of Patrick Dixon, *The Rising Price of Love* (Hodder & Stoughton, London, 1995) who researched the extent of the astonishing financial drain caused by the sexual revolution. Dr Dixon's figures (now over 20 years out of date, so things would be even worse now) are speculative; but to make an informed estimate at all is a cut above going with the drift. The prime ways he analyses the sexual revolution to have been a financial drain are the following. First, in health (AIDS and other STDs; resultant loss of years of productive work; cervical screening; IVF; 'family-planning' clinics for teenagers; abortion advice; affair-related stress and guilt). Then, in the proliferation of divorce (legal costs; splitting into two homes; resultant additional household costs; absence from work; counselling). Further miscellaneous costs include single-parent welfare payouts; youth crime among products of broken homes; children in care; increase in social workers.

[47] C Ellison et al., 'Does Religious Commitment Contribute to Individual Life Satisfaction?' [1989] Social Forces 68.1; C Lim & R Putnam, 'Religion, Social Networks, and Life Satisfaction' [2010] American Sociological Review 75.6; and the ongoing research of the Austin Institute for the Study of Family and Culture.

[48] See the 2016 Mississippi State University study cited at ncregister.com/blog/segelstein/regular-family-attendance-at-church-can-help-kids-thrive-say-researchers/#ixzz42yUohfoz. Children were found to benefit in the areas of eagerness to learn, variety of interests, creativity, persistence, and responsibility.

[49] For example, G J Gates, *How Many People Are Lesbian, Gay, Bisexual and Transgender?* (Williams Institute, 2011): 1.7% lesbian or gay; 1.8% bisexual – this amid a massive growth in bisexual self-identification.

[50] In December 2013, the London Borough of Hounslow launched a poster campaign accurately highlighting that domestic abuse has a disproportionately large prevalence in gay households. It rehearsed 21 words comprising 5 repeated words ('straight', 'lesbian', 'gay', 'bisexual', 'transgender'). In each of the poster's 4 variant versions, 'gay' came 6 times, 'bisexual' 5 times, and 'lesbian' and 'transgender' 4 times each. 'Straight' – which was also the only one of the 5 words that was never highlighted in any of the posters, appeared just twice in each poster. What unreal imagined proportions, even outdoing those in Channel 4's offerings such as *Big Brother* and *Skins*.

[51] In accordance with the findings of the Social Readjustment Rating Scale devised in 1967 by T Holmes and R Rahe.

[52] On the quite horrible callousness of divorcing adults towards their children, see the study of J S Wallerstein *et al.*, *The Unexpected Legacy of Divorce: A 25-Year Landmark Study* (Hyperion, New York, NY, 2000). It's not clear why the word 'unexpected' is used. Child victims of divorce/remarriage are (xxiii) more likely to end up in mental health clinics and in hospital; more likely to indulge in early sex and to have children out of wedlock; less likely to marry, but more likely to divorce. Worse: the 2013 internet survey by Netmums found parents to be in denial about the actual effects on their children: three-quarters of the 1000 parents surveyed judged that their children were coping well with the divorce/separation, whereas just one-fifth of the 100 children surveyed judged themselves to be happy in their new circumstances. See telegraph.co.uk/women/sex/divorce/10541451/warring-parents-in-denial-about-effects-of-divorce-on-children.html.

[53] Chesterton makes this point in *Orthodoxy* (Baronius, London, [1927] 2005) chapter 5; Lewis in *Surprised By Joy* (Collins, Glasgow [1954] 2011) p.206.

[54] On abortion and worsened mental health, see recently (2016) D P Sullins on *Sage Open Medicine*: www.papers.ssrn.com/sol3/papers.cfm?abstract_id=2813546

[55] UK Census 2011.

[56] See www.sixteensmallstones.org/interesting-statistics-contrasting-atheism-and-christianity/.

[57] This point is central to E S Williams, *Lessons in Depravity*: for an explicit statement of this anti-marriage ideology see p.27. See too V Riches, *Sex Education or Indoctrination? How Ideology Has Triumphed Over Facts* (Family & Youth Concern, Whitton, 2004); E S Williams, *The Outrage of Amoral Sex Education* (Belmont House, Sutton, 2006).

[58] Nor could Christians see why the excuse of not being able to afford a wedding was used. There is no actual need for weddings to be lavish: that is merely culture-specific, and even *within* the culture is a recent development. To say that people need to complete their education and/or earn for some years before marriage is simply to *describe* what is happening in this culture at this time (which we already knew) without explaining why that should be taken as either normal or necessary. The inevitable result of increasing the typical age for marriage is the same as the result of making marriage optional: few will 'hold out' till marriage and the pool of potential sleeping-partners increases exponentially

given a secular culture, which is no doubt why these spurious arguments that no-one can marry young (which also help delay psychological maturity, and remove any timetable or motivation for its attainment) were employed in the first place.

[59] Prior to the UK Teenage Pregnancy Strategy of 1998-2010, there was an ignominious decade 1976-86 when the Family Planning Association launched targets to reduce abortions and illegitimate births. In those 10 years they distributed over 50m items of literature paid for by public money. Yet in those years abortions rose by 42,000 (from 130,000 to 172,000); and illegitimate births more than doubled, from 19,600 to 39,600: E S Williams, *The Outrage of Amoral Sex Education*, p.17. Now, on Christian assumptions that was exactly what would be expected, and it is clear that one follows the world-view whose predictive power is best. What followed instead (E S Williams, *Lessons in Depravity*, chapter 14) was the Gillick saga, where a mother's temporarily successful challenge to the permission of under-age girls to attend so-called 'family-planning' clinics without parental permission saw the number of visits to those clinics fall by one-third, and abortions from 5.6 to 5.4 per 1000. This progress was, however, soon reversed by the law.

[60] Just as the African countries flooded with condoms had AIDS epidemics and the one country Uganda who suggested abstinence as an option saw AIDS brought under control. See A Ivereigh, 'On Condom Use, The Pope May Be Right' (guardian.co.uk 19.3.2009). Condoms presuppose promiscuity: a self-fulfilling prophecy. Not only AIDS but abortion is (unsurprisingly) brought under greater control through abstinence education: www.104babcock.wordpress.com/2009/07/07/abstinence-only-states-more-effective/. Christians tend to prefer the positive word 'chastity' to the more negative word 'abstinence'.

[61] One is reminded of George Otis's series of *Transformations* videos published by CWM around the turn of the millennium. These showed a series of locations where Christianisation had been the key to transforming the entire community for the better.

[62] On the flaws of secularism, see M Poplin, *Is Reality Secular? Testing the Assumptions of Four Global World-Views* (IVP-USA, Downers Grove, IL, 2014). It is remarkable how often the main secularist gurus are found to have had psychologically troubled backgrounds and lives. See P Johnson, *Intellectuals* (Weidenfeld & Nicolson, London, 1988); D Di Marco & B Wiker, *Architects of the Culture of Death* (Ignatius, San Francisco, CA, 2004); R de Toledano, *Cry Havoc! The Great American Bring-Down and How It Happened* (Anthem, Washington, DC, 2006) – on the Frankfurt School.

[63] On the sexual revolution, see primarily G Kuby, *The Global Sexual Revolution: Destruction of Freedom in the Name of Freedom* (Angelico, Kettering, OH, [2012] ET 2015); and also M Eberstadt, *Adam And Eve After The Pill: Paradoxes of the Sexual Revolution* (Ignatius, San Francisco, CA, 2012).

[64] The human cost, largely among the young and easily-led, is the main factor here: Jennifer Roback Morse's Ruth Institute has recently produced a 'Twelve Survivors of the Sexual Revolution' Chart, each survivor-type being listed alongside the lies they may be imagined to have been told to justify what they suffered. The types are: child of divorce; child of unmarried parents; reluctantly divorced man/woman; reluctantly single parent; heartbroken career woman; donor-conceived person; pornography-addict (& families); post-abortive woman/man; gay-lifestyle refugee; refugee from the hook-up culture; cohabiter with regrets; person with health problems as a result of hook-ups, abortion or contraception.

[65] Both Disability and Sexuality are included among the 6 titles in the Inclusive Church Resource Book Series, published by Darton, Longman and Todd.

[66] Even commercially, supermarkets such as Aldi and Lidl have capitalised on the fact that customers can get exhausted by having too wide a choice – which will happen if choice is uncritically seen as a good.

[67] Recent well-publicised cases of mass city-wide sexual exploitation of girls in England have often involved English girls and Pakistani men. But no-one has mentioned that since Pakistani girls seem to be clearly off-bounds, replicating the relevant features of *their* upbringing and culture would make *English* girls equally off-bounds, and actually *did* so till the sexual revolution came. These cases indicate how problematic, fuzzy, inadequate, and harmful is the reliance on so-called 'consent'.

[68] The best-known saying in this regard is that no-one would buy a cow whose milk was already free. It is a foregone conclusion that secularists will (in real or feigned ignorance of the function of examples and comparisons in academic discourse) take this to be a direct comparison between wives as a class and cows as a class!

[69] A view that makes the same error as evolutionists typically do: both fail to see that the issue of whether or not there was/is a creator is separate from the issue of how whatever was created subsequently developed.

[70] The fact that MPs are typically white, educated urban liberals with a law/politics background means that much voting is effectively democratically skewed. The 'Brexit' from Europe was supported by 52% of the populace but just 20% of MPs. The same-sex marriage Bill was not opposed by a single political party, though the country was closely divided. And polls suggest a public vs politicians clash on the death penalty which even the normalisation provided by a law change cannot remove: see yougov.co.uk/news/2014/08/13/capital-punishment-50-years-favoured.

[71] Compare the case (reported in newspapers 10.12.2008) when Mrs Justice Dobbs refused as 'without merit' the joint request of the Christian Legal Centre (the legal branch of Christian Concern) and Comment on Reproductive Ethics for a judicial review into how three bodies could be licensed by the Human Fertilisation and Embryology Authority (HFEA) to create human-animal hybrids *before the relevant vote had even taken place that would determine whether any such thing was to become legal or not*. These three cases involving Christian Concern all show how even the law is at times powerless in the face of a greater power in the land: undemocratic and often anti-intellectual political correctness. So does the more recent case of Aisling Hubert, whose legal challenges to girl-aborting lawbreaker doctors have resulted in massive bills for the whistleblower in her poverty rather than for the lawbreakers in their wealth – together with the extraordinary assertion that to pursue her challenge would not be 'in the public interest'. This astonishing conclusion was not calculated either by large numbers of legal minds nor by actually asking any of the public, making this a classic example of Orwellian Newspeak. See www.christianconcern.com/gender-abortion.

[72] Around this time, instances of anti-Christian discrimination were proliferating (see R Scott, *Christians in the Firing Line* (Wilberforce Publications, London, 2013); G Kuby, *The Global Sexual Revolution*, chapter 14; M Eberstadt, *It's Dangerous To Believe: Religious Freedom and Its Enemies* (Harper, New York, NY, 2016)), and at the time of writing they show no sign of abating. Most such discrimination now centres on attitudes to same-sex marriage. The Coalition For Marriage published a list of thirty cases of discrimination including those of Chick-fil-A, Asher's Bakery, Brendan Eich the CEO

of leading search-engine Mozilla, and Bryan Barkley of the Red Cross: c4m.org.uk/downloads/30cases.pdf.

[73] Thus the strict discipline of *Supernanny* Jo Frost (ABC / Channel 4 2004-12) proved TV-worthy because it is currently so unfamiliar. Likewise Headteachers of turn-around schools are invariably disciplinarians and achieve astonishing results and happier, more motivated children by the application of basic principles. But the necessity of structure and discipline to many, Christians included, seemed common sense. If we applaud its re-entry, why was it abandoned? On 'freedom' see J Marsh, *The Liberal Delusion* (Arena, Bury St Edmunds, 2012) chapter 2.

[74] As it is used (as an unthinking cliché) by secularists: not in its historical sense within 1920s-30s US Presbyterianism.

[75] On difficulties caused by this word, see P Morgan, *The Marriage Files* (Wilberforce Publications, London, 2014) pp.80-6.

[76] Often thought to have been coined by G Weinberg, *Society and the Healthy Homosexual* (St Martin's, New York, NY, 1972).

[77] This point was confirmed to me in conversation with the Public Enquiry Point of the Crown Prosecution Service in 2015.

[78] F Turek, *Correct, Not Politically Correct: How Same-Sex Marriage Hurts Everyone* (MorningStar Publications, Wilkesborough, NC, 2008) gives the following figures for the USA. 60% of rapists, 63% of youth suicides, 70% of long-term prison inmates and reform-school attendees, of teen pregnancies and of high-school dropouts, 72% of adolescent murderers, 85% of youth prisoners and youth with behavioural disorders, and 90% of youth runaways – these are all from fatherless homes. Products of such homes are 7 times more likely than the average to be poor, 6 times more likely to commit suicide, and more than twice as likely to commit crime or become pregnant out of wedlock. S Baskerville, 'Divorce as Revolution' [2003] Salisbury Review 21.4 found that 'fatherlessness far surpasses both poverty and race as a predictor of social deviance'.

[79] See P Morgan: e.g., *Are Families Affordable? Tax Benefits and the Family* (Centre for Policy Studies, London, 1996); *Farewell To The Family? Public Policy and Family Breakdown in Britain and the USA* (Health and Welfare Unit, [1995] 2nd edition 1999); *Family Policy, Family Changes: Sweden, Italy and Britain Compared* (Institute for the Study of Civil Society, London, 2006).

[80] Attitude magazine interview, 8.4.2009.

[81] Psalms 84.11.

[82] See p.264 for ideologues' love of 'interpretation'.

[83] For example, if Queen Elizabeth II came to the throne in February 1952, think how many months of how many years there are when she did not come to the throne.

[84] A random example. If an object blown in the wind 'pirouettes', it may be performing *precisely* the same movement as the ballerina who pirouettes. Who therefore is to say that the term is metaphorical in the first instance and literal in the latter?

[85] Giles Fraser, for example, takes the Resurrection of Jesus (specific type of event; specific person; specific putative date) to 'mean' *any* transformation for the better experienced by *anyone* (*Church Times*, 28.4.2011).

[86] 1 John 4.8,16.

[87] See section A above.

[88] In PM David Cameron's 20.11.2012 phrase.

[89] This was agreed, albeit from different premises, even by those who (with skewed

WHAT ARE THEY TEACHING THE CHILDREN?

priorities) failed to grant civil partnerships to types of cohabitees assumed to be in non-sexual relationships. The recent publication A Davison, *Amazing Love* (Darton, Longman & Todd, London, 2016) at least twice blurs the edges between sexual and non-sexual relationships. On p.54 it is said that some Christians 'oppose same-sex relationships'. Quite the opposite: I have never heard of *any* that do! But I have heard of plenty, the vast majority both historically and internationally, that oppose same-sex *sexual activity*. Later, on p.101n13, the book speaks of 'same-sex desire, sexual activity, and enduring romantic attachments' – notice how the rogue element was smuggled in, cushioned in the middle of the three positions (it could scarcely have been put in either first or last position without being noticed and commented on). On p.88 the book says that some are excluded because of 'who they love': see p.279 for this elementary error.

[90] See p.256.

[91] P Edwards (ed.), *The Macmillan Encyclopedia of Philosophy* (Macmillan, London, 1967) *s.v.* 'Vagueness': 'religion' is the article's chief example of a vague word.

[92] The finding of a survey done jointly by the Church of England, the Evangelical Alliance, and Hope (published in September 2015) was that a much-increased 39% of UK adults have become so historically uninformed as to consider Jesus to be mythical, and that this figure rises 25% among young adults: precisely the group who have grown up in a world of procrustean, one-size-fits-all, 'religious studies'.

[93] The mystery is no mystery to Gene Veith who explains, plausibly, that postmodernists exalt tolerance because they want a convenient licence-plus-approval cocktail: *Guide to Contemporary Culture* (IVP, Leicester, 1994) pp.195-6.

[94] D L Sayers, An Address Given To The Public Morality Council at Caxton Hall, Westminster, 23.10.1941: *s.v.* 'Sloth'.

[95] 1 Corinthians 13.13; Galatians 5.22; Colossians 3.14. Note, however, that this Galatians verse also includes 'longsuffering', which is not so far from the better kinds of tolerance.

[96] Media framing has recently been studied by Matthew C Nisbet in numerous papers.

[97] This happens, for example, when those holding unevidenced ideological positions aim to be the reconcilers, valuing unity *per se* – which is a never-attained chimaera (nor is it ever explained why we should see it as being a good thing) – rather than unity in the truth. (This orientation towards human feelings and solidarity *rather than* truth is characteristic.) Thus, an organisation called *Via Media* was recently set up by some (Jayne Ozanne, David Ison, Angus Ritchie and others) whose entrenched position is at one extreme. Further, I have several times been in meetings where debate *itself* has been said to be off the agenda – though it is never the 'side' that characteristically prioritises evidence, in the normal scholarly fashion, that says this. If the emphasis is on unity, the scope for warranted criticism is then lessened, which can sometimes be useful. Such meetings have been: *The Lust For Certainty*, St Mary's, Putney, 21.11.2006; the launch of the Cutting Edge Consortium, Parliament, 24.11.2009; the Abortion Rights Pro-Choice Parliamentary 'Open' Meeting, 17.5.2012. The Shared Conversations within the Church of England which concluded in July 2016 were also of this nature; but the idea is that debate will follow in due course.

[98] It makes sense that ideas that have shown their staying-power will sometimes have a lot to be said for them. They may often just be common sense, which is what led to their being widely-held in the first place. Such ideas may frequently be classified as 'conservative' or 'traditional', but there is no intrinsic merit (or demerit) in being either of *those* things. The ideas' merit is located elsewhere.

Chapter Eleven

BRITISH VALUES: A PANDORA'S BOX?
THE DIAGNOSIS
Dr Christopher Shell

The characteristics of a truth-seeking approach

Truth-seeking prioritises evidence, reality, research, facts, and truth. Evidence is twofold: observational evidence that a given theory or hypothesis demonstrates *correspondence* with the way the world actually works; and logical evidence that the resultant world-view demonstrates *coherence* and lacks self-contradiction.[1] Because we have no preconceived conclusion in mind, there is no talk of 'conceding points', no persuasion, and no tactics.

Rather, we are engaged in the truth-seeking adventure, so the subject-matter will be reality, and not some human-made closed world like law or 'religion'. Investigations will be undertaken case-by-case, with the result that inaccurate sweeping generalisations are avoided.[2] And there will be a tentative preliminary expectation that investigations *will not all be easy, nor all difficult*, but rather will vary from very easy to very difficult in a standard-deviation curve.

The main two heresies of this scholarly approach are firstly 'agree to disagree' (or: 'good disagreement') and secondly relativism: 'true *for me*'/'true *for you*'. As soon as either of these enters, the process becomes unscholarly, and truth is not the goal. But attaining truth is the goal of all debate. Accordingly, to utter either of these things is to withdraw from the debate altogether, and relinquish any part in the decision-making process. And there are good reasons why those whose position is merely ideological and not evidence-based would be only too happy to withdraw from debate. If either of these two errors is allowed, ideology (the enemy of scholarship) can not only be admitted, but can flourish *just as much as* its antithesis, disinterested scholarship. Many so-called 'disagreements' are nothing but truth-seeking versus spin / ideology / wishful thinking.[3]

Correct world-views or answers can best be attained by ranking questions according to how fundamental they are;[4] and by ranking statistics according to how striking and clear-cut they are.[5] The most foundational data of all can then be bedrock, central to all debates on the topic; upon this data, one can then erect the only-slightly-less compelling statistics; and so on in progression, level by level. Debaters who are more selective and less objective in what they prioritise need to be called to account.

The characteristics of an ideological approach

An ideological approach disregards truth, evidence, and reality.[6] It is happy to 'agree to disagree' or seek 'good disagreement'; for then its preferred stance, however un-evidenced, need never be altered or even scrutinised; and it prefers hand-picked Trojan-Horse slogans to sustained arguments or nuance,[7] in order that any given issue can be *framed* in a particular (advantageous) way. It also considers 'fashionability' important,[8] and believes in the myth of inevitable progress.[9] And it puts feeling above thinking, or conflates them. Thus, all who oppose *anything* connected with homosexuality are 'the haters'.[10] In the same way, it puts style/image above substance[11], or conflates them too. Thus, an opponent's understandably exasperated or justly angry manner is thought relevant to a debate's result: a diversionary tactic which conveniently 'prevents' the ideologue needing to address the *questions*. A key requirement is to avoid being laughed at – which means in practice that stances will demonstrate unquestioning cultural conformity. Waverers will regard truth-seekers as 'brave' for sometimes holding a minority position, not realising that the truth-seekers could not possibly claim to be either scholarly or truthful if they *always* went with the majority whether or not the evidence pointed that way.

The ideological approach is also highly self-contradictory. For example:

(a) 'A march involving hundreds of thousands of protesters is of no importance.'[12]

(b) 'The Lord's Prayer, a huge cultural icon loved by multiple millions and scarcely ever specifically criticised, must not be broadcast in cinemas; but all kinds of questionable and unverified secular and capitalist messages about the way to true happiness may be endlessly repeated there.'[13]

(c) 'Abortion is fine, but pictures of it are upsetting.' (Which on any assessment is odd, because the latter are caused by the former, and mere pictures have never hurt anyone.)

(d) 'It is immoral to abort girls. To abort *both boys and girls*? No problem.'

(e) '"Pro-life: that's a lie: you don't care if women die" makes sense as a slogan even though maternal mortality is lowest in Poland, Malta, Ireland and Chile, the countries that predictably wouldn't dream of invading women's wombs.'[14]

(f) 'A child can have an abortion without parental permission, but not an aspirin.'[15]

(g) 'A child does not need a parent's permission or even knowledge to embark on a transitory, unsafe sexual relationship even at 15; but does need parental permission to embark on a secure marital relationship at 16.'

(h) 'The more one supports same-sex marriage, the less one should support marriage in general.'[16]

(i) 'I don't agree that ex-gays even exist; but homosexuals ought to comprise 8%[17] of those who appear on the BBC.' (In truth, ex-gays are far *more* numerous than present self-identified homosexuals.[18])

(j) 'It is fine for someone to undergo a major operation that changes their entire biological gender; but for them even to claim a change in sexual orientation, *where this change is from gay to straight*, is unthinkable, even though it is a mere mental change (of the sort that can potentially happen 1000 times a day) and is therefore far more minor than a change in bodily structure.'

(k) 'Evidence of gender derived from a person's body, which is (i) observable, (ii) not subject to change/fluidity, (iii) not requiring to be taken on trust – this evidence is *less* conclusive than that derived from their present mental state and self-testimony, which is none of the above (i-iii); and therefore the latter should trump the former when it comes to which bathroom they enter. Whether or not any young girls may be present there.'[19]

It is plain to anyone that these things do not add up; but the ideologues don't care, since they are not truth-oriented or reality-oriented, but goal-oriented: they are in the business of getting what they want, or think they want.

So ideologues think in terms of so-called 'conclusions' already pre-emptively reached, *faits accomplis*, and not in terms of a (surely necessary) investigative process. For example, when Vicky Beeching speaks of her new doctoral research topic, there is no indication that a conclusion will emerge at the end of research; rather it seems *already* to have been arrived at in advance. This alone would be startling enough – but when the 'conclusion' in question goes against all the existing large scholarly commentaries on 1 Corinthians[20] and Romans[21] *and* against nineteen centuries of Christian thought, *and* just so happens to match up with (and therefore to be potentially explicable by) movements within a person's own limited culture and historical context – then that is a very serious matter. Are such ideological (non-scholarly) approaches taking root in *universities*, of all places?[22] Relatedly: one often finds the fallacious argument from authority: a listing of scholars who have reached contradictory conclusions, in order to indicate that there is scholarly disagreement and that all kinds of views may therefore legitimately be held. Such lists are worthless, first because no argument that jumps straight to the conclusion can be remotely valid, and secondly because any 'conclusion' is only as good as (and is in fact no more than the distillation of) the evidence and arguments that it is based on: so all discussion should be about the evidence and arguments, not about the 'conclusions'.

Unsurprisingly, an ideological approach often shuns debate. This was illustrated in 2013, when both William Lane Craig and Abort67 had trouble finding opponents who would debate them in London. But debate can also be closed down by reference to 'sacred text'. This is no different from Christian proof-texting, and no more legitimate: it just refers to a different text. Sometimes this text is the law of the land, which ideologues tend to regard as infallible – until, that is, it states something with which they don't agree.[23] But the 'sacred text' can equally well be 'company policy', held up as the final word. When this tactic is employed, it tends to astonish spokespeople to be told that 'company policy' (which sometimes seems to be held by them to be equivalent to the great stone of Artemis that fell authorless and contextless from the sky[24]) is irrelevant to the issue,[25] and was likely worded to maximise the company's own interests. We already know what the policy *says* – but is it *good or beneficial or coherent* policy?

If a person takes the ideological non-evidence-based approach, they will often claim (surely high-handedly?) that they have the right to terminate a debate pre-emptively.[26] This 'right' is typically called in aid when a point has just been made that cannot be answered,[27] and it contrasts unfavourably with truth-seekers' commitment (including my own) to address *any* point that is raised. Debate can conclude only when truth has been reached and light shed; and obviously the *last* person who can claim the right to conclude a debate (unilaterally!) is the one who is currently losing it. Such an approach denies free speech (even words that are 100% true can be censored[28]), but it also tends to work on the assumption that *everyone* is inevitably employing the same dishonest tactics! – just for different ends.[29] It is, however, obvious to any scholar that this assumption is false. If there is no quest for truth, there is no scholarship; and true scholars, by the law of averages, inevitably find themselves coming to uncongenial conclusions much of the time.

Ideology in action

In this 8-part final section we see how blatantly contemptuous ideology can become if it is not recognised, named and shamed.[30]

UK media, 1960s–1970s

Over the course of 1964, Clean-Up-TV campaigner Mary Whitehouse was lampooned in the satirical BBC documentary *Swizzlewick*, most notoriously when her husband had recently unavoidably run over and killed a deliberate suicide. Later she experienced her name being used for satirical purposes by, successively, a pornographic magazine and shop belonging to David Sullivan and Mary Millington, and a 1990–2 TV comedy. When her former opponent Joan Bakewell[31] admitted Mrs Whitehouse had in essentials been right,[32] one thought, 'Why must people wait for media figures to attain sufficient maturity and understanding, rather than (as the Christians had always done) just following the more mature in the first place?'

The now-shamed DJ Jimmy Savile was capable of open contempt, most notoriously when he groped a teenager Sylvia Edwards in full view of the camera on *Top of the Pops* in 1976. But his regular behaviour towards the young on the *TOTP* set was also highly questionable, according to Dame Janet Smith's enquiry, and so was the overall ethos of the *TOTP* studio. Far from being a one-man problem,[33] this was pan-cultural.[34]

The *Sun* advice page is a further example of contempt for the public's intelligence. Is it, for example, coincidental that every problem in each photo-story just happens to involve half-undressed couples? And what are we to make of the fact that each letter's *second* paragraph almost invariably begins 'I am age X, and [the other person I'm talking about] is age Y'? That demonstrates a high level of 'editing' and string-pulling, at the least. And is it coincidental that a very high percentage of the letters involve people enacting (unsurprisingly, not without mishap!) the new sexual norms? Or is the real aim simply the normalisation of behaviours for the 'benefit' of readers and predators alike?[35]

Then there was the *Carry On* film series. Humour is the perfect Trojan Horse for recruitment to the amoral revolution. After all, most people will think they can't criticise *anything* about a comedy without being thought a killjoy;[36] and in any case, Christians, like others, obviously appreciate fun and light-heartedness. But, especially as the 1960s turned to the 1970s, what about their message? The girls in *Camping*[37] – in whatever state of dress or undress – are still *school pupils*. In *Matron*,[38] a wife gets picked up by the ambulance only for the husband to rush back to the house where the twist is that his hidden (much younger) mistress suddenly emerges. Cue a big laugh: infidelity rules in 1972. In *Girls*,[39] the moral at the conclusion is (as also in *On The Buses*) that the dirty old man gets the girl.

In the Christmas holidays 1972–3, when I was 6, I was in the audience for the pantomime *Cinderella* at the Odeon Theatre, Golders Green, starring Barbara Windsor and Ed Stewart. There was one totally irrelevant scene, whose title 'In Another Part Of The Forest' only emphasised its irrelevance. It consisted of a guitarist (who never otherwise appeared) leading the communal singing of a then current Chuck Berry song, *My Ding-A-Ling*. In the context of the UK's Operation Yewtree (2012-), it is relevant that a six-year-old (myself) could at the time see ten suspicious anomalies. Adults, no doubt, could see even more. What were these anomalies?

First, the scene was irrelevant to the pantomime. Then, the eponymous toy was obscure; as were the events referred to; and there was certainly no reason for audience members to share the songwriter's emotional attachment to his toy to *any* degree. Yet we were expected to *celebrate* it. Further, this was (I was reliably informed) a pop-song – yet, very atypically (especially from a rock star), one with a nursery-rhyme tune[40] that a younger audience could very easily catch onto while unaware that the tune's innocent nature was a deliberate and cynical cloak for the less innocent words. The tune was also highly unoriginal and banal – so I deduced it must have been *something else* that made the song a hit. Finally, the particular variant version used on this occasion, which was the more risqué one that includes the word 'you' ('I want *you* to play with…'), gave rise to two anomalies: this 'you' was unexplained, abrupt and unnatural to someone hearing the song for the first time, as the words would have flowed better without it; and no identity for the 'you' was suggested.

People expect pantomime *doubles-entendres* to go over children's heads. But this was not a *double-entendre* but a double-meaning; and one of the meanings did not even exist prior to the song, leaving only the more obscene one, which was unsurprisingly obvious even to a 6-year-old. Not that I actually thought the song was obscene despite this surface evidence. For because I didn't notice, and would anyway have been unable fully to understand, the final verse's giveaway climax, I stuck with the view that a present from a relative was being referred to (verse 1). But still the mass of anomalies in the song (and in its especial selection), made a child wonder.

WHAT ARE THEY TEACHING THE CHILDREN?

The penny didn't drop until much later, when it first occurred to me that adults can have bad intentions towards children. Yes, children left to their own devices might well devise *worse* songs; but it looks likely that youthful, semi-unaware singers, by now in fully-acquiescent pantomime-mode,[41] were being exploited, and their modesty eroded, to pander to the adult-dictated sexual imperatives of an increasingly morally lax society.

Least of all did I suspect, at 6, that those bad intentions could be institutionalised and attain a 'top'-down false respectability stemming from Hugh Carleton Greene's BBC,[42] which patronised *Top of the Pops* and prioritised Radio '*One*'. The pantomime's adult organisers (and probably many children present) already knew that Chuck Berry openly paraded his song's actual intent,[43] because his voice-overs on its song-track seek to embarrass those who won't join in, the penalty for which is to be stigmatised in the final verse as self-abusers. At the same time, he singles out for special praise those who sing in harmony (almost in worship-mode). The words Berry uses here, 'It's a free country: live like you wanna live', link the message inescapably with sexual 'freedom'. What we now know about the amorality of much of the 1970s was actually blatantly apparent even at the time.

The four-letter word, 1960s onwards

The BBC, like many other broadcasters, has embraced[44] the main four-letter word. Its normalisation (it has become the default swear-word, as in 'What the ****?', 'Get the **** out of here') is clearly contemporaneous and parallel with the sexual revolution: in fact, no word more succinctly encapsulates that revolution. Yet the word's internal contradictions, with its multiplicity of meanings *that give divergent messages*, are obvious. As commonly used, the word means any of the following:

(1) sexual intercourse;
(2) exciting and/or intensified (adjective '****ing');
(3) a replacement for God ('for ****'s sake'; 'thank ****');
(4) the most worthless thing of all ('I don't care a ****');
(5) something which is a curse ('**** off', '**** you');
(6) something which causes chaos and destruction ('****ed up').

One might expect the meanings to have family resemblances, else why would this particular word have been thought apt in each case?

So is there, even within such apparent contradiction, a unifying thread? *Yes* – and here the Christian world-view again demonstrates its strength through its explanatory potential. Points (1)–(2) suggest that extramarital and/or libertarian sex produces the triple thrill of transgression, power, and temporary enjoyment. Point (3) demonstrates that this draws people away from God, whom they now mock; and 'free' sex replaces God as their new ultimate. Point (4): though this is barely acknowledged, too late people realise it is a scam, producing zero benefit and much loss. Finally, points (5)–(6). As a now-indelible part of an individual's personal history, it produces unwanted deep connections ('soul ties') that can change and confuse one's entire sense of identity, along with harmful 'mental' effects like regret and depression. What, then, are the grounds for embracing this unutterably depressing word for mass-broadcast? The deceitful nature of the activity in question is openly paraded in this widespread collection of phrases, when viewed together as a whole.

The post-AIDS reinvention of homosexuality, 1989[45]

Kirk and Madsen's *After The Ball* [46] advertises its brainwashing plan equally openly. It is concerned not with actual statistical facts on fruits of homosexual behaviour, but with 'spin' that will change public *perception* of homosexuals. *And it admits as much*. This dishonesty is not regretted,[47] because the authors know that their proposed jamming conversion-method[48] is tried and tested and will succeed (as indeed it did); and they cynically take the end to justify the means. The historical/ educational slant of this method makes it a small step to the classroom, where children are already familiar with the acceptance/anti-bullying narrative. Though this book is from the USA, the UK, as often happens, swiftly followed suit. From around 1994 (coinciding with the launch of Radio 5 Live), friendliness to the LGBT activists' cause suddenly became clear editorial policy, even though dissenters would at that time have comprised a substantial proportion of the UK.

Abortion in the UK, 2007 to date

There was an astonishing exchange in the House of Lords during July 2007, when the Leader of the Lords, Baroness Royall, reiterated that abortion policy should not be driven by moral concerns.[49] To keep morality out of it is to keep the issue of *good* out of it (though self-interest remained firmly in place). Without regard for the good, what are legislators for? Perhaps we should not have been surprised, since (similarly to the USA) the Emily's List system still operates whereby female Labour Party candidates can receive special funding and backing, the *one and only* non-negotiable requirement being that they are 'pro-choice'. The killing of infants is thus ranked as the chief cause of all.

In October 2008, ahead of an important vote, I emailed all 350 'pro-choice' MPs with 301 rational arguments (largely derived from Alcorn[50]) against their 'position'. Of the total of 15 points made in reply, not one addressed any of the 301 arguments. The result of my experiment was clear: truth, which ought to be the central consideration in any debate, was not even of peripheral importance within their 'perspective'.

On 30 March 2012, 'The Battle of Bedford Square' took place next to the London abortion clinic situated there. Abortion-supporters openly and admittedly employed: raucous noise, drumbeat marches, menacing bicycle rushes, attempts to encircle, taunting, swearing, abuse, and simplistic slogans. The 'other side' remained quite still; they prayed, sang, and (in my case) debated. The 'side' that was adult in behaviour is opposed by the law; the other's supported by it. Could the law and its guardians therefore be regarded as other than adolescent or irresponsible in this matter?

Two months later (16 May 2012) I was at a pro-'choice' 'public meeting' in a committee room in Parliament. A few MPs joined the 130 who attended. Yet, as a dissenter, I was greeted with slow handclapping and loud demands from one MP to sit down as soon as I opened my mouth. That MP and a journalist both said they knew what my counter-arguments were. I responded: 'What? All 301 of them?'. My challenge to answer these 301 within a year was unmet: not a single answer to any point by the 30 who took handouts. No debate; no truth-seeking. All unsupported ideology.

December 2014 saw three separate illogical abortion-related initiatives:
(1) Christ Church, Oxford, cancelled a forthcoming debate on abortion because of a threatened protest. Yet a tutorial essay by any student protester would need to face at least some of the 219 separate logical

and compassionate[51] arguments against their stance contained in one book.[52] What stance on *any* other topic ever gave rise to 219 separate counter-arguments? So the most questionable stance of all gets special protection. That is not merely illogical: it is the reverse of logic, and of all that this or any University stands for.

(2) Shadow Home Secretary Yvette Cooper called for buffer zones outside abortion clinics. Yet people can protest about *any* issue. Pay-levels (the main protest topic) don't compare to life-and-death. But Ms Cooper relegated the latter to the bottom: to be protested about only under restrictions that prevent any impact on the very people the message is relevant to. Again: the very reverse of the logical pecking-order.

(3) The Supreme Court ruled it compulsory for *midwives* to be involved in 'terminations'. Midwives join the profession to bring life, and because they love babies. The 'Royal College of Midwives' (actually a Trade Union)[53] had challenged the previous contrary ruling because it was so important to them not merely that midwives help to bring death (!) but that *every one* of them should do so.

There's a ladder of illogicality and of deadened conscience here. Step one: defy the baby's interests. Two: harm the baby. Three: 'abort' (in accurate biology: kill). Four: require some others to do the same. Five: make *all* midwives do the same. We have stage-five illogicality and cruelty.[54]

The Queen's Diamond Jubilee and London Olympics, 2012

On 4 June 2012 (as in 2002) a Jubilee pop concert was held in front of (and on!) Buckingham Palace. Early in the BBC coverage, a joke was cracked classifying the monarch as 'a queen', so treating the homosexual sense as prior to the monarchical sense.[55] The Queen didn't show overt pleasure at the concert, which was somewhat imposed upon her; but why would she? The genre of music was that whose main practitioners, from the 1960s onwards, mostly[56] promoted sexual anarchy, drug use, destruction of hotel-rooms and musical instruments, and the occult. They were now invading her residence, even its roof. Was this perhaps a statement about which forces were really in charge?

Speaker John Bercow appeared to act cynically in hailing the Queen at the Palace of Westminster[57] as 'kaleidoscope Queen of a kaleidoscope country in a kaleidoscope Commonwealth' when an organization especially close to his own heart, of which he remains patron, was The Kaleidoscope Trust, which works in favour of gay and lesbian rights.

Later that summer the London Olympics Opening Ceremony on 27th July included backing footage of the violently-voiced anti-monarchist song *God Save The Queen* by the Sex Pistols (who also performed at the ceremony), a song previously banned during the 1977 Jubilee; and a performance by the rapper Dizzee Rascal, who had tarnished the previous night's pre-Olympics Hyde Park concert with repeated swearing. The euphoria of the Closing Ceremony later proved the perfect arena to attempt a public consciousness-shift while the world looked on, by making *all* the various cultures of a 90% religious world sing together of Lennon's 'no heaven ... no religion', and showcasing the unrepentant pensioner-baiting Russell Brand singing the very Beatles song[58] condemned by Mrs Whitehouse. Culture-loosening efforts are typically scheduled for music-performances and advertisements at maximum-viewing time: as, for example, a Superbowl[59] or X Factor final.[60] Jesus by contrast delighted in children's innocent shouting or singing: Matthew 21.15–16.[61]

The Queen's Opening Of Parliament Speech in May that year had not unreasonably been expected by some to contain a reference to one of the very largest items on the following year's agenda: the introduction of Same-Sex Marriage. Perhaps as the result of people being ashamed of making a good and highly-respected senior citizen intone intentions opposed by most of her generation, excuses were made and the matter was left unmentioned in the Speech. A year later, for 2013's Speech, the further excuse was made that this Bill was *already* passing through Parliament, so could no longer be classified as forthcoming. Thus one of the most radical legal changes imaginable received no more mention in any Queen's Speech than it had in the Conservative election manifesto.

Same-sex marriage, 2013 to date[62]
In 2013, the particular Trojan-Horse phrase that was everywhere was 'equal marriage'. But we shall now investigate how much intrinsic equality actually exists between the two groupings labelled 'heterosexual' and 'homosexual'.[63] Incredibly, in a purported large-scale enquiry/

debate, the following evidence on whether homosexual practice or the average homosexual lifestyle *was* 'equal' (or indeed good) scarcely got a look-in: for the ruling ideology made some true things 'unsayable'.

Do self-identified heterosexual and homosexual people share basic human equality?
Heterosexual and homosexual couples are equal *in humanity and human dignity* (as is every pair of humans). They are also equal in being *two in number*; but that is true simply by definition, and numbers other than two are not our present topic anyway. They are equal in both being 'in a loving relationship' – but of course most of us have several simultaneous 'loving relationships'.

Are their respective sexual/quasi-sexual pair-bondings equally valid natural phenomena?
Both these types of human relationship are attested in nature; but so is everything else, whether beneficial, harmful, or neutral. However, there is an infinite percentage difference between their respective *natural fruitfulnesses* (nature's *imprimatur*): one produced all of us, the other none.[64]

What of homosexuality in animals?[65]
First and most obvious, many things are 'same-sex behaviour' but not homosexual, like attending football matches, pubs or makeovers together. Second, some behaviours (dog with table leg, etc.) are just mating-season hyper-sexuality indifferent to object and gender: males may be 'next-best' where females are absent. Third (and related), as it is very rare for animal sexual behaviour to be *exclusively* same-sex, and also for same-sex affection to be witnessed, it is unsurprising that homosexual *orientation* in animals is doubted by a leading gay researcher.[66] Fourth, even when orientation does appear, there is often more to be said: the domestication of rams by definition involves a degree of artificial emasculation. Finally, one day we will laugh at the self-aware human race trying to *copy* (but very selectively) the instinctive animals whom we actually outstrip. We do not do that in other spheres of life!

Are their respective behaviours equally genetically determined?[67]
In the genetics-environment question, much hinges on which percentage-discrepancies between homosexuals and heterosexuals are largest: those connected with environment (which research has already shown to be huge) or with genetics and/or intrauterine environment, where we await the fuller publication of newly-announced initiatives.[68] The honest approach here is to make the *most* striking statistical discrepancies the *most* foundational – and so on.

Before we begin, three preliminary points on genetics must be made. First, genes can cause only predisposition, not action. Second, any one character trait will be at least *somewhat* more correlated with some gene profiles than with others – it could scarcely be otherwise. And third, even where there's a genetic correlation, that obviously doesn't make the said behaviour beneficial![69]

And there are also two preliminary problems with 'born gay' claims that even the layperson will already be aware of. First, most people can't remember *anything* that happened to them before around the age of three. And second, they certainly aren't sexually attracted to *anyone* till long after even *that* age.

But there are also multiple scientifically-based objections, as evidenced by eight massive environment-related discrepancies:
– E O Laumann *et al.*[70] found *urban environment* to increase male gay self-identification by 708%.
– The same study found *college environment* to increase lesbian self-identification by 900%.
– *Molestation when young* apparently increases such self-identification by (average finding) 500%.[71]
– As for the effect of *culture and cultural change*, the 2013 UK National Survey of Sexual Attitudes and Lifestyles found that the number of women reporting same-sex partners increased from 1.8% to 7.9% in 20 years. And gay-friendly societies can see gay lifestyle proliferate.
– On the *misleading nature of the word 'lesbian'*, what we regularly see in lesbian behavior is less 'orientation' than simply what a sexual-revolution environment permits. Lesbians on average not only have regularly slept with men, but their median number of male partners is *twice* that of self-described 'straight' women.[72] Others take female partners not because of

'orientation' but because once the sexual revolution takes hold it becomes nigh impossible for a large number of women to form an exclusive bond with a man, since it has come to be regarded as acceptable for men to play the field, and if they can they will.

– On the *fluidity* of the self-designation 'homosexual', Savin-Williams and Ream[73] found all gay identity to be 3-4 times *less* stable than heterosexual identity, and 25 times less so in adolescence, since the vast majority of 'gay' 16-year-olds were 'straight' by 18. So, by self-identification (normally the main criterion), there are far more ex-homosexuals than current homosexuals. However, the former don't officially exist (to judge from the 2012-14 London bus campaign dispute involving Core Issues Trust), whereas the latter are perceived to be everywhere.

– On *home environment*, the meta-analysis of Stacey and Biblarz[74] found that girls raised by lesbians are at least 400% more likely to identify as lesbians themselves.

– On *identical twins*, several studies from around 2000 converge in concluding that identical twins, *even though* they are so often prone to copy one another, will fail to share their twin's homosexual 'orientation' (or proclivity) in 89% of cases for males, or 86% for females.[75]

Are they equal in relation to pederasty or paedophilia?[76]

Laumann *et al.*[77] found a disproportionately high 21% of all adult-preteen sexual bonding to be same-sex. J M W Bradford *et al.*[78] gives a higher figure of 33%, with an additional 10% mixed: findings which were subsequently cited favourably by a Home Office document.[79] K Freund *et al.* [80] gave a similar figure of 35%; while W D Erickson *et al.* reported an 86% finding, though this included bisexuals.[81]

Proportions of homosexual child-abuse *offences* seem much higher than proportions of homosexual child-abuse *offenders*: Freund *et al.* (above) found homosexual offences to be 80% of the total; and Freund's later paper with R J Watson[82] found that on average homosexual paedophiles molest 7-8 times as many victims as do heterosexual paedophiles.

The meta-analysis of J R Hughes,[83] which reviewed 554 papers, concluded that it is impossible to view homosexuality and paedophilia as completely unrelated.

That didn't stop the UK Home Office – which as mentioned had earlier referenced Bradford's paper favourably – from sacking Hans-Christian Raabe from their (unrelated!) drugs division in 2011, for having some years earlier *correctly* cited this overwhelming consensus. When challenged, Minister James Brokenshire failed to cite even one scientific paper when specifically asked which papers he was relying on; of course, he would have needed to cite many more to make a case. This was a clear travesty of justice. Had there been an equal number of papers on both sides, the position would have been equivocal, but would still not have justified sacking. In reality the vast consensus supported Dr Raabe's position, *and* the statistics involved were stark; but the Minister apparently thought he did not need to cite, refer to, or even know about the research! Result: uninformed might-is-right ideology wins.

Are they equal in degrees of promiscuity?
Bell and Weinberg[84] reported that 84% of white homosexual males and 77% of black had had 50+ homosexual partners; of these, 28% of white and 19% of black had had 1000+. The San Francisco Bay area which was the topic of the study was atypical; but, it emerged, not atypical enough.

Among subsequent researchers, A Kaslow[85] found that 69-83% of gay men reported 50+ lifetime sexual partners. J Lever[86] found that 2% of adult male homosexuals had had one lifetime sexual partner, 57% had had 30+, and 35% had had 100+. P van den Ven *et al.*[87] found that 82% reported 50+ lifetime partners, while nearly 50% reported 100+; this study gave a lifetime average of 251. C H Mercer *et al.*[88] found that the median numbers of partners for UK heterosexual, bisexual and homosexual men were respectively 2, 7, 10 within the preceding 5 years. E S Rosenberg *et al.*[89] found that of those with a primary sexual partner, 68% had at least 2 other partners per year.

Summaries of peer-reviewed science on homosexual promiscuity, covering 20 or so studies altogether, are given by R A J Gagnon[90] and M L Brown.[91] Results generally converge to give the following picture: Around 90% of homosexuals are not in a couple. Of those who are, only 10–25% were monogamous in the last year. A given heterosexual couple is about 41 times more likely than a given homosexual couple to be monogamous, and it is hard to find a faithful male pairing of over five years.[92]   The picture is even worse for lesbian couples, who stay together on average two-thirds as long as do their gay male counterparts.[93]

This stark picture isn't denied (and is sometimes celebrated) by gay activists Kirk & Madsen, Silverstein & White, Altman, and Savage.[94] Clearly, intolerance and resulting despair is not the cause of this common inability to form and sustain monogamous sexual relationships, since promiscuity doesn't decrease in gay-friendly San Francisco, Amsterdam, Sweden, or New Zealand,[95] but is more generally and universally exhibited by homosexuals.[96]

But how does all this compare with married (heterosexual) couples? Perhaps they too are similarly promiscuous. No. Even in the USA (the country worst hit by the sexual revolution), and even as recently as the mid-1990s (as much as 30 years into that revolution), it was reported by three separate studies[97] that 80% of married people had never been sexually unfaithful to their present spouse. Such a discrepancy is so great as to be definitive.

Are they equal in their mental health?
High promiscuity rates are not calculated to improve mental health or sense of identity. J E Phelan *et al.,*[98] in a meta-analysis of experimental evidence and research over 125 years, concluded that more than 33% of homosexuals are substance-abusers,[99] while 40% of homosexual men report suicidal histories,[100] and a disproportionate number report eating disorders and depression. This study found that social bias and discrimination (as opposed to the inevitable results of promiscuity) do not in themselves contribute to the majority of homosexual maladaptivity. Neither, one might add, need unpopularity lead to any notable degree of promiscuity: it does not do so among groups such as Catholics and Jehovah's Witnesses, who often suffer social stigma.

Again, the meta-analysis of ME King *et al.* found 'a twofold excess in suicide attempts' for LGB people, compared to the population average; and a 1.5 times higher rate of depression and anxiety disorders, and of alcohol-/substance-dependence.[101]

Several studies also show a startling discrepancy in levels of domestic violence between heterosexual and homosexual households.[102]

Mental health among the same-sex attracted was improved by their adoption of greater chastity and by religious participation.[103]

Are they equal in STI-contraction?
E S Rosenberg *et al.*[104] concluded:
– Homosexual men account for 61% of the new HIV infections in the USA – yet only 2% of the population.
– Infections among young black homosexuals increased 48% between 2006 and 2009.
– 20% of homosexual men have HIV; nearly half unknowingly.
– Syphilis rates among homosexual black men rose 134% in a single year (2009-2010).

The antibiotic-resistant flesh-eating bacterium MRSA USA300 began at around the same time to spread among gay males wherever promiscuity, drugs and antiretroviral-based complacency combined. There have since been resurgent epidemics of syphilis, rectal gonorrhoea and new HIV infections among homosexual men. All of these, together with herpes, the cancer-causing Epstein-Barr virus, HPV-related oral cancers (rarely detected before stage III-IV), and anal cancer, occur very disproportionately among homosexual men. In addition, same-sex attracted men are twice as likely to contract *any* cancer as other men, and first do so (on average) 10 years earlier.[105]

2013 rates of gay-male HIV contraction in the USA meant that men who have sex with men were *over 1000 times* more likely to contract HIV than men who don't.[106] (Equality?) However, abstaining from promiscuity (as opposed to abstaining from homosexual sexual activity) is not the remedy, since one study found that 86% of new HIV infections occurred within 'steady partnerships'.[107]

The most recent report of Public Health England[108] found that men who have sex with men were responsible for more than 70% of new cases of gonorrhoea and a simultaneous increase in syphilis. Advice ranged from 'avoiding overlapping sexual relationships' to undergoing 'HIV and STI tests every three months if having unprotected sex with new or casual partners'. No advice was given to *avoid* such Russian roulette; and nothing within a million miles of the Christian teaching which is incomparably more successful and far more prone to honour human value and integrity.

Is there equality in the physical dangers of the different kinds of intercourse open to them?

Historically, homosexual men have been at greater risk of infection partly because, whatever is tacitly assumed, even *taught to children*, there's *no equality* whatever between anal and vaginal intercourse:[109]

– A single instance of anal intercourse carries 20 times more risk of HIV contraction than a single instance of vaginal intercourse.[110]

– Anal intercourse is medically risky, even without promiscuity, because of both the relative dirtiness of the anal area, and the relative difficulty of cleaning it when one cannot directly see what one is doing.

– The rectum has a sphincter: so it is a non-entrance exit. The vagina, however, has a hymen, which, unlike a sphincter, is broken with 0% medical harm.

– The rectum has much less natural flexibility and stretch than the vagina.

– The rectum has no natural lubrication, a fact which shows that it is not biologically intended for quasi-sexual intercourse.[111]

– The rectal lining is precisely one cell thick: as thin as it is possible to be. That would spell injury-risk anywhere in the body. But when we add to that the unusual strain caused on this part of the body, with the attendant risk of cuts and bleeding; the increased pressure and rubbing caused by the use of contraception; and the fact that we are talking about a part of the anatomy particularly susceptible to harmful disease – then the risks are clearly massive.

– Worse: inside the rectum are microfold cells which actively attract, embrace and envelop those very harmful microbes which cause STIs.

It's illogical to call sexual practices natural or acceptable when they can never safely take place without a condom. What of the 99% of history when less technology attended contraception? Such acts would therefore have been even less safe then – yet they are extremely unsafe even now. How then can they be part of the 'natural' pattern? Rather, just as in other realms such as diet, we learn from nature itself what is natural and what is artificial and man-made. Nature shows that the only sexual practice that can be conducted safely without either technology or disease intervening is marital vaginal intercourse where it involves two people who married as virgins.

Is there equality in average life-expectancy?
R S Hogg *et al.*[112] concluded that the life-expectancy of gay or bisexual men at age 20 is 8–20 years lower than that of heterosexual men.

One denomination's discussion of homosexuality, 2013–14 [113]

On 28 November 2013, a Church of England report chaired by Sir Joseph Pilling was published, claiming strong disagreement among scholars about the New Testament's prohibition on homosexual activity. This was mischievous. Of course *any* document will have interpretative issues; and the older and more culturally-distant it is, the more it will have. But when it comes to *the main point* under discussion, there has never been scholarly or common-sense doubt (nor any warrant for doubt) that homosexual behaviour is proscribed by both[114] biblical Testaments – pervasively, severely, and absolutely,[115] just as is the case for lying, murder and adultery.[116] Such inevitable disagreement as there is, is not about that main point. I therefore issued a double challenge to *Church of England Newspaper* readers. Find a New Testament scholar who disagrees;[117] and find a young person (since so many were so keen to 'keep up with' the young) who has ever known what the counter-arguments[118] are.

Neither challenge was met, though the correspondence extended over nearly a year (13 December 2013 till 5 October 2014). But this was not seen as a 'result'. Debates are now not expected to be won or lost, even in Christian organisations. That, by definition, is an ideological takeover.

Around the same time (26 September 2014), Dr Chris Cook asserted in the *Church Times* that the variety of translations of the key word *arsenokoites*[119] cast doubt on whether we know its meaning. That is untrue. 'Men who have sex with men'[120] is the agreed meaning, avoided in translation only because of its infelicity. *Arsenokoites* is a compound of two very common, general, and unambiguous terms meaning 'lie [with]' and 'male'. These terms precisely echo the Septuagint of Leviticus 18.22, 20.13.[121] Paul's vice-lists cover only a handful of vices each, so there is space only for general (not recondite) ones. Romans 1, where homosexual practice alone is singled out as the most characteristic and telling pagan sin, makes such an inclusion in the 1 Corinthians and 1 Timothy vice-lists unsurprising. The term is most probably a neologism; Paul *did* several times coin words,[122] and to avoid incomprehension there would have been a clear need to be literal and plain when so doing – a requirement admirably met by *arsenokoites*. Moreover, there is no strong or widespread alternative theory.[123] I think we will soon be amazed that weak cultural conformity has lately produced such counter-intuitive[124] Scripture 'interpretation'.[125]

Epilogue, 2016

The following cautionary tale struck me as a good typical example containing several perennial elements of the ideology problem:

I was recently handing out a leaflet on the influence of environment and culture upon homosexual behaviour. A predictably clichéd complaint was made that this was 'overtly homophobic'. What lack of thought that shows. There are statistical measures where homosexuals come out worse than heterosexuals; but there are so many thousands of possible areas of comparison, and even by the law of averages homosexuals would score worse in 50% of these: no harm in that. But what gives cause for concern is massively worse scores in central matters. If *that* doesn't get reported, it must be otherwise publicised, in order to prevent ignorance and/or misinformation.

I replied by saying my leaflet concerned published scientific conclusions. The complainant said the cited papers were *all* 'utter tosh', by this incisive analysis gaining the advantage, in security's eyes, over a truth-seeker and science-publiciser. I was escorted away.

The next day I bumped into the complainant, who said the science quoted was too partial or selective: to which I responded by asking them to point out any errors in my handout. It is at this point that they acted dishonestly in as many as six different ways.

First, they refused, so failed to show they were capable of stepping up to the debate at all. Then it became clear that they were not aware whether I had cited one paper or several. Further, they were incapable of naming even one of the papers referred to. That being the case, they also could not give any detail of what any of the papers said either. Nevertheless, they rejected wholesale the claim of each and every one of these peer-reviewed scientific-journal papers (which they knew nothing about) to be science at all. And stood by their assessment that it was all 'tosh'.

The foresight of C S Lewis in his book *That Hideous Strength*[126] provides food for thought, with its disturbing parallels to today. Back in 2007, Lord Brennan was driven to the end of his tether and collapsed, rather like Lewis's Canon Jewel, while protesting the Orwellian illogicality of the Embryology Bill in the Lords.[127] Our present mental health crisis[128] is partly administered by the NHS's Bracton Centre (Bracton was the College central to Lewis's book). And we even have, like Lewis, an apparently friendly, but in fact undermining, public organisation called the NICE. Ours advises teenage girls to stockpile Morning-After Pills and wants to give condoms to 13-year-olds.

So we fight on against the principalities and powers, 'demolishing arguments'[129] on the occasions where they deserve that. Hitherto, and scandalously, it is only on rare occasions that the ideologues have taken the trouble to supply *arguments* of any sort at all. That's why they should jump ship and join the truth-seeking adventure.[130]

Notes

[1] 'Family campaigners' often identify abortion and homosexual practice as two key 'battlegrounds'. Although I rate divorce as more pernicious than homosexual practice (according to the measure of the extent to which permanent and settled irresolution and harm is being deliberately adopted), I agree that abortion is unparalleled in errors of *coherence*, while advocacy of homosexual practice is unparalleled in its lack of *correspondence* with what real-world statistics tell us. I also don't count as a 'battleground' any arena where so high a proportion of the evidence points strongly one way.

[2] Monty Python's *Life of Brian* (HandMade Films, 1979) comes to mind here. For some reason, people often try to elicit the conclusion that the film *as a whole* is or is not blasphemous. The truth is quite different: films are long enough to have both blasphemous and non-blasphemous parts. Here, the portrayal of Jesus is respectful; whereas the mocking use of 'I was blind and now I see' (John 9.25: a testimony echoed by many through the ages for various reasons), and calling the gift of life itself excrement: these two things look blasphemous, not least because they are plain wrong. And it is the least surprising thing possible that die-hard satirists known for a combination of university-style and schoolboy-style humour should at least occasionally fail to accord some topics the seriousness they deserve.

[3] Particularly and (in this instance) progressively since the 1960s, spin and perception have come to take centre-stage, displacing transparency: among advertisers who want us to associate their product with pleasant and memorable (and sometimes quite irrelevant) images, music and ideas without ever mentioning competitors or counter-arguments; and also among politicians, who have taken to relying on spin-doctors and focus-groups. Colossal expenditure attends this in both these arenas. Even in the world of publishing (and of course more so in journalism), there is an obligation to honour the publisher's ethos, which can potentially mean that the author's original words never appear, while the readership are fed back what they are presumed to want in an unedifying circular process.

[4] The most fundamental being, for example, 'How is it possible that it should have come about that anything should have existed at all, rather than nothing?'.

[5] I would give two examples of especially striking and clear-cut statistics. First, the colossal discrepancy between the almost-guaranteed STI-free state of married virgins, such as are customary in many real-world cultures, and the average 2,811,024 aggregated former (mostly indirect) 'partners' that the average adult who has slept with 7.65 people might potentially catch a disease off (as calculated by Lloyds Pharmacy in 2009: see onlinedoctor.lloydspharmacy.com/blog/sex-degrees). Second, the fact that every single person bar none has had precisely two parents, and that these have without any exceptions been one male and one female.

[6] Research and statistics mean nothing: bald unsupported generalised assertions can be made such as 'We don't favour one way of family life over another' – the words of Harriet Harman as co-author of the 1990 Institute for Public Policy Research thinktank report *The Family Way*. In that document, Harman and her associates also 'wondered [whether] the presence of fathers in families is necessarily a means to social harmony and cohesion'. Where researched and unresearched positions are treated as being on a par, there are no limits to what stances may be adopted: Harman's own National

Council for Civil Liberties provided a platform for paedophiles in the 1970s, a scandal which received due acknowledgement from the Press only in 2014. A Fathers4Justice demonstrator, Mark Harris, was so infuriated by the laziness of Harman's approach to evidence that he mounted the roof of her home on 8th June 2008 to draw attention to his book and its research findings on fathers denied access to their children. See news. bbc.co.uk/1/hi/uk/7442435.stm. For the utter 180-degrees inaccuracy of Harman's claims about fathers, see p.276. Ms Harman exemplifies the harmfulness, dishonesty and intellectual bankruptcy of secularism in advocating that something that has highly deleterious effects (fatherlessness) should be treated as the equal-best option. Besides assertions that ignore evidence and research, a further and related fruit of this ideological approach is *relativism*. The idea, for example, that a woman who is pregnant ought to receive *non-directive* counselling in order to come to the decision that is 'best *for her*' not only makes little sense in itself but also is based on the obviously false idea that a person of the female gender can never be mistaken in what they choose, nor do a wrong action such as wilfully choosing to kill her own child. In truth, it is likelier that *very few* parents of either gender are unaware of the obvious truth that to 'abort' is to kill their own child. Yet even 'evangelical Christian' pregnancy-crisis organisations are taking the non-directive and relativistic route, which besides its other errors is also without any foundation in their own tradition. See E S Williams, *What Is Going On In Christian Crisis Pregnancy Counselling?* (Belmont House, Sutton, 2005).

[7] Never better illustrated than when amid a high school otherwise devoted to critical thought and debate one comes across Stonewall posters proclaiming 'Some People Are Gay – Get Over It', and the like. This forecloses the debate before it ever happens. It is therefore lazy. It is also bullying, aggressive, and patronising.

[8] See E Noelle-Neumann, *The Spiral of Silence* (University of Chicago Press, Chicago, IL, [1980] 2nd English-language edition 1993) on how people are inclined to flock to what is *perceived* (doubtless with some media help) to be a new majority view. A recent example of this c.2012–13 was Western politicians' helter-skelter spate of coincidental Damascus Road 'conversions' to 'belief' in same-sex marriage (or perhaps prudent avoidances of political suicide). In America, even Barack Obama, an icon of the 'left', did not pledge support for it as President till as recently as 9th May, 2012 (abcnews.go.com/ blogs.politics/2012/05/timeline-of-obamas-evolving-on-same-sex-marriage). Nor did equally far-'left' Hillary Clinton endorse it till a year later (theatlantic.com/politics/ archive/2014/06/hillary-clintons-gay-marriage-problem/372717). Yet a reasonable, mild-mannered academic, Ryan Anderson, who dared to echo what even the far-'left' were saying just two years earlier, was deprived of his microphone on MSNBC network rather than be allowed to debate (dailysignal.com/2015/03/31/msnbc-cuts-ryan-t-anderson-mic-as-he-defends-indiana-law).

[9] It follows logically that some ideologues' inability to deviate too much from contemporary fashion (which we can term 'social deviance intolerance' or 'low social deviance tolerance') would, paradoxically, have led to their being equally in tune with the fashions and mores of the very eras which they now criticise, had their lifespans happened to occur earlier. Those who now criticise the 1970s do so because the cultural climate now allows that criticism; it looks like thousands of complaints could and surely should have been made at the time, but were not, the cultural climate again being the culprit.

[10] See *Metro* 8.9.2014, an issue of the newspaper where rainbow-coloured football-bootlaces run *unbroken* from first page to last. Similarly on 15.5.2015 LGBT regalia

took over a whole street (Church Street!) in Twickenham. One point about rainbows (which of course have long pre-existed and will long survive all who, not without hubris, seek to purloin or 'own' them for their own ends) is that they encompass the entire spectrum of colour: there is no 'outside' position. This is the saturation approach: no space for disagreement.

[11] The ultimate *faux pas* for David Steel, the architect of the 1967 Abortion Act, is to use green ink to write to him. The fact that what he patronizingly stereotypes as 'the green-ink brigade' may be correct in what they assert about the murderous nature of 'abortion' seems not to be of comparable importance to him – so long as they do not use green ink, since any point that would be true in black ink could never be true in green. See theguardian.com/politics/2004/jul/06/society.health. The identical wrong-headed green-ink point is made by Bishop Alan Wilson, www.kiwianglo.wordpress.com/2011/11/11/bishop-alan-wilson-on-gaystapo-homophobia. With similarly skewed priorities, Sam Leith, *Evening Standard* 8.2.2016, opines that 'the' problem with *Playboy* 'is not that it objectifies women; it's that it's so...naff.'. Three elementary logical errors in one sentence: style above substance; unsupported assertion; and false either-or, as though only *one* problem can possibly exist. And even then it is not explained *why* objectifying women is all right.

[12] One of several huge marches barely covered by the world's press for ideological reasons was the Circus Maximus event in Rome (30.1.2016) opposing same-sex marriage and gay adoption.

[13] The ban was first reported in the Press on 22.11.2015, and was addressed by Abp R Williams, *Evening Standard* 7.12.2015, from whom I derive this comparison.

[14] See, e.g., nationalreview.com/corner/300129.

[15] Further appalling argumentation regarding abortion is found in Ann Furedi's speech at the 2008 UK Battle of Ideas (www.abortionreview.org/index.php/site/article/442). In her first paragraph, she claims the right to avoid the central scientific/medical dimension altogether (in other words, she will hand-pick which questions she does and does not address). In her fifth paragraph, she says that the fact that some people 'want to have ... control' (don't we all?) is the conclusive factor: if they want it, they must have it. The ninth paragraph begins with a double-error: 'For me, the question is....' In debate, you must argue, and 'for me' is nothing but assertion. And since when has there been just one question?

[16] This is the apparently counter-intuitive finding of the U S Health and Human Services Survey based on 2011-13 data: see lifesitenews.com 21.3.2016. It is backed up by D Blankenhorn's findings on Norway in D Blankenhorn & J Rausch, *The Future of Marriage* (Encounter, New York, NY, 2007). Some countries, such as Spain, are hard to assess in this respect, since their marriage rates were already clearly falling by the time of the introduction of same-sex marriage.

[17] www.pinknews.co.uk, 23.4.2016.

[18] See p.309. We also have to ask whether ideologues would allow people self-confessedly to turn from straight to gay or not, given that they are 'not allowed' to do the opposite – even though any initial claim to be gay at all may rest on as little as (a) initial indoctrination that gay and straight are two equal options both involving innumerable masses; or (b) an initial molestation incident; or (c) an initial hyper-sexual release where a partner of the opposite gender cannot realistically be found; or (d) growing up in an environment where many of one's peer-group are experimenting in this way.

[19] In addition, there are the multiple self-contradictions found within the homosexual programme: see J Satinover, *Homosexuality and the Politics of Truth* (Baker, Grand Rapids, MI, 1996). A list is found in F Turek, 'Eight LGBT Contradictions That Blow A Gaping Hole In The Movement' [2016] *Charisma* News, Aug. 4th. He quotes Pascal: 'People almost invariably arrive at their beliefs not on the basis of proof but on the basis of what they find attractive.' Among Turek's list of contradictions are the following. There are no men-woman differences – until someone wants to marry what they are still happy to call a 'same-sex' person. Judging is condemned – yet lavishly exercised. Tolerance and inclusion are commended – yet withheld. Discrimination is wrong among bakers who don't want to commend same-sex marriage, but right among those who don't want to bake cakes opposing it. There is no gay agenda – apart from when Paypal cancel business plans. For the dishonesty of the claim that there is no gay agenda, see M L Brown, *A Queer Thing Happened To America* (EqualTime Books, Concord, NC, 2011) chapter 1. Not only is it unbelievable that single-issue activists would have no agenda (!) but there is no reason to get bashful about admitting to having any agenda in the first place. *Of course* we will want the thing(s) that we most believe in to be spread or universalised; and *of course* there will generally be at least one cause, out of all the millions of causes that exist, that a given person will rate that highly. What else would one expect?

[20] The main 1 Corinthians commentaries used in universities would include those of C K Barrett, G D Fee, R F Collins, A C Thiselton, and J A Fitzmyer.

[21] The main Romans commentaries used in universities would include those of C K Barrett, C E B Cranfield, J D G Dunn, D J Moo, J A Fitzmyer, N T Wright, R K Jewett, and R N Longenecker.

[22] See vickybeeching.com/blog/lgbt-theology-2. That universities should be at the forefront of blocking free thought, free speech and free discussion (see too p.305) is an extremely serious matter when by definition they are the first places intended to promote it. They are abolishing their whole *raison d'être* if they accede to student demands to create 'safe spaces' where only comfortable perspectives can be voiced. Safe spaces (which are impossible anyway, since the views comfortable to one group will be uncomfortable to another) are a much-discussed recent feature on US and UK campuses: see spiked-online.com/freespeechnow/fsn_article/university-should-never-be-a-safe-space#.V7oHQo-cHIU. It is also a matter for concern that leading academics unimpeachable in their *own* field of physics (Stephen Hawking), biology (Richard Dawkins) or philosophy (A C Grayling), should so often demonstrate meek, uncritical acceptance of the package of 'progressive' dogma of the sort critiqued in this and the previous chapter, as opposed to independent thought.

[23] Ironically, that's actually the same as the Christian position: Christians always have civil disobedience as a live option if necessary. But unlike ideologues, educated Christians don't proof-text, but rather aim to present the reasons undergirding a stance.

[24] See Acts 19.35.

[25] Just as people can be astonished that one might not believe in (for example) the broadcast watershed, or Civil Partnerships, in the first place. Certain unquestioned things rest on a flimsy foundation. The watershed suggests that things unsuitable for children will always be suitable for adults, whereas there will be plenty of cases where those things are, by virtue of their immaturity, therefore *less* suitable for *mature* people than they are for children; and the option of simply not broadcasting at all things that

bring no obvious benefit but also the possibility of harm (things, too, which plenty of societies have always done very well without) has been excluded as though it did not exist. In the case of Civil Partnerships (and not believing in these is mainstream, since till extremely recently almost nobody believed in them), the idea was that sex or quasi-sex gave a status to the relationship between two people (otherwise blood-relationships and house-sharing would have been similarly recognised, which they were not), without ever questioning whether the quasi-sex in question was healthy by nature, or of equivalent status to marital sex.

[26] Of course, 'no comment' *is* a comment, and, like it or not, is effectively a concession of the debate ('I can't answer that point').

[27] See Epilogue.

[28] See, again, Epilogue.

[29] This has been stated to me as self-evident by the spokesperson for an LGBT group. Also a liberal Jew debater demonstrated that no other possibility (such as disinterested scholarship – or scholarship of any nature at all) had occurred to him, by reiterating the same point uncomprehendingly.

[30] That this kind of contempt is easily recognised for what it is by the general public can be seen from the film *Keeping Mum* (Summit Entertainment, 2005). In the script of the football scene, Lance (the golf-coach, played by Patrick Swayze) deliberately says to the vicar, 'I see your wife.' (a *double-entendre*) to give himself the double thrill of (a) not needing to go to the slightest length to hide the true situation and (b) mocking his despised interlocutor by parading his brazenness under his very nose.

[31] Bakewell was enough of a 1960s devotee to remark with chilling contempt for her husband that '1960s London was a good place to have an affair': *The Daily Telegraph*, 12.6.2011.

[32] *The Mary Whitehouse Effect*, Radio 4, 5.6.2010, 20.00.

[33] Smith's enquiry also makes clear that the *Top Of The Pops* cameramen customarily focussed on the legs of the dancing girl members of the public.

[34] Complaints do not appear to have been received about the cameramen's angles. Compare the testimony of A Tilby, *Church Times* 12.2.2016: she judged the attitude of the leering cameramen in a school documentary to be utterly unworthy of complaint *because of* contemporary mores – even though those mores were so atypical and so utterly and obviously unchristian. We are not at all talking of an unusually large number of abusive men having unluckily coincided in this era, but about the widespread and prevalent cultural norms and expectations created and normalised around this time, which in their turn effectively 'created' such men.

[35] William Oddie (see Polly Toynbee, *The Independent*, 9.12.1996) pointed out that agony aunts as we now understand them came along together with the sexual revolution; were more than averagely likely to be divorced and in various ways to have made comparatively avoidable messes of their own lives (so were filling posts that would more suitably have been filled by the mature people who were thereby deprived of them); and would not have been appointed were they not signed-up evangelists for, and subsequently normalisers of, the sexual revolution – for the 'benefit' of their huge readerships.

[36] See note 2 above: people cannot be incapable of seeing that films are long enough to contain *both* plenty that's good *and* plenty that's bad.

[37] Rank, 1969.

[38] Rank, 1972.

[39] Rank, 1973. Moreover, the on-screen relationship between Sid James and Barbara Windsor was replicated in real life. So how much was acting and how much was reality-documentary not only promulgating the film's questionable moral but even enacting it?

[40] Also akin to well-known folksongs: First Couple Up, Little Brown Jug.

[41] Compare notes 59-60 below.

[42] The 'left-wing' bias of the BBC continues. (In Chapter 10, we identified 'left-wing' and 'right-wing' as nonsensical positions; but people do sometimes adopt nonsensical positions.) Eric Hester (*Catholic Herald*, letters, 23.12.2011) demonstrated that they paid 5.7 times as much to advertise in the *Guardian* as in *Times* and *Telegraph* combined – even though *Guardian* sales totalled only 22.5% of the sales of the other two. Therefore the BBC was 25 times (2400%) more anxious to court *Guardian* readers (i.e., 0.38% of the UK population of 61.1m) than to court the others combined. Quite apart from their employing 22.5% Christians in a then c.60% Christian country.

[43] This is what takes it beyond, for example, George Formby's *My Little Stick of Blackpool Rock*.

[44] Since Kenneth Tynan on the programme *BBC3*, 13.11.1965.

[45] See the analyses of D Kupelian, *The Marketing of Evil* (Cumberland House WND, Nashville, TN, 2005) chapter 1, and R R Reilly, *Making Gay Okay. How Rationalising Homosexual Behavior Is Changing Everything* (Ignatius, San Francisco, CA, 2014).

[46] M Kirk & H Madsen, *After The Ball: How America Will Conquer Its Fear And Loathing Of Homosexuals in the '90s* (Plume, New York, NY, 1989).

[47] The strategy is openly acknowledged to involve lying: p.154.

[48] This method involves presenting repeated positive images of homosexuality and homosexuals, including historical exemplars (some, like Socrates and Alexander the Great, being dubious choices, given that they were deeply embedded in their own culture). The idea was also to present the homosexual movement as akin to Civil Rights or Women's Suffrage – and this has indeed become the dominant narrative. And, allied to this, to present 'bigoted' dissenters as freedom-haters.

[49] *House of Lords Hansard*, 9.7.2007.

[50] R Alcorn, *Pro-Life Answers to Pro-Choice Questions*: expanded edition (Multnomah, Colorado Springs, CO, 2000).

[51] Given that no ten-year-old girl would contemplate killing her baby in the course of her lifetime, when and by what stages does this startling attitude-change for the worse take place? For very many, it never does: such a thing remains unthinkable. All those who can bring themselves to do such an act have one thing in common: they have indulged in sex, generally outside marriage. The theory that extramarital sex deadens conscience and feelings would explain why they can bring themselves to do such a thing. More wholesale evangelisation of the young towards a no-qualms attitude to abortion received a potential boost with the 2012 appointment of Julie Bentley, former CEO of the Family Planning Association, to lead Girlguiding UK at around the same time as the dropping of God from the Promise, for which the executive had already prepared the way. It was said at this time that the Guides had never been a Christian organisation. We are left to gape uncomprehendingly not only at the evidence of the erstwhile Promise, especially in its earlier manifestations, but also at the proportion of hymns in Guide songbooks, and at the proportion of troops who meet in Church halls, and who present colours in Church.

[52] R Alcorn, *op. cit.*.

[53] Like the Royal College of Obstetricians and Gynaecologists; but quite unlike most

Royal Colleges, e.g. the Royal College of Music.
[54] Carol Everett, a former Texas abortion clinic owner (lifesitenews.com, 12.5.2014) says pushing sex education on children can create a demand for abortion.
[55] BBC Radio 4's *Don't Make Me Laugh* on 20.4.2016 'celebrated' the Queen's 90th birthday no less boorishly. Another example of lack of respect for the elderly came in 2005 when Michelle Bass's grandmother was so horrified by her granddaughter's antics on Channel 4's *Big Brother* that it made her physically ill. This was reported in the Press (see, for example, standard.co.uk/showbiz/michelle-nan-ill-with-shame-6967195. html); but it was never implied that the grandmother had right on her side. In less than a year she had died: chroniclelive.co.uk/news/north-east-news/michelle-grieves-loss-gran-1522056. A final example came from Richard Godwin, *Evening Standard* 22.5.2013. He wrote of Gerald Howarth MP, who had spoken against same-sex 'marriage': 'Or perhaps, like so many of his generation, he really does dream that everyone in Soho wants to bum him.' He also used the word 'relic'. This is an unintelligently sweeping generalisation *and* utterly inaccurate *and* insulting *and* showing disrespect to our wisest generation. Despite that, when I three times asked the female sub-editor sitting across from Mr Godwin on the other end of the telephone whether she saw anything wrong with it, she predictably claimed that she could not, try as she might.
[56] A good idea of how many did so can be gained from J Blanchard, *Pop Goes The Gospel*: revised and enlarged edition (Evangelical Press, Darlington, 1989). It is no coincidence that Queen's highly-rated *Bohemian Rhapsody* both invokes Beelzebub and ends in the utter selfishness (*and* nihilism; *and* sleight of hand) of equating 'nothing really matters' with 'nothing really matters *to me*'. This song was played at both the Opening and Closing Ceremonies of the London 2012 Olympics, on the former occasion accompanied by a pentagram formation.
[57] See, for example, *The Daily Telegraph*, 20.3.2012.
[58] *I am the Walrus*: see mentalfloss.com/article/50128/11.
[59] For example, Justin Timberlake and Janet Jackson in 2004.
[60] For example, Rihanna and Christina Aguilera in 2011.
[61] Contrast Chuck Berry's corruption of children's innocent singing: pp.301-2.
[62] On same-sex marriage, see especially: M J Anderson & R Bernhoft, *Male And Female He Made Them* (Catholic Answers, San Diego, CA, 2003); D Blankenhorn, *The Future of Marriage*; J Corvino & M Gallagher, *Debating Same-Sex Marriage* (OUP, Oxford, 2012); S Girgis, R T Anderson & R P George, *What Is Marriage? Man And Woman: A Defense* (Encounter, New York, NY, 2012); R S Harris, *Is There A Case For Same-Sex Marriage?* (Anglican Mainstream, Eynsham / Voice For Justice, Swindon, 2012); A Esolen, *Defending Marriage: Twelve Arguments For Sanity* (Saint Benedict Press, Charlotte, NC, 2014); P Morgan, *The Marriage Files: The Purpose, Limits and Fate of Marriage* (Wilberforce Publications, London, 2014).
[63] See www.lifesitenews.com/opinion/top-12-studies-showing-risks-to-couples-in-same-sex-unions.
[64] There are implications here for the integrity of the teaching profession. No teacher with a grain of truth in them could see 0% as equivalent to 100%. But as we see on pp.308-9 massive discrepancies are to all intents and purposes assumed without arguments or research to be parity. 900% equals zero, for example. That is an inaccuracy-level intolerable in schoolchildren, let alone teachers, who inhabit a fact-imparting (but sack-fearing?) profession.

[65] A full treatment is J Balthazart, *The Biology of Homosexuality* (OUP, New York, NY, 2011). See too the summary in P Morgan, *The Marriage Files*, pp.143-6.

[66] S LeVay, *Queer Science: The Use and Abuse of Research into Homosexuality* (Massachusetts Institute of Technology Press, Cambridge, MA, 1996) p.207.

[67] See N & B Whitehead, *My Genes Made Me Do It! A Scientific Look At Sexual Orientation* (Huntington House, Lafayette, LA, 1999).

[68] Such as those of William Rice and Tuck Ngun.

[69] Since the decoding of the Human Genome, the importance of environment has regularly been emphasised above that of genetics. See, for example, O James, *Mind Your Genes: The Real Reasons Children Are Like Their Parents* (Vermilion, London, 2016). On calculating the genetically-influenced proportion of various traits (for which identical twins are useful), see for example J A Schermer *at al.*, 'A Behavior Genetic Study of the Connection between Social Values and Personality' [2011] Twin Research and Human Genetics 14.3.

[70] E O Laumann *et al.*, *The Social Organization of Sexuality* (University of Chicago Press, Chicago, IL, 1994): sample-size 8744 adults.

[71] R L Johnson & D K Shrier, 'Sexual Victimization of Boys' [1985] Journal of Adolescent Health Care 6.5; E O Laumann, *op. cit.*; R Garofalo *et al.*, 'The Association between Health Risk Behaviors and Sexual Orientation among a School-Based Sample of Adolescents' [1998] Pediatrics 101.5; W C Holmes *et al.*, 'Sexual Abuse of Boys' [1998] Journal of the American Medical Association 280.21; S Jones & M Yarhouse, *Homosexuality: The Use of Scientific Research* (IVP-USA, Downers Grove, IL, 2000); M Tomeo, 'Comparative Data of Childhood and Adolescent Molestation in Heterosexual and Homosexual Persons' [2001] Archives of Sexual Behavior 30.5.

[72] See factsaboutyouth.com/posts/female-homosexual-behavior.

[73] R C Savin-Williams & G L Ream, 'Prevalence and Stability of Sexual Orientation Components during Adolescence and Young Adulthood' [2007] Archives of Sexual Behavior 36.3. For details of the great fluidity and elasticity in homosexual attraction that casts doubt on whether homosexuality is normally a fixed orientation, see too: V Dickson *et al.*, 'Same-Sex Attraction in a Birth-Cohort: Prevalence and Persistence in Early Adulthood' [2003] Social Science and Medicine 56.8; L M Diamond, 'Female Bisexuality from Adolescence to Adulthood: Results from a Ten-Year Longitudinal Study' [2008] Developmental Psychology 44.1; S E Mock & R P Eibach, 'Stability and Change in Sexual Orientation Identity over a Ten-Year Period in Adulthood' [2012] Archives of Sexual Behavior 41.3. E Whiteway & D Alexander, 'Understanding the Causes of Same-Sex Attraction' [2015] Science and Christian Belief 27, also accept the difficulty of speaking of 'orientation' as something innate. The on-the-ground campaigning for honesty in this matter has been led by Core Issues Trust (www.core-issues.org), whose archives detail the progress of the notorious London-bus-adverts case of 2012-14, where the well-moneyed Mayor's office deployed the whole armoury of the law (and since when has it ever been possible to purchase true justice?) to force a penniless organisation, voicing unwelcome truths, to be kept in check.

[74] J Stacey & T J Biblarz, '(How) Does The Sexual Orientation Of Parents Matter?' [2001] American Sociological Review 66.2.

[75] For example, J M Bailey, 'Genetic and Environmental Influences on Sexual Orientation and its Correlates in an Australian Twin Sample' [2000] Journal of Personality and Social Psychology 78.3; K S Kendler *et al.*, 'Sexual Orientation in a US National Sample of

Twin and Nontwin Sibling Pairs' [2000] American Journal of Psychiatry 157.11; see too P S Bearman & H Brueckner, 'Opposite-Sex Twins and Adolescent Same-Sex Attraction' [2002] American Journal of Sociology 107.5. For a summary of recent convergent studies, see www.patdollard.com/2014/12/identical-twin-studies-prove-homosexuality-is-not-genetic/#ehmuFW1QgYU9qyFw.99. For 20th-century studies see tim-taylor.com/papers/twin-studies/studies.html.

[76] Julia Gasper's work, at academia.edu/17168650/Homosexuality_and_Paedophilia_A_ Reference_Guide, is not only well-referenced but also excellent on the logic of the question. It addresses widespread *canards* such as the glib generalisation that gender is of no import to paedophiles, and the idea that (given that there is a widespread sexual preference for youth anyway, not least among homosexuals) one can draw a clear dividing-line between the two categories of behaviour mentioned in the title.

[77] *Op. cit..*

[78] J M W Bradford *et al.*, 'The Heterogeneity/Homogeneity of Pedophilia' [1988] Psychiatric Journal of the University of Ottawa 13.4.

[79] D Grubin, 'Sex Offending against Children: Understanding the Risk' (Police Research Series, paper 99. Home Office, 1998) p.14, para.2.

[80] K Freund *et al.*, 'Pedophilia and Heterosexuality vs Homosexuality' [1984] Journal of Sex and Marital Therapy 10.3.

[81] W D Erickson *et al.*, 'Behavior Patterns of Child Molesters' [1988] Archives of Sexual Behavior 17.1.

[82] K Freund & R J Watson, 'The Proportions of Heterosexual and Homosexual Pedophiles among Sex Offenders against Children: An Exploratory Study' [1992] Journal of Sex and Marital Therapy 18.1.

[83] J R Hughes, 'Review of Medical Reports on Pedophilia' [2007] Clinical Pediatrics 46.8.

[84] A P Bell & M Weinberg, Homosexualities (Simon & Schuster, New York, NY, 1978): sample-size around 1000.

[85] A Kaslow, 'The Multicenter AIDS Cohort Study' [1987] American Journal of Epidemiology 126.2: sample-size nearly 5000.

[86] J Lever, *The Advocate* magazine 1994: sample-size 2500.

[87] P van den Ven, 'A Comparative Demographic and Sexual Profile of Older Homosexually Active Men' [1997] Journal of Sex Research 34.4: sample-size 2583.

[88] C H Mercer *et al.*, 'Behaviorally Bisexual Men as a Bridge Population for HIV and Sexually Transmitted Infections' [2009] Journal of STD and AIDS 20.2: sample-size 5168.

[89] E S Rosenberg *et al.*, BMC Public Health 11: www.biomedcentral.com/content/ pdf/1471-2458-11-189.pdf.

[90] R A J Gagnon, *The Bible and Homosexual Practice* (Abingdon Press, Nashville, TN, 2001) pp.452-60.

[91] M L Brown, *A Queer Thing Happened To America*, pp.382-6.

[92] D P McWhirter & A M Mattison, *The Male Couple* (Prentice-Hall, New York, NY, 1985) suggest this happens less than 1% of the time, according to their own sample.

[93] See W Schumm, 'Comparative Relationship Stability of Lesbian Mother and Heterosexual Mother Families: A Review of Evidence' [2010] Marriage and Family Review 46.8. Also, 40% (so far) of the lesbian couples who had had a child by AI (artificial insemination) were found to have parted: N Gartrell & H Bos, 'U S National Longitudinal Lesbian Family Study: Psychological Adjustment of 17-Year-Old

Adolescents' [2010] Pediatrics 126.1.

[94] See B Muehlenberg, *Strained Relations* (2014) introduction.

[95] See note 98 below for evidence on the lack of difference between the outcomes for homosexual people whether they live in a gay-friendly culture or not.

[96] Jayne Ozanne (*Church of England Newspaper*, letters 6.11.2015) denies that homosexual desires are more promiscuous than heterosexual, *and proposes that no contrary view be allowed to be published*. Desires aside, homosexuals' *acting upon* those desires is certainly more promiscuous; tellingly, she cites no evidence to the contrary! The call for censorship of peer-reviewed science is unreasonable to the fifth degree. First, most uphold freedom of speech, even for lies and abuse – and we have neither of those here, which means that Ms Ozanne is both in theory and in practice happy to ban truthful, accurate material. Second, all agree that arguable positions can be published. Third, the position to which Ms Ozanne objects is not just arguable, but a scientific/ statistical consensus. Fourth, this particular consensus is especially clear-cut, involving as it does massive discrepancies between heterosexual and homosexual behaviour. Fifth, by what right does someone ask for a ban without citing one single piece of contrary evidence? And far more than one piece of evidence would be needed to outweigh that already cited in this section.

[97] E O Laumann, *op. cit.*; A Greeley, 'Marital Infidelity' [1994] Society 31.4; M W Wiederman, 'Extramarital Sex: Prevalence and Correlates in a National Survey' [1997] Journal of Sex Research 34.2.

[98] J E Phelan *et al.*, 'What Research Shows: NARTH's Response to the APA Claims on Homosexuality' [2009] Journal of Human Sexuality 1. See too N E Whitehead, 'Are Homosexuals Mentally Ill?' [2002] NARTH Bulletin 11.2; C Björkenstam *et al.*, 'Suicide in Married Couples in Sweden: Is the Risk Greater in Same-Sex Couples?' [2016] European Journal of Epidemiology 31.7.

[99] *L A Times* 11.4.2007 reported methamphetamine use to be 20 times higher than average among the gay population.

[100] One study found that the suicide risk for same-sex registered partners was 8 times greater than for married men: R Mathy *et al.*, 'The Association between Relationship Markers of Sexual Orientation and Suicide: Denmark, 1990-2001' [2011] Social Psychiatry and Psychiatric Epidemiology 46.2.

[101] M E King *et al.*, 'A Systematic Review of Mental Disorder, Suicide, and Deliberate Self-Harm in Lesbian, Gay and Bisexual People', www.biomedcentral.com 18.8.2008. A more recent large-scale study, based on the U S National Health Interview Survey and identifying substantially worse readings for LGB people, is G Gonzales *et al.*, 'Comparison of Health and Health Risk Factors between Lesbian, Gay and Bisexual Adults and Heterosexual Adults in the U S' [2016] JAMA Internal Medicine, published online 27.6.2016. On LGB youth and risky behaviour, see recently www.cdc.gov/mmwr/ volumes/65/ss/ss6509al.htm.

[102] G Greenwood *et al.*, 'Battering Victimization among a Probability-Based Sample of Men Who Have Sex With Men' [2002] American Journal of Public Health 92.12: 7% of heterosexual males but 39% of homosexual reported being abused. A similar figure of 32% is given by E Houston & D J McKiman, 'Intimate Partner Abuse among Gay and Bisexual Men: Risk Correlates and Health Outcomes' [2007] Journal of Urban Health 84.5. Two meta-analyses likewise found alarming rates: C Finneran & R Stephenson, 'Intimate Partner Violence among Men Who Have Sex With Men: A Systematic Review'

[2012] Trauma, Violence and Abuse 14.2; A Buller *et al.*, 'Associations between Intimate Partner Violence and Health among Men Who Have Sex With Men: A Systematic Review and Meta-Analysis' [2014] PLOS Medicine 11.3.

[103] S Harris, 'Mental Health, Chastity and Religious Participation in a Population of Same-Sex Attracted Men' [2009] Doctoral dissertation.

[104] E S Rosenberg, *op. cit.*.

[105] U Boehmer *et al.*, 'Cancer Survivorship and Sexual Orientation' [2011] Cancer 117.16.

[106] The figures used were from a US Centers for Disease Control and Prevention presentation on HIV prevalence in young males. See the analysis of Peter Ould at www.peter-ould.net/2013/09/16/some-staggering-statistics.

[107] M Xiridou *et al.*, 'The Contribution of Steady and Casual Partnerships to the Incidence of HIV Infection among Homosexual Men in Amsterdam' [2003] AIDS 17.7.

[108] See *Evening Standard* 6.7.2016, p.27.

[109] For the whole physiological angle and a frightening look at how sex education ignores the realities and put children at peril, see M Grossman, You're Teaching My Child What? (Regnery, Washington, DC, 2009). In her interview with National Review Online's Kathryn Jean Lopez (www.article.nationalreview.com/?q=YTQwY2U1ZDExN2QxAxYjIhYjE5MWFkOWE1YjcwZmI) Dr Grossman emphasises how out of date is the science on which sex education often depends. No mention of the oral sex – throat cancer link: are educators seriously saying that children should *not* be protected from this? No mention of 100% use of condoms decreasing STI-contraction by only 30%. But advice from SIECUS that 'it is up to you how much risk you are willing to take'. Especially ignored, as Dr Grossman highlights, has been the physiology of attraction between still-immature adolescents. On this, see also J S McIlhaney jr & F McKissic Bush, *Hooked: New Science On How Casual Sex Is Affecting Our Children* (Northfield, Chicago, IL, 2008). Sexual activity releases brain chemicals that create emotional bonds, and breaking of these bonds causes depression and make future close bonding difficult: these facts make lifelong marriage the only psychologically healthy option, as has long been instinctively known. Dr Grossman had herself seen the physiological and psychological fallout of the US campus hook-up culture first-hand, and published anonymously her findings in *Unprotected: A Campus Psychiatrist Reveals How Political Correctness In Her Profession Endangers Every Student* (Sentinel, New York, NY, 2007). L S Stepp, *Unhooked: How Young Women Pursue Sex, Delay Love, And Lose At Both* (Riverhead, New York, NY, 2007) emanates from the same environment; as does the fictional work of T Wolfe, *I Am Charlotte Simmons* (MacmillanPicador, New York, NY, 2004).

[110] S D Pinkerton *et al.*, 'Cost-Effectiveness of Postexposure Prophylaxis after Sexual or Injection-Drug Exposure to HIV' [2004] Archives of Internal Medicine 164.1.

[111] Here, pro-homosexual-practice thinkers are forced to contend that anal intercourse, already intrinsically dangerous, was acceptable even in the 99% of human history when it would have been even more dangerous because of the lack of safe-lubrication science.

[112] R S Hogg *et al.*, 'Modelling the Impact of HIV Disease on Mortality in Gay and Bisexual Men' [1997] International Journal of Epidemiology 26.3.

[113] Four full analyses: T E Schmidt, *Straight And Narrow? Compassion And Clarity In The Homosexuality Debate* (IVP-USA, Downers Grove, IL, 1995); J B De Young, *Homosexuality: Contemporary Claims Examined in Light of the Bible and Other Ancient Literature and Law* (Kregel, Grand Rapids, MI, 2000); R A J Gagnon, *The Bible and*

Homosexual Practice; S D Fortson & R G Grams, *Unchanging Witness: The Consistent Christian Teaching on Homosexuality in Scripture and Tradition* (Broadman & Holman Academic, Nashville, TN, 2016).

[114] The Sodom story (Genesis 18-19) is often cited, with the line taken being, at least since D Sherwin Bailey, *Homosexuality and the Western Christian Tradition* (Longmans, London, 1955), that '*the* sin of Sodom' was inhospitality. First, Sodom quite obviously did not have just one sin (cf. Ezekiel 16.46-50)! Second, Jesus (Matthew 11-20-4 // Luke 10.13-15) will naturally use Sodom as a benchmark for *any* kind of sin, whether or not it is one they were especially known for. Tyre is equally cited here – but was *that* city notable specifically for inhospitality? Third, inhospitality there was, but it *consisted in* rude homosexual advances. Fourth, it cannot escape notice that Lot's proposed remedy, the sacrifice of his daughters' virtue, involves replacing homosexual with heterosexual; nor that that remedy is so drastic as to mark the alternative (whether that be conceived as homosexual intercourse or as rape of angels who are also viewed as male) as an even worse, ultimate abomination. Fifth, is it coincidence that the city acknowledged as worst just so happens to have been that characterised by homosexuality – scarcely a common feature? Sixth, if the men merely wanted to 'know' (become acquainted with) the angels (a minority view sometimes found), that would not be a deficit of hospitality but hyper-hospitality shown by the whole city (the Judges 19-20 parallel also confirms the centrality of imposed sex of some sort, as does Jude 7).

[115] See Gagnon, *op. cit.*, 449-50.

[116] If there are cultural differences between first- and twenty-first-century homosexual practice, as there must be, no less are there cultural differences between first- and twenty-first-century lying, murder and adultery. A major line in recent discussion has been to classify homosexuality as culturally/socially constructed, given that its manifestations differ so strongly from culture to culture. See M Foucault, *The History of Sexuality 1: An Introduction* (ET: Knopf Doubleday, New York, NY, [1980] 1990); J Thorp, 'The Social Construction of Homosexuality' [1992] Phoenix 46.1.

[117] The Pilling Report, despite its strong focus on biblical issues, did not contain input from any leading biblical scholar. One might compare the way that Steve Chalke, who would not even claim to be a New Testament scholar, is endlessly quoted on the topic of homosexuality and the Bible.

[118] See pp.308-9.

[119] 1 Corinthians 6.9; 1 Timothy 1.10.

[120] As in NIV2011.

[121] D F Wright, 'Homosexuality: The Relevance of the Bible' [1989] Evangelical Quarterly 61.4.

[122] For example: *syn-* compounds in Romans 8.17 and in various parts of Ephesians. Paul may have coined a word here because no single Greek word existed that could be used to refer specifically to these Leviticus passages.

[123] Dr Cook also stated that it is scarcely possible that the evidence of a small independent organisation like Core Issues Trust on the biological or other origin of homosexuality should be preferable to that of the more grandly named Royal College of Psychiatrists. In fact: (a) On this occasion it was the former that cited plenty of chapter and verse; the latter cited very little. (b) Must the RCP know more than CIT in *every one* of the thousands of areas of psychiatry, including CIT's specialist area? Why? (c) It is a philosophical error to use the arguments from authority and from supposed lack of authority. Both

border on snobbery. Assessment must, of course, always be on the basis of quality of argumentation, and not in terms of the preconceived worth of the messenger. (d) CIT's evidence on this occasion came from the RCP's cited sources anyway. (e) The RCP had already modified its position statement on the matter in April 2014, taking on board some of CIT's criticisms. Here CIT, not RCP, made the running. (f) In general, when one speaks of official statements of official bodies, it still remains the case that they often emanate from very few people indeed, and sometimes from as few as one. Dr Cook continues in the same vein in *Church Times* 16.9.2016.

[124] The most egregious case is that of the Centurion's Servant story (Matthew 8.5-13 // Luke 7.1-10: cf. John 4.46-54). In a way that is utterly appalling to those who understand the amazing strength and beauty of war comrades' friendships (and David and Jonathan fall in this category), this is sometimes twisted into a story of pederasty. Never mind that *pais* could not be a more common or mundane word, meaning simply 'child'; nor that the John parallel (and it must be a variant of the same story since (a) only here do we have a Roman official – and a Capernaum Roman official at that – in a miracle story; (b) only here, other than at Mark 7.30 // Matthew 15.28, do we have a healing at a distance) has it that this male child was the official's *son*. Only one of the three accounts, Matthew, uses *pais* to describe the boy: John has 'son' (*huios*) and Luke, perhaps clarifying Matthew, has 'slave' (*doulos*; though there is a sole reminiscence of Matthew's *pais* at Luke 7.7).

[125] Since Christians and others alike often confuse the very different issues of what the text says and what the interpreter thinks (this confusion is of the essence of ideology), I should emphasise that I speak here of what the first-century text says, not what I would like it to say (!), nor anything to do with my own thoughts on the matter. I do not believe that any text is self-evidently true (though various individual statements may be); assertions made in texts can be seen to be true only insofar as the evidence suggests that they are. In this particular case, Paul correctly identifies that homosexual behaviour is unnatural and harmful.

[126] (Simon & Schuster, New York, NY, [1945] 2003).

[127] *House of Lords Hansard*, 18.11.2007.

[128] See p.259.

[129] 2 Corinthians 10.5.

[130] End Note: I'm especially glad to have the chance to contribute to a book in honour of June Cash. She was exactly the kind of family-loving, sane, mature, and extremely determined Christian who these days is in danger of being sidelined, and even sometimes criminalised. (The new class of 'criminals' are chalk to the old class's cheese: the discrepancy in character between the two groups is readily apparent.) June, as you yourself knew, the battle is already won. No-one (least of all in the arena of education, and least of all for their own ends) has any business going against logic, nor against statistical consensus, nor against common sense. And on all those fronts we have a walkover.

Chapter Twelve

HOLDING THE LINE –
A PERSONAL REFLECTION
The Baroness Cox

By background I am a nurse and social scientist, and it was something of a surprise in 1983 to find myself appointed to the House of Lords – an illustration, I think, of God's sense of humour! Up to that time I had never actually been 'into politics'. In fact, I was the first Baroness I had ever met, but I asked God how best to use the unexpected and immense privilege I had been given of speaking in the House of Lords. He answered, 'It's a great place to be a Voice for the Voiceless.' So ever since, that is what I have tried to do, speaking out at home and abroad for those suffering persecution and oppression, many trapped behind closed borders.

As those familiar with my career will know, I have always been interested in education, but today – and again, to my surprise – I see a clear link between school age children and those suffering persecution and oppression. Which is why I am contributing to this book. To those feeling equally surprised, I should explain that in my view young people today are being increasingly subjected to a state-sanctioned educational programme that promotes indoctrination over the impartation of knowledge, the effect of which is to prioritise the normalisation of secular values standing in direct conflict to what are now deemed the old-fashioned teachings of traditional 'Christian' morality.

Speaking personally, I have a long-standing commitment, going back many years, to recognition of the enormous importance of teaching Religious Education (RE) in our schools, and the progressive and deliberate downgrading of this by secular activists has been key to enabling and facilitating the secular and often distinctly anti-Judaeo-Christian values now being promoted throughout our culture. It is for this reason that I reiterate my strong support for the teaching of RE.

In this chapter I shall address five themes:

1. Some of the reasons for the importance of teaching RE, including knowledge of our Judaeo-Christian faith and heritage.
2. Challenges of recent years confronting the teaching of RE, with particular reference to decades following the 1960s.
3. A brief 'trip down memory lane' to 1988, when I and others worked to try to amend the 1988 Education Reform Act – with a recollection of the dire state of affairs at that time, and some of the political challenges we encountered.
4. Inspirational examples from partners on the frontlines of faith and freedom abroad.
5. Challenges and opportunities on the home front today.

1. Some reasons for the importance of teaching RE, including knowledge of our Judaeo-Christian faith and heritage

A. Spiritual: we are blessed to live in a country identified as Christian. But this means we have a duty to pass on to successive generations the knowledge of that faith, which has been handed down to us often at great cost. Opponents, such as secular humanists, may challenge this duty, arguing that we are no longer 'a Christian country'. But, as T.S. Eliot claimed in *The Idea of a Christian Society*: 'A society has not ceased to be Christian until it has become positively something else.'[1] As a nation, we have not yet declared ourselves to be something else.

A second challenge is the allegation that teaching religion is a form of brainwashing. This is a false argument because, whatever the issue, for anyone to make up their mind they need first to have full knowledge of the facts so that they can make an informed choice. To deny the teaching of Christianity (and other faiths) is to deny any possibility of that happening, because it deliberately withholds information. True choice regarding faith comes then – and can only come – when people have full knowledge, and can assess for themselves whether or not to believe. This is not coercion but, in its purest sense, education – helping the student to decide for themselves.

The argument used by secularists, with barely concealed triumph, is that it is inappropriate to teach religion in a multicultural society. Far better, they urge, to ignore religion entirely, lest offence be caused. Religion should be practised in private! But strangely this is an argument not generally supported by believers of other faiths – and I believe indeed that it is easier to understand other belief systems and cultures when approached from a position of 'faith', than from the innately sceptical approach of secularists.

B. Historic: It is impossible to understand and fully appreciate our history of art, music, architecture, parliament, the economy, voting rights – and so many other aspects of our culture – without understanding the faith which inspired, nurtured and preserved them.

C. Legal: There is a legal requirement to teach RE, and unless that changes, this stands.

D. Political: Knowledge of Christian beliefs is essential to any understanding of the development of the fundamental values, principles, policies and laws of our country – and indeed extends beyond that to the whole of what is deemed 'Western civilisation'. Critics of Christianity often point to the negative aspects of our faith over history – such as the Inquisition or the 'cultural imperialism' of Christian mission. But, as we shall see, this is a biased assessment and most definitely not the whole story, while at the same time there are many ways in which the world can be deemed to be a better place because of Christianity.

John Bradley in his new book *The Mansion House of Liberty* writes:

> This book records the motivation of our predecessors in building our country into the way it is today, men and women of the Christian faith… (who) strove over the centuries to build British society and the values we now have.
>
> These attributes matter. They are worth retaining … so, if we are to maintain them vigilantly, we need to know how and where they came from. Their preservation is important, not as nostalgic museum pieces but in a way which encompasses their values and insights, from which we benefit, adapted to our modern conditions. My aim…is to demonstrate how Christians have applied their faith

to their part in the building of Britain...*for many of the principal players, faith was their motivation...*[2] (emphasis added)

2. Challenges confronting the teaching of RE, post 1960

Some personal experiences may perhaps help to illustrate the bigger picture. During the early 1970s, I found myself as Head of Department of Sociology at the then Polytechnic of North London. I arrived totally politically naive to find myself with an academic Department of twenty staff, sixteen of whom were members of the Communist Party, or further Left. Their definition of higher education was not mine! Mine was and is freedom to pursue the truth within the canons of academic rigour. Theirs was hard-line indoctrination, and they displayed absolutely no compunction in resorting to academic blackmail, physical violence and harsh censorship of any and all views they found politically unacceptable! Their primary foci for assault were religious faith and traditional family values.

This may perhaps sound far-fetched and even alarmist, but let me offer three examples to illustrate the ferocity of the attacks:

(a) A student who followed me into the women's cloakroom looked around with fear to make sure no-one was there and blurted out: 'Please may I come to see you? I'm finding it really difficult to maintain my Christian faith with all this teaching. But I daren't be seen entering your office or the other staff will take it out on me.'

(b) Another student, a recently widowed woman, came to see me in floods of tears. She had just presented a seminar paper on 'The Family', which was not based on the Marxist critique of family values. The response of the lecturer had been to tear it up in front of the class and call her a 'bourgeois bag'.

(c) A violent occupation of college buildings was based on false allegations that the about-to-be appointed Director was a 'Racist' and a 'Fascist'. These were cruel lies: he had taken part in the Battle of Arnhem where he saw many of his friends dying alongside him, fighting Fascism, and he had got into trouble in Northern Rhodesia for helping black students. The occupation was dominated by an 'Occupation Collective' which authorised the subjects which were allowed to be taught each day – nothing to do with the curricula for which students had paid, often sacrificially. I persisted in teaching my 'unauthorised' seminar on Criminology. It ended in physical assault – but the happy and somewhat surprising outcome was that the following year the student who led the assault asked me to be his academic tutor. I was only too happy to agree: I told him, 'I love living dangerously!' Later he told me, 'It takes a lot of courage to ask to have you as a tutor. Most of the final year students would like to do so, but dare not because of reprisals from other staff.'

I knew this kind of indoctrination was not only happening at the Polytechnic of North London, but that the soft underbelly of Higher Education was being targeted in many universities and polytechnics. For this reason, and to highlight the dangers, with two colleagues I wrote a book, *The Rape of Reason*.[3] It need hardly be said that I was very nervous. If you have any integrity, you don't 'write and run', and I knew I was going to have to face a backlash – not just from disgruntled colleagues but from the wider academic and politically 'Left' worlds. Mercifully, however, on the day of publication, out of the blue God sent a lifeline. The columnist Bernard Levin rang me to say he would be writing about the book as he deemed it to be immensely important for the future of democracy. The next day he wrote an opinion editorial article in the centre of *The Times*, concluding that this was such an important book that he would devote his remaining two articles that week to discussing it. He had only previously written a trilogy for Mozart and Solzhenitsyn. The timeless relevance is encapsulated in these excerpts:

> (*The*) *Rape of Reason* tells, with an astonishing degree of judicious calm, of the planned destruction of an institution of higher education, with the use by the destroyers of physical and psychological intimidation, of totally unscrupulous dishonesty, of violence, theft and vandalism, of obscenity and defamation and of a wide range of literally criminal actions. It tells also of something worse: that is, the resignation and retreat, in the face of this campaign, by those whose undoubted task it was to resist and combat the corruption. And it tells, finally of something worse still: of the way in which the assault was actively aided by some of those who had the duty of defending free inquiry, intellectual tolerance and integrity of thought but who instead connived at the assault on all three and indeed frequently

helped to instigate it....

If I say "Send not to ask for whom the bell tolls" you will yawn at the cliché – well, yawn away, for there are clichés even worse than that one, as Orwell knew...

What exactly has happened at the Polytechnic of North London? You can find out, in horrible detail, by reading *Rape of Reason* and I hope many people will. I can summarise it, however, by saying that what has happened is that a few people have determined to turn it into a place where twice two do not necessarily make four, but forty, or four hundred, or nineteen and a bit, if they say so.

Yet Orwell was right: freedom is the freedom to say that two plus two make four. And that is why I do not much care if you do yawn when I begin "Send not to ask for whom the bell tolls", provided you realise that it may well be tolling, at the Polytechnic of North London, for thee.'[4]

In these passages, Bernard Levin illustrates the powerful forces sweeping through higher education at that time; we are currently reaping the whirlwind.

The extreme relativism of 1960s 'Flower Power', combined with the widespread and systematic attack on faith and fundamental values, created a spiritual vacuum which was reflected in the culture, including the education system, of subsequent years that has lasted right up until the present day.

This brings me to my third theme – the political and legal battle in the 1980s to reinstate the teaching of RE in all schools and to preserve the teaching of our Judaeo-Christian heritage in the syllabus.

3. The battle for the reinstatement of teaching RE in schools and the inclusion of our Judaeo-Christian heritage

During the latter years of the 1980s, I was involved with research into aspects of teaching in secondary schools, including the situation with regard to RE. I undertook research with John Burn, subsequently Head of a Christian Academy in Newcastle on Tyne.

Our findings were deeply disturbing. In many schools we discovered that RE was not being taught at all, despite requirements stemming from 1944 legislation. But in others we discovered an almost worse situation, because what was being taught under guise of 'RE' included political indoctrination, such as promoting the Campaign for Nuclear Disarmament with no countervailing views on any merits of defence, as well as an extreme form of syncretistic relativism which destroyed the integrity of any faith, and therefore of all faiths. We even found that some schools, under the mantle of RE, included the occult!

Coming towards the end of the decade, however, the 1988 Education Reform Act provided a welcome opportunity to try to address these issues, and in particular to reinstate the requirement that RE be taught in all schools. Naturally, this carried the concomitant requirement that such teaching should include knowledge of our Judaeo-Christian heritage.

An examination of the text of some of the contributions to Parliamentary debates, recorded at the time in Hansard[5] is instructive and worth quoting at length:

Christian Teaching in Schools, Friday, 26 February 1988

Parents and teachers in many other places have expressed anxiety over two issues. One is the dilution of Christian teaching in a multi-faith mish-mash. The other is secularisation by concentration on social and political issues.

For more than 20 years after the 1944 Act, RE syllabuses were Christian-based, but over the past 15 years many have been influenced by the Shap working party on world religions and have developed multi-faith syllabuses in which Christianity is treated as just one among many faiths and perhaps not even the predominant subject for study. Moreover, some multi-faith syllabuses are so worded as to allow inclusion of secular and political creeds such as humanism and the militant atheism of Marxism. Their inclusion seems, to say the least, a contradiction in terms. Of course there is a strong case—and I must emphasise this—for including some teaching about the other great world religions, especially in a society where these religions are practised. Such teaching can increase understanding and respect, which are essential values in a pluralist society.

But that is very different from presenting young people with a position of extreme relativism in which all belief systems are presented in a value-free hotchpotch as exemplified in a book which I am told by teachers is widely used in RE. It is called 'Beginning Religion'... It shows page after page of grotesque and sometimes frightening pictures of religious rituals such as human sacrifice and a spine-chilling photograph of an Aborigine initiation ceremony. The Lord's Prayer is discussed on the same page as Shamanism. There is considerable emphasis on the occult. This edition actually suggests that children should try to find out what happens at a séance. I gather this has been omitted from a later edition. However, preoccupation with the occult and with phenomena such as witchcraft is a recurring theme in many RE courses.

Parents in York report that a class used all its RE lessons for a whole term to learn about witchcraft, including the use of videos of witches' covens. A number of RE inspectors in ILEA sent a letter to all schools warning against the traumatic psychological effects of teaching the occult in London's schools.

How has this situation deteriorated so drastically? Some of the developments are, I suggest, a result of confusion of multi-culturalism, multi-racism and multi-faith education. The fact that Britain is a society of many races and faiths is highly significant. But many who have come to live here from other countries, especially from the Caribbean, are Christian. Christianity remains the dominant religion in this country, and without an understanding of Christianity no real appreciation of our history or our culture is possible....

So it is important to put recent attempts to broaden RE into multi-faith syllabuses into context. The initial endeavours to include an understanding of other faiths were laudable. But that does not justify a transformation of the entire RE syllabus into a kaleidoscope of shallow ideas about myriad belief systems from Shamanism, ancestor worship and the occult, to a study of other faiths which leaves pupils ignorant of the basic tenets of Christianity.

Graham Turner, in the Daily Mail of 25th November 1987, describes a school in Sussex where children said that they learnt about Hinduism and Sikhism, but hardly anything about Christianity. He writes: Eleven Out of 15 youngsters said they had no idea who Pontius Pilate was. "'Wouldn't even know how to spell it', said one. 'Not a clue who he or she is', said another'." Some of the most surprising teaching material has been produced by an organisation with the word "Christian" in its name: the Christian Education Movement. Its book on Spring festivals gives graphic accounts of the Chinese New Year, of Krishna festivals, before coming to the Jewish Passover and then giving only a very cursory account of the Christian Easter, before concluding with "Making a Mobile for Chinese New Year"...

Before I begin to draw a conclusion perhaps I may briefly mention the other aspect of RE which many parents are finding unacceptable. I refer to its use for partisan political purposes. For example, the GCSE religious studies syllabus from Doncaster is heavily laced with CND material with no comparable discussion on defence and disarmament or alternative views. The syllabus from Alperton School in Brent shows how RE is to be part of an integrated humanities course with highly politicised messages. Of course there is a case for consideration of social, political and moral issues from a Christian perspective. But that is a world away from using RE to legitimate one-sided, simplistic answers to complex, controversial problems.

Education Reform Bill, Monday 18 April 1988

.... Many people believe that we should now rectify the omission of the 1944 Act which failed to specify the predominantly Christian or biblical nature of RE and worship. Of course the right to withdraw children must be safeguarded, and there must be an opportunity for all to learn about other major world religions. But we are still a predominantly Christian country and we need to ensure that our young people do not grow up ignorant of the faith of their forefathers or of the great Christian influence in our nation's spiritual heritage, culture and history.[6]

Amendments to reflect these concerns were eventually included in the Bill, but not without considerable effort – as demonstrated by some of the political machinations to which we had to resort in order to gain support! For example, when my colleagues and I were working to prepare the amendments, it was obviously important to seek the backing of the Bishops in the House of Lords. However, when I approached one of them, to my astonishment I was asked not to move the amendments. When I asked why not, I was told that it would *'divide the College of Bishops'*.

Incomprehensible as it seems, it would appear that so-called 'unity' was more important than safeguarding and passing on the spiritual heritage of our faith to our children! But it meant, of course, that we had to proceed without their initial support.

Then I was told that the Chief Whip had been heard to say that arrangements would be made to ensure that Lady Cox's amendments would always come on late at night. Naturally that meant that there would be few people to engage in the debate – and so it followed that there would be no votes.

Well, rules, as we all know, are made to be broken – and this is where, I am afraid to say, I had to learn to play their game and use the same sort of tactics myself, in the process decisively breaking convention! With the encouragement of some doughty Peer supporters keen to see the safeguarding of our spiritual heritage included in the Bill, I had the temerity to move a vote at some unearthly hour in the early morning – virtually unprecedented behaviour. Exactly as I had hoped, it caused a furore! There were not enough Peers to form a quorum and the House had to dissolve immediately. Which meant, in turn, that the amendments had to reappear at prime time the following Monday afternoon.

When I arrived, already somewhat nervous, I was immediately summoned to meet a furious Chief Whip, who was especially angry because he said that, as a Deputy Speaker, I should know and abide by the rules! That in itself was bad enough, but news of my misdemeanour was by then common knowledge, and when I later rose to my feet to speak to a packed House, it was to meet with a distinctly chilly reception.

I then indulged in even more impudence. Over the weekend I had received a phone call from a Muslim friend, who was distinctly unhappy with RE teaching at the time, because he said it violated the integrity of not just Christianity, but of all faiths, including his own! He told me that on the previous Friday, many Muslims in his mosque had been praying for the issue, including a prayer that the name of Christ would be revered in British schools – at which point I could not resist glancing over at the Bishops' Benches, and remarking that I wished our Bishops could be heard praying the same prayer!

Notwithstanding the Bishops' lack of enthusiasm, however, it would appear that the prayers were efficacious, because shortly afterwards the then Bishop of London undertook to take responsibility for the Amendments, which later became part of the 1988 Education Reform Act.

I subsequently heard from many Christian teachers in State schools that those amendments had made life a lot easier for them, because as a result they were able to teach about the UK's spiritual heritage without the vehement and sometimes vitriolic opposition so many had previously faced.

More recent developments and challenges are explored in detail elsewhere in this book, so I shall not go into them here. But I wanted to describe the historical background of recent decades to show that this is not a 'new' problem, and to give some idea of the challenges confronting us. Many of our adversaries are both formidable and determined, and compromise is not possible, because they will not rest until they have achieved victory – which is the complete removal of Christianity from public life. We either fight to defend our spiritual heritage, therefore, or lose it altogether.

But lest this sound overly pessimistic, I would like to turn to the inspiration I and colleagues in my small charity, HART (Humanitarian Aid Relief Trust), receive from our partners battling on the frontlines of faith and freedom around the world. Not only are their faith and testimony relevant to our own situation here in the UK, but they model the responsibility we all bear to cherish and pass on our spiritual heritage – and to guard and educate our young. More than that, their brave example – often at great personal cost – demonstrates the supreme importance of Christian values in promoting and protecting fundamental values of freedom and democracy. No other belief system in the world, be it secular ideology, conventional religions, or derived from so-called

New Age spiritualties, cares for and defends to such an extent the value, rights, and fundamental freedoms of the individual.

4. Inspirational examples from partners on the frontlines of faith and freedom abroad

My first example comes from Burma, where HART is working with ethnic national peoples still suffering from military offensives and violations of human rights by the Burmese Army. Inspirational stories of living faith abound, but one example in particular stands out as relevant to the concerns of this book: we are told by our partners there that the Burmese Government doesn't 'like' Christianity because it fosters genuine democracy by encouraging individuals to think for themselves. What a tribute to our faith and its underpinning of fundamental freedoms! On the evidence of this book, could the same be said of secularist educational policies?

My second example comes from Sudan and the war which raged there from 1989 to 2005. During that time hundreds of thousands of women and children were abducted into slavery by the Islamist regime in Khartoum. At the time I had the immense privilege and opportunity to work with Christian Solidarity Worldwide (CSW) to redeem many hundreds of these women and children from slavery. Tragically, it was only a drop in the ocean of numbers – but we were doing what we could to fulfil the biblical mandate to free the oppressed and those suffering the ultimate oppression of slavery. It meant, however, that I witnessed first-hand the horrors of the reality of contemporary slavery, which made me appreciate with especial fervour the contribution of our Christian heritage to global initiatives to promote freedom, seen in the transformational work of William Wilberforce and his colleagues, who were responsible for the breakthrough legislation to abolish the slave trade in the British Empire.

Thirdly, a brief mention of the contribution of 'Christian Mission': When I was fighting the Marxist-Leninists dominating higher education in my college, there was a sustained commitment by them to denigrate Christianity and Christian mission as a form of cultural oppression. Now, it is undeniable that over the centuries mission work has not been without its faults, but there are equally many examples of cherished legacies to the protection and well-being of mankind, seen especially in the provision of life-saving health care and education. In so many countries in Africa and Asia, people in remote areas will point to a hospital, saying 'That hospital would never have been there if it hadn't been for the British'.

A propos of which, I will never forget, during the war in Sudan, walking for many hours through the destruction and death perpetrated by the Khartoum regime in the South. We arrived eventually at a remote village where we were welcomed by the tribal chief. Everything was destroyed, but as we sat on the ground among the ants, he spoke these words:

We will always be grateful to the British because you gave us education; and education gives us the freedom to think for ourselves. You cannot give anyone a greater gift or a greater freedom than that.

These are just some examples of a response to the guilt complex about our faith which was generated in those days, and which still persists in many quarters. Many of these phenomenal achievements in promoting health, education and freedom were rooted and grounded in Christian values, and achieving them called not just for commitment, but often resulted in the ultimate sacrifice.

Fourthly, we do well to remember that the commitment to define and apply the concept of Genocide, which now has far-reaching application, was first developed by Raphael Lempkin, a Jew and therefore deeply committed to Judaeo-Christian tradition, who was profoundly moved by the fate of one-and-a-half million Armenians in the Armenian Genocide perpetrated by Ottoman Turkey.

All these examples, which admittedly don't even scratch the surface of what we today accept as 'human rights', testify to the fact that it is the Judaeo-Christian tradition, with its inherent respect for the human individual and its cherishing of the concept of individuals' rights and freedoms, which has generated and sustained the most humanising and humanitarian internationally recognised laws and policies, such as the abolition of slavery and the concept of Genocide. Other faiths such as Buddhism – and faith leaders, such as Gandhi – offer profoundly significant spiritual and political contributions to humanity, but the Judaeo-Christian faith has made uniquely the most distinctive world-changing contributions to international law and universal human rights.

It is, for example, impossible to imagine the Universal Declaration of Human Rights without the Judaeo-Christian context of Western civilisation.

Finally, I would like to highlight the situation in northern Nigeria, where thousands of Christians have been killed and hundreds of churches destroyed. In fact, since the rise of Boko Haram, persecution has escalated into what may accurately be described as a reign of terror. As a part of that horror, we all heard about the appalling fate of the 250 girls kidnapped from Chibok. But when we from HART were last in the region, we were told that a thousand had been kidnapped before the Chibok horror, and many hundreds since. And here in the West, we have never heard about them!

It is our privilege to support some partners in that much-beleaguered country, including the Anglican Archbishop of Jos in Plateau State, the Rt. Revd. Benjamin Kwashi, where he has founded the Christian Institute to train men and women in ministry, maternal and child health, IT, and other important subjects. During a recent visit, he gave us a message:

> 'If we have a faith worth living for, it's a faith worth dying for. Don't YOU betray the faith we are living and dying for....'

5. The battle on the home front

In conclusion, the truth is that in the UK today we are betraying that faith. To give an obvious example, we have allowed the growth of sharia Courts, which operate as a parallel and highly discriminatory legal system, inflicting extremely disturbing forms of religiously sanctioned gender discrimination on Muslim women, which causes great suffering.

Islam teaches that women are worth less than a man,[7] and under the edicts of sharia law, a husband can divorce his wife simply by saying three times, 'I divorce you'. This sounds harsh, but it can get worse. Recently, one of my Muslim woman friends showed me a piece of paper sent through the post with just the words 'I divorce you' written on it, signed by her husband – and that was apparently it. Her marriage had been ended.

Sharia law also allows polygamy, so that a man can 'legitimately' have four wives – though of course the reverse is not true because, as we have already seen, women under Islam don't have the same rights as men. But bigamy – usually confined to a mere 'two' spouses – is illegal in this country. So why this apparently sanctioned exception for Muslims, upheld by the sharia courts? Why too are Muslim men allowed to 'chastise' their wives, in behaviour that under any other jurisdiction would be classified as domestic violence?

The conclusion is inescapable that women under sharia law endure legally endorsed abuse, and are routinely and systematically exploited: as described by Habiba Jaan, another courageous Muslim friend, who wrote a chilling report detailing the suffering of fifty Muslim women in the West Midlands.[8] Hardly surprising then that another Muslim woman told me bitterly,

I feel betrayed by this country. I came here to get away from all this; and it's worse here than in the country I came from.

Yet not only is sharia law causing great suffering to many Muslim women in our country; its application also poses a major threat to the fundamental principle of liberal democracy, enshrined in the tenet, 'One Law For All'. It is for all these reasons that I introduced my Private Member's Bill to restrict the power of sharia courts in Britain. But the problem will only finally be dealt with by a more wholesale and rigorous approach, and it is vital that any education policy we now develop acknowledges and protects our Christian heritage, because only on that basis will we be able to defend the values on which our nation has been founded.

Back in Nigeria, Archbishop Ben gave us another challenge: 'If you don't fight these battles now, your grandchildren are going to have to fight the battles you have not had the courage to fight.'

In the UK today political Islam is growing in both strength and force, and it is exploiting the freedom given by democracy to try to destroy our democratic system of government and the freedoms it enshrines. The recent 'Trojan Horse' attempt to subvert schools in Birmingham[9] is a disturbing and well documented illustration of this, and we must be robust in our response, not allowing 'political correctness' or 'cultural sensitivities' to override the law of the land. As things stand, it is not surprising that the commitment to Islamist ideology is growing among the younger generation of Muslims, so that increasing numbers are becoming what is termed 'radicalised'. But this makes it only more imperative that we teach a counter-ideology of love, genuine compassion, justice and freedom. Based on our faith.

When we see our fundamental freedoms under threat – from whatever source – we must pray for wisdom and discernment. But, in love, we must also *act* to defend those freedoms, lest we lose them. Our heritage is indisputably Christian. Our laws were first formed and developed in accordance with the values of our faith, and our kings explicitly ruled *under God*. But more importantly, no other belief system in the world is as committed to defending the rights and freedom of the individual – as a being of infinite worth made in the image of God, and so worthy of respect. Which is why our calling to protect, preserve, promote and pass on our Christian heritage in and through education is so precious, and of fundamental importance.

May we not leave our children to fight the battles we have not had the courage to fight, but may we strive to ensure that we pass on our spiritual, cultural and political heritage undiminished, that subsequent generations may flourish in peace and justice. The future of our nation is at stake and the time for action is NOW.

Notes

[1] T.S.Eliot, *The Idea of a Christian Society* (originally delivered as three lectures at Corpus Christi College, Cambridge, 1939. Published by Harcourt, 1960).

[2] John Bradley, *The Mansion House of Liberty, the untold story of Christian Britain* (Roper Penberthy Publishing, 2015).

[3] Keith Jacka, Caroline Cox, and John Marks, *The Rape of Reason: Corruption of the Polytechnic of North London* (Churchill Press, 1975)

[4] See *The Times*, 30 September 1975; 10 October 1975; 30 October 1975.

[5] See http://hansard.millbanksystems.com/lords/1988/jun/21/education-reform-bill

[6] HL Deb 03 May 1988 vol 496 cc450-557, http://hansard.millbanksystems.com/lords/1988/may/03/education-reform-bill-1

[7] E.g., Quran (4:11) – (Inheritance) "The male shall have the equal of the portion of two females" (see also verse 4:176). Quran (2:282) – (Court testimony) "And call to witness, from among your men, two witnesses. And if two men be not found then a man and two women."

[8] https://www.secularism.org.uk/uploads/aurat-report-dec2014.pdf

[9] See http://www.bbc.co.uk/news/uk-england-birmingham-35615798

CONTRIBUTORS

Edmund P. Adamus was Director for marriage and family life in Westminster Archdiocese from 2004-2016. He is now Professional Adviser to the Episcopal Vicar for Education and Schools Commissioner in Portsmouth Diocese. From 2007-2012 he established and managed the St. John Southworth Fund awarding several million pounds to alleviate poverty and deprivation across London. In 2011 Edmund was a co-recipient with Philip Blond (Founder of the Res Publica Think Tank) of the 2011 Family Values Award. He has helped develop resources to aid parents in their indispensable duty to provide formation for children in human sexuality.

Anthony Busk specialises in forensic social dynamics analysis, working within the diverse and conflicting cultural activist tensions of present day Western society. He is a former Senior Lecturer in management, and as a Research Director focused on social issues relevant to the interplay between employment and enterprise development, and the role of education. More recently he has researched the resurgence of Marxist-Engels dogma, and the subsequent systematic campaign within schools to disintegrate Judaeo-Christian family units. He believes it is a behavioural norm which already is bringing social chaos, and ultimately will have profound effects on national economic wellbeing.

June Cash was a Church minister, worship leader and intercessor. She was also a founder member of Voice for Justice UK, serving as company secretary. Throughout her life she campaigned for the defence of Christian values – in church, education, politics, and in the family. She battled against cancer for three years, and was promoted to glory on 2 May 2015, leaving behind her husband Tony, two daughters, and four grandchildren. Greatly loved and missed.

The Baroness Cox was created a Life Peer in 1982 and was a deputy speaker of the House of Lords from 1985 to 2005. She was Founder Chancellor of Bournemouth University, 1991-2001; Founder Chancellor of Liverpool Hope University 2006-2013 and is an Honorary Vice President of the Royal College of Nursing. She is heavily involved with international humanitarian work. She is Founder and President of HART [Humanitarian Aid Relief Trust]. She was also a founder Trustee of MERLIN [Medical Emergency Relief International].

Baroness Cox's humanitarian aid work takes her on many missions to conflict and post-conflict zones, including, amongst others, the Armenian enclave of Nagorno Karabakh; Sudan; South Sudan; Nigeria; Uganda; the Karen, Karenni, Shan, Chin and Kachin peoples in the jungles of Burma. In Indonesia she helped to establish the International Islamic Christian Organisation for Reconciliation and Reconstruction (IICORR) with the late former President Abdurrhaman Wahid. She has also been instrumental in helping to change the former Soviet Union's policies for orphaned and abandoned children from institutional to foster family care.

Publications include *Cox's Book of Modern Saints and Martyrs*, with Catherine Butcher, Continuum 2006, 4th reprint 2011; *This Immoral Trade: Slavery in the 21st Century* 2006 (new edition 2013); *The West, Islam and Islamism: Is ideological Islam compatible with liberal democracy?*, co-authored with John Marks; *The Very Stones Cry Out. The Persecuted Church: Pain, Passion and Praise* with Benedict Rogers, Continuum, 2011. Two biographies have also been published by Monarch/Lion Hudson: *The Baroness Cox: Voice for the Voiceless*, by Andrew Boyd and, more recently, *The Baroness Cox: Eyewitness to a Broken World* by Lela Gilbert.

Brian Hadley Working with several pro-family organisations, Brian is an independent researcher into the top-level issues underlying global culture change. A Natural Sciences graduate from the University of Cambridge, for three decades he pursued a professional career in occupational health, safety and the environment, areas where facts and fiction are increasingly in competition. Having worked for organisations in both the public and private sectors, this technical, legal and organisational experience has given him unique insights into how special interest groups seek to influence politicians and shift public opinion. He now applies this framework in his research across a range of societal stressors related to marriage and family issues. His attention has recently focused on how and why primary schools are being targeted as hotbeds for social engineering.

Robert S. Harris is the Joint Convenor of the Lords and Commons Family and Child Protection Group and is a Director of *Voice for Justice UK*. He is the author of the acclaimed book, *Is There a Case for Same-Sex Marriage? Questions of Eligibility and Consequences*. He has organised conferences and spoken at events in parliament and elsewhere, covering a wide spectrum, from family issues to religious liberty. Robert holds a degree in philosophy from University College London and a Diploma from the College of Law in London.

Edmund Matyjaszek was born in London, and now lives in Ryde, Isle of Wight with his family. He was educated at Wadham College, Oxford, where he studied Classics and Law. His prize-winning play "The Consultation", a modern day psycho-analysis of Christ, has been twice performed. He has published two poetry collections "Walsingham: England's Nazareth", and "The Rosary: England's Prayer". Since 2009 he has been Principal of Priory School, an independent Christian school at Whippingham, Isle of Wight.

Dr Alastair Noble BSc PhD studied chemistry and did research work at the University of Glasgow, Scotland. He has been a secondary school teacher, adviser, schools inspector and deputy director of education. He has also worked on educational programmes within the BBC, the CBI and the Health Service. He was the Field Officer for School Leaders Scotland from 2001-2013 and in the same period was an educational consultant for CARE in Scotland. Alastair is married to Ruth and lives in the village of Eaglesham near Glasgow, Scotland.

Philip Quenby is a writer and film-maker. His book *Redeeming a Nation* looks at how God has worked in English history over the centuries. His five-part documentary Magna Carta Unlocked (available from www.magnacartaunlocked.com) examines how and why modern civil liberties grew on the back of a failed peace treaty – and what part the Bible played in that process.

Lynda Rose is an Anglican priest and writer. Originally called to the Bar, she subsequently went into ministry and was amongst the first women to be ordained in the UK. She served for a number of years in parish ministry in and around Oxford, but more recently has devoted her energies to campaigning on pro-life and related Christian issues. She is CEO of **Voice for Justice UK**, and also serves as Joint Convenor of the *Lords and Commons Family and Child Protection Group*. She is author of several books for both the religious and general markets.

Christopher Shell is married with three primary-age daughters, and manages a large Christian store. He gained a double-first from Oxford and a Ph.D. from Cambridge, together with seven university prizes in various subjects from the two institutions.